Necessary Evil

Necessary Evil

How to Fix Finance by Saving Human Rights

DAVID KINLEY

OXFORD
UNIVERSITY PRESS

OXFORD
UNIVERSITY PRESS

Oxford University Press is a department of the University of Oxford. It furthers
the University's objective of excellence in research, scholarship, and education
by publishing worldwide. Oxford is a registered trade mark of Oxford University
Press in the UK and certain other countries.

Published in the United States of America by Oxford University Press
198 Madison Avenue, New York, NY 10016, United States of America.

CIP data is on file at the Library of Congress
ISBN 978–0–19–069112–7

1 3 5 7 9 8 6 4 2

Printed by Edwards Brothers Malloy, United States of America

Sapere aude

TABLE OF CONTENTS

PREFACE

The cavalcade of social and economic consequences of living in a world dominated by finance is spectacularly varied and seemingly unending.

As I write these words I listen to President Donald Trump declaring his intention to introduce tax reforms that may well widen rather than narrow the already crippling wealth gap between the rich and the rest in the United States. Reports from the World Bank tell me that the world is richer today than it has ever been, and that such wealth has enabled the truly remarkable achievement of slashing levels of extreme poverty from more than 40% of the global population to under 10% in just thirty years. The financial system has played its part in reaching this milestone. Yet, think how much more could be achieved if the financial system did not also facilitate the huge flows of illicit finance that are draining from developing countries at rates far greater than their economies are growing. I read how information technology has so overtaken the modus operandi of banks today that they operate (and accordingly hire) more like tech firms than old style banks. But with this revolution come problems of privacy, commercial exploitation, and gargantuan risk-taking, as well as the benefits of convenience and speed. Newly released data from the OECD show significant increases in development aid being spent by rich countries *inside* their own borders, as they struggle to accommodate tides of refugees from poor or strife-torn parts of the globe. Meanwhile, we are told that our distrust of banking and finance has reached epic proportions, with one recent survey showing that barely 50% of general populations around the world believe banks to be trustworthy institutions (the lowest of any industry sector surveyed), and another study showing that many bankers don't even trust each other to act ethically or honestly.

And this is just a sample of the myriad of ways finance profoundly impacts our lives today.

It is the many and varied financial circumstances such as these that got me—a human rights law professor—seriously interested in the financial system some

ten years ago. Financial wealth and the roles played by governments, corporations and individuals in its generation, distribution, investment, and expenditure are all matters that bear directly or indirectly on levels of human rights
fulfilment. The financial resources of individuals and communities are important because they strongly determine our capacity to secure our human rights to
be fed, free, safe, and treated with respect. With sufficient individual wealth and
fair, competent government, these rights are likely to be adequately protected.
But where financial wealth is minimal or non-existent and governance is unfair,
weak or dysfunctional, then these rights are vulnerable and often abused. This
holds true in rich countries as well as in poor ones.

Understanding how global and local financial systems work, therefore, is
of vital importance to those concerned to protect and promote human rights;
or at least it ought to be. In fact, for too long the human rights community has
ignored or dismissed finance as antithetical. It has not helped, of course, that
financiers—and by extension, the financial system—have returned the favor by
spurning human rights matters as irrelevant and someone else's problem. Both
sides are wrong, and both suffer as a consequence. The fact is that the two desperately need each other; like Elizabeth Bennet and Mr Darcy, their destinies
are tied, whether they like it or not. For while human rights guarantees depend
heavily on the purchasing power of finance, the financial system needs to deliver
beneficial human rights outcomes if it is to secure and retain its social legitimacy.

Questions about the nature of this fraught relationship, its past and present
characteristics, and what can be done to make its future prospects brighter and
fairer, have been the driving forces behind my research over the past decade, and
this book is my attempt to provide some answers.

I have not been alone in this quest and have leant on many individuals and
institutions while writing the book. Over many years, the Sydney Law School,
and especially my colleagues in the Sydney Centre for International Law, have
provided the encouragement and freedom that enabled me to begin the project and, more importantly, to get it finished. Sciences Po Law School, its Dean,
Christophe Jamin, and his colleagues, generously hosted me on a sabbatical
for six months during which time much of the writing was completed; and the
Australian Research Council provided funding for the research upon which the
writing was based. My many students over many years in global economy, development and human rights classes in Sydney, Oxford and Paris contributed more
than they realize to sharpening my thinking on the topic, though some, notably
Jessica Werro, Jahan Navidi and David Hamer, who provided research assistance
for the book, know only too well the debt I owe them.

I benefited enormously from other colleagues, interviewees, acquaintances
and friends too numerous to list comprehensively. Notably, however, I'd like
to register my particular gratitude to the following: Mary Dowell-Jones, Boni

Meyersfeld, Juan Pablo Bohoslavsky, Danny Bradlow, Margaret Wachenfeld, Aoife Nolan, Aldo Caliari, Ryan Brightwell, Joanne Bauer, and Mike Posner—fellow bridge-builders between the worlds of human rights and finance who shared their experiences and expertise; Ross Buckley, Charlie Taylor, Jeni Klugman, Colin Christie, Katherine Teh-White, Josh Dowse, Justin O'Brien, Micah Burch, Jennifer Hill, Pip O'Keefe, David Livingstone, Sheelagh McCracken, Liv Armytage, Murray Bleach, John Findlay, and Kym Sheehan who lifted the lid for me on all manner of matters financial; and on matters of human rights I was kept honest by Chip Pitts, Justine Nolan, Conor Gearty, Liz Umlas, Daniel Augenstein, Jeremy Perelman, Chris Sidoti, Philip Alston, Nicola Jägers, Patrick Earle, Ralph Steinhardt, Shiyan Sun, John Pace, Radu Mares, Christof Heyns, Susan Karamanian and Magdalena Sepúlveda.

I must also make special mention of those who contributed to this book's eventual publication in its present format. For this is a book intended for wider audiences than specialists and academics, and has been written and researched accordingly. The transmutation of deep scholarship into wide readership is never easy and can result in something more mutant than trans. You, the reader, will be the judge of that of course; but in so far as this book has avoided that fate it is due in no small part to the support and good counsel of Leif Wenar, Nikki Goldstein, Rowan Jacob, Sarah Turnbull, Fred Veniere, Jo Nell, John Nell, Jason Greer, Mike Atkinson, Judith Kinley and Catherine Kinley; my indefatigable agent, Jim Hornfischer, David McBride and Claire Sibley at Oxford University Press, and Cheryl Merritt and her editorial team at Newgen. Thank you all.

David Kinley
Sydney
November 2017

Necessary Evil

Introduction

Finance* ensnares the globe in a web of almost unimaginable complexity. It governs almost every aspect of our lives. Every day and everywhere, we use the financial system to mortgage our homes, to insure our health and our death, to invest in our futures through education and pension funds, to feed and clothe ourselves and our children, to be paid when we labor, and to help others in need. Banking services offer transactional guarantees and security, and they help curtail corruption; their denial can also be used as a weapon against tyrants and despots. For the poor especially, even rudimentary services, from microfinance in South Asia to mobile banking in sub-Saharan Africa, can transform lives simply by cutting out loan sharks and mercenary middlemen. Finance, it is clear, can be benign, safe, convenient, and a force for good.

But in just our generation, over the last twenty-five years, something momentous has happened. Finance, in myriad ways, has undergone a foundational transformation. Its institutions and practitioners have embraced and advanced its dark side, where its very ubiquity turns it from a useful everyday service to a menacing fiend. For the utility of the financial system derives from trust. Trust that promises will be honored; that deals will be done honestly and openly; and that risks will be made known. So when trust is shattered and faith lost, the repercussions threaten not just the money in our pockets but also the larger system, and thus our way of life.

From the crude manipulation of currency exchange rates that enriches autocrats from Myanmar and North Korea to Uzbekistan and Zimbabwe, to

---

* A note on terminology: where I use the word "finance" as a noun throughout the book it is generally intended as shorthand for "the financial system, its governance, institutions, services and practitioners." Where any particular aspect of finance is being singled out I have endeavored always to make that clear.

the sophisticated rigging of lending rates between banks that benefits bankers in London and the duplicity of Wall Street banks betting against their clients, greed has driven finance over the edge. Financial institutions all over the world piled into the U.S. subprime mortgage market without understanding or caring about the lies that propped the market up. The poor and the gullible were duped into greater penury by unscrupulous mortgage brokers who had eyes only for their commissions. International aid and development resources have been bled almost dry by a lethal combination of pilfering by host state rulers, the impotence of aid agencies in the face of corruption, and the indifference of Western banks to the corruption of clients on their books. The scale of this larceny is so extensive that poor countries give to rich states more than they receive in return.[1] Even so, Western creditors, including notorious vulture funds, chase down every debt owed by poor states, no matter how squeezed they are in the task of meeting the basic needs of their people. Like a massively upscaled version of the subprime fraud, the citizens of poor states have had crippling debt forced upon them by corrupt, tyrannical rulers aided by compliant and careless international financiers. Such "odious debt" is well named.

Banks and other financial institutions are not only party to these abominations; they have been the architects. Over the past quarter century, limits on bank borrowing have been relaxed and debt has soared; regulatory controls of capital markets have been loosened and extreme risk-taking has been institutionalized. Financiers have held governments hostage by convincing them that what is good for the finance sector is good for the economy and that what is good for the economy is good for society. Bankers have tagged themselves the smartest guys in the room and demanded to be paid accordingly. Tax regimes overwhelmingly favor the rich over the poor, capital over income, and big corporations over small. Most incredibly, the financiers have effectively recast the social contract between governments and their citizens. With a state-backed guarantee against failure, banks and insurers have procured a license to bet with other people's money, keeping the gains from the massive risks they take, and passing on the losses to society when those risks turn sour. The 2008 taxpayer-funded bank bailouts amounted to socialism *for* Wall Street.

Taming the Money Monster

But finance's monster, like Frankenstein's, has developed a life of its own and escaped the control of its creators. Where financial institutions might once have been too big to let fail, they are now too big to save. A repeat of the 2007/08 crisis today would find the West's coffers bare. Even China's massive rainy-day currency reserves would not suffice to reverse a global liquidity crisis on that scale.[2]

Outrage over the finance sector's special pleading, gargantuan bailouts, tax dodging, and resistance to increased scrutiny and regulation is a sign of an awakening consciousness. But the protests are no more than pinpricks to an elephant, and finance's monster is far from tamed. The major banks are now bigger than they were ten years ago, and they still hold debts so large that failure of even a modest portion would bring the financial system to its knees; levels of cynicism within the sector itself, and distrust outside it, remain sickeningly high and are, if anything, rising (barely 50% of us trust banks, the lowest of all the major industry sectors surveyed by the Edelman Trust Barometer);[3] and wealth disparities continue to expand, reaching levels last seen one hundred years ago on the eve of the Great War and the Great Depression.[4] Beneath it all, around 1.5 billion people still struggle daily to find enough to eat and clean water to drink, to enjoy even the most basic levels of health care for themselves, or education for their children, or power for their homes, and whose access to anything resembling adequate legal or financial services, still less political representation, is nonexistent.[5]

This is not the way things should be. Wealth is not the problem; its allocation is. The world's total financial assets (valued at a staggering $294 trillion) are four times larger than the combined output of all the world's economies.[6] So there is, apparently, plenty to go around. Finance argues that the trickle-down effect is its contribution to wealth redistribution, but evidently a trickle is not enough. The median income of U.S. households has in fact significantly dropped over the last seventeen years, while that of the rich has steadily risen. For the ultra-rich it has risen stratospherically.[7] For those at the very bottom of the wealth table, the trickle has not registered at all, with the proportion of Americans living beneath the poverty line rising during that same period.[8] There can be little doubt that such systematically lopsided sharing of the enormous wealth gains made over the past two decades fed directly into the "deep vein of distress and resentment"[9] that led millions of working- and middle-class Americans to elect Donald Trump to the presidency in November 2016.

We forget (or do not care to remember) that the financial system is a means, not a goal. Its object is not just to bake the biggest wealth pie possible, regardless of ingredients and recipe, texture and taste. It must also be to slice and serve it in ways that increase the sum of human welfare and happiness; in short, in ways that protect, promote, and fulfill the human rights of everyone. The proof of the pie is in its eating: who gets to eat, when, and how much. Finance can enable the good life—a life in which one's individual security, dignity, and worth are recognized and respected. Its service to the needs of the wider community is what provides finance with validity, as it is these basic "good life" rights that constitute fundamental precepts upon which our societies are built. The continuing failure to recognize the impact that finance has upon them is crippling our efforts to better understand finance and to make it work for all of us, not just a privileged few.

Reclaiming finance by bending it to society's needs is the mission of this book. Its message is a call to action. For governments and financiers to accept the need for change and to effect the necessary reforms; and for the rest of us, including human rights advocates, to better understand finance and what we can, cannot, and should expect of it. In an exploration of this complex and fascinating landscape, the book uses human rights as the gauge through which to investigate, test, and evaluate finance. How, it asks, can the financial sector be encouraged to spread wealth, not just make it? To reduce poverty, not entrench it? To protect human rights and security, not endanger them?

The Argument

It turns out that the answers to these questions lie in tackling two elemental obstacles presented by the financial sector itself. First, its narcissism—the perception that such unquantifiable "externalities" as human rights exist beyond the realm of finance and are therefore irrelevant to it. They are somebody else's problem; neither the concern nor the responsibility of finance. Second, its "financial exceptionalism"—the view that given its immense size, power, and prevalence, the sector justifies its own existence; it is an end in itself, in other words, rather than a means to help achieve other ends.

These are, in fact, perversions of what finance is meant to be. Finance *is* a mere utility. A vital one to be sure, but one nonetheless intended to serve society, not to subvert it. The institutions of finance are licensed to promote broad community interests, not just to satisfy the narrow interests of their immediate stakeholders. Even financial insiders concede the point. William Dudley, former CEO of the Federal Reserve Bank of New York and former managing director of Goldman Sachs, opened a 2014 workshop on reforming banking culture with the words: "Financial firms exist, in part, to benefit the public, not simply their shareholders, employees and corporate clients."[10] The protection and promotion of human rights is one of the most important ends to which finance must be put. This is something that finance itself can neither ignore nor avoid, as it is by way of delivering such service that the financial system obtains its very legitimacy, its social license to operate.

It is also something that the sector is quite capable of achieving. For alongside finance's negative entries in the human rights ledger, there are also some notably positive ones. Finance has helped liberate individuals and peoples alike by providing them with greater independence, freedom, security, and self-respect. It has further enabled states to improve the basic living standards of many and to provide particular help to those most in need. Relatively small but significant increases in individual income and wealth have also lifted hundreds of millions of people out of abject poverty. Finance's engagement with human rights, therefore, is not just about the damage it causes. Its contribution can and should be much more constructive.

We all have a responsibility to work harder to make this turnaround happen. Our governments need to take control of the financial system, rather than continue to behave like teenagers in a pop star's fanzone. Arch critics of finance, including social justice and human rights advocates, need to step out from behind rhetoric and convey more clearly and convincingly how their concerns should bear on the conduct of finance. This requires cultivating a much deeper and more sophisticated understanding of how finance actually works, and what it means for human rights. Only then will human rights advocacy acquire the expertise and the credibility required to give it any real chance of influencing how finance operates. Reconciling finance and human rights is necessarily a two-way process.

The global financial crisis (GFC) was a hard-hitting wakeup call for everyone. Certainly, the crisis, and the economics of austerity that followed, caused standards of living to decline sharply for millions who could least afford it. The experience underlined how vital finance is to the fulfillment of our most basic rights, such as housing, education, health care, job security, and welfare support. But the most profound revelation was to show how poorly we all understand how finance really functions, what drives it, and how it impacts the communities we live in and the individual rights we each hold. At a time when grass-roots political revolts in the United States and Europe reflect concerns all around the globe of the deleterious effects of finance on ordinary people's way of life, outraged calls for reform in the name of human rights and social justice have been genuine and well intentioned, but have also lacked depth, engagement, and credibility. They have been easy, therefore, for the finance industry to dismiss.

Amid the torrent of literature that has flowed out of the GFC, serious human rights commentary has been notably absent. This omission both diminishes the nature of debate over financial reforms and, thereby, provides the platform upon which this book is built.

This book's origins lie in the conclusion of another. In the fall of 2008 I was grappling with the final chapters of *Civilising Globalisation*, exploring how the global economy has helped raise our standards of living, while at the same time perverting our standards of fairness and justice. The extraordinarily swift and sweeping effects of the credit crisis then unfolding made clear to me what had been hiding in plain sight: namely, the power and pervasion of global finance over just about all forms of social, economic, and political interaction, including human rights. "With what consequences?" and "how to respond?" were the questions that kicked off my research agenda and set the tone for the decade that followed, as I tried to make sense of this often-fractious, always complicated, and yet surprisingly intimate relationship between finance and human rights. The results of these efforts are this book, in which I endeavor both to explain how and why finance and human rights interact in the many and various ways they do, and to lay out the arguments for what must, and can, be done to reclaim the dark heart of finance by reinstating finance as humanity's servant, not its master.

The Journey

The research for this book spans some ten years and has taken me on journeys back and forth across the globe, allowing me to bear witness to finance's greatest triumphs (like helping lift hundreds of millions Chinese out of dire poverty in just twenty years),[11] and its greatest failures (such as leaving behind 760 million people worldwide in extreme poverty, with more than half of those living in just two countries—India and Nigeria).[12] Meeting with bankers, economists, lawyers, politicians, and policy-makers, as well as human rights activists, aid and development specialists, philosophers, historians, and anthropologists, I came to understand the way finance works for the fabulously wealthy in the grand cities of the West, as well as how its absence impacts the poorest of the poor in the slums of Mumbai and the Dayak villages of Kalimantan. I sifted through a wide array of data from behavioral economic studies of the ultrarich and the ultrapoor, the mathematics of risk, and the psychology of cheating, criminal complicity, and whistle-blowing. I delved into the ethics of empathy and the psychology of esteem, as well as the reasons behind global flows of illicit finance, the economics of debt and development, and the politics of international relations. Above all, I reflected on how well governments respect and protect the human rights of their people.

As the research progressed, I found myself time and again drawn back to the realm of politics in my quest both to understand the causes of the problem and to find its solutions. Financial regulators in the West proved to be so beholden to the exceptionalist demands of the finance sector that they were powerless to prevent, or even adequately predict, the latest global financial crisis. Even in its aftermath, they have been able to make few significant changes to the global financial architecture. The situation, however, is neither monolithic, nor permanent. Finance's wildly successful onslaught on the institutions of government— enabling Wall Street and the City of London to capture or neuter their respective government regulators—has been a political battle, fought with armies of lobbyists promising wealth for all if they get their way, and economic doom if they don't. But politics, by its very nature, swings and turns.

Today, evidence and voices that argue against the sector's claims for special treatment are mounting: banks are now more scorned than admired; disgust over widening inequalities of wealth is increasing; movements toward greater tax transparency are being made; and the urgent need to tackle global corruption is widely accepted. Across the politics of finance, it seems, the time is ripe for change, despite the enormous obstacles. The research for the book was driven by the desire to add a distinctive human rights voice to this reformatory movement.

In all these ways the research helped me understand the extraordinary impact of finance on ordinary lives, and what really lies at the bottom of the relations between finance and the essential human rights we all believe we are entitled to and expect to be protected. It also showed me what is wrong with the relationship and what the options are for its reform and renewal. How, that is, finance could shed its worst conceits and return to its role as fuel for the economy's engine, rather than its driver. How, by helping human rights, not harming them, it can regain the public trust and credibility it has so spectacularly lost over the past decade. The world's financial system can be made to better help defend the rights you and I cherish, and that others so badly lack.

The Finance/Human Rights Relationship

Across the millennia, money has been scorned as constituting "the root of all kinds of evil,"[13] and its pursuit pilloried as "an instrument of slavery."[14] It might seem odd, therefore, even perverse, to argue not only that we should acknowledge the intimacy that exists between finance (that is, money's systemic incarnation) and human rights, but that we should actively encourage it. Yet, this is precisely my contention. The relationship is often tempestuous and sometimes catastrophic, and is presently in dire need of repair. But it is nonetheless one that is essential to the fulfillment of human rights goals, and vital to the legitimization of finance.

This is so even if, as some claim, the global financial system can be likened to a crime against humanity. In March 2009, just as the wider consequences of the GFC were becoming apparent, Shoshana Zuboff, a then recently retired professor at the Harvard Business School, published a piece in the Bloomberg Businessweek that lamented the GFC's disfigurement of millions of lives and compared the design faults of the global financial system to those that sustained the Weimar Republic's Holocaust.[15] The same "remoteness and thoughtlessness, compounded by an abrogation of moral judgement," she argued, is to be found in the attitudes of the perpetrators in both systems. Borrowing from Hannah Arendt's piercing account of watching the trial of Nazi war criminals and her characterization of them as "terribly and terrifyingly normal," Zuboff is struck by how apt a description that is for bankers and financiers today. The institutionalized narcissism of finance and its readiness to quarantine its operations from scrutiny based on ethical or consequentialist grounds produce the same widespread abnegation of responsibility for the consequences of its actions. This is precisely because such outcomes seem so removed from the everyday experience and behavior of those who operate the system.

In terms of the objectives of this book, however, there exists a vital distinction between the two systems. Whereas the grotesqueness of the Weimar Republic was unsalvageable, that of finance can, and must, be rescued. The only defensible moral and legal responses to the philosophy of the former were to reject and erase it. In the case of global finance, the philosophical foundations are broader and more varied. There exists legitimate contestation as to what are its purposes and what are the best ways to go about achieving them. Finance clearly has redeeming features that are not just useful and even laudable, they are essential to the realization of many of the most basic elements of our individual welfare, security, and social existence.

Stages in the Relationship

The narrative that drives the book is the story of a relationship. A relationship that on its face seems unlikely and antagonistic, but which on examination reveals itself to be sincere rather than just peevish, and interdependent, not merely coincidental. Each chapter progresses through a particular stage or aspect of the relationship, uncovering lessons of the many ways in which finance affects the human rights upon which we rely and through which we construct our lives. Together, the seven chapters that follow build a complete picture of the ways the two phenomena attract and repel each other, the highs and lows of their relationship, why they desperately need counseling, and what that might achieve.

Beginning with the notion that the two do indeed make strange bedfellows, the first part of the book (chapters 1–3) focuses on which of the essential ingredients of finance and human rights make the relationship compatible (common concerns for liberty and security), and which are combustible (financial hubris that breeds contempt for all beyond its borders). It shows how finance and human rights have often occupied the same stage in history, with finance driving just about every significant advancement in modern human society, from the civilizations of ancient Babylon and Greece, to the industrialization of Europe, North and then South America, and now Asia. The post-1945 new world order was founded on a belief that peace and security are best secured through the combination of economic strength and individual freedoms. The fact, in tandem with these advancements, that throughout history the pursuit of financial advantage has also fueled the atrocities of war, genocide, famine, state-funded oppression, and corporate crimes and corruption illustrates just how complex the relationship is and how important it is to better comprehend it. This opening part is rounded off with an examination of the human rights consequences when the controls on financial risk are loosened and greed is unrestrained. While it is argued that greed is good—in moderation—its malign excesses are intolerable when the prudent management of risk is abandoned by incompetence or design, and greed is allowed to run rampant.

The capacities of private and public finance to do good as well as harm are the focus of the book's middle section (chapters 4 and 5). For the vast majority of people many of our day-to-day rights and basic securities are financed through our own, private means. Payment for our toil, for the goods or produce we sell, or the financial returns from our investments, (big or small) provide an essential means by which most us feed, clothe, house, educate, entertain, and even heal ourselves; how we establish families, socialize, pray, pontificate, participate in political processes, and even settle disputes between ourselves. The availability of jobs and work opportunities, as well as the existence of safe communities in which to live and regulated markets in which to trade, are, therefore, critical to securing such private means. We cannot, in other words, do it alone.

We need corporate investment, at home and overseas, to create jobs and help people to help themselves. Globalization has expanded and strengthened national economies and allowed families to flourish, fed by the enormous rivers of remittances that now traverse the globe. Global poverty has halved in the last 20 years, and in the West, old-style corporate investment is now supplemented by newly styled investment with social impacts. But we also need some significant level of responsible, publicly funded state intervention for ordered, healthy, and prosperous societies to thrive, to have safety-nets to help those in need, and to curb capitalism's tendencies toward exploitation and kleptocracy. So here the book interrogates the time-honored controversy that taxes are the price we pay for civilization, lamenting the crippling paucity of tax dollars in most of the world's countries, and lambasting legalized tax dodging of epidemic proportions in rich states. It is here, too, that aid's checkered and diminishing role as the economic engine of development is considered as it struggles to remain relevant. We also engage with the moral and practical questions surrounding the rising levels of private philanthropy as driven by desires ranging from meanness to magnanimity, vanity to guilt, and from eccentricity to efficacy.

The destabilizing context of colossal and growing wealth inequality worldwide in which all of these tribulations of private and public finance are played out provides the backdrop for the book's final two chapters.

In societies that claim to be democratic, fair, and egalitarian, there is no greater injustice than when one section of the community cheats on another, especially when it is the most powerful that cheat. That governments may be complicit in the deceit adds insult to injury. And further, that human rights responses should too often be politically naïve and myopic in their view of finance and how to fix it are opportunities forsaken. These are the concerns of chapter 6. It looks first at the ways in which governments are subverted by financially driven criminality. The staggering levels of the *trillions* of dollars of illicit funds washing through the world's financial systems are the direct result of such open defiance. The fact that this is due in part to finance systematically rigging the powers of governance and regulation in ways that benefit private interests at the expense of broader public needs is laid bare. Such appropriation of the instruments of government, it shows, has allowed our largest corporations to avoid paying tax with ease, and it helps explain why, after the GFC, so many banks were prosecuted and fined, but none of their senior management.

How to reestablish trust in finance's capacity to serve the interests of our communities, by shifting its core values from ruthless self-interest to responsible economic stewardship is the task taken on by the book's final chapter. While acknowledging the importance of state intervention to regulate the industry, I argue that ultimately it is in persuading finance to promote these virtues from within its own ranks that the real battle will be won or lost. This chapter uses evidence of modern society's heightened levels of rationality (even if at times we can be forgiven for doubting it) to show how appeals to "empathy" can push financiers down the road toward caring more about the impact of their actions on others. This basic human virtue, as argued by great philosophers and increasingly practiced by ordinary folk, cannot be forsaken in any social order, including that of finance.

Noble though this may be, however, it is hardly enough. So the chapter also explains how the intriguing notion of appealing to the desire for professional "esteem" can apply to financiers in ways that will persuade them to behave more responsibly. For this to happen, the book concludes, professional incentives that venerate a winning-at-all-costs mentality must change, and the glamour of avarice has to be repudiated. Above all, both financiers and governments must acknowledge that there is a deep-seated problem and accept the need for reform. The path to changing the heart of finance is through its head. This is finance's predicament, but it is also human rights' opportunity.

1

Strange Bedfellows

"If we do not find anything pleasant, at least we will find something new."
—Voltaire, *Candide* (1759)

Hubris

As Alan Greenspan climbed the steps of the U.S. Congress on the morning of October 23, 2008, you could sense the first real hint of fall in the air; few, however, had any inkling of the bombshell that he was about to deliver inside. Greenspan was there to provide testimony to an inquiry by the House Oversight and Government Reform Committee into the causes and effects of the worldwide credit crunch that was then unfolding and threatening to engulf the economies of many states including, and indeed especially, the United States. There was intense media interest in Greenspan's appearance before the committee precisely because, as Chairman of the U.S. Federal Reserve for nearly twenty years between 1987 and 2006, he was considered by many to have been the architect of the longest and most lucrative bull market in modern economic history—a market that had now come crashing down around us all. During that time, with his hand on the lever of monetary policy of the nation that boasts the world's default currency, and his highly regarded and persuasive policy pronouncements directed at the legislators of the world's largest economy, the markets had developed a hypersensitivity to all that he said and did, no matter how complex or nuanced. Thus, despite the fact that he once quipped that "if I turn out to be particularly clear, you've probably misunderstood what I've said," the sobriquet "Master of the Universe" stuck.

There was nothing nuanced about what the media wanted to hear from Greenspan that day. They wanted to know not only what he thought about the ongoing crisis, but also whether and to what extent he would concede responsibility for his own role in building the house of cards so high and so fast. They did not get a mea culpa, despite some indelicate pushing in that direction by the chair of the committee, the redoubtable Henry Waxman. But they did get an extraordinarily frank admission from Greenspan of an error of judgment. "I've found a flaw," he declared. "I made a mistake in presuming that the self-interest of organizations, specifically banks and others, was such [that] they were best capable of protecting their own shareholders and their equity in the firms."[1] In other words, he believed, as did so many others, that bankers' self-interest would always, ultimately, guard against the taking of excessive risk.

In this respect, Greenspan's thinking is redolent of Adam Smith's contention some 250 years earlier that the butcher's or baker's (or banker's) pursuit of his or her own interests in the market coincidentally serves the interests of the community (by delivering a desired service for a fee that would otherwise not exist or have to be provided by individuals themselves).[2] A critical difference, however, is that Smith's faith in the market was both backed and limited by his unshakeable moral sentiment that the market must do good, including, and especially, for those on the margins of society even if, at the same time, it handsomely rewards the market makers and players. This is a critical feature of Smith's advocacy of the market. The market for Smith, in other words, is, or can be, an effective and efficient economic vehicle by which to achieve desirable social outcomes.

Too often in recent times, this condition has been forgotten or overlooked, to the detriment of the economy and society as a whole. But the fact remains, whether we like it or not, that finance is a necessary evil for the promotion and fulfillment of human rights.

Finance as a Utility

My aim is to refocus attention on this conditional feature of finance; to go beyond regarding finance merely as a goal by reasserting its role as a means. That is, to *re*argue the point that as a means, one of the most important ends toward which it must work is the betterment of human rights protection. For this not only benefits all of us as rights holders, it also underwrites the very existence of finance by justifying the part it plays in our societies. Indeed, this invocation of the life-supporting qualities of human rights can even be seen as helping to effect finance's change of heart. By redesigning the warped incentive structures through which esteem is won and lost inside the sector, while at the same time appealing to financiers' (collective and individual) senses of empathy for the circumstances of others affected by their actions, I build the argument that by fixing finance we can save human rights.

This grand task falls within the broad domain of what John Maynard Keynes identified as *the* major political challenge of mankind, namely, to reconcile economic efficiency with social justice and individual liberty.[3] In his demand for full employment that best and most fairly achieves social welfare, while also insisting on liberty such that it "give[s] unhindered opportunity to the exceptional and to the aspiring," Keynes betrays his liberal sympathies. Even as he stipulates that economic efficiency "needs criticism, precaution, and technical knowledge," thereby revealing his analytical rigor, he also understands economics as a vehicle to achieve goals and purposes outside itself.

It is in this vein that here, at the very outset, I want to clarify that the relationship between human rights and finance is in fact close and enduring, even though in practice this is seldom acknowledged, still less understood. As with many relationships, such intimacy can bring great pain as well as pleasure, and yet neither can live without the other. Finance, as I will show, is at the center of many human rights atrocities, while also, at times, enabling their salvation. Further, it can and should be restructured in ways that will expand these benefits and diminish the harms it causes. But before we reach into the future of the relationship, we must establish how we reached the present. And to do that we must first explain the basic chemistry that connects the pair.

In formal terms finance's primary function is to optimize the allocation of capital by channeling funds from savers to borrowers—what economist John Kay labels its "search" and "stewardship" function.[4] In fact, finance works in a myriad of ways that are today so familiar to us that we hardly notice them: money in our hands, credit on our cards, checking account books in our bags, ATMs everywhere, transactions online, transfers by phone, all sorts of loans from banks, deposit accounts, pension funds, weekly or biweekly pay checks and salaries, paying income tax annually and sales taxes daily, and the insuring of just about everything we own, everywhere we travel, as well as our health, our lives, and our deaths.

Finance also performs functions equally varied, but far less familiar, affecting us all in ways that we do not expect, nor realize. Every day billions of transactions across the world's financial markets are made by individuals, financial institutions, corporations, and governments trading in securities of every kind (stocks, shares, bonds, commodities, currencies, interest rates, and the seemingly neverending variety of derivatives contracts), as well as undertaking all manner of payments, transactions, and clearing house transfers between financial institutions. The scale of all this activity is astonishing, pushing more than $14 trillion in U.S. dollar-denominated trades alone through the global banking system every day.[5] Finance also encompasses other no less exotic and potent phenomena—the $20 trillion-plus rivers of illicit funds that flow through the world's banking systems, much of it in tax havens, but also significant amounts deposited in main street retail banks in the West; the billions of dollars of foreign direct investments (FDIs) made by corporations every day and the international laws that protect their outlays; the financial activities of rich states' Sovereign

Wealth Funds, and of rich individuals through their philanthropic funds; and the desperately needed, often-criticized, and always politically charged funding of aid projects in developing countries by Western aid agencies (and, increasingly, also by middle-income states like China and Brazil), the World Bank, the International Monetary Fund (IMF), and regional development banks. How each of these critical features of finance impacts on human rights will be explored and explained as we progress through the book.

In its extraordinary breadth, depth, and variety, therefore, finance provides the lifeblood of the economy. But finance is also meant to "enrich society," as Christine Lagarde, the head of the IMF, has put it.[6] Indeed, in this book I argue that all of these components of finance have a responsibility to serve the interests of the community as a whole, including the protection and promotion of human rights. For in the world of finance, context is everything. By considering the financial system in its broader economic, social and political contexts, one comes to recognize the importance of defining it in utilitarian terms. Thus, alongside the accumulation of capital, a necessary and core rationale of finance has to be the manner of its distribution, including how that underwrites the fulfillment of human rights.[7] Finance is truly a utility, a social service, not unlike power or water, and therefore always a means to an end, never an end in itself.

There is an understandable temptation to assume that the fortunes of human rights protection wax with the financial boom times and wane with the busts. In reality, the poor and marginalized whose human rights are most at risk tend to be more affected by long-term trends (upward or downward), than the immediacy of the peaks and troughs. As I maintain throughout the book, the recurrent boom/bust cycles that have dominated the history of global finance, and especially the last three decades or so, have impacted directly those long-term trends in ways that do not necessarily correlate with the human rights experiences of the wealthier and more mainstream groups in society.

Financial Ownership

Greenspan's faith in self-interested market behavior as being for the benefit of all through such self-correcting booms and busts was not, evidently, well placed—even by his own admission.[8] What is especially disturbing about this situation, however, is not so much that Greenspan was proved wrong, but that he, as head of the Federal Reserve and at that particular time, ever held such a belief in the first place. For it necessarily assumes both the existence of an umbilical link between owners of capital and its managers, and that the link is long-term in perspective. This is an astounding assumption to make. Because one of the defining features of the changing structure of corporations during Greenspan's tenure and beyond has been the marked shift from "ownership capitalism" to "management capitalism,"[9] which essentially severs or shrivels the umbilical cord and has both pushed, and been pushed by, shorter and shorter time spans. While short-termism drives management—by way of performance targets, balance sheets, and regulatory hurdles—many (though by no means all) share-holding owners are typically focused on the longer-term goal of capital growth through increasing share prices. It would be a mistake to believe, however, that this has all been orchestrated by corporate executives without the knowledge of shareholders, or somehow against their wishes. Shareholders have been party to the shift by way of their ever-eager delegation of strategic as well as operational power and control to management, too often showing little or no interest in the direction and details of a company's actions provided their investment returns remain positive.[10]

Nowhere has the pusillanimity of owners been more apparent than in the banking sector. Consider, for example, the lightning-rod issue of ballooning remuneration packages doled out to staff in the boom years before the 2007–08 credit crisis, in respect of which shareholders displayed "all the resistance of a doormat."[11] Even after the chastening of the crisis and the ignominy of needing government bailouts to keep functioning, the big global banks brazenly and immediately returned to looking after the interests of their executives above all else with salaries and bonuses paid in 2009 equating, on average, to between a quarter and one-half of the core capital held by a firm.[12] Shareholders, it seems, have become "the new proletariat,"[13] whereby, in a curious reversal of Marx's original formula, the capital of many is exploited by the labor of an elite few.

The tendency of management professionalism to move away from stewardship and toward salesmanship[14] not only fractures the relationship of trust and understanding between management and owners, it also directly impacts the role that corporations play in the wider community in terms of the benefits and problems they bring. These shifts in the operational philosophy and structure of corporations are seen by many—especially following the crash of 2008—as indicators of what has gone wrong with free market capitalism. More specifically, they are talismans of how removed global finance had become from the reality of all except the very few employed at the top of the financial services sector. Now more than ever, finance shapes the economies we live in. The availability of finance, its cost, format, associated risk, and quantity are determinants not only of whether you are rich or poor, but also, to a significant extent, the state of your individual health, safety, security, and freedom—factors that bear directly on your enjoyment of human rights. And yet the global and local regulatory systems governing finance pay little if any heed to the impact of finance on these daily struggles of individuals' lives. It has, in fact, been designed that way.

A central tenet of the modern free market economy in which finance plays such a vital role is to distance it as far as possible from social circumstances not deemed relevant to its operation. State intervention and regulation should be kept to a minimum, and where it does exist, relate only to those social and economic features essential to the functioning of the market. Human beings and the natural environment are nonetheless both relevant and vital in this way of thinking. But as labor and clients, not as bearers of human rights; and as property and resources, not as common wealth. This is what the great wartime economist and philosopher Karl Polanyi scathingly characterized as the market economy's commodification of human beings and nature,[15] borne directly of the "extraordinary assumption" that an economy works best when "directed by market prices, and nothing but market prices . . . without outside help or interference."[16] Modern finance's introspection and claims of "exceptionalism," with which much of this book is concerned, draw directly on this assumption together with the sector's economic and political clout that enables it effectively to ring-fence much of what it does from outside concerns.[17]

Financial Weapons of Mass Destruction

The core features of the finance sector are remarkable not just for their apparent blindness to human rights concerns, but also for their representation of the way the global financial system has been constructed. Its systematic orientation toward risk-taking behavior, while it may not be unlawful, is nevertheless inherently destabilizing and too frequently unethical. So comfortable have we become with this circumstance that we express little surprise over the fact that today there is scarcely anything that has not been converted into a monetary value.[18] More than just mortgages, bank loans, and every conceivable commodity, nearly everything around us and even inside us has been financialized, from earthquakes, drought and pollution, health, and education, to our emotional states, bodily organs, and quantities of fat tissue.[19] Many aspects of our well-being as individuals, including risks associated with our anxiety levels or body mass index (BMI),[20] can be converted into insurable costs, which can themselves become tradable commodities. For not only are there insurers and those wishing to have their health insured, there are also reinsurers and others interested in betting on whether the insurance will ever be needed, and if so, when. This is the essence of derivatives trading. The original insurance contact sets in motion a slew of derivative contracts involving third parties (that is, neither the insured, nor insurer) directly associated with it, and whose execution are wholly dependent on the outcomes of the primary contracts.

Financial derivatives, such as futures, options, and swaps, are just the same. The critical price points are distant (in terms of contractual relationship or time, or both) from the circumstances of the original or underlying entity. It is their derived nature that makes them so tradable, for their attraction has less to do with the inherent value of the underlying entity, and more to do with how one can exploit speculation on price movements in their particular derivatives market. It is also what makes them so dangerous—"Financial weapons of mass destruction," as Warren Buffett labeled them in 2002.[21] While one would expect those few directly involved in derivatives trading to be exposed to the negative consequences of their actions (which, given the sheer size of the derivatives market, can be overwhelming),[22] it would seem hugely unjust if those many who had no knowledge of, let alone any input to, the relevant trades are negatively affected.[23] Especially if they are already the poorest and most marginal members of society, and the detrimental effects are to their human rights. Yet this is precisely what is happening.

In a classic case of the tail wagging the dog, trade in derivatives can have significant and contradictory impacts on the price of the underlying assets, no matter how sound (or unsound) the fundamentals of those assets are. This, vividly, was the case with the food security crisis that occurred in the midst of the GFC in 2007–08. The price of staple food commodities such as corn, wheat, rice, and soybean skyrocketed during this period, causing global food prices to rise sharply. According to the World Bank, the price hike drove an estimated additional 44 million people into poverty.[24] The UN Food and Agriculture Organization's cereal price index (which calculates changes in international prices of wheat, corn, and rice) increased by 37% in 2007 and then by a further 42% in 2008.[25] Such increases are devastating for the poor, especially those in least-developed countries, "who even at the best of times must spend up to four-fifths of their income on food," as Olivier de Schutter, the former UN Special Rapporteur on the Right to Food, noted at the time.[26]

One might have assumed that such price spikes were caused by shortages in the relevant crops, with demand far outstripping supply. In fact, there were no such shortages. What had caused this hyperinflation was the massive injection of funds into commodities markets by large institutional investors as they sought refuge from collapsing shares and property markets at that time. These pension funds, hedge funds, large banks, and even sovereign wealth funds were not, of course, interested in wheat or corn as commodities in their own right, and still less did they wish physically to hold, store, or transport them. Rather, they wanted to trade—that is to speculate—on the *future* prices of such commodities. Thus, they poured billions of dollars into purchasing commodities futures contracts, pushing demand and prices upward and creating what were, in effect, enormous stockpiles in commodities futures.[27] This, in turn, directly impacted the then current prices of the actual commodities themselves, as their perceived present value increased in anticipation of their inflated future prices. As one hedge fund manager put it in a U.S. Senate Committee hearing in May 2008: "You asked the question: 'are institutional investors contributing to food and energy price inflation?' And my unequivocal answer is 'YES.' "[28]

While the inherent risks in derivatives trading may be the spark for such staple food price hikes, what fans the flames of their ruinous human rights effects is the magnifying impact of leverage in finance. The loosening of restrictions on both institutional and individual borrowing that occurred throughout the industrialized economies in the late 1980s and early 1990s permitted and encouraged the taking of ever- larger positions in efforts to maximize gains, even if that also meant risking maximized losses.[29] Either way, global finance has reached truly gargantuan proportions. The world's stock of financial assets (that is, all shares, bonds, and derivatives) is estimated to be $294 trillion (in 2014), which is some four times larger than the total output of all the world's economies as measured by global gross domestic product (GDP) ($75.5 trillion in 2013).[30]

With such size and attitude, finance today has attained extraordinary power and significance. No longer is it merely an auxiliary to the economy's quest to ensure that goods and services are produced for, and distributed to, those who need them.[31] Rather, today it is finance that dictates how the economy operates and, thereby, exercises enormous sway on what national governments do and think. "The finance industry has effectively captured our government," as Simon Johnson, a former chief economist of the IMF, has noted about the situation in the United States.[32] Kevin Dowd and Martin Hutchinson (economist and former merchant banker, respectively) agree. They describe how, by way of powerful political friends, immense salary differentials between bankers and their regulators, and the capacity to game the system borne of the complexity of financial market transactions, Wall Street has effectively won the protection of government against disgruntled investors, rather than attracted its censure.[33]

Importantly, in neither its past auxiliary, nor present despotic, formats has finance contemplated the human consequences of its actions and outputs; nor, indeed, has that been expected of it. In its former role as an economic facilitator, this was arguably a less serious matter, as one could have reasonably expected that the political and economic masters of finance would be more keenly aware of wider social implications. But in its contemporary role as the economy's dictator and key driver of broader agendas, such disregard for the impact it has on the lives of others beyond its realm is unconscionable. A foundational concern of the book, therefore, is to establish how and why this circumstance has come about by explaining the content and consequences of the interrelations between finance and human rights. Only then, when we understand the nature of the culture, incentives, and practices that have created and sustain finance's sense of

self-entitlement, will we be in a position to challenge and change it for the benefit of the human rights to be enjoyed by all of us.

Transformative Powers

Power lies at the heart of any such explanation and understanding, and the power
of finance is immense. Despite a general recognition of the control finance has
over our lives and societies, most people, it is fair to say, are likely to underestimate its true scale. Not so Roger Altman. In late 2011, three years after the onset
of the GFC, Altman, an investment banker and prominent finance commentator, argued in a piece in the *Financial Times* that

> the financial markets act . . . like a global supra-government. They oust
> entrenched regimes where normal political processes could not do so.
> They force austerity, banking bail-outs and other major policy changes.
> Their influence dwarfs multilateral institutions such as the International
> Monetary Fund. Indeed, leaving aside unusable nuclear weapons, they
> have become the most powerful force on earth.[34]

By comparing the power of finance to that of fission (together with Buffett
[above] there seems to be a theme developing here), Altman clearly points to
its destructive potential while promoting its constructive capacity. His article
was prompted by the role that the GFC had played in instigating the economic
stagnation and austerity measures that were then gripping much of Europe, and
yet he muses that the power of financial markets is "a double-edged sword," with
history suggesting that "the longer-term effects can be often transformative and
positive." Altman's own career has provided him with experiences of both the
positive and negative sides of finance.

Altman served as a U.S. Deputy Treasury Secretary in the Bill Clinton administration in 1993–94, during which time changes to the *Community Reinvestment
Act* (CRA)[35] regulations were negotiated to reduce the compliance and cost
burdens to mortgage lenders when issuing housing loans to borrowers in low-
income neighborhoods (which was the central aim of the CRA). The inevitable
consequence of these amendments (enacted in 1995) was to relax lending standards, as financiers sought to approve as many such loans (soon to be dubbed
"subprime") as possible. The intent, and result, of the legislation was to make
access to housing finance easier for those who were otherwise effectively locked
out of acquiring finance under normal, more rigorous, as well as discriminatory,
conditions set by lenders. It was, as President Clinton argued at the time, an economic initiative that "is supposed to have a civil rights impact," to be achieved by

giving low-income households "a chance to build homes, to build businesses, to create jobs [and] to build neighborhoods."[36] Adequate housing, including security of tenure, is an important right in itself, but, as implied by Clinton, it is also often critical to securing other human rights such as access to adequate health care, individual safety and security, privacy, and work, as well as concomitant children's rights.

Today, however, it is widely accepted (though not, interestingly, by Roger Altman)[37] that the combination of this deregulatory green light and the careless and venal attitudes of banks, mortgage brokers, insurance companies, and rating agencies to the huge expansion of their business based on U.S. subprime loans (whether directly, as lenders, or indirectly, as insurers of the loans) pumped much of the air into the housing bubble that was to burst some twelve years later with the GFC. As a result, many of the human rights gains of the CRA, and much else besides, were duly lost in the severe financial constriction and prolonged global economic downturn that followed.[38]

Another, less turbulent, but no less significant, example of the global power of finance is provided by what it can do for the education of girls. It is estimated that for every 100 out-of-school boys worldwide, there are, on average, 120 girls out-of-school.[39] In many developing countries the imbalance is much worse, such as in South and West Asia (especially Pakistan, Afghanistan, and Bangladesh), where the gender gap is widest in its out-of-school population, with 80% of its out-of-school girls unlikely ever to start school compared to 16% of its out-of-school boys.[40] There are many and varied reasons for the disparity, but chief among them are the lower social status of girls, discriminatory cultural beliefs and practices, early marriage, and lack of safety and inadequate sanitation at schools. Poverty is often a trigger. As the UN Girls' Education Initiative (UNGEI) puts it: "If a family has limited funds and has to be selective on [sic] whom to send to school, more often than not, it is going to be the boys."[41] That said, remarkable progress can and has been made, with just about all developing countries showing huge improvements in the ratio of girls enrolling at primary, secondary, and tertiary levels of education over the past twenty-five years.[42] Even in the problematic area of South Asia, India has been a standout performer reaching near gender parity in 2013 for secondary school enrollments, when barely six girls for every ten boys attended high school twenty-five years earlier.[43]

The benefits to be gained by addressing the educational gender gap are enormous, as are the costs of its neglect. In a study of sixty-five low- and middle-income and transitional countries, the children's rights organization Plan International, for example, estimates that the cumulative economic cost of not educating girls to the same extent and standard as boys across the sixty-five countries amounts to $92 billion per annum. This figure represented an opportunity cost incurred by these countries whereby, on average, a 0.3% growth in each country's per capita income would have been gained for every 1% increase in the share of women with secondary education.[44] These potential gains of educating girls stem directly from the demonstrably fewer children had by educated women, the increased survival chances of the children they do bear, and the better health and welfare choices they make for themselves and their children. Indeed, the benefits of education tend to be self-perpetuating, as healthier and more educated women work more productively, obtain better jobs, are more financially astute, and are better able to articulate and pursue their demands.[45]

When finance is injected directly into girls' education, the results are often startling. So-called cash-transfer programs, as initiated in Latin America in the 1990s and now replicated across the developing world,[46] have proven to be especially effective in raising the schooling standards of girls. The pioneering *Bolsa Família* program in Brazil provides direct cash payments each month to poor households based on the number of children in the family. Conditions are attached, including compulsory school attendance of children up to fifteen years of age for no less than 75% of the school year. The results reflect solid increases in attendance for all children, but are especially impressive with respect to girls, with nearly 12% increases in school attendance in the six- to seventeen-years category. What is more, even in the fifteen- to seventeen-years age range (that is, *beyond* the specified "under 15" condition of the program), the girls' attendance rates remain high, with more than 9% increases recorded in rural and impoverished regions.[47] The accumulated effect of these gains has led to women now making up more than half of all tertiary-level students in Brazil,[48] and an improvement in their representation in the workplace. In a 2013 survey of Brazil's most powerful businesswomen, *Forbes* magazine claimed that "women now hold more than 50% of the postgraduate qualifications in the [business] market. They occupy as many positions as men in industries such as finance, and are gaining ground in traditional male strongholds such as construction and engineering." The report noted further that "14% of the CEOs of large companies in Brazil are women," as compared to barely a third of that percentage in the UK and the United States.[49] While it is true that gender disparities in the workplace still exist in Brazil (especially with respect to pay disparity, with women earning, on average, just 64% as much as men),[50] Brazil's experience demonstrates that given sufficient political will and financial backing, improvements in gender parity can certainly be made.

Interdependency

Finance is indisputably essential for the protection and promotion of human rights. Economic and social rights, such as access to adequate food and clothing, housing and shelter, primary education, access to health care and a clean environment, remunerative work, and basic social welfare, all require financial backing. So, too, do civil and political rights to free speech, privacy, religion, assembly, movement and equal treatment before the law. To put all these rights into practice, individuals must be able to purchase or pay for the conditions that will allow this to happen or, where they lack the individual capacity to do so, minimal levels of financial assistance or the services themselves must be provided by the state. Finance, in other words, is a necessary means for the achievement of human rights ends at their most basic, as well as when they are enjoyed in abundance.

The dependency also works in the opposite direction. Finance needs human rights, because its very legitimacy is contingent upon the contribution it makes to fulfilling society's conditions and expectations made of it, including human rights goals. Finance must be interpreted broadly in this context, encompassing public and private; global, national and local dimensions; and both small and large movements (or promised movements) of money. It covers the raising and spending of tax revenues, retail banking (deposits, lending, and mortgages) and shadow banking (investments and insurance), microfinancing, FDI, financial markets trading (in shares, bonds, derivatives, and currencies), and also overseas development assistance (ODA). To view finance through such a wide lens helps us to envisage the multifarious ways in which finance drives and directs the operations of commercial enterprise, the functions of governments, and the livelihoods of individuals across the globe. An appreciation of the breadth, depth, and complexity of global financial relations today also helps us better understand both their impact on human rights standards and what can be done to increase the benefits and decrease the damage of such impacts.

The financial circumstances of individuals and communities bear directly on their capacity to secure basic levels of human rights protection and enjoyment. Other factors that directly affects whether and how human rights are respected include (1)opportunities and abilities to earn a living; (2) people's access to financial services, and the integrity of the services on offer; (3) the costs of capital and credit (for individuals, businesses, and governments); (4) the reliability of capital flows; (5) the prudence of institutional and individual investors; (6) taxation requirements; and (7) the availability of social welfare support. As such, when funds or financial services are absent, or where the cost of their access is prohibitive, then individuals families and whole communities, especially already poor ones, will struggle to obtain acceptable levels of protection of their rights to health, education, shelter, and even to food and clean water. When a state has crippling debt levels, FDI has shrunk, and (for developing states) aid has dried up, governments will themselves struggle to assist people in obtaining or maintaining these essential services. But when the financial circumstances of states and individuals are healthier and funds or their access are more available, then the impact on people's living standards and hence their human rights circumstances will likely be positive.

These general rules—or rather tendencies—are helpful, but they are by no means certain, nor are they necessarily linear. Identifying broad correlations between financial and human rights circumstances tells only part of the story. An enduring set of questions concerns the determinative properties of such correlations; that is, how do decisions taken on Wall Street bring about good or bad human rights outcomes on Main Street or No Street? What are the lines of cause and effect? And how clear or certain or circuitous are they? Yet the asking of these questions, still less their answering, is all but neglected in today's literature. Typically, conclusions are reached more by way of assumption and assertion than by supposition and analysis. It is not hard to see why this is the case. The task is extraordinarily difficult. The causal directions are often complicated and nearly always opaque. And prejudices about finance and about human rights are as entrenched as they are ardently promoted. The opportunities for, as well as inclinations toward, truly interdisciplinary research on the two subjects are very few and far between.

Choosing a workable prism through which to observe the relationship is essential. Poverty is an excellent candidate for the role, not only because it graphically illustrates the human rights consequences of insufficient or misdirected finance, but also because it shows the manifest human rights benefits to be gained from sufficient and effective financial support, as, for example, with the *Bolsa Família* program described above. It is poverty to which we return time and time again throughout the book as we investigate the relationship between finance and human rights and devise ways to make its benefits more widely felt and more fairly distributed.

The Poverty Prism

At the launch of the *Make Poverty History* campaign in London's Trafalgar Square in February 2005, Nelson Mandela proclaimed that "overcoming poverty *is* the protection of a fundamental human right."[51] It is precisely because the poor have little or no buffer against economic loss that when their finances are diminished, even minimally, it can imperil the very fundamentals of their physical and social existence. Most obviously, their rights to food, shelter, education, and health care are threatened as their capacity or opportunity to access these necessities is curtailed. Their civil and political rights are also negatively affected, including, for example, the right to nondiscrimination (women, children, and ethnic minorities are almost always the ones that suffer the most); the right to free speech, association, movement, and participation in government (capacities often lost when one's energies are focused on survival or basic comforts); and even the right to privacy (the price often paid for greater reliance on state welfare). The poor, in other words, have more to lose than those whose economic circumstances are less parlous precisely because what they might lose is so vital not only to their physical well-being but also to their sense of self-worth and dignity.[52]

The alleviation of poverty is the stage upon which human rights and finance so often meet and where their combination of aspiration and tragedy unfolds. It is not the only stage—conflicts over land, resources, and environmental policies are examples of others—but it is surely the most desperate. In the years immediately preceding the credit crisis, the World Bank had tentatively trumpeted the fact that the number of the world's abjectly poor (then deemed to be those living on under $1.08 per day) had dipped beneath 1 billion (approximately 985 million in 2004).[53] That figure crept above the talismanic mark of 1 billion people in the years following the GFC, before once again returning to its steady downward trend.[54] In terms of the scale of the moral outrage that such numbers ought to invoke in us all as we live through the most prosperous times human civilization has ever known, marginal breaches of the billion barrier in either direction are inconsequential. Even on the basis of the latest figures (using 2013 data), more than 10% of humanity (or nearly 800 million people) still live in situations of economic deprivation, social exclusion, and personal degradation that surely beggar belief for anyone able to read these words.[55]

Such data remain a crude indicator of the breadth and nature of impoverishment.[56] Poverty is not just a matter of lack of money. It can stem from money's misuse or underuse as much as from its absence. How well the poor are able to manage what money they do have often influences the standards of human rights they enjoy on a day-to-day as well as long-term basis. The extraordinary experiences of microfinance over the past twenty-five years have been most revealing in this regard. One illuminating study of the money management techniques of the poor in Bangladesh, India, and South Africa conducted by four public policy and development specialists in the mid-2000s and entitled *Portfolios of the Poor* makes the point vividly.

> Not having enough money is bad enough. Not being able to manage whatever money you have is worse. This is the hidden bind of poverty. For lack of a tool to marshal money into the right sums at the right times, a missed doctor's visit tips into a full-blown family health crisis. A lack of ready cash deprives a child of a place at school, or prevents an adult from seizing an opportunity to increase income and gain greater economic stability.[57]

By reviewing the participants' diarized accounts of their daily financial transactions, the authors of the study found that the inhibitions encountered by the poor were often systemic rather than personal. Indeed, at an individual and family level, they found that the subjects invested astonishing amounts of time and energy in dealing with financial problems. But their ingenuity in financial matters was matched by their frustration at not being able to do more with their money. Too often they had no or very limited access to formalized financial services to help facilitate savings or negotiate loans or investments, despite their willingness to pay for such services.

So, while financial solvency and services are crucial to defining and tackling poverty, there are, clearly, other nonfinancial factors at play in understanding how poverty is felt and dealt with. The new breed of so-called multidimensional poverty indices (MPIs) measure average education levels, health levels (including life-expectancy and infant mortality rates), access to clean water, sanitation, and power sources, as well as incomes. This broadened perspective has provided a greater understanding of the nature, causes, and distribution of poverty, and—most significantly—the aggregate numbers of the global poor calculated by way of the Oxford University–based MPI have remained steady around 1.5 billion or so for the last seven years.[58] That is in stark contrast to global level of poverty measured by way of the simpler (and revised) $1.90 per day poverty line, which, according to the latest calculations of the World Bank, sits at 766 million people.[59]

The fact that most of these people live in countries that have pledged to respect and protect the human rights of their citizenry under both domestic and international laws appears to amount to the cruelest of ironies or the grossest of derelictions of duty. This applies to wealthy and middle-income nations as well as to poor ones. For make no mistake, while many of the poor people live in the poorest countries—mainly in South and South-East Asia and sub-Saharan Africa—a significant number, and an alarmingly growing proportion (now more than 70%), live in "middle-income countries" such as China, Pakistan, Indonesia, and, especially, India and Nigeria. The problem is also evident even in the richest states. In the United States some 43 million people (that is, approximately 13.5% of the population) live beneath the national poverty line.[60] The abiding lesson to be learned here is that poverty knows few boundaries and respects few rules.

Despite their huge numbers of poor, the constitutions and legal regimes of the five middle-income countries mentioned above (including, notably, China)[61] all solemnly guarantee economic and social rights, as well as civil and political ones, while struggling in practice to secure either set of rights. Rich Western states also expressly declare their adherence to protecting and promoting human rights, typically by way of constitutional guarantees. However, they tend not to enshrine protections for economic and social rights in the same way they do civil and political rights, the latter being historically considered more germane to the forms of democratic government they espouse and practice. That said, nearly all industrialized states have extensive legislative programs that essentially do much the same job as constitutional guarantees by providing minimum standards of education, health care, housing, and welfare support.

The record among all states (whether low, middle, or high income) of signing and ratifying relevant international human rights instruments is also, on the whole impressive. Out of the 193 member states of the UN, the vast majority have ratified UN Conventions covering the rights of children (192),[62] of women (189), and against racial discrimination (178). The seminal Covenants covering civil and political rights and economic social and cultural rights are also well subscribed to (169 and 166, respectively).[63] On the basis of these bare figures alone there appears to be a significant appetite among states to submit themselves to international human rights obligations. What impact this may be having on their actual protection on the ground, however, is another matter altogether. We can say of human rights, as the inestimable Yogi Berra said of baseball, that while in theory there may be no difference between theory and practice, in practice there is.

So, notwithstanding the constitutional assurances, the rafts of domestic legislation, and the healthy sign-up rates to international instruments, the gap between promise and practice remains lamentably wide for most states. On either side of the middle majority, the human rights records of some states (like Canada, Finland, the Netherlands, Norway, New Zealand, and Sweden, and possibly also (as fast improvers), Brazil, the Czech Republic, and South Korea) are creditably good, while others are tremendously bad (Afghanistan, Belarus, Chad, Democratic Republic of Congo, Equatorial Guinea, Laos, Niger, North Korea, Pakistan, Saudi Arabia, Syria, Uzbekistan, Zimbabwe). The positioning of these states, and all others in between, on the human rights–respecting league table, reflects the relative beneficence or toxicity of a blend of key governance capabilities, such as respect for the rule of law, levels of good governance (that is, representative, fair, transparent, and effective), and competency in economic management, and degrees of international integration and cooperation.

The particularities of each of these factors, their respective balances, and the potency of their mix are difficult to gauge, and so the human rights direction in which they are likely to propel states is hard to predict. The causal relationship between human rights and just one of these factors—economic growth— yields inconveniently conflicting data. Take, for example, a 2011 report by *The Economist* using IMF data on the world's fastest-growing economies. On the one hand, among the top ten fastest-growing economies between 2001 and 2010 were Angola, Ethiopia, Chad, Mozambique, and Rwanda, all of which over the past decade have greatly improved their performances in respect of noneconomic indicia (including, to various degrees, human rights), as well as economic indicia. On the other hand, on the same top ten list are China, Myanmar,

Nigeria, Kazakhstan, and Cambodia, whose records outside the economic realm are far less commendable.[64]

Poverty and its alleviation provide the canvas upon which to paint the various features of the financial/human rights nexus. But so much more can also be seen in the picture. Household finances are held in the thrall of global finance. Personal security concerns intersect with matters of national security, and standards of individual freedom reflect standards of governance. The bigger picture is not outside or beyond the finance and human rights relationship; it is constitutive of it. "True individual freedom," as Franklin D. Roosevelt argued, "cannot exist without economic security and independence. 'Necessitous men are not free men.' People who are hungry and out of a job are the stuff of which dictatorships are made."[65] More than seventy years on, his argument still rings true.

The Public Problem of Private Poverty

By definition, the poor are often the least likely to be able to obtain minimal levels of rights protection by their own means and so are the most reliant on the state. The private plight of the individual thereby becomes a public problem. If finance is to provide the social services we expect of it, the state must necessarily play a key role in orchestrating the raising and dispensing of the largesse. The greatest problems arise when the state does not fulfil the role, either because it is unwilling or unable, or both.

For example, the degradation of the Myanmar economy over the fifty years of authoritarian rule between 1962 and 2012 left the vast majority of its 50 million people impoverished and destitute. From its status as the "rice bowl" of the region early last century and despite its vast timber, oil, gas, and mineral wealth, the country tumbled to near the bottom of the United Nations Development Programme's (UNDP's) Human Development Index (150th out of 187 countries by 2012), with an estimated per capita income (in "purchasing power parity" terms) of just over US$3 per day.[66] Some 26% of the population lived beneath the country's own pitiful poverty line of 754 kyat (about US$0.85) per day.[67]

During this time, the government was unable and apparently unwilling to secure basic social services for its people. Power blackouts were frequent; clean water and sanitation systems were decrepit or absent for many, especially in rural areas; medical services were sparse and severely underresourced; and social welfare schemes were almost nonexistent for the most vulnerable and marginalized. Such neglect has a long trailing impact. Even today, with democracy largely restored, education beyond primary school is basic or absent, and what little tertiary education there is struggles to overcome the former military rulers' systematic dismantling and severe underresourcing of the sector.

The circumstances of the most needy, such as orphaned (or abandoned) disabled children, were truly shocking. When working in the country some fifteen years ago, a colleague and I visited what was then the only institution in the country that cared specifically for the education of children who were both mentally and physically disabled. It was small (with perhaps twenty children in care), utterly overwhelmed by demand, and relied entirely on international aid and private handouts. The staff there were heroic and what they were able to achieve with so little was almost magical, but there was no escaping the searing desperation of the situation. When states are starved of financial resources—no matter the cause, or who or what is to blame—it is always the most vulnerable who suffer the greatest.

Yet, of the abjectly poor states, Myanmar is one of the lucky ones, for it now has hope. Since mid-2011 the political circumstances in the country have changed direction. The then-president Thein Sein presided over genuine moves toward democratic government, the restoration of the rule of law, and the revival of the economy. The first open elections for decades were held in 2012, which established a bona fide opposition party, Aung San Suu Kyi's National League for Democracy (NLD), followed by a landslide victory for the NLD in the general election in November 2015. An NLD candidate, Htin Kyaw, was installed as the country's president in March 2016. Kyaw openly admits to being a proxy for Aung San Suu Kyi—a surrogacy necessitated by the fact that The Lady (as she is often referred to) remains constitutionally barred from holding the presidency.[68] Today things are very different. Many political prisoners have been released,[69] the state's iron grip on the media has been relaxed, and lawyers are no longer cowed into doing the government's bidding. The West has lifted trade sanctions; the kyat has been effectively floated,[70] and FDI has flooded into the country.[71] And while discrimination against and displacement of the Rohingya Muslims remains a grave and systemic problem, ceasefires have been negotiated with various disquieted ethnic groups.

Starting from what is admittedly a very low baseline, there are reasons to believe that human rights standards in Myanmar will benefit from the freer and healthier political and economic circumstances. That is despite the military's lingering power, with 25% of seats in Parliament nominated by the commander-in-chief of the Defence Services and large parts of the economy still controlled by men who have simply swapped khaki fatigues for business suits. Certainly, the country's ability to fund basic economic and social rights, as well as many civil and political rights (a fairer justice system is never cheap), is being strengthened by marked increases in trade and investment, and burgeoning taxation and royalties receipts. Myanmar is now Asia's fastest-growing economy.[72] Whether and how quickly the country will be able to effect these beneficial outcomes in practice is of course a different question altogether. For it is a cardinal rule of the relationship between finance and human rights that while an increase in financial capacity is very often a necessary feature of raising human rights standards, it is not alone sufficient. There is no simple linear progression from a position where there is more money in businesses' bank accounts and the state's coffers, to the outcomes of more freedom, equality, comfort, and respect for all citizens.[73]

The economic tiger of India has averaged an annual growth rate of more than 6% since 1951 (including a peak of 11.4% in 2009–10), [74] and has increased its per capita income from $330 in 1993 to $1,590 in 2015,[75] yet these impressive statistics have not yielded a more equitable distribution of wealth. The share of national income commanded by the bottom 40% of Indians actually fell from 22% to 20% between 1993 and 2011, while that of the richest 20% grew from 40% to 44% in the same period.[76] Most tellingly of all, 260 million people, or 21% of the entire population, still live in extreme poverty, as measured by the World Bank, at less than $1.90 per day.[77] Misguided policies that fail to focus on those whose need is greatest; incompetent or corrupted implementation of food and other welfare programs; and vested interests that create political obstacles to changing antipoverty programs, all combine to stymie the financial benefits of the world's seventh-largest economy[78] from flowing through to uphold the most basic human rights of nearly one-third of the world's poorest people.[79]

In the end, it boils down to capacity. Financial flows are only effective in human rights terms when there are sufficient institutional, procedural, and individual capacities to direct and deliver the desired outcomes. Politicians and policy-makers, bureaucrats and businesses, lawyers, the media, and civil society all rely on adequate funding to do their jobs, and their capacity can be increased with increased funding. But this takes time and commitment. The international aid community has learned this lesson over and over. Flooding a newly anointed preferred donor-recipient country with development programs of every sort, such as happened with Timor Leste after independence in 2002, or Myanmar after 2012, at the same time as FDI surges into the economy quickly soaks up all available domestic capabilities to handle the influx. The resulting bottleneck (or "absorptive capacity" in aid-speak) tends to slow or halt public and private sector development at least for as long as it takes for capacity to be invigorated and expanded.

Indonesia went through this process after its liberation from the authoritarian Suharto regime in the late 1990s. Today, though still not without manifest problems in translating financial wealth into human rights benefits, the Indonesian government has learned from its experiences and now pursues smarter antipoverty programs rather than simply relying on the ineffective "trickle down" of wealth from ever-increasing national economic growth. Targeted programs pick out community organizations as the vectors by which cash, food, and other aid benefits are delivered, thereby bypassing endemically corrupt governmental bureaucracies. Recognizing how parlous is the position of the poor—even, indeed especially, those who are one step above the very poorest—the government has devised a raft of antipoverty programs, including a universal health care system,[80] that seek to combat the devastating consequences that come from sudden mishaps that are the stuff of ordinary life. A lost job, an accident or sudden illness, an eviction, a failed harvest, or the loss of a vital piece of machinery or equipment can each on their own pitch an individual or family back down the poverty ladder.[81]

Evidently, the extent and efficacy by which finance provides a social service to the poor has to be supervised or facilitated to a significant degree by the state. The manner in which a state (or states collectively, in respect of global finance) regulates the financial sector is critical. And never more so than how a state permits or promotes the culture that characterizes the sector, and the incentives that drive it.

Incentives and Exceptionalism

The predominant incentive in the finance sector is financial enrichment—be it personal or institutional. Crucially, however, it is not just about "how much?" but also "how much compared to others?" Indeed, the relative component is often the most important, even all-consuming, concern.[82] Nowhere is this more strikingly illustrated than through remuneration in banking and finance, where bonuses typically constitute a significant part of total earnings (from 50% to 200% above one's base salary), even after the chastening of the 2007–08 GFC and some subsequent, lackluster efforts to reform bankers' pay structures.[83] Beyond a certain amount to live comfortably (or very comfortably, by any normal metric),[84] the quest, come bonus time, is to garner a bigger payout than others in your peer group. It is a league table of your value to your employer and you want to be heading it, or at least heading up it.

This incentive process also helps explain the extraordinary gap between salary packages in finance and those in other industry sectors, the inequity of which has been a matter of enduring criticism. As John Maynard Keynes put it more than one hundred years ago (and even then he framed it as "the old question"): "How long will it be necessary to pay City men so entirely out of proportion to what other servants of society commonly receive for performing social services not less useful or difficult?"[85] It needs to be made clear that the highly elevated levels of bankers' pay in comparison with other professions was not a given across the intervening decades. In fact, following the Wall Street Crash in 1929, pay in the finance sector fell precipitously and did not fully recover in relative terms until the 1980s.[86] Evidently, the same remunerative chastisement of excessively incautious financiers has not occurred following the credit crisis in 2007/08.

An illuminating example of the consequences of today's competitively acquisitive culture is provided by the circumstances in which Stuart Gulliver, CEO of HSBC, found himself on the afternoon of February 25, 2015. Following findings in 2012 of the extensive use of HSBC accounts held in Mexico and the United States to launder the illicit funds of drug cartels and terrorist organizations—in respect of which the bank agreed to settle by signing a U.S. Justice Department "deferred prosecution agreement" for $1.9 billion—HSBC then became embroiled in a scandal involving accusations concerning its widespread facilitation of tax fraud.[87] That day Mr. Gulliver had been called before a UK Parliamentary Treasury Select Committee to explain his bank's repetitively errant behavior.

Such was the litany of criminal charges and investigations then facing HSBC—as listed, in a withering tone, by the committee chairman[88]—one might have expected Mr. Gulliver to have been notably crestfallen when further allegations emerged that he personally was involved in tax evasion by sheltering several millions dollars of bonus payments in a Panamanian company as channelled through that company's private Swiss bank. Not a bit. His unapologetic response was to claim that the purpose of the arrangement was "nothing beyond the desire for privacy" and to prevent general HSBC staff from finding out how much he had been paid.[89]

Now, whether or not this was the true reason behind the ploy, the fact is that Gulliver clearly considered it to be a perfectly acceptable, even sensible, reason to explain his actions. But is it an acceptable reason, especially coming from the chief executive of one of the world's largest financial institutions? Why must he hide information about his pay? Is he worried that if its true extent was known he would be embarrassed or ashamed, or find it difficult to defend, or that it really was a ruse to evade or avoid tax? It is notable in this respect that Gulliver specifically nominates his HSBC colleagues and staff as those from whom he sought to conceal the information. Perhaps when you reach the rarefied heights of senior banking executive pay, the league table no longer matters; you are beyond and above it. So much so that rather than yearning to secure bragging rights, you are content to retire from the competition as quietly as possible, comforted by the knowledge that you have already won.[90]

The significance of this tale lies not in what we think of HSBC or of Mr. Gulliver, but in what HSBC's serial misbehavior and Gulliver's attitude says of the culture that prevails in the financial sector, what motivates its actors, and what rules they play by. These questions have attracted the attention of anthropologists and psychologists, as well as economists.

In late 2014, a team of behavioral economists from the University of Zurich published the results of their study of 128 employees from a major international bank in which they sought to determine whether it was banking culture that engendered dishonest behavior, or whether it was simply that the industry attracted more dishonest people to work within it.[91] The researchers employed a psychological technique known as "priming" whereby individuals are first prompted by different considerations before they all then perform the same tasks. The cohort of bank employees was split into two groups—a "professional identity" group and a "control" group. Members of the former were asked a series of questions about their roles and responsibilities within the bank; the latter were asked questions about their personal life, unrelated to their job. Members of both groups were then asked to toss a coin ten times and record the results, all unobserved by the research team, the subjects having been told that they would be financially rewarded the more "heads" they recorded. This apparently innocent experiment returned some interesting results. "Heads" was recorded in the professional identity group 58.2% of the time, which is a statistically significant deviation above that of chance, while in the control group the instance of "heads" was 51.6%, which does not constitute a significant deviation above chance. Drawing on this, and other supplementary, empirical data, the team concluded that the prevailing business culture in the banking industry "favours dishonest behaviour."[92]

Anthropology on Wall Street

A partial explanation for this propensity to cheat might be found in the work of anthropologist Karen Ho. A former bank employee herself, Ho's *Liquidated: An Ethnography of Wall Street* is a fascinating study of the attitudes and aspirations of workers in finance. What stands out in her research is the conceit and sense of entitlement that pervade those who work in the sector. Throughout her many interviews, the same themes are raised time and again by interviewees as justifications for their actions, no matter how morally repugnant or legally questionable. They repeatedly stress the smartness of those they work with and (by implication) themselves. "Wall Street, in their view," she writes "ha[s] created probably the most elite work-society ever to be assembled on the globe," which was a confirmation of what they were typically told by their employers when first they started working in the sector.[93] They wear their immense capacity for hard work as a badge of honor. Logging twelve hours a day was a minimum, with the norm being more like 110+ hours per week, which would necessarily include "four or five all-nighters a month."[94] Even if, on further examination, this proved to be more about one's stamina to stay in the office all hours, rather than working productively, their resultant sacrifice of any meaningful life outside work was widely seen as further validation of the financial rewards that they would reap now, or in future.

The intense competiveness of bankers' work environment was also offered as justification for their propensity for extreme behavior. This applied not only to their relations with each other (the determination to be smarter, more hard-working, and better remunerated than one's peers), but also in relation to other businesses and professions, none of which were considered to be anywhere near as gladiatorially combative as finance. The consequences of all of this, Ho records, is a strongly held sense of superiority among finance workers, who viewed the rest of corporate America (and the "real world" generally) as slower, softer, and dumber. Even corporate lawyers were considered inferior beings, with one former lawyer-turned-banker admitting that he had been enticed to move into finance after being told that on Wall Street "you tell the corporate lawyers what to do and make much more money."[95] Another interviewee—a former Morgan Stanley analyst—explained to Ho that the firm's new recruits were typically told that they would be working with the greatest minds of the century.

Yet, even if such a pep talk were halfway accurate, great minds are no guarantees of great success. The fantastically catastrophic 1990s riches-to-rags story of the hedge fund Long-Term Capital Management (which was run by celebrated financiers, two Nobel Laureates, a host of professors, and scores of PhDs) is still the textbook illustration of the plain fact that being the smartest guys in the room does not prevent you from making colossally bad financial decisions.[96]

In the end, what Ho concludes is that these alpha attributes have not just contributed to finance's transformation from being a sector that serves the rest of the economy, to one that now dictates to the rest of the economy. They have also justified a "doing whatever it takes" work ethic that pays little, if any, heed to interests and concerns beyond the financial.

To be sure, this culture and these incentives reap substantial financial rewards for banks, bankers, their clients, and even (albeit attenuated) wider society. But this alone cannot legitimate the legal and political exceptionalism that finance demands and is largely accorded. Still less can it excuse the harms—financial and otherwise—borne by individuals and society as a consequence of this special treatment. The fact that an incentives regime strikingly different from that existing in other parts of the economy has emerged in finance does not justify itself. Nor does the fact that its emergence was superintended and even encouraged by governments and lawmakers. The prevailing culture is not preordained and can be altered in ways that better serve the interests of the economy and society as a whole. This does not mean, however, that the rewarding of self-interest must be removed as a motivating factor. It is, and will remain, an important tool and a consequence of financial markets, but it is not the goal.

The Mission

The institutions and services of finance are social functionaries, vectors of wealth creation and economic management that can help us live lives that are safer, healthier, and more fulfilling. In this way, finance can contribute directly to the building of societies that are fairer as well as freer. Finance *can* breathe life into human rights, helping translate them from aspirations into practice. The potential is enormous. The challenge—our mission, as it were—is to realize that potential, both to fulfill human rights goals and to validate finance's social contract. An essential step along this road is to agree no longer to be mesmerized by the claims that the finance sector makes of its own validity. The standards it sets itself are not, or should not be, the standards that the rest of society must accept. Rather, it is our responsibility to insist that the metrics against which the value of finance is to be measured be set by the society to which finance owes service and from which it derives legitimacy.

That these metrics must include the nature and extent of finance's contributions to the promotion and protection of human rights is the argument I've outlined in this chapter. In the next I investigate what common ground is shared by finance and human rights, upon which such a rewarding relationship might be built.

‖ 2 ‖

Living Together

> "We companies are all birds of prey; mere birds of prey. The only question is, whether in serving our own turn, we can serve yours too; whether in double-lining our own nest, we can put a single lining into yours."
>
> —Charles Dickens, *Martin Chuzzlewit* (1843)

Ends and Means

In 1998, economists Uri Gneezy and Aldo Rustichini, from Israel and Italy, respectively, conducted an experiment on the impact of monetary fines on people's behavior.[1] After observing the rates at which parents arrived late to collect their children at day-care centers, they introduced a fine for latecomers. They were testing the so-called deterrence hypothesis, which assumes that the introduction of a penalty will produce a reduction in the targeted behavior. The results of their study, however, pointed in precisely the opposite direction. Indeed, not only was there no deterrent effect, the number of tardy parents actually increased to double the rate recorded before the fine was imposed. What is more, the elevated rates of late parents remained so even after the fine system was removed.

After analyzing the data, the two researchers reached an intriguing conclusion. The introduction of a fine system appeared to sanitize the relationship between the late parents and the day-care centers. In effect, it rubbed away the uncomfortable and messy indebtedness the late parents otherwise felt toward the staff who had to stay behind to look after their children. As the parents were now "paying" for this after-hours service, it seemed that they were more (not less) willing to flaunt the pickup deadlines. As psychologist Christian Jarrett observed of this outcome, "By introducing money into the equation, the day care centers undermined an unspoken agreement built on social trust and good morals."[2]

If a monetary incentive really is capable of desensitizing us to the social consequences of our actions, then might this be a root cause of why so often the various iniquities and wickednesses of the global finance system are excused or overlooked? Well, yes, quite possibly. But ultimately our susceptibility to money's seductive powers depends on a number of other factors, including, in particular, the nature and extent of the regulatory regime within which money is managed.

In the case of the day-care centers, the fine was introduced into the grey area of after-hours responsibilities, an issue that was not explicitly addressed in the contracts existing between parents and the centers. Rather, it was left to an implied sense of propriety expected of parents (to be late only in exceptional circumstances) and the staff (to look after uncollected children). As the researchers note in their study, had the fine been much larger, then they would very likely have observed a deterrent effect.

In the world of finance, questions about the sufficiency and magnitude of sanctions to deter inappropriate or illegal actions, as well as the extent and manner of their enforcement, are also subject to much debate.[3] This is because such regulatory concerns reflect the very purposes of the financial system itself, namely, to generate *and* protect wealth through the prudent allocation of risk. It is in the inevitable tension created by the co-existence of these two objectives that we find a place for human rights arguments.

The pressing and never-ending obligations of universal human rights protection play a critical role in the legitimization of finance. The facilitative and potentially life-enhancing functions of finance are utilitarian in nature. Financial products, the people who produce them, and the manner in which they do so, all have the capacity to enhance the human condition and thereby justify their existence. But equally, when they fail to do so, do so poorly, or operate in ways that diminish the rights of the many in favor of a few, then the rationale of finance is damaged or destroyed. As individuals, communities, organizations, corporations, and governments, we have great expectations of services offered by finance. We make use of them to purchase, invest, borrow, repay, donate, lend, insure, and underwrite in so many areas of our daily lives. So much so that it can be fairly said not only that money makes the world go around, but also that the world revolves around money. Its pre-eminence threatens to overwhelm, at the same time as it promises to deliver, which tension is reflected in finance's long history.

Across time and all over the world, from Mesopotamia, through Qin Dynasty China, Mauryan India, and in ancient Greece and Rome, monetary transactions predate (and eventually displaced) the time-honored systems of barter. They did so by permitting one side of the exchange to use the medium of money to fulfill the conditions of the transaction, thereby cracking open the almost endless possibilities of commercial intercourse.[4] The pace of social progress accelerated in Europe, for instance, when during the late Middle Ages, contracts replaced custom, serfdom declined, and capitalism flourished. Money's fungibility and capacity to multiply have, over time, expanded our horizons in ways that our forebears could have barely imagined. The author of one of the very first books published on money and financial markets, Walter Bagehot, essayist and former, long-time editor of *The Economist*, wrote in 1873 that even the citizens of Elizabethan England (an unprecedentedly prosperous time in its history) "would have thought that it was of no use inventing railways (if [they] could have understood what a railway meant), for you would not have been able to collect the capital with which to make them."[5]

It is the extraordinary utility of money that has established it as the lifeblood of the economy. Its relative value, mass mobility, and volatility all profoundly affect the way economies work and thereby directly impact on social and political affairs. At an individual level, money also operates as an indicator of wealth; it is a representation of one's financial capacity that translates directly into social status and political power.

That the acquisition of wealth amounts to personal virtue (as Plato had the mythical Meno proclaim in his dialogue with Socrates), is, however, another matter altogether. It is true that today, as in ancient Greece, much time and effort is invested in the getting and spending of money, and that some degree of esteem is granted to those who excel in both respects. Wealth can be generated in noble and beneficial ways and it can be dispensed with virtuous intent (as might be claimed of the so-called philanthro-capitalists we will encounter in chapter 5). But such a correlation is coincidental rather than necessary. Virtue, as Socrates so clinically exposed to Meno, is no more assured by one's hordes of gold and silver, as it is by one's lack of them.[6]

Money as an Instrument

Money, despite all, remains merely an instrument, inert and eminently transferable. The manner in which it is acquired and the uses to which it is put are not determined by the medium itself, but rather by the objects and designs of those who raise, allocate, and spend it. Like a gun, money can liberate or kill, depending on the hand that holds it. As we are unable to guarantee the virtuousness of those who wield the instrument, it is susceptible to abuse. There needs to be, therefore, some level of public or state intervention that both permits and restricts the actions of financiers. That is the job of the financial system, and it holds true whether the state is inclined to regulate so as to allow market forces as much freedom as possible with only a broadly conceived goal in mind (simply to "create as big a pie as possible"), or the purpose is much more specific ("how precisely the pie is to be made and divided up"), and where market forces are

constrained accordingly. Advocates of the former approach may be fond of pit-
ting government regulation against market regulation, as did Alan Greenspan in
his infamous remark that "there's nothing involved in federal regulation which
makes it superior to market regulation."[7] But the difference is a matter of degree,
not kind.

A free market in finance, as in all other aspects of the economy, is not in fact
free of *rules*. Some rules, including those that effect government intermediation,
are always necessary in order to allow the market to function, however freely, as
Mr. Greenspan himself was all too aware. During his time as head of the Federal
Reserve he was an arch exponent of the most manipulative of all interventionist
devices in the financial markets, the setting of interest rates. His orchestrated
slashing of the base U.S. interest rate (that is, the interest rate that banks charge
one another for one day [overnight] lending)[8] from 9% to 3% between May
1989 and September 1992, and then again from 6% to 1% between January 2001
and June 2003, flooded the U.S. economy with cheap credit and expanded the
capacity of financial markets exponentially.[9]

The essential feature of all rules of any financial system are that they ought
to impose order according to the overarching goals that society expects of
capital—how and by whom it is raised, allocated, and used. Thus, while it is generally accepted that a few might profit enormously, the financial system ought
to be expected to assist in the betterment of society as a whole by improving
the conditions of everyone, including the standards of human rights protection
that they enjoy. The formally widespread prohibition against charging interest in
ancient economies (and still nominally today within Islamic banking) is a clear
example of a rule designed to strike what was considered to be a fair balance
between the market dynamics of lenders and borrowers on the one hand, and
the broader community's economic and social interests on the other. The whole
idea of taxation—on income, consumption, and transactions—is another example of a grand policy to spread wealth and its benefits, as we will investigate at
length in chapter 5.

At their base, most, if not all, financial systems will claim that they are serving
the "betterment of society" objective, even if their methods, standards of service,
and, indeed, definitions of "society" differ markedly between systems and over
time. Financial systems are, like all other aspects of modern societies, affected
by an array of economic impulses, political prejudices, and social mores, which
emanate from local and global sources and which swirl around, complement,
and contradict each other. Sometimes the impetus is morally based. The rise of
Christianity during the later stages of the Roman Empire inspired the Roman
rule against usury (the charging of excessive interest on lending money) on the
basis that early Christians considered the practice to be immoral. No matter that
while it may have helped the poor by freeing them from financial exploitation, it

also hindered them by restricting their access to financial opportunity. At other times, the rationale may be much more pragmatic. The decision, for example, by the U.S. Federal Reserve in 1981 to restrict money supply and let interest rates float was aimed at curbing rampant inflation. Inflation was drastically cut in the immediate aftermath, but the newfound volatility of interest rates, inadvertently awoke the then-somnolent, predictable, and relatively insignificant bond markets, which quickly grew to become the unruly and enormously powerful behemoths they are today.[10]

Evidently the impulses as well as the impacts of financial regulation can be variable, unpredictable, and difficult to control. But they can also be very significant in social as well as economic spheres, including with respect to standards of human rights protection.

A Common Liberal Heritage

Historian Niall Ferguson argues in *The Ascent of Money* that finance has fuelled just about every significant advancement in human society.[11] The civilizations of ancient Babylon and Greece, the industrialization of Europe and now Asia, and the professionalization of today's Western economies have flourished, and sometimes fallen, on the back of finance. Such is the power of its lure and leverage and the torment of its squander and absence. The dawn of the "Age of Rights" has been no exception.[12]

The rights revolutions in eighteenth-century France and the United States were inspired by peoples' desires to shake loose the shackles of not only political repression and social immobility, but also commercial nepotism and usurious financiers. The revolutionaries' concerns were as much to do with private inequities as with public injustices. As such, they drew on the potent though still- emerging strain of liberal philosophy espousing individual rationality and rights, alongside the demands of the social contract (between the governed and the governors) and the dismantling of constraints of political preordination.

But there were also more prosaic financial reasons for the unrest. Fomenting in the minds of the American colonists in the late 1760s, for instance, was an acute sense of injustice over the British Empire's ruthless milking of the colonial economies to fund the imperial homeland's astronomical national debt following its victory over the French in the North American leg of the eighteenth-century Great War for Empire. Through the Imperial *Navigation Acts* (which directed nearly all the proceeds of colonial trade to London) and the *Stamp Act* (which directed colonial tax receipts the same way), Britain seriously stifled private commercial enterprise in its American colonies, and also trampled on civic pride and a sense of fairness, giving rise to the War of Independence that followed.

The French Revolutionaries were, if anything, even more embittered and determined to right private wrongs and public prejudices. The Jacobins' focus was on overturning the socially and economically destructive and self-serving privileges of the aristocracy and the church's attendant religious hierarchy (the so-called first and second estates) to the benefit of the peasants and professionals (the third estate). Again, it was the dire circumstances of the state's coffers, exhausted by the Great War for Empire, that precipitated the crisis when Louis XVI tried to enforce the cripplingly regressive taxes to which the ordinary people were subject but the aristocracy and clergy were exempt. Though the revolutionaries prevailed in the events that followed, there remained an uneasy tension between their individual and social sentiments as reflected in the very first article of the iconic *Déclaration des Droits de l'Homme et du Citoyen* (1789), which proclaimed both that men are free and equal in rights, and that, nevertheless, social distinctions can legitimately exist provided they are for the public good.[13]

Human Rights Globalization

The internationalization of human rights, whose modern epoch extends from 1945 onward, also has a financial tale to tell. The conferences on peace, security, and social stability, held in Dumbarton Oakes (in October 1944) and San Francisco (in June 1945) that established the United Nations, followed hot on the heels of the economic- and finance-focussed congress in Bretton Woods (in July 1944) that established the International Monetary Fund (IMF) and the International Bank for Reconstruction and Development (IBRD), the foundational institution of the World Bank Group. And while the original intention had been neatly to carve up global institutional responsibilities according to these subject areas, conceptual intersections and practical realities rudely intervened. Neither the Articles of Agreement of the IMF nor those of the World Bank could avoid related social concerns (so both stress the necessity of promoting standards of living and labor conditions),[14] and the UN's mandate was stretched not only into the economic realm (the UN Charter created the Economic and Social Council), but also the political realm, with the express inclusion of human rights in the Charter's Preamble (the Member States reaffirming "our faith in fundamental human rights") and elsewhere throughout the Charter's text.[15]

The insertion of proclamations of support for human rights in the UN Charter was a foundational moment in the evolution of the modern era of international human rights standards. Legal scholar Mary Ann Glendon's characterization of the occasion as a "glimmering thread in a web of power and interest"[16] elegantly captures the promise as well as the peril of human rights in the postwar world. At the time, no one seriously believed that appeals to human rights would prevent states from using their sovereignty in time-honored ways as either a sword or a shield to protect or advance their interests,[17] still less that they would be considered necessary to legitimate exercises of economic power.

In fact, the cruel despotisms that so dominated Europe's horizon before, during, and after the Second World War had profound effects on philosophy and economics that were to bear directly on the relationship between human rights, economics, and finance at a global level. Young intellectuals such as Ayn Rand (an émigré from Russia in the 1920s) and Milton Friedman (whose Hungarian Jewish parents migrated to the United States in the 1890s) were antagonistic toward statist government, having been scarred by the calamities they witnessed (directly, in Rand's case) unfolding in Germany and Russia in the interwar years at the hands of all-powerful state apparatuses. In the United States, both found a receptive and nurturing home for the development of their thinking in the 1950s, 1960s and 1970s. Rand's radical "objectivist" brand of moral philosophy stressed the paramountcy of the individual as a vehicle of rational self-interest, to be left to his or her own devices and destiny, almost wholly untouched by state interference.[18] Friedman's perception of individual freedom was less utopian, grounded as it was in the imperative of economic freedom. Friedman considered the former to be possible only through the latter, and furthermore, that a robust, free-market economy would be best able to serve the welfare needs of society as a whole.[19] Alan Greenspan, among many other powerful economic lever-pullers in the late twentieth century, was an acolyte of both of these iconoclastic thinkers.

Paying for Rights

The connections between prosperity and financial security on the one hand, and individual rights and social justice on the other, are clear to see. During the same postwar period, much of the effort expended in international relations was in the name of securing peace and stability through a combination of economic strength and individual freedoms, although the methods used were somewhat more statist and communitarian. The rebuilding of Western Europe after the war was being underwritten by the U.S. Marshall Plan, and to a lesser extent the World Bank. Institutions of social welfare were being established in all countries in the West, and the initial steps toward a European Economic Community (later the European Union) were being taken along a path signposted with the four freedoms of movement of people, goods, services and capital. The United Nations, the Organization of American States, and the Council of Europe were all promulgating charters of human rights that guaranteed civil, political, economic, and social rights, and the European imperial powers were busy divesting themselves of their dominions, while leaving behind legal, political, and, most crucially, economic legacies upon which they drew for decades to come.

During the height of the Cold War, there was a sort of uneasy detente between the Left and the Right in Western politics and economics. The Left was willing to tolerate some degree of market freedom provided it filled the state coffers as well as individual pockets, and the Right was prepared to tolerate financing a welfare state provided that the captains of capitalism were otherwise given a fairly free rein. The position of human rights has in fact vacillated in the space between the two. Marxist orthodoxy derided the notion of rights of the individual as atomistic and socially destructive, a capitalist prop that championed freedom of the few over equality between the many.[20] Variants of this orthodoxy were propounded by the Left for as long as the political culture in the West associated human rights with the classic liberalist vision of civil and political *freedoms*—that is, individual liberties that are both protected by the state and protected against unwarranted state interference or coercion.[21] In this sense then, human rights were more the preserve of the antistatist conservatives or right-wing sympathizers; a natural ally of economic liberalism that lent support to the likes of Ayn Rand in her heroic tale of man-against-state in *Atlas Shrugged*.[22]

From the mid-1970s onward, however, the perception of what constituted human rights recovered somewhat from the Cold War's snap-frozen labels of civil and political rights as Western, and economic and social rights as Socialist. There were a number of reasons for this. The UN's International Covenant on Economic, Social and Cultural Rights (ICESCR) came into force in 1976, alongside its fraternal twin, the International Covenant on Civil and Political Rights (ICCPR), with the principal aim of redressing social and economic inequities. The newly independent and the recently more vocal nations of the South and East (that is, in South America, Africa, South and South-East Asia and the Pacific, and, after 1989, Eastern Europe) were showing heightened interest in the value of economic and social rights as their economies started to develop. The Left worldwide softened its approach to human rights as a whole, seeing communitarian worth in individual rights to achieving such fundamental goods as sufficient food and water, adequate housing, and access to health care and education. All of these, it was recognized, required a highly proactive state, and effectively counterbalanced the claims of small state proponents that all governments need do is not to interfere with people's freedoms.

Finding Rights

Across the political spectrum, human rights were enjoying a surge of interest as they began increasingly to be deployed in arguments for why states should and could do more to protect the poor and vulnerable at home and overseas, and as rhetorical weapons against bad or tyrannical governments, wherever they ruled. Democracies appeared to relocate their human rights souls with, for example, a very sudden spike in the mention of human rights in the U.S. media in the mid-1970s. Samuel Moyn notes that in 1977 the term "human rights" appeared five times more often in the pages of the *New York Times* than in any previous year.[23] There is no doubt that this was due to the prominent place given to human rights in Jimmy Carter's presidential campaign speeches in late 1976, and then again in his inaugural address in January 1977. But the newfound favor in the notion also reflected the growth in international human rights instruments, especially under the auspices of the UN.

In the two decades following the coming into force of the two Covenants mentioned above, three further seminal treaties were negotiated and adopted by the UN, and widely ratified by states: the Convention on the Elimination of Discrimination against Women 1979 (CEDAW), the Convention Against Torture 1984 (CAT), and the Convention on the Rights of the Child 1989 (CRC). This activity reached its apotheosis with the CRC, which holds the records for both attracting the greatest number of ratifying or acceding states (that is, all, except the United States),[24] and in the quickest time. It was opened for signature on November 20, 1989, and received the requisite number of ratifications (twenty) less than a year later (it had taken both the ICCPR and ICESCR 10 years to reach that stage),[25] coming into force on September 2, 1990.

The coincidence of this rights and freedoms fervor with the dismantling of the Berlin Wall created something of a dislocation in the favor and fortunes of the human rights standard-setting at the international level. For while the clamor within international organizations, scholars, and civil society was to accelerate the expansion of the human rights universe, many of the states themselves were much more tentative, and some decidedly skeptical. In the nearly thirty years since, the UN has continued to churn out human rights treaties covering human rights defenders, human trafficking, enforced disappearances, child soldiers, migrant workers, indigenous peoples, and persons with disabilities, among others.[26] At the same time, the protection and promotion of human rights has been invoked in support of a widening array of matters of international concern, including humanitarian law, environmental protection, the treatment of refugees, punishing war crimes and crimes against humanity, and even justifying the use of armed force (that is, on the basis of a "responsibility to protect" individuals and communities from egregious rights violations).

Yet, in key respects, states have not followed on an individual basis that which collectively they have promulgated through the good offices of the UN. The Migrant Workers Convention, for example, took thirteen years to attract a sufficient number of ratifications to come into force in 2003, and by the end of 2017 still had only fifty-one signatories, among which, significantly, there are no rich, predominantly migrant-recipient, states. An Optional Protocol to the ICESCR permitting its supervisory committee to hear individual complaints of breaches of economic, social, or cultural rights was not finally agreed to until 2008, some twenty-five years after the same facility was attached to the ICCPR.[27] And finally, despite more than two decades of negotiation, the rights of indigenous peoples have managed to obtain no more protection than a nonbinding UN Declaration in 2007, and even that was initially renounced by key nations with indigenous populations such as Australia, Canada, New Zealand, and the United States, before each of these states eventually endorsed the Declaration by early 2011.

Human Rights and the Global Economy

There are in fact many reasons for states' hesitancy. They include the predictable inclination of governments and others in positions of power to be resistant to the claims made on them by international human rights laws, precisely because such claims limit the scope and content of their authority, notwithstanding the fact that acceding to such limitation can itself be a source of respect and authority. There are also ever-present relativist challenges to the proclamations of the universality of human rights, based on assertions of substantial cultural, religious, political, and economic differences between states. And finally there is also the palpable sense of rights treaty fatigue among states and their representatives. As a result, there exists a healthy body of critical analysis, essentially querying whether respect for human rights really is either the solution to a seemingly ever-expanding menu of the world's nastiest problems, or the object of a worthwhile human endeavor.[28]

To my mind, this strengthens the human rights project, by helping to ensure that its tenets are made more robust and defensible through adversity, rather than overprotecting them, as one might do a child.[29] This is so even when critics suggest, for instance, that the presence of human rights has "contributed to making mass murder more, rather than less, likely," because, argues Charles Blattberg, their expression as abstract entities desensitizes us to the actual realities of their abuse or deprivation in practice.[30] Or when legal theorist Costas Douzinas argues that the very success of the mainstreaming of human rights today has stripped them of their essential power of antiestablishment, revolutionary promise.[31] To engage with such critiques, by addressing, rebutting, or even accepting points they contain helps to build stronger and better-directed arguments in support of the human rights project. So, in response to Blattberg's "mass murder" barb, for example, it might be that the problem lies not so much in the reification of human rights in more legal instruments and heavier political rhetoric, but in the fact that there is presently not enough understanding of their on-the-ground impact. And in response to the Douzinas's denouement message, it might be said that the cutting edge of human rights need not be dulled just because more of its precepts are embraced by establishment entities, but it does mean that the ways in which the instrument is used must necessarily change.

The apparently unpromising prospects and problems of integrating human rights with the global economy are no exception in this regard. Movements on the triple fronts of philosophy, development, and international law have pressed for the express consideration of human rights in the execution of economic policy and the prosecution of commercial practice. John Rawls's highly influential theory of justice, which so invigorated political science in the 1970s and beyond, argued that rights were to be underpinned by the notion of a fair distribution of goods and necessities throughout society.[32] During the 1980s and 1990s in particular, a discordant collection of academics, policy wonks, development practitioners, and civil society activists advanced various forms of a so-called human rights–based approach to development, which forged an instinctively appealing, but practicably problematic, union between the aims of human rights and development.[33]

More recently, legal theoreticians and practitioners have spawned an interest in determining to what extent nonstate actors (NSAs) are legitimate and practicable agents within international law, including as duty-holders of international human rights obligations. The significance of this last point in the current context is that these NSAs include multilateral economic and finance bodies such as the World Bank, the IMF, and the World Trade Organization (WTO) (to the extent that it regulates cross-border financial transactions).[34] They also include globalized private actors, like transnational corporations (including banks), philanthropic foundations, and public-private partnerships, like the Global Fund or GAVI (the Global Alliance for Vaccination and Immunization), which over the past fifteen years has immunized 500 million of the world's poorest children against such preventable diseases as cholera, polio, meningitis, measles, rubella, and rotavirus.[35]

Rights Politics

These efforts all assume a level of substrata interconnection between the global economy and human rights, and they also assume that by exposing these connections, the former would be better able to service the latter. Yet, the very elasticity in the definition and application of human rights that permits such links to be made can also provide cover for abusing rights. The apparent bendability of the obligations attached to economic and social rights in international legal texts has long been a source of frustration and confrontation between and within states. The overarching mandate of the ICESCR obliges each state party (in article 2(1)) "to take steps . . . to the maximum of its available resources, with a view to achieving progressively the full realization of the rights recognized in the present Covenant."[36] These qualifications are considered by many to be political necessities, written in so as to entice states to sign up in the first place, and further, they reflect the inescapable reality of the widely differing state capacities to provide for basic economic and social rights. Certainly, these "let-out" provisions are not themselves unlimited—the Covenant's overseeing committee has made it clear that there are "core minimum standards" beneath which the Covenant permits no state to descend—they nonetheless provide states with plenty of wiggle room.[37]

Though the ICESCR was signed by the United States under the Carter presidency in 1977, successive U.S. administrations have refused to ratify the Covenant (as have nearly thirty other states), on the grounds that the objectives expressed in the treaty, such as the provision of adequate food, education, housing, and health care, are not properly the province of human rights.[38] More specifically, the argument goes, they are not the proper subject of human rights *law*, in the sense of being legally enforceable claims against the state, but rather are public policy goals, to which, nevertheless, "the United States is committed," as it has stressed during Universal Periodic Reviews before the UN Human Rights Council.[39] Even American human rights advocates are skeptical of the legal status of economic and social rights. Aryeh Neier, who founded Human Rights Watch, dismissed such "broad assertions . . . of a right to shelter or housing, a right to education, a right to social security, a right to a job, and a right to health care [as occupying] territory that is unmanageable through the judicial process and that intrudes fundamentally into an area where the democratic process ought to prevail."[40]

Interestingly, China argues much the same point but in an entirely different direction. China signed both the ICESCR and the ICCPR in the late 1990s, but has only gone on to ratify the former, in 2001.[41] From its initial blunt and archly defensive foray into the international debate on human rights in its 1991 white paper *Human Rights in China*, the government has consistently argued that civil and political rights, such as freedom of expression, association, movement, political and religious beliefs, and the right to free elections, are desirable goals. However, they must be secondary to the pursuit of securing peoples' basic economic and social rights, which is to be achieved through a focus economic growth and prosperity. The language in which China engages in international debate today is certainly less strident and more nuanced,[42] but its steely resolve to suppress civil and political rights has, if anything, increased in recent years,[43] as enabled by the ruling Communist Party's ready use of state security and public order exceptions to the list of civil and political rights protected by the *Constitution of the People's Republic of China* (1982).[44]

In common with international human rights instruments and many national constitutional right provisions, rights guarantees are subject to conditions under which they may legitimately be circumscribed by the state. It is, however, in the articulation and application of these limitations that China exhibits particular zeal. Thus, for example, the right to privacy is restricted "in cases where, to meet the needs of State security or of criminal investigation, public security or procuratorial organs are permitted to censor correspondence in accordance with the procedures prescribed by law" (Article 40), and freedom of speech in so far as it relates to criticisms of the government is qualified by the simple, but effective, prohibition of "fabrication or distortion of facts for purposes of libel or false incrimination" (Article 41). Above all, the decisive power to interpret any statute, and to interpret and supervise the enforcement of the *Constitution* lies not with the judiciary, but with the Standing Committee of the National Peoples' Congress, the state's most powerful political body (Article 67). Together, these limitations and assignment of constitutional powers provide more than enough latitude for the Chinese state to control the peoples' exercise of their civil rights according to whatever economic or political demands it sees fit to impose.

The politicization of rights has also made itself apparent in debates over the conditions that can permissibly be attached to international trade.[45] Given that, by definition, no trading regime is ever truly free from conditions, and that international trade law does as much to supervise the maintenance of trade restrictions as it does to dismantle them, it is unsurprising that human rights grounds have been raised as legitimate concerns for trade to consider. In the most concerted effort yet to introduce human rights conditions into mainstream international trade rules, Western powers, led by the EU and the United States, advocated that minimum labor standards (beyond the lone existing prohibition of the use of prison labor) ought to form part of WTO law. This proposition was aired first at a meeting of trade ministers in Singapore in 1996 and then again, four years later in Seattle, and was greeted on both occasions by fearsome opposition from developing states on grounds that had little or nothing to do with human rights, but far more to do with economics.[46]

As is the way with so many trade disputes, both sides allege that there are ulterior motives behind the other's position. Developing states have argued that the real reason for imposing minimum standards governing wages, working conditions, collective bargaining rights, workplace health and safety measures, and more is to nullify that most potent of the developing world's comparative advantages—cheap labor. Western states are concerned, they add, to protect their own domestic workforces and appease their own restless trade unions worried about being undercut by low overseas labor costs. The Western states, for their part, have argued that many developing states are sacrificing human rights at the altar of economic growth, by using international trade law as an excuse and duplicitously claiming that the West's reasoning was trade protectionist and self-serving.[47] While there is truth in both sides of the argument—and the stalemate meant that the proposed labor standards were never introduced—what is most noteworthy about the episode is how far the rhetoric of human rights was bent to the exigencies of economics.

The fundamental point demonstrated by each of these examples is that the relationship between economics on the one hand, and human rights on the other is one of an open partnership: sometimes flexible and accepting; at other times secretive and seditious. And while they are prone to separation and even divorce, the demands of political responsibility and social legitimacy keep them in bed together. David Hume's observation some 250 years ago, that all economic questions are, ultimately, questions of the principles and passions of human nature, bears well the test of time.[48]

Complicated Confederacy

It is within this broad economic context that the peculiar confederacy of finance and human rights is to be understood and assessed. It is peculiar because while the ubiquity of finance in everyday life—whether small or large, sophisticated or rudimentary—is obvious, its institutional and systemic features are nearly always one or more steps removed from direct impact on peoples' lives. Even the more or less straightforward examples of positive and negative human rights effects caused by financial actions tend to prove this rule.

Thus, while the expansion of subprime mortgages in the United States in the 1990s and 2000s brought house-ownership within reach of many who were otherwise locked out of the housing market, the predatory lending practices of banks and brokers that characterized the sale of these mortgages precipitated serious social consequences. The housing market collapsed, with the loss of some 8 million to 13 million homes in the United States according to the Financial Crisis Inquiry Commission,[49] and the living and human rights standards of many Americans plummeted. The collateral damage of the crisis, as the commission put it, were "real people and real communities."[50]

In a similar vein, the financing of mining projects or utilities installations can also have adverse social and environmental consequences, but equally it can provide jobs and livelihoods, increase education opportunities, and improve access to health care for employees and local communities.[51] On their face, these connections between financier and human rights beneficiary or victim appear more or less binary. On a closer look however, the relations in both cases are more convoluted, with multilayered intersections and diffuse lines of responsibility and liability.

A key driving force behind the subprime mortgage market was a huge and complex web of collateralized debt obligations (CDOs), whereby individual loans were first aggregated and then putatively insured against default by being bought and sold in tranches by a host of financial actors, including retail and investment banks, insurance companies, institutional investors, governments, and ordinary shareholders. As a result, though the reprehensible and at-times illegal actions of the "face to face" mortgage retailers certainly played a part in the financial calamity that befell so many home owners, the causal roots of their misfortune were in fact widely dispersed throughout the whole of the financial system.

The circumstances that typify corporate or project financing are similarly indirect and unclear, even if less extensively so. Thus, a mining or utilities corporation might obtain funding through a range of channels, from using its own cash reserves to raising capital by issuing stock or bonds, taking out bank loans, using funds from private sector or host government partners, or accepting investments from multilateral agencies such as the World Bank's International Finance Corporation. In addition, corporations will have obtained insurance, from private sector insurers or from public sector guarantors, like national export credit agencies or the World Bank's Multilateral Investment Guarantee Agency. The point is that here again we see that the "direct" financial relationship with the individual human rights holders is only a part of a much bigger and more complicated story. Parts are played by a host of other actors whose relationships with the affected individuals are not only indirect, but their motives and interests in the particular project and its impact on those individuals can vary considerably.[52] The private sector financiers will be focused on investment returns, whether or not they are committed to considering the social and environmental impacts of their project financing decisions as one of the eighty-five or so financial institutions signed up to the *Equator Principles*.[53] In contrast, the interests of the host state government, home state export credit agencies, and development agencies will place greater emphasis on the project's socioeconomic outcomes, alongside the project's financial viability.

In this context, consider, for example, the complicated matter of the complicity of financial institutions in the mining of coltan in the Democratic Republic of Congo (DRC), where 80% of the world's reserves of the element are to be found. Tantalum, a derivative of coltan, is an essential component in a wide range of high-tech devices, including cell phones and laptop computers, as well as pacemakers and prosthetic hips. Accelerating demand has wildly inflated the commodity's value, with its market price more than trebling between 2011 and 2012.[54] The tremendous riches to be gained from mining it have attracted both heavy investment and a unenviable record of widespread abuses of the rights to life, personal security, health, housing and labor, in particular,[55] all fuelled by corruption, lawlessness, and violence.[56]

The local and international mining companies (from Australia, Canada, China, the UK, and the United States) operating in Eastern DRC and neighboring Rwanda, Burundi, and Uganda, together with their chain of corporate clients (from Kemet, a major capacitor manufacturer, to phone makers Apple and Samsung),[57] have all obtained funding from, or through, banks. All interested parties, including corrupt government officials and warlords, are also utilizing various banking services to handle the proceeds from coltan sales. The four states mentioned are also receiving financial assistance from international development agencies as such as the World Bank, EU Aid, and several bilateral agencies. To what extent these banks ought to be held responsible for human rights abuses occurring further down the supply line is clearly a moot point.[58] That said, the argument that they should and could do more to try to prevent such abuses occurring in the first place is persuasive,[59] especially as the *Dodd-Frank Act* disclosure requirements regarding dealing in conflict minerals now make their job of identifying potential problem clients that much easier.[60] Either way, the extent to which they *can* be held responsible depends on there being some evident line of cause and effect between the actions of the financier and the rights abuses, which can often be very difficult to establish.[61]

Such complex patterns of interconnection between financial inputs and human rights outcomes are endemic to the everyday social settings of human interaction in which they occur. We are, individually and collectively, "the bedrock" of any economic system, argues Mary Dowell-Jones. "Human beings are . . . the fundamental unit of any economic system. Lost jobs and savings = lost spending power = lower economic growth = lower financial returns. The whole is irreducibly symbiotic," as she neatly puts it.[62]

Speaking Different Languages

These practical difficulties in charting the precise lines of connection between finance and human rights are reflected in conceptual clashes, ignorance, and misunderstandings of each other's objectives, methods, terms, and conditions. Even when they do earnestly try to understand and relate to each other, the two disciplines resemble as much ships passing in the night as a day-time car crash.

To some extent this is just a particular circumstance of the dissonance on a broader plane between the "languages" of economics and human rights. Manuel Couret Branco—a Portuguese economist who is one of the few scholars to address the issue in any depth—puts his finger neatly on their different approaches by characterizing economics' language as one of "wants, [where] ability to pay is the key question," whereas "within the language of rights, it is entitlement."[63] This, argues Branco, leads inevitably to a clash of social perspectives, whereby in economics, exclusion and inequality are expected and tolerated, while in human rights, inclusion and equality are the "only acceptable situation." What makes this clash significant is that while immediately following the Second World War there might have been some grounds to believe that the politics of human rights would hold sway on a global scale, the idea was short-lived. It has since been qualified by the politics of economics, and especially by the demands of finance, which together have become the predominant sources of global power.

This circumstance presents two foundational propositions that underpin the aims and objects of human rights. First, the fact that economics and finance are the pre-eminent focuses of global politics (no matter that they are normally mixed with any number of other concerns, be they social, environmental, cultural, or geographical), is not something human rights advocate can ignore, still less try to defeat. And second, that the intentions and goals of human rights need to be reconciled, to some degree, with those of economics and finance. Not, I hasten to add, that this requires the supplication of human rights to the demands of economics and finance, but because financial capacity and economic efficiency are vital to the promotion and protection of human rights. They are "instruments for the bettering of human life," as the father of welfare economics, Arthur Pigou, succinctly put it nearly a century ago.[64]

Seeking such reconciliation between finance and human rights is hampered not only by language and the shifting priorities of global power bases, but also by their respective cultural and technical peculiarities. There can be no doubt that the inscrutability of modern financial systems is daunting, not least because the analytical rigor by which they claim to be driven and explained is as flawed as it is adamant. The mathematical formulae of so-called quants (quantitative risk analysts) who model not just market behavior but also that of humans, are only fully predictable in their eventual failure. In the end they are always "fooled by randomness," as author and former trader Nassim Taleb famously labeled it.[65] So while both financial insiders and outsiders are urged to believe in the power of the market *and* in its tameability by the smartest analysts that money can buy, such a stance is conceptually contradictory and evidently false in practice. It is also especially unhelpful to efforts trying to bridge the gap in mutual understanding between the world views of human rights experts and financial specialists.

Minding this gap is something that Mary Dowell-Jones has been doing for more than a decade. Mary holds the rare distinction of being both an accomplished human rights scholar and an expert in finance. She is also unafraid to call out the imperfections in the efforts of players on both sides of the finance/ human rights divide to take each other seriously and thereby try to bridge the gap between them. Mary and I began to work together after we met in Geneva in January 2009 at a gathering of would-be bridge builders from both camps.

By that time, the breadth and depth of the social consequences of the 2007– 08 financial crash were readily apparent. And yet, conspicuously absent from the main proposals to reform finance then being considered was any discussion of the relevance of human rights principles. In part this was due to the ignorance (or dismissal) of human rights among the financial sector contributors to these discussions. But it was also due to the lack of the necessary technical understanding among rights advocates of how financial systems really function.[66] The financial reform agenda was thereby robbed of an important perspective on account of the two sides talking past or at each other, rather than with each other. An essential first step to repairing this circumstance, we argued, was that human rights advocates must put themselves in the shoes of the financiers and reflect on what might best convince them of the value of serving rather than subverting human rights goals.[67]

Missed Opportunities

The corollary of the absence of human rights expertise within finance is, naturally enough, the fact that human rights considerations constitute no part of the architectural deliberations on how global finance is regulated presently, and how it might be regulated in the future. That is, despite grand and repeated calls for human rights principles to "form the cornerstone of financial regulatory efforts from the design to implementation to monitoring stages."[68] Without any concrete proposals backing up these calls specifying *how* human rights principles might be viably translated into the practice of financial regulation, such rhetoric, no matter how politically appealing, disappears into thin air. Such proposals need to be detailed and practicable.

It is not enough to call for reforms to "ensure that all economic policy at the domestic and international levels be carried out in accordance with the body of standards and principles offered by the human rights regime." [69] Explaining what precisely those principles mean in practice for economic policymaking is also needed. As they stand, international human rights laws provide no such detailed prescriptions. Rather, they do what was originally intended of them, namely, articulating desired rights outcomes of more freedom, safety, and comfort. If they are to do more, then a lot of extra work needs to be done by all of us in the human rights community to retrofit those outcomes with viable economic and political processes by which they might best be achieved. Engaging in the debate at the level of political principle is certainly necessary and important in order to attract attention, to raise profile, and to stake out moral and political territorial claims. But where serious engagement is lacking at the level of financial practice, then no matter its moral message, human rights advocacy will founder on the rocks of finance's existing vested interests, institutions, and political power.

The failure to interact on meaningfully detailed terms is, however, not all in one direction. It remains a problem for both sides of the divide, as economists and finance specialists are equally guilty of superficiality in their understanding of human rights. Take, for example, Yale economist Robert Shiller's engagement with human rights. Shiller's revealing work on the irrationality of human behavior by which financial markets are designed and driven marks him out as a high-profile financial commentator seemingly well-disposed toward the idea of making finance better serve the interests of human rights. In *Finance and the Good Society*, Shiller argues for what he calls a more "democratic" financial system, one that "takes account of the diversity of human motives and drives."[70] Adopting a somewhat Hobbesian perspective on human nature, he sees the opportunities provided by finance to take risks, to compete, and above all to win as a sort of essential pressure valve for society—"an outlet for our aggressions and lust for power." He may be right in this, and in his view that it is preferable to such alternatives as physical violence,[71] but despite his talk of finance being all about the stewardship of society's assets, he surely misunderstands the place of human rights vis-à-vis finance.

Certainly, the rights impacts of finance can be and often are beneficial. Finance is essential in helping motivate industries, job creation, medical advances, technological innovations, welfare benefits, and much else besides. But this "financial reality" does not and cannot support the claim that finance must in some way take precedence over the ends to which it is put. However, this is exactly what Shiller appears to suggest when he chastises the "traditions behind" human rights as being "sometimes in conflict with financial reality."[72] Sometimes they are, as I noted earlier in this chapter, especially when rhetoric triumphs over thoughtful engagement, but not always, and not conceptually. The problem is not that "the rights of man are set down in financially inconsistent ways."[73] The line of reasoning travels in exactly the opposite direction. Fundamentally, it is finance that must bend to the reality of the needs of human rights.

To add further, as Shiller does, that these conflicts and inconsistencies stem from the "arbitrary or traditional framing of [human rights] concepts," rather than by way of "some *sensible* philosophy," is perplexing, to say the least.[74] Shiller cannot be unaware of the vast body of philosophical endeavor since the Enlightenment trying precisely to make sense of the "rights of man"; and if not, does he mean to scorn such efforts? In any event, modern—that is to say postwar—human rights proclamations are imperfect in many ways, but they are certainly not unrealistically inflexible or uncompromising. In fact, the bulk of human rights policymaking and jurisprudence today is focused on delineating the boundaries of the extensive qualifications, including in respect of economic realities, written into the many international human rights instruments that have followed the Universal Declaration of Human Rights (UDHR) in 1948.[75]

Evidently, there is much work yet to be done on both sides of the gap before it is to be successfully bridged. The cardinal principle that the betterment of human conditions, including through the raising of human rights standards, is or ought to be a core object of finance has yet to be fully understood, let alone widely accepted. What the human rights community can do to provide clarity as to what are or ought to be these standards, while at the same time better comprehending the ability of finance to deliver, is central to the bridge building. An essential step in that enterprise is for rights advocates to be prepared to explain not only why human rights are relevant to finance, but also what demands they do and do not make of financiers and financial institutions.

Human Needs and Human Rights

To accept the plasticity of human rights, and to acknowledge that beyond the establishment of individual claims they also have broad and contested policy dimensions—that they may be justifiably limited, for example, by demands of national security, public order, or public health—is not to cave in to compromise.[76] In fact, one of the great strengths of human rights in theory as well as practice is their potential to embrace broad social, political, and economic perspectives. Why this potential has not been more actively exploited—especially in the fields of economics and finance—has a lot to do with the colonization of the human rights field by law and lawyers and by notions of legal entitlement, responsibility, and enforcement. It is not that these features are unimportant or unwanted; far from it. They are the spine that keeps the whole human rights body upright. But they are not the full corpus; there are other reasons that make human rights the practical and rhetorically powerful force that they have become over the past seventy-odd years.

One important way to understand how socially interconnected human rights are is to analyze them in the context of what humans need to live a life worth living. It is from the eighteenth-century Prussian rationalist Immanuel Kant that we draw philosophical inspiration for the linkages between human needs and human rights. Kant talked of the moral imperative of treating human beings as ends and never merely as means (like chattels or other owned or disposable goods), whether that be from the perspective of a fellow human being or an institution. Such treatment of the person was, for Kant, not just any old imperative and certainly not one based on mere faith, but a "*categorical* imperative," based on pure, deductive reasoning. According to Kant, no abrogation of a categorical imperative is permissible; and from it come certain fundamental individual rights that can be claimed against those in authority.[77]

That said, however, the basic human "needs" to which end human rights are committed (securing individual liberty, respect, and dignity, within a safe, ordered, and justly governed society) are not met by human rights alone. Achieving such ends is necessarily dependent on there being in place an efficient and fair government, a complementary legal order, and adequate financial resources. The protection of human rights, then, is a necessary but not sufficient condition to the process of fulfilling human needs.

This situating of human rights has been especially well conceived by pioneering work on the notion of human "capabilities" by Martha Nussbaum and Amartya Sen—a philosopher and an economist, respectively. Nussbaum's original interest in the idea was in addressing the entrenched inequalities and injustices endured by women, and Sen's was in addressing entrenched poverty and the apparent inability of the theory and practice of development to combat the problem. Both were united in seeing the capabilities approach as a means (i) to determine *what* it is that each human being requires to live a life of some minimal level of dignity, and (ii) to devise a methodology for *how* these requirements can be justly met. Such basic needs range from health and longevity, through the development and use of the core human faculties of the senses, imagination, emotions, and reason, to affiliation, recreation, and material well-being.[78] The central tenet of the capabilities approach is the proposition that while it is accepted that individuals clearly differ one from another in terms of innate characteristics and circumstantial capacities, all are capable of reaching, and are entitled to reach, at least the minimum levels of the needs listed above. Whatever freedoms, education, health care, or material goods that it takes to ensure that everyone reaches these minimum levels *must* be provided. And it is at this point—the point of obligation—that human rights and their spine of legal enforceability find a place in Nussbaum's and Sen's thinking.

The capabilities approach is attractive because it properly places human rights within the wider context of meeting human needs, while continuing to highlight the contribution they can make toward achieving that goal. The approach also tends to reflect the true scope of what human rights seek to achieve, rather than the sometimes overeager claims made in human rights rhetoric. It will acknowledge, for instance, that Article 12 of the ICESCR does not provide for the right *to be* healthy (rather, it provides for "the right of everyone to the enjoyment of the highest attainable standard of physical and mental health"); and that Article 14 does not guarantee the right *to have* work (rather, it includes the "right of everyone to the opportunity to gain his living by work which he freely chooses or accepts"). In other words, these articles oblige states to ensure access to adequate health care and to provide opportunities for employment, among other things. A focus on capabilities necessarily invites considerations of the financial wherewithal of individuals to obtain their basic needs and of the public or private institutions that might provide for those who fall short of being able to provide for themselves.

Rights Differences

A further insight critical to understanding human rights is that there are differences between *which* rights individuals—and especially certain groups of individuals—see as being the most important or urgent for their own circumstances. No matter how rhetorically attractive is the argument that all rights are "universal, indivisible and interdependent and interrelated,"[79] people and states do prioritize some rights over others, or at least they prioritize particular needs and thereby the rights that accompany them. Immutable, universal rights in the Kantian sense of constituting a categorical imperative as referred to above do not exist in practice. As the pragmatist philosopher Richard Rorty puts it, "The Kantian picture of what human beings are like cannot be reconciled with history or biology. Both teach us that the development of societies ruled by laws [including human rights laws] was a slow, late, fragile, contingent, evolutionary achievement."[80] An evolutionary process, one might add, that is ongoing and will remain forever unfinished. This is not lamentable, morally or legally,[81] it is just an accurate representation of the rights (and needs) distinctions that peoples and societies make often and unavoidably.

It is clear, for example, what the poor see as their greatest needs and the most important rights, as graphically illustrated by the outcomes of the World Bank's monumental survey *Voices of the Poor* in 1999. The survey asked 60,000 poor people from across the globe (in rich as well as poor states) what they needed most in order to live a "good life." Unsurprisingly, being adequately fed, healthy, and free from fear, violence, and abuse were high on their list, as were notions of self-respect, forming loving relationships, and a sense of belonging to a community. But above all else, the survey respondents made it clear that it was their access to material assets that was paramount: their capacity to own or use means of production, whether land, crops or animals, a means of transport, a job, and access to credit or savings. These were seen not just as valuable assets in their own right, but also, crucially, as the means by which people could achieve their other needs and desires.[82] For the poor, at least, it seems that it is the human right to securing property ownership, to seeking employment, to obtaining fair wages and a safe workplace that they are primarily interested in securing. Sure, it appears that they are also interested in rights to nondiscrimination, movement and association, and privacy, but mainly because it is the protection of these rights that help the poor to obtain work, to increase their personal safety, and to gain greater security and control over their own lives.

Rights Impacts

Global and local finance materially impact on whether and how such human rights are enforced and whether the relevant human needs are met. For many of the world's poorest, their capacity to obtain and enjoy many vital human rights hinges directly on the rivers of remittances crisscrossing the globe; on the grants, loans, and lines of credit issued by international development agencies; and on the divestments of governments and philanthropists. And for all of us, our human rights fortunes float imperceptibly on the tides of the speculated billions churned daily through banks on Wall Street and in London's Square Mile; on the usury of retail banks; and on the vast commercial investments made by corporations locally and across the globe. The variety of impacts on you and me, and the more than 7 billion people with whom we share the planet, is mediated through layer upon layer of financial transactions, and by way of countless commercial intercourses in the "real" economy. Certainly, the particular human rights impacts of a microfinancier's $100 loan to a basket-weaver in Dhaka will differ from China holding $1.185 trillion of U.S. debt,[83] but only in terms of the number of intermediaries and individuals, all of whom are subject to the vagaries of finance. The understanding, mapping, and measuring of the extent and significance of this byzantine relationship between human rights and finance are tasks that neither community can continue to neglect, no matter how daunting the challenge.

The two chapters in the middle of this book undertake these tasks according to private-sector and public-sector perspectives (chapters 4 and 5, respectively), but first, in chapter 3, I tackle the question of how to reconcile the apparent gulfs in attitude, ethos, and practice when human rights goals are placed within the cauldron of managing monetary risk, the nerve center of any financial system.

‖ 3 ‖

Flirting with Risk

"The chance of gain is by every man more or less overvalued, and the chance of loss is by most men undervalued, and by scarce any man, who is in tolerable health and spirits, valued more than it is worth."
—Adam Smith, *The Wealth of Nations* (1776)

"Let go thy hold when a great wheel runs down a hill, lest it break thy neck with following."
—William Shakespeare, *King Lear*, Act 2, Scene 4 (Fool)

The Attraction

Cleopatra is surely history's greatest femme fatale. Fabled not only to have seduced her arch enemies Julius Caesar and Mark Antony on her way to nearly conquering Rome,[1] she also married two of her own brothers. All predeceased her. Cleopatra's allure was not just her legendary intelligence and beauty, but also her wickedness. She was both forbidden and dangerous. The intoxicating effects of high arousal and deep fear are, as psychologists readily affirm, very similar in nature, and all too often equally irresistible.

Any relationship, especially in its early days, involves an element of risk. Indeed, it is often an essential ingredient of attraction. The prospect of what is hinted at, but yet unknown, conjures up exciting possibilities, both pleasing and worrying, even if not necessarily at Cleopatran levels of intensity. So it is with finance's relationship with human rights, even if neither is yet prepared (or sufficiently aware) to admit it. Individuals and communities suffering from poor housing and nonexistent health care, whose voice is ignored or silenced, or whose children lack schools to go to and jobs to aspire to, will relish the possibility of increasing their wealth. It might give them a chance to address their problems, even if, at the same time, they accept the risk of failure or loss. Financiers who are made aware of the impacts of their actions on the human rights standards of individuals and communities beyond their professional orbit may be attracted by the altruistic possibility that such impacts could be beneficial, even while accepting the risk that they might also be detrimental. Equally, they may simply not care either way.

The challenge in establishing a mutually agreeable, respectful, and long-lasting relationship is to balance the risks incurred by both sides. What counts in making a happy marriage is not so much how compatible you are, but how you deal with incompatibility, as Leo Tolstoy investigates in his masterpiece *Anna Karenina*, while demonstrating, in the reality of his own profoundly unhappy marriage, a complete failure to put words into action.[2] Likewise, with human rights and finance, reconciling their incompatibilities is easier said than done. When assessing risk in financial relations, one cannot merely assess in isolation either the potential losses or gains facing those directly involved. The circumstances of those who stand to lose or gain *indirectly* from the consequences of the transaction must also be taken into account, insofar as such consequences are relevant and reasonably foreseeable. Above all, gains must be distributed and loses borne appropriately and fairly according to the levels of risks knowingly taken. This should mean, in the first place, that those who have, consciously, gambled hugely, should reap commensurate costs and benefits. And second, that those whose livelihoods and standards of human rights protection are unwittingly exposed to financial risks as a consequence of the actions of others should benefit to some degree from any gains made, and be largely, if not wholly, shielded from any losses.[3]

This, however, is not always how risks and responsibilities are presently apportioned in the finance/human rights relationship. Rather, while the benefits accrue largely to those who have directly borne the risk, the flow is sometimes reversed when it comes to losses. That is, the risk-bearers are indemnified against all or some of the losses by those whose exposure to the risks was indirect, such as the government or the public. This phenomenon was especially evident during and after the latest global financial crisis (GFC), and especially among banks whose traders were risking mostly other people's money (that of depositors and investors), rather than their own, and whose losses were therefore limited to fees and bonuses, not their own capital. How we reached such a circumstance is not only a story worth telling, it also provides the key to how risk can play a different and fairer part in the relationship between finance and human rights.

From Boring Banking to Fantasy Finance

Banking used to be boring. In the fifty or so years between the Great Depression in the 1930s and the Great Deregulation in the 1980s, banking was characterized by conservatism, stability, and prudence. It was an era of thrift and risk aversion, when the services provided by bankers were simple—namely, to act as guardians of other people's money, which they held, lent, and invested according to strict regulatory conditions and ethical standards. The essential equivalence of deposits with loans, as depicted in Frank Capra's 1946 classic *It's a Wonderful Life*, represented the central principle of banking, such that the inadvertent loss of a relatively small quantity of deposits (just $8,000, in the case of the Bailey Bros. Building and Loan Association in the Capra movie) could catapult a bank into bankruptcy and a banker, quite likely, into jail.

All this was to change in the 1980s and 1990s. Between 1986 and the late 1990s, a succession of broadly complementary government policies and legislation deregulated the financial markets in the key centers of London and New York.[4] This precipitated a major restructuring and expansion of the financial services offered by banks, not just in the City of London and on Wall Street, but across the globe. The lifting of restrictions prohibiting proprietary trading by banks (investing their own funds in securities and other financial instruments) effectively removed the strict separation between retail and investment banking that had been in place since the Great Depression. At the same time, controls on the levels of how much banks could borrow and lend were substantially relaxed. The single, most important, consequence of these reforms was a vast increase in both the capacity and willingness of banks to take on financial risk.

As a result, whereas in the 1970s and early 1980s, the level of debt held by large financial corporations was broadly similar to that held by most large nonfinancial corporations (normally less than 50% the value of the corporation's assets), in the late 1980s through the 1990s, bank borrowing skyrocketed. By the mid-2000s, the debt-to-assets ratio for banks was typically in excess of 90% and, with the biggest banks, regularly more than 97%,[5] a level that the Bank of England was subsequently and rather sheepishly to admit was a "huge mistake."[6] This exponential growth in borrowing—or 'leveraged' debt—fueled financial capacity and, with it, brought promises of even greater returns. That is the majesty of leverage. There is, of course, a downside of equivalent dimensions, because moving risk around does not remove it. That is the tragedy of leverage.

The Majesty and Tragedy of Leverage

The attraction of leverage is tied up with the society-wide eagerness to binge on debt. Debt itself is not necessarily the concern. It has a long history of personal and commercial usefulness, predating even money, as anthropologist David Graeber makes clear.[7] Likewise, the fact that banks, businesses, and governments have long factored debt into their financial arrangements need not be a worry. What is of concern are the enormous and accelerating levels of such debt that banks, businesses, governments, and all the rest of us are now routinely willing

to take on. Rich or poor, for holidays or houses, the capacity of private individuals today to finance their lifestyles on credit and borrowed money is breathtaking. Adair Turner, the former head of the UK's now-defunct Financial Services
Authority, calls this the "Utopia of finance for all."[8] In many countries, the real
estate market has been the principal source of the debt binge. Residential mortgages today make up around 65% of all bank lending in the UK (the next biggest
category, at 14%, is commercial real estate),[9] with similar or higher proportions
in the United States and other Western nations. Some thirty years ago the bulk of
bank lending in these same countries was for nonmortgage business purposes,
not real estate borrowing.[10]

It is not hard to see how the lure of living the good life let this occur, even if
we cannot quite shake off the haunting suspicion that it is too good to be true.
Indeed, for many, it proved to be a disaster. For around the corner of lifestyle
utopia lay financial dystopia. When a housing market the size of the United
States' has a total loan-to-value ratio for mortgages of more than 5 to 1 (that
is, total home loans were 5 times larger than the total value of the homes), as it
did in the late 2000s,[11] you can be certain that the dream is going to turn into
a nightmare for many people. The housing bubble was even more ludicrously
inflated in Ireland, despite being colorfully serious for the Irish (Michael
Lewis referred to Irish banks as ranging between "dirty little secrets" to "the
world's worst" in his irresistible *Vanity Fair* article on the crisis in Ireland),[12]
but the size and reach of the U.S. housing market failure was in a different
league altogether.

Personal financial leverage is the vehicle by which such differentials in loan-
to-value (and debt-to-income) are created, and bank leverage is the engine that
drives that vehicle. Daunting though such risk exposure is for many millions of
mortgage holders around the world, it is a mere bagatelle compared to the levels
of leveraged debt borne by banks. This, as mentioned earlier, is routinely in the
order of a ratio of 50 to 1; that is, where total shareholder equity represents only
2%, or less, of the bank's total assets and liabilities. Even this is a gross underesti-
mation if a broader view of debt is employed, as Oxford economist John Kay has
so graphically demonstrated.

In his book *Other People's Money*, Kay reveals the full extent of big banks'
exposure by lifting the lid on how derivatives are accounted for on their balance sheets.[13] Banks like JP Morgan and Deutsche Bank hold mind-bogglingly
large quantities of derivatives, including many backed by mortgages. In the case
of Deutsche Bank, its total derivatives exposure in 2012 amounted to €55.6
trillion—more than 1,000 times the bank's shareholders' equity, and some 20
times the gross national income of Germany! On its books, however, the bank
recorded the value of these instruments as a tiny fraction of that amount. The
disguise is achieved by way of the standardized and legal accounting mechanism

of "fair value," which focuses on the differences between the current and future value of a derivative (that difference being where gains and losses are made by those trading in them), rather than on its total value. These differences are nearly always small, so their "fair" value is recorded as correspondingly small on the bank's balance sheet. The method in this madness, it is argued, is underwritten by the fact that big derivatives traders like banks will always comprehensively hedge their positions—that is, by holding roughly equivalent values of long (price rising) and short (price falling) derivatives contracts, thereby limiting their net exposure

However—and this is the key point—no matter how small the differences in the present and future prices of individual contracts, and irrespective of how finely tuned their hedging, the vast numbers of contracts held, together with the sheer size of the overall derivatives exposure of a bank like Deutsche Bank, point toward potential catastrophe. All it takes for that potential to become a reality is for pricing errors to occur—such as happens when the worst subprime mortgage-backed derivatives are mistakenly rated AAA instead of C ("junk"), which are small mistakes individually, but cumulatively are devastating.[14] Like the failure of a humble O-ring that precipitated the destruction of the Space Shuttle Challenger in 1986 (caused by unexpectedly cold temperatures on the morning of the launch), so a loss of just 0.1% of Deutsche Bank's total derivatives exposure (namely, €55 billion of €55 trillion) would be sufficient to destroy the bank.[15] The margin for error in both space travel and high-flying banking is very slim indeed.

Banks may, or may not (as we see later), be aware of the precariousness of their circumstances, but if we assume that they are, or at least suspect as much, the question arises—why do they do it? How come, as the U.S. Financial Crisis Inquiry Commission put it, "like Icarus, they [the banks] never feared flying ever closer to the sun?"[16] The answer, it seems, is simple enough. It is all about size— the bigger, the better. If the bank is big enough, and its potential losses so great as to threaten the stability of other parts of the financial system, then governments will intervene to save it or bail it out. The big banks know this; the governments know this; and taxpayers have come to know it. So, when the potential rewards of hyper leverage are so mouthwatering, and there exists an implicit state-backed guarantee against huge losses (but only, counterintuitively, huge ones, nothing less), the decision to leverage for all they are worth and much more is, for banks, a no-brainer. If "too-big-to-fail firms" believe that they will not be allowed to fail, then "private firms capture any additional profits that result from high-risk activities, while the government bears any extreme losses," as economist Marc Labonte from the U.S. Congressional Research Service explains. To this he adds, ominously, if they believe that they will be rescued, "they have an incentive to behave in a way that makes it more likely they will fail."[17]

Aside from the market-distorting moral hazard created by such guarantees against gargantuan failure (a point further pursued later in this chapter and picked up again in chapter 6), the story of leveraged debt is underpinned by two further factors. One is political, the other psychological. In the political arena, the taking on of debt has been promoted by such aggressive government policies as the 1993–94 amendments to the *Community Reinvestment Act* (CRA) in the United States discussed in chapter 1, which heralded the subprime mortgage storm in the 1990s and 2000s, and more generally, by the propensity in the West to provide tax breaks for all sorts of consumer debt, including mortgage repayments, which are tax deductible in more than half of the rich-world economies. Nearly all countries, rich and poor, also allow corporations to write off loan repayments against taxable earnings.[18]

These public policies chime with the persistent psychological trait to underestimate risk when faced with the opportunities promised by debt. So potent are the latter attractions, that even after the 2007/08 financial crisis, debt levels among private and public borrowers have remained high, as enabled by the still-enormous and—remarkably—still-growing levels of leverage debt generated by the banks and governments.[19] It seems, therefore, that not only have the lessons of the latest financial crisis not been heeded, the implications of another failure have been magnified because many of these banks are now "too big to save." The coffers of most, if not all, states are so depleted after ten years of global economic anaemia that they are no longer financially able to bail out big banks should they push themselves once again to brink of failure. Even if they had the funds, governments' political appetite for stepping in to save the banks again is close to zero, such would be the public outrage should they suggest that they might do so.

Human Rights Risks

There is always a certain degree of risk in any financial investment, including the risk of damaging impacts on people's rights standards. Leveraged investment accentuates that risk, but also the potential gains. Throughout the past quarter century, individuals and communities have been financially enriched both directly and indirectly in ways that have enhanced the protection and promotion of their fundamental rights. Directly—through employment and trading opportunities, as well as through basic legal protections of contract and property ownership, many individuals have been able to expand their capabilities to provide for themselves, their families, and communities lives that are safer, freer, healthier, better fed, housed, and educated. Indirectly—the budgetary capacity of many states has been greatly increased, enabling publicly funded support to be provided to those who are unable to secure minimal levels of those same rights-respecting circumstances for themselves and their families.

This twofold enhancement of people's rights can be self-perpetuating, in that increasing individual and community wealth can lead to extra income for the state through the levying of taxes on the revenue-generating activities of those individuals and their businesses. This, in turn, should lead to better standards of public services that enhance still further the opportunities for individual wealth. This virtuous circle goes some way to explain the burgeoning middle classes in many developing states whose human rights fortunes are today markedly better than they were twenty-five years before. In China, for example, the World Bank estimates that some 800 million people have been lifted out of extreme poverty since the early 1980s.[20] It is, in fact, an incredible feat, unprecedented in human history in its proportions and pace. In 1981 88.3% of China's population lived in abject poverty, struggling to survive, let alone live a life with dignity and self-fulfillment. According to the latest available data to the World Bank, that figure has, incredibly, dropped to just 1.85%.[21] So today, nearly everyone in China enjoys material protection of their basic rights to health, education, and an adequate standard of living that could not have been imagined little more than one generation ago.[22]

As attractive as this equation might be on the global plane, it is marked by imperfections and breakdowns. Aside from the incontrovertibly serious obstacles posed by the fact that some 5.2 billion people, about 73% of the world's population, still have inadequate or no access to publicly funded social protection,[23] and that more than $1 trillion of illicit funds per annum flow out of developing states,[24] shocks from financial risks gone bad impact greatly on middle classes and the poor, albeit in different ways.

The GFC that began in the rich world in 2007 precipitated economic and social crises in the years that followed. For those in the West, this manifested itself in rising unemployment, property losses and devaluations, and the cutbacks in social protection. The apparently worthy aim to expand home ownership to high-risk, often low-income families in a number of developed countries (but most notably in the United States) by way of subprime mortgages was a key ingredient in the GFC recipe. The "commodification" of housing—whereby it is perceived "as a mere good that can be bought and sold like many others,"[25] and which encouraged the predatory, imprudent, and illegal lending practices of banks and other financial institutions specifically targeting these high-risk clients—was extremely risky and, as it turned out, extremely costly.[26] Not only did the (predictable) rising rates of defaults on these loans precipitate a cascading destruction in the value of mortgage-based derivative financial instruments, and from there to a worldwide credit crunch, they also left families homeless and, in many cases, destitute.

Foreclosure filings by homeowners in the United States, for example, reached record levels after the crisis, with more than 14 million filings registered from 2007 to 2014, leading to more than 6 million eventual foreclosures.[27] The vast majority of these home losses involved families (either as the property owners or tenants of the foreclosing owners) whose precarious situations were often made irretrievable by even relatively small commonplace events, such as relocation expenses, relationship problems, or the birth of a new child, let alone more serious setbacks such as a job loss or a major health problem. The situation was made worse by the marked trends in many developed countries to reduce public housing stocks and privatize the management of state-funded housing thereby diminishing public sector capacity to meet needs when the market fails to do so.[28]

Rich-World Austerity

The central purpose of social welfare programs, where they exist, is to provide a financial safety net for those who find themselves in such circumstances of vulnerability. That is why the austerity measures curtailing public expenditure, introduced with varying degrees of severity in many developed states in the years following the 2007/08 financial crisis, were so damaging for those who were most in need of a social safety net. And they were unfair. The need for public sector austerity arose from the huge increases in public debt incurred as a consequence of taxpayer-funded bailouts of banks and other financial institutions in 2008–09, losses in tax revenue as economies contracted in the face of the financial crisis, and the increasing demands on the social welfare programs themselves as financial hardship tipped increasing numbers into the safety net. Many financiers and investors had taken substantial risks in the pursuit of substantial gains. Many had failed in the process, and while undoubtedly they felt some pain, the defining feature of the 2007/08 financial crisis and its aftermath has been the very significant sharing of the pain far and wide. As political scientist Mark Blyth puts it: "Austerity is not just the price of saving banks. It's the price that the banks want someone else to pay."[29]

The impact of austerity measures on human rights standards in economies worldwide has been palpable. According to the UN's High Commissioner for Human Rights:

> The ability of individuals to exercise their human rights, and that of States to fulfil their obligations to protect those rights, has been diminished. This is particularly true for the most vulnerable and marginalized groups in society, including women, children, minorities, migrants and

the poor, who suffer from decreasing access to work and social welfare programmes, and reduced affordability of food, housing, water, medical care and other basic necessities. The negative impacts of the financial crisis and subsequent austerity measures are also seen to exacerbate existing structural inequalities.[30]

This report makes clear that the impact has been severe on the levels of protection for many rights guaranteed by the International Covenant on Economic, Social and Cultural Rights (ICESCR), especially adequate housing, access to health care, and social security for families and the jobless.[31] And while it is true that states' commitments to the realization of the rights contained in this Covenant are conditional on their doing so "progressively" and "to the maximum of [their] available resources," these are not conditions that permit states to do whatever they please in terms of funding these rights. The flexibility suggested by these terms is meant to reflect real world exigencies, rather than to diminish the Covenant's overall objective to have states guarantee basic, minimum levels of rights protection.[32] As such, argues the UN Committee that oversees the implementation of the Covenant, any regression in rights protection prompted by an economic downturn has to be explained and justified by a state as necessary and proportionate, must not be discriminatory, and can only be temporary.[33] In particular, states are expected to demonstrate why any chosen austerity measure is *less* detrimental to economic and social rights than not acting at all.[34]

The need to shield the weakest and most vulnerable from the ravages of public-sector cuts is justifiable not only for social reasons, but also for economic ones. The effects of austerity measures on women, for example, are especially significant as they impact not only women themselves but also all those around them—husbands, partners, children, and other dependents, such as elderly relatives.[35] When people's income security is threatened and their access to health care and other social services is diminished or denied, their ability to take advantage of any economic opportunities that do arise is undermined.[36] The austerity packages adopted by some of the EU states worst affected by the 2007/08 financial crisis, such as Portugal, Ireland, Greece, and Spain (the so-called PIGS), as well as the UK and Italy, have also been condemned for being socially unjust and economically counterproductive.[37] The *Financial Times'* Martin Wolf lambasted them as imposing "huge and unnecessary costs, not just in the short run, but in the long term as well: the costs of investments unmade, of businesses not started, of skills atrophied, and hopes destroyed."[38]

Though many of the poorest citizens in these and other developed economies suffered from restrictions in the provision of basic public services and assistance,[39] few states weathered austerity waves of the number and depth as those that rolled across the Greek economy in the years following 2008. With general unemployment in 2015 running at 25% and youth (under 24) unemployment at a ruinous 50%,[40] the average annual wage dropping by more than 10% in real terms between 2003 and 2013,[41] and government spending in 2013/14 sitting at more than 5% below that of 2006 in real terms (in comparison, UK public spending increased by just under 9% in the same period),[42] it surprised few that the Greek electorate voted against its government honoring another installment of debt repayments in a snap referendum called in July 2015. While this piece of political theater did nothing to alleviate Greece's dire economic circumstances, it did highlight the fundamentals of risk in global finance. In the opinion of one economic commentator at the time, the event provided the Greeks with the opportunity to send a strong message to their country's creditors (most especially Germany):

> Debt is not a guarantee of future payments in full. Rather, it is a risk that creditors take, in hope of maybe being paid tomorrow. The key word here is "risk." If you're willing to take the risk, you'll get a premium—in the form of interest. But the downside of that risk is that you lose your money. And Greece just called Germany's bluff.[43]

Here we return to the modern manifestation of risk in global finance, namely, that it is rigged in favor of powerful creditors, whether systemically important private-sector financial institutions, or (as here) states' Central Banks and multilateral financial entities. For while it might be said that Greece's principal creditors—the so-called *Troika* of the European Commission, the European Central Bank (behind which stood the Bundesbank), and the IMF—felt pressurized during the July 2015 hiatus, pushback from the Greek electorate served only to harden their resolve.[44] Eventually Greece had no option but to seek further credit from these same creditors and in circumstances where its citizens were suffering still-further social and economic hardships. Even a series of legal "rulings" that the austerity reforms instituted by Greece at the behest of the *Troika* amounted to violations of minimum labor and welfare rights protected by the Council of Europe's European Social Charter, did nothing to lessen the severity of the belt-tightening measures imposed on Greece's citizens.[45]

What is perhaps most notable about this Greek imbroglio is that the game of financial brinkmanship was being played with a Western nation one within the fold of the EU. As we will see now (and later, in Chapter 5), such invidious dilemmas are commonplace experiences for many of the poorest nations.

Poor-World Impacts

The economic, social, and human rights impacts on poor states of the 2007/08 financial crisis and its aftermath, though different from the experience of rich states, have been no less serious. In a report reviewing the initial consequences of the GFC for developing states in November 2008, the World Bank estimated that crisis-related spikes in the prices of food and fuel had already driven some 100 million people into poverty in the developing world. The impact was harshest in those states least able to cope: "Many countries most exposed to rising global food and fuel prices are those with high pre-existing levels of malnutrition. Burundi, Madagascar, Niger, Timor Leste and Yemen are among the ten most affected countries for both [children] stunting and wasting indicators. All of these countries experienced double-digit food inflation in 2007-08."[46] The report pointed out that governments in these and other least-developed states had sought to offset the inflationary pressures on basic commodities by extensive use of tax reductions as well as increased spending on subsidies and income support. By so doing, however, they depleted their budgetary capacity either to provide for those who still required welfare support, or to respond to any additional economic contractions. This latter point was especially serious, as the forecasts for emerging economies were, at that time, unpromising. The World Bank projected further calamities for the world's poor as "current estimates suggest that a 1% decline in growth rates of developing economies trap an additional 20 million people into poverty," with all the negative implications for standards of living and rights protections that brings.[47]

As a matter of fact, the rates of growth of developing states' economies in the years that followed the financial crisis did slow a little, falling from an aggregated average of 5% growth per annum in 2000–09 (mainly the precrisis period) to 4.3% in 2009–14 (the postcrisis period).[48] In an article written in 2010, when he was the UK's Secretary of State for International Development, Douglas Alexander highlighted the three ways by which emerging economies were affected by the crisis.[49] First, through capital flight, as foreign direct investment flows into developing states were stifled (FDI inflows dropped precipitously for developing countries from $587 billion in 2008 to $354 billion in 2009);[50] second, through decreasing remittances, as job opportunities in rich countries (from which 80% of developing country remittances are sourced) disappeared and pay rates stagnated or regressed (thus, having more than tripled between 2001 and 2008 to a total of $323 billion, remittances dipped to $305 billion in 2009);[51] and third, through diminished export revenue, as international trade contracts (year-on-year growth in exports from developing economies collapsed from positive 22% in 2008 to negative 22% in 2009).[52]

The hardships suffered by the poor and marginalized in developing states were in many ways more acute than in rich states, because they had less to lose before hitting rock bottom. The fact that these groups were suffering on account of a risk-induced crisis not of their own making added to the sense of injustice. Many a leader in the developing world may have shared the sentiments of one Latin American finance minister's response to news of the GFC ("Thank God at least this time it wasn't our fault"),[53] but the sense of relief would have been utterly lost on those who bore the brunt of the downturn.

In developing countries the poor and the disadvantaged are always the most susceptible to even minor diminutions in access to basic necessities. Catarina de Albuquerque, the former UN Special Rapporteur on the Right to Water, for example, charted a pattern of neglect across the planning, institutional responsibilities, and allocation of water resources to disadvantaged groups typically defined by ethnicity, gender, class or caste, disability, and geographical location.[54] In times of economic crisis, she noted, "such inequality tends to become even more aggravated," as states and service providers incline toward easier-to-reach communities, neglecting the most marginalized groups who are often living in remote rural areas.[55]

Perhaps the most significant human rights impacts of severe financial shocks on the poor in poor countries are long-term. "Whereas the actual economic slowdown may be limited in time, its effects on many people may last for generations," as Magdalena Sepúlveda, the UN Independent Expert on Human Rights and Extreme Poverty, put it in her 2009 report. For the poor, a severe financial crisis can trap them in an unending cycle of little or no income and consign their children to similar prospects.[56]

> Whereas the actual economic slowdown may be limited in time, its effects on many people may last for generations. The crisis may trap those who are unable to afford basic needs during a prolonged period of unemployment and very scarce income in extreme poverty for the rest of their lives, and their children may also face a lifetime of poverty.[57]

The experiences of the most disadvantaged in societies during and after times of economic crisis reflect the need for human rights protection in its rawest form. For human rights proclamations are not merely (or only) aspirational standards for a better life, they are also expressions of the minimal standards for a life worth living. Human rights laws impose minimum core obligations on states to guarantee basic levels of individual freedom and social protection, which are neither discretionary nor tradeable. So when, for example, significant numbers of individuals in any state party to the ICESCR are deprived of essential foodstuffs, essential primary health care, basic shelter and housing, or the most basic forms of education, then that state is deemed to be "failing to discharge its obligations under the Covenant."[58] To read the Covenant in a way that does not establish such a minimum core obligation would be, according to its supervisory Committee, to deprive the Covenant of its raison d'être.[59]

While the fulfillment of such obligations clearly imposes a financial burden on the state, it is not, typically, one that is unbearable. "Countries can afford safety nets," the World Bank insisted at the height of the recent financial crisis, pointing out that on average, social protection expenditures in developing countries hover between 1% and 2% of GDP, with "some of the most successful programs, such as Mexico's *Oportunidades* or Brazil's *Bolsa Família*, cost[ing] about 0.4% of GDP." [60] The Bank conceded that the financing of safety nets may require the reprioritization of public expenditures, but the increased spending on basic welfare programs "often pales in comparison with other interventions to counter crises, such as public works programs, increased unemployment insurance, or the cost of financial sector bailouts."[61]

Important though it is for those suffering the consequences of egregious financial risk gone wrong, the critical question is not whether the state can afford to provide the necessary extra welfare support, but how did it come to be called upon to do so in the first place. In other words, what are the methods, motivations, and incentives that lie behind the highly leveraged financial risk-taking that leads to financial crises and economic depressions? The answers to these questions are to be found in two age-old human traits: faith and greed.

Faith

On October 8, 2003, at the University of Massachusetts in Boston, Roger W. Ferguson, Jr., Vice-Chairman of the Board of Governors of the U.S. Federal Reserve System, delivered a speech on the future of financial services.[62] Mr. Ferguson was in an optimistic mood. He was confident in the strength of the U.S. banking system as it left the prosperous late 1990s and embarked on the new century. He acknowledged that the current period was more stressful in light of the then-recent corporate governance scandals that had brought giants Enron and WorldCom to their knees, but believed that the combination of enhanced disclosure and accounting requirements introduced by the *Sarbanes-Oxley Act* (2002) and punishing market responses to corporate misfeasance would provide "powerful incentives for virtually all market participants to maintain high standards." His most remarkable expression of faith, however, was directed toward what he referred to as the new technologies of risk measurement. These, he believed, were delivering "truly impressive improvement[s]" in the capabilities of financiers to manage risk. "Modern advances in the quantification of risk," he pronounced, "have provided bank management with a far more disciplined and structured process for evaluating loans, pricing risks, and deciding which risks to retain. Careful judgement by experienced credit officers of risk is still required," he conceded, "but the modern techniques developed by both academics and market practitioners are tools to facilitate a much deeper evaluation of risk than has been possible even a decade ago."

The revolution Ferguson was referring to was, of course, the then-growing trend toward the mathematical modeling of risk, directed by algorithmic rule-setting and driven by amplified computing capacity. But his faith in the combined power of mathematics and microprocessing that yielded such deceptively accommodating predictive tools such as Value-at-Risk (VAR)[63] was in fact a classic example of the triumph of hope over expectation. It may have seemed that the face of trade in financial products was being irrevocably altered by the application of these hyperbolic capabilities, but in fact the results were only as good as the assumptions upon which the algorithms were based.

Put simply, the baseline assumption made about the actions of other investors (upon which an algorithm would then build a set of rules to be followed by the investor) was that they would operate rationally; that is, in ways that would invariably maximize the financial outcomes of the choices before them. Even if this assumption may be true of most investors most of the time, it is not true of all investors all of the time. Irrational financial actions, for whichever of the multiplicity of reasons human beings have for taking them, are not, and cannot be, adequately factored into mathematical equations. Whether these all-too-human impulses are labeled "animal spirits" (as Keynes called them),[64] or "irrational exuberance" (in Greenspan's words),[65] or simply "jumping on the bandwagon," they elude effective algorithmic expression precisely because by their very nature, the consequences of such actions are almost impossible to pick.

In hindsight, of course, such gross errors in judgement now seem obvious, but Ferguson was not alone in making them.[66] Far from it. Indeed, regulators and bankers alike were united in their expressions of surprise at the onset of the 2007 financial crisis and, perhaps most disturbingly, were initially utterly perplexed by its causes. To a substantial degree their confusion stemmed from the fact that they simply did not understand the true nature of the financial products they were dealing with. The pivotal scene in the 2011 movie *Margin Call*, when the mathematically gifted junior risk analyst (played by Zachary Quinto) discovers the full extent of his firm's gargantuan risk exposure and his (Wall) street-wise, but mathematically uninitiated, boss (played by Jeremy Irons) asks him to explain his findings "as you might to a young child, or a golden retriever," was an accurate artistic representation of life.[67]

The "life" it represented was of one of a serious disconnect between the back-room, quantitative analysts (or "quants") who were writing the risk algorithms and the front-room bankers who were selling them. There were fewer clearer illustrations of such dislocation than the lame incoherency of some of the excuses that senior bankers were making in the early days of the financial crisis Take, for example, how in August 2007, David Viniar, the CFO of Goldman Sachs, sought to explain the recent dramatic losses suffered by the firm's flagship hedge fund as the consequence of "25-standard deviation moves [away from the mean price]," happening "several days in a row." Viniar was referring to the likelihood of events occurring at the extremes of a standard deviation curve (that is, at the two thinning and endless tails on either side of a classic bell curve), as predicted by the models or algorithms applied by Goldman Sachs to that particular financial product.

A 25-standard deviation (or "sigma") event, on the face of it, might be considered very remote. Evidently, the message Viniar was trying to convey was that Goldman's fund was experiencing a run of bad luck and that its modeling showed that fluctuations in prices and returns were bound to revert to normal, predictable patterns very soon. At that time, the CFOs of many financial firms, including Bear Sterns, Citibank, Merrill Lynch, and UBS, were also posting substantial losses while offering much the same bad-luck stories by way of explanation.[68] Their faith in their capacity to predict and manage risk remained strong. But they were all wrong.

The problem was not lousy luck, but warped mathematics. In a brief paper published in early 2008, four academics from three British and Irish business schools asked the question, "How unlucky is 25-sigma?"[69] Their answer was both extraordinary and revealing. They found that the probability of a 25-sigma event was—quite literally—off the scale of measurability. Assuming that losses were normally distributed in accordance with a classic bell curve, the authors calculated that a 2-sigma event would occur on approximately 1 day out of 44; a 3-sigma event, once every 741 days; and a 4-sigma event once every 31,560 days. By the time you reached a 6-sigma event, the probability was already over 1 trillion (that is, more than 1,000 billion) days, and by 8-sigma, the expected occurrence of the event was beyond the normal numeric counting scale, being expressed instead as a formula, which the authors thoughtfully explained in plain terms, as "a period (considerably) longer than the entire period that has elapsed since the Big Bang."[70]

Faith No More

Clearly, therefore, the probability of a single 25-sigma event, let alone several in a row, is incomprehensible. The senior management of the world's leading finance firms plainly had no idea (or worse, didn't care) what they were talking about when trying to explain the levels of risk that their firms' financial products were exposed to. Yet the most important skills that bankers claim to possess are their knowledge of, and capacity to manage, financial risk. If nonfinanciers cannot trust the financiers who are the best in the business to do that job competently (not *perfectly*, let us be clear, just competently), then something is seriously wrong with the system. As Bill Bonner (another critic of the financial sector's manifest incompetence in the lead-up to the GFC), pointed out at the time, when these big banks fail in their task to manage risk it is not only they who suffer, if they do so at all. Many people who are not even aware of their exposure to the mismanaged risk may suffer cataclysmic losses, as was the case, referred to earlier, for the 2 million American families whose homes were subject to foreclosure proceedings as an immediate consequence to the 2007 credit crunch.[71]

There is, at least in theory, another category of financial actor that ought to be helping financiers and nonfinanciers alike to understand levels of risk. Credit-rating agencies (CRAs) evaluate the creditworthiness of organizations that issue debt in public markets, and of the debt instruments themselves, such as government or corporate bonds, collateralized securities, and certain stock issues. [72] Fundamentally, as Standard and Poor's (the world's largest rating agency) puts it, CRAs offer an opinion on the likelihood of default.[73] Such opinions are, in nearly all cases, purchased by the issuers of the debt. So, while the rating agencies may or may not be providing opinions that are in fact accurate, they are not disinterested. The potential for conflicts of interest is obvious. Obvious or not, it is especially harmful when third parties rely on those opinions in order to gauge the risk levels associated with any particular financial venture. These third parties may be other financially savvy entities such as banks, or they may be individuals or institutions with little financial knowledge, such as mum-and-dad investors or local councils. In any case, in practice, third parties do place considerable store in the ratings provided by these agencies.[74] So, when these ratings prove to be wildly inaccurate, investors can suffer enormous losses.

Just how much so was starkly illustrated as the impact of the GFC began to hit public-sector institutional investors across the globe, including governments, public pension funds, and municipal authorities. The largest pension fund in the United States, the California Public Employees' Retirement Scheme (CalPERS), estimated that as a consequence of its reliance on the very high (that is, safe) ratings provided by all three of the biggest rating agencies (Standard and Poor's, Moody's, and Fitch) on certain financial products in which CalPERS had invested heavily, the fund had lost some $800 million when they turned toxic. Three of the so-called structured investment vehicles (SIVs) the fund had backed contained the highly contaminated securitized subprime mortgages. When CalPERS filed a case in 2009 for negligent misrepresentation against all three agencies, it argued that the agencies knew or ought to have known that these

SIVs were in fact extremely risky and not worthy of the high ratings assigned to them. CalPERS further alleged that the rating agencies had knowingly worked with the issuers to structure the deals on these "so they could rate them as highly as possible," thereby maximizing their fees.[75]

The rating agencies raised a number of defenses, but the most notable was, remarkably, a human rights one. They invoked First Amendment protection, based on the claim that the opinions of rating agencies were in fact an engagement in free speech rather than (less well protected) commercial speech.[76] This peculiar line of reasoning (which, incidentally, U.S. corporations have previously shown themselves not shy to invoke)[77] was eventually effectively closed off by the California Court of Appeal.[78] Indeed, on the strength of this adverse ruling, Standard and Poor's had little option but to settle the case in early 2015 (for a reported $125 million), as did Moody's, one year later, in March 2016 (for $130 million).[79]

This did not, however, bring an end to the hemorrhaging of CRAs' reputations, as the U.S. Justice Department, in conjunction with nineteen U.S. states, continued to pursue the big three agencies on grounds similar to CalPERS. This time, however, the stakes were much higher. The biggest case of all—a $5 billion suit against Standard and Poor's—was filed by the plaintiffs in 2013. It, too, was settled in early 2015 for an eye-watering $1.375 billion.[80] When announcing the terms of this settlement, the U.S. Attorney-General Eric Holder spelled out in blunt language the nature of Standard and Poor's culpability: "[o]n more than one occasion, the company's leadership ignored senior analysts who warned that the company had given top ratings to financial products that were failing to perform as advertised," he noted. Yet, damningly, "the company declined to downgrade underperforming assets because it was worried that doing so would hurt the company's business." He then added, sardonically, "[w]hile this strategy may have helped S&P avoid disappointing its clients, it did major harm to the larger economy, contributing to the worst financial crisis since the Great Depression."[81]

It was concern over the wider societal implications of the agencies' massive mispricing of risk, as much as the market distortions this mispricing caused, that prompted regulatory responses in both the United States and Europe aimed at protecting investors (and society) by making CRAs more accountable.[82] Whether these added constraints are sufficient to ensure greater independence and more accuracy in ratings assessments remains to be seen, given that CRAs are still being paid by the issuers of debt for the ratings. This critical detail has helped maintain demand for their services, as the return in lower borrowing costs consequent upon a favorably high rating "can be up to ten times as much as the fees paid for the rating."[83]

The misplaced faith in the capacity of individuals or institutions to assess financial risk reliably, and therefore to forecast financial outcomes accurately, can have grave consequences for all those who rely on flawed assessments, including the financially savvy who are aware of the risks they are taking. For those who have little or no knowledge of the financial risk they are exposed to, let alone its extent, the consequences may be especially serious and unjust. When consequences include lost jobs, homes, education opportunities, welfare support, or access to health care, the matter is not just unfortunate but a calamity. Financial risk-taking is typically founded on a combination of emotion, knowledge, and reason. But as the proportions of each differ depending on the levels of the risk-taker's financial literacy, so too do the respective degrees of responsibility for the resultant outcomes.

Enlightenment philosopher David Hume maintained that it is our desires and passions that motivate each of us more than any preordained conception of rational action.[84] In the ongoing quest to make macroeconomics and finance more scientific, it has been a monumental mistake to focus on what markets ought to do, rather than on what they actually do, even if the "is" and the "ought" are often, *but not always*, the same. This, in terms of risk management, is a crucial point. As behavioral economists George Akerlof and Robert Shiller argue, to construct a conception of how the economy works based on people who only have economic motives and whose actions are always fully rational is absurd. For a start, economic rationality itself eludes accurate estimation, as memorably demonstrated by Keynes in his beauty contest parable. This is where contestants are asked to choose the six most attractive faces from hundreds of photographs presented to them. The winners are those who correctly identify the six faces most voted for. The most sophisticated contestants (that is, the most rational) will not merely rely on their own judgment, but will try to anticipate what others might consider to be attractive, the permutations of which make accurate prediction of rational action effectively impossible. And so it is, argues Keynes, with predictions in market economics. [85]

Even more damning is the fact that the rational economic actor model excludes the very questions as to other motives, some of which are irrational, that one needs to ask in order to understand how the economy actually works in practice.[86] It is to one such expansive motive that we turn next. For alongside faith, the second indelibly human trait that helps explain how our attitudes toward risk have brought us pain as well as pleasure is greed.

Greed

Greed occupies a curious place in capitalism. In their book *How Much is Enough?* economists and father-and-son duo Robert and Edward Skidelsky argue that "capitalism rests precisely on [an] endless expansion of wants. That is why, for all its success, it remains so unloved. It has given us wealth beyond measure, but has taken away the chief benefit of wealth: the consciousness of having enough ... The vanishing of all intrinsic ends leaves us with only two options: to be ahead or to be behind."[87] The Skidelskys' comment on the futility of this self-consuming impulse echoes Shakespeare's *The Rape of Lucrece*:

> And so, by hoping more, they have but less;
> Or, gaining more, the profit of excess
> Is but to surfeit, and such griefs sustain,
> That they prove bankrupt in this poor-rich gain.[88]

Sentiments such as these may go some way toward explaining our ambivalence about avarice. It is at times loudly championed by some as an admirable quality. More often and by many more, it is despised and derided. Most often of all, it is tacitly acknowledged as a key driver in capitalism,[89] to be nurtured and encouraged as the mother of endless innovation (or "creative destruction," as economist Joseph Schumpeter labeled it),[90] while ultimately guarding against its excesses and its carelessness. At the heart of the economic role of greed lies the question of how to practice the delicate art of curtailing the damage it does to others while exploiting its productive capacities for the widest benefit possible. How, that is, can we harness the energy and entrepreneurism that individuals invest in pursuit of their own personal wealth for the good of society as a whole.

That such redoubtable power can be used to provide adequately for those whose welfare is threatened or whose human rights are denied can be one important reason for permitting greed such a free rein in the first place. We may accept, therefore, as did Adam Smith, that "beneficent actions might well be influenced by the basest of passions."[91] In the process, we need not extinguish the prospect of personal gain, even great personal gain, but with such gains come conditions. The accumulation of financial wealth is subject to legal requirements and social expectations regarding both the manner of the accumulation and the ends to which the wealth is put. The impacts on others of the wealth accumulator's actions are relevant considerations. The challenge boils down to harnessing the social benefits of pursuing self-interest, while curtailing the destructive consequences of outright selfishness. The evident difficulty we have had, and still have, in striking this balance constitutes one of the great cultural contradictions of capitalism.[92]

Greed in Finance

The particular place of greed in finance, it is argued, is not just that it comprises a key driver, but that it is deified. This beatific perspective tends to obscure its detrimental consequences and blind its protagonists. In a tremendously acerbic article in 2010 regarding the rapacious behavior of some of finance's highest flyers before, during, and after the 2008 credit crisis, journalist and author Matt Taibbi asks whether now, in fact, "Greed *is* God?"[93] Taibbi was directing attention to the attitude as much as to the actions of Goldman Sachs (which he saw as talismanic of the financial sector generally) regarding a series of inquiries into the legality of certain speculative positions it took in 2006–07, which pitted the interests of one client against those of another, to Goldman's significant benefit.[94] The ethics as well as legality of the deals were in question,[95] but despite this unwelcome attention, the firm's senior personnel appeared to be genuinely bemused by all the fuss. Had they not just brokered a deal that was especially clever, a product of their superior business nous? Underhanded, maybe; even borderline illegal. But should they not be rewarded for their intelligent gaming of the market, and shouldn't those they had bet against suffer losses for being less smart (no matter that those who lost out included their own clients, notably, the European Banks ABN Amro and IKB)?[96] "*Caveat Emptor* dude," as Taibbi characterized this mind-set.

Like the tango, however, it takes two for greed to weave its magic into the financial markets. On the other side of those who, like Goldman, win big, are those who lose big, like IKB. Both sides are driven by the desire to profit as handsomely and usually as quickly as possible from the deal. This is the essential dynamic in every financial transaction. The "consideration" supplied by both sides (or rather "all sides," as many of these financial products are multiparty and multilayered) to the contract is their promise to pay up, or bear the loss in any transaction. The product of such financial transactions is nothing tangible, no "visible" goods; rather, there is just a movement of "invisible" capital from one account to another. Even insiders are apt to describe such insular activity as "socially useless," [97] at least in the sense that the transactions themselves do not yield useable outcomes, or even realizable wealth. As veteran banker-cum-author Satyajit Das explains in *Extreme Money:* "[l]ess than 8 per cent of all dollars are in the form of paper money or coins. The vast majority of dollars exists in the form of entries in the accounts of borrowers or lenders. Paper money is an abstraction, or, as most of it does not exist physically, an abstraction of an abstraction."[98]

In its focus on the creation, accumulation, and expenditure of monetary wealth, the financial system is at heart a control system. Yet we all suspect and have long feared that the desire for money and wealth knows no limits.[99] One might suppose, therefore, that finding within such a system the means by which to strike an equitable balance between personal cupidity and societal need might be especially difficult. Certainly, as discussed in chapter 1, the performance-based bonus schemes in finance are skewed toward rewarding avarice. But while bankers' pay and the incentives behind them are unquestionably important factors in the equation, greed's distinctive place in finance is propped up by foundations that are more substantial than the attraction of generous compensation packages. Essentially, the acceptance of greed reflects a societal tolerance, even commendation, that disparities in financial wealth (including egregious ones) can be justified. Not only is the embedded sense of entitlement that prevails inside the finance sector typically met with resigned expectation by the rest of us outside it,[100] we outsiders routinely rely on the products and services that the sector offers and eagerly consume them when we invest, borrow, hedge, trade, or transact.

So we are complicit in the grip that greed holds over finance, if only because we seem so inclined to appreciate its convenience and covet the wealth it can deliver. Adam Smith recognized the perniciousness of society's "disposition to admire, and almost worship, the rich and the powerful" as nothing less than "the great and most universal cause of the corruption of moral sentiments."[101] Whether or not greed, and our veneration of it, ranks as such a grave moral consequence today may be moot, there is no denying the continuation, even accentuation, of the disposition to celebrate the rich in popular culture, not only through the Western media, but in São Paulo soap operas, on Shanghai billboards, and all in between.

In any case, succumbing to temptations of avarice provides no guarantee of beneficent outcomes. Rather, in terms of financial risk and its consequences, the part played by greed is best seen as a sort of "psychological leverage." That is, while the risk of financial failure or success correlates directly with the extent of your financial commitment, your financial commitment is dependent on your aptitude for greed. The greater the greed, the greater the risk. Similarly, wider society's tolerance of the risks taken on by sections within it is essentially dependent on society's collective facility for greed and its depth of addiction to debt.

When Risk Goes Bad

Even if we agree with Adam Smith that mankind is characteristically overoptimistic in the matter of financial risk,[102] the task of how to maximize outcomes beneficial for human rights while minimizing those that are detrimental is arduous indeed. It is made all the more so when the behavior of the financial sector resembles that of a "sugared-up toddler."[103] In the late 1990s and early 2000s the "sugar" was of course the enormous levels of leveraged debt that were sloshing around the financial system,[104] but it was reckless greed that lay behind the hyperenergetic, hedonistic, and heedlessly demanding behavior that blinded the sector to the wider social and economic consequences of its actions and that led eventually to its epic meltdown in 2007–08.

As with all parents or guardians confronted with a string of tantrums like those comprising the financial crisis, the choice of responses ranged from giving in to giving out. Ireland, for instance, opted for the former path. In an effort to save its banking system, which was crippled by massive holdings of mortgage-backed assets that had turned toxic, the Irish government decided to recapitalize a number of financial institutions, including the country's three main banks: the Bank of Ireland, Allied Irish Bank, and Anglo Irish.[105] To finance the venture, the government committed €35 billion of public funds (nearly 40% of its annual GNP and the highest per capita input of any state in the Eurozone),[106] on top of €50 billion in loans from the IMF, the European Union, and several other EU member states.[107]

Iceland, on the other hand, chose the latter path and let the banks fail. Faced with a domestic financial crisis in 2008 as grave as Ireland's, the Icelandic government contemplated a bailout. But in the end it opted to let the country's main banks default on the bulk of their debts of approximately €85 billion,[108] much of which was held by governments (especially of the UK and the Netherlands), banks, and other private investors throughout Europe.[109] In what must rank as one of the remarkable statements by any world leader about the crisis, the country's president, Olafur Ragnar Grimmson, argued:

> Why are the banks considered to be the holy churches of the modern economy? Why are private banks not like airlines and telecommunication companies and allowed to go bankrupt if they have been conducted in an irresponsible way? The theory that you have to bail out banks is . . . about bankers enjoy[ing] the profits of their success, and then letting ordinary people bear [the costs of] their failure through taxes and austerity. People in enlightened democracies are not going to accept that in the long run. [110]

President Grimmson was in fact declaring what many people believed, but were afraid to say—the Emperor really was wearing no clothes.[111] By taking this path, the Icelandic government was able, initially at least, to protect state-held funds that could be used to refinance personal mortgages that banks were no longer able to maintain, and to preserve levels of social welfare support.[112] After these funds were expended, however, and as access to international credit evaporated, the currency plunged, inflation soared, and economic growth went into reverse, the government had no choice but to hike tax rates and seek a loan from the IMF.[113]

President Grimmson certainly struck a chord; but he may have been some-what optimistic in his claim that "enlightened democracies" would not, in the long run, tolerate bank bailouts. If evidence from the short and medium terms is anything to go by, the world's major economies are showing no such intolerance. In fact, in the immediate wake of the 2007/08 crisis, Iceland's response turned out to be a classic case of the exception that proves the rule. Nearly all Western economies tended strongly toward the Irish response by bailing out or national-izing their major financial institutions. Whereas some states did let certain banks fail (for example, Bear Sterns and Lehman Brothers in the United States) before saving others, only a few states (Australia joined Ireland in this regard) went so far as to provide state-backed guarantees for depositors.[114]

The economies of Ireland and Iceland were plunged into deep recessions and the citizens of both nations endured considerable financial and social hard-ship in the years following the crisis. During that time, UN human rights bodies documented broadly similar stories of privation in the two countries—marked rises in the number of unemployed, more people living in poverty, and widening social exclusion. Cuts in public services and welfare support in both countries hit single-parent families, children, persons with disabilities, the homeless and inadequately housed, and migrants.[115]

By taking what the IMF labeled an "unorthodox" approach to the crisis, Iceland did not avoid pain, but it did offer (as the IMF also acknowledged) a via-ble alternative response to a financial crisis caused by exposure to excessive risk. For the vast majority of economic commentators, this outcome was unexpected. Indeed, when Iceland signaled its intentions to orchestrate the banks' strategic failure, many of them predicted economic Armageddon.[116] To its credit, how-ever, this did not include the IMF. Despite its image as a harsh enforcer of strict neoliberal orthodoxy, the IMF was accommodating in its negotiations with Iceland over the life-saving loan it extended to the stricken state in November 2008. In stark contrast to its dogmatically critical response to economies that sought to implement currency controls and other protectionist measures dur-ing the Asian financial crisis in the late 1990s, the IMF on this occasion took a more open stance and was praised by the Icelandic government for "its flexibil-ity and willingness to engage . . . and [for] leaving as much space as possible to elected politicians to take the decisions and do the hard work to select their own rules."[117]

The IMF's confidence in Iceland's approach was duly rewarded—three years down the track the economy had retreated from the brink and was showing good signs of recovery. So much so that when the Fund and the Icelandic government co-hosted a conference in Reykjavik in October 2011 to mark the successful conclusion of the loan program, there was a palpable sense of pride alongside relief that the experiment had worked. In terms of what are normally dry and stale affairs to all but insiders and aficionados, this conference was refreshingly different. Not only did it present the unusual spectacle of a debtor government and a creditor financier enthusiastically exchanging compliments about each other's behavior, it also provided economists and financiers who were skeptical of the bank forgiveness and austerity measures being followed by the rest of the developed world with a living example of an economy successfully bucking the trend. These skeptics included Nobel Prize–wining economists Joseph Stiglitz from Columbia University—who said that "it would have been wrong to burden [Iceland's] future generations with the mistakes of the financial system,"[118] and Paul Krugman of the *New York Times*—who argued that "Iceland's heterodoxy gives us a test of economic doctrine."[119]

Risky Lessons

Clearly, then, lessons were there to be learned. Subsequently, the IMF was the somewhat unlikely source of one important lesson in terms of promoting human rights standards. Reflecting on the Iceland experience, Nemat Shafik, the Deputy Managing Director of the IMF, highlighted two key takeaways. The first of these was fairly straightforward—it is easier for the Fund to deal with countries that have clear economic strategies in mind. The second, however, spoke to the nature of the strategy, and specifically to the one Iceland had in mind. Shafik was now of the view that a state faced with a financial crisis may increase rather than restrict its economic policy options when it makes the preservation of the welfare state a priority above the bailing out of errant banks.[120] For those familiar with the dry, belt-tightening strictures of the IMF of old, this perspective was iconoclastic indeed.

The most important message, however, was hinted at by conference participants rather than explicitly drawn out. One example of this came when Willem Buiter, the colorful chief economist at Citibank, received a standing ovation at the Reykjavik conference when he referred to the cause of the gargantuan size of Iceland's banking sector immediately prior to the crash (the capitalized value of which had grown to ten times the country's entire economy)[121] as "an example of collective madness." Another came, when looking ahead, Simon Johnson of MIT and former IMF chief economist, warned that the global financial system still resembled "a big house of cards."[122] The message here is that the finance sector's attitude toward financial risk and its economic and social consequences has changed little. We, moreover, continue to accept finance's pleas of exceptionalism during bad times when the rest of society must bear the mammoth costs of systemic financial failures; not to do so would destroy the financial system and, with it, the capacity to create wealth during the good times. This is a classic example of "moral hazard" (or the "doom loop"):[123] believing that ultimately they will always be insured against complete failure, financiers are emboldened to take on yet more risk, with all the wider and deeper social consequences that implies when another crash inevitably occurs.

One response to this sobering thought is to point to Iceland's experience as a quintessential example of the benefits of *not* permitting moral hazard. In other words, big risk-takers ought and can be forced to accept losses when their investments fail, in the same way as they pocket the gains when they succeed. As Juan Pablo Bohoslavsky, the UN Independent Expert on Foreign Debt and Human Rights, concluded after his 2015 mission to Iceland, the country's "human rights compliant response" to the crisis provides an example from which "bigger and less developed countries, with more complex problems, can learn . . . and cherish the value of having a social security net in place to ensure a basic protection floor for all."[124]

Another response is to focus on the social implications of the "normal" operation of finance—that is, in the periods between crashes—rather than just on the crash alone. The grossly disproportionate distribution of the costs and the benefits of finance between the rich and the rest occur when finance is working in both ordinary and extraordinary conditions. The system is designed that way. The distributional imbalance is the unavoidable and intended consequence of a system that permits and encourages increasing disparities in wealth created by rampant greed, untrammeled debt, and an overblown faith in methods of risk management. Inequality is in fact built into risk, in that the greater the opportunity for the latter, the wider the disparity in the former. And the relationship is self-perpetuating. Thus, economist John Quiggin argues that "inequality particularly encourages a search for opportunities to capture the benefits of risky actions while shifting the costs onto others, or onto society as a whole."[125]

What this tells us is more about politics than about finance and economics. It was politics that permitted the financial system to be constructed in this way, so it is politics that can effect its redesign. In this, the financial crisis provides both a reminder and an opportunity (even ten years on) for reform. For Quiggin, the democratic response to the crisis must be to reassert the state's crucial role as the ultimate risk manager.[126] By so doing, not only is the state then better able to mitigate the detrimental consequences suffered by those in society least able to bear them when risk goes bad. It also meets its political responsibilities as trustee of the people and its legal obligations under international and national human rights laws to promote equality and freedom for all, especially for those deficient in both respects. Banks must be compelled or otherwise persuaded to find the middle ground in risk management "between gut feeling and number fetishism,"[127] and investors must be forced through legal sanctions to bear responsibility for the consequences of the financial risks they wittingly take.[128]

Leadership needs be shown in tempering excessive individual and institutional risk-taking when society's interests as a whole demand it. Free financial markets that facilitate extreme risk are creatures of state power, as political philosopher John Gray argues in *False Dawn*, that "persist only so long as the state is able to prevent human needs for security and the control of economic risk from finding political expression."[129] The state, therefore, has both the power and the responsibility to curb the creatures' excesses.

Friends with Benefits

We conclude this chapter back where we started. The attraction, necessity, and inevitability of risk are all integral parts of the relationship between human rights and finance. In this context the goal is to control it, not eliminate it; to harness its beneficial outcomes; and to do our best to avoid or limit its detrimental impacts. The principal beneficial outcome of successfully negotiating financial risk is the generation of wealth. Wealth enhances the lot of successful risk-takers, and thereby directly promotes their enjoyment of their human rights (here noting that the poor, as well as the rich, court financial risk). In addition it may also, indirectly, enhance the capacity of others, including the state, to promote human rights standards more broadly and effectively. It is to financial wealth and its patterns of distribution and movement that we now turn, looking first at private wealth (in chapter 4) and then public finances (in chapter 5).

|| 4 ||

Private Matters

"I'd like to say 'no' to the cold hard cash, but starving just would not make sense."

—Hunters and Collectors, *Where do you go?* (1991)

What Money Can Buy

It is not without some irony that the man whose image adorns the largest denomination U.S. dollar banknote still in circulation is widely reputed to have scorned money. Poor by birth and thrifty by philosophical inclination, Benjamin Franklin amassed a fortune during his lifetime on account of his extraordinary industry.[1] It is odd, therefore, that he is so often incorrectly attributed with the adage that "[m]oney never made a man happy yet, nor will it" (it actually belongs to an obscure nineteenth-century English clergyman named David Alfred Doudney).[2] Franklin was in fact both knowledgeable and prudent in financial matters, being well aware of the value of money and the benefits of spending it wisely.[3] Perhaps the temptation to have even the "Father of America" believe—as do so many of the rest of us—in the bitter sweetness of money was too appealing to resist. But whatever the reason, there can be no doubting our near-universal cynicism toward cash. True love and genuine friends, as well as happiness, are all said to be important things that money cannot buy. But what of the important things that money can buy, especially when "today, almost everything is up for sale," as public philosopher Michael Sandel tells us?[4] Health care, education, a home, food, a fair trial, free speech, personal safety, and even national security are all available at a price, whether to us personally, or to the state on our behalf. Not only are these commodities and services important in their own right, they are also essential ingredients in love, happiness, and friendship. They help make these desirable circumstances of existence happen; or, to put it another way, their lack or absence makes life a whole lot harder.

Monetary wealth is, therefore, both necessary and desirable in the pursuit of our sentient pleasures and even of life itself. Its "generous and fecund power," as Émile Zola put it,[5] has the potential to transform the way we live. For some, financial wealth provides the means to secure the bare essentials of sustenance, clothing, and shelter; for others, it literally buys better health, education, comfort, space, privacy, voice and influence, and more. This transformative capacity is true of both public wealth (wealth that is in the possession and control of the state), which is the concern of the next chapter, and private wealth (wealth that is in the hands of individuals, corporations, and other nonstate entities), which is the focus of this chapter.

The manner whereby private wealth is generated, in what it is invested, and how it is distributed are all matters of critical importance to people's enjoyment of human rights and are necessary for establishing a justification for the acquisition and divestiture of wealth itself. Still, problems in recognizing and understanding the nature of the interdependency between private wealth and human rights, alongside questions of the fair and appropriate regulation of the relationship, are foundational concerns that we encounter time after time in this chapter and throughout the book. I recall, for example, an event some years ago that neatly illustrates this disconnect. I had been invited to give a talk to a group of lawyers at a large global law firm in London on the topic of human rights and finance. The senior partner who hosted the event was a specialist in finance law, and by way of introduction he admitted being curious to hear what the two matters could have in common, for in all his years sitting in meetings with bankers, investors, insurers, and all manner of other financial actors, he could not recollect the words "human rights" and "finance" ever being used in the same sentence.

Today the situation is changing, but it is still far short of mutual comprehension and intimate engagement. Over time, banks have been sued for complicity in human rights–abusing regimes, such as Nazi Germany (Credit Suisse and UBS)[6] and apartheid South Africa (Barclays),[7] while others have faced criminal charges for knowingly engaging in money-laundering ventures on behalf of terrorist organizations (BNP Paribas, breaching U.S. economic sanctions)[8] and criminal gangs (HSBC, with regard to Mexican and Colombian drug cartels).[9] More generally, the financial institutions (and even the law firms they engage)[10] are now at least aware of the relevance of human rights and have begun to try to make sense of that relationship.

The Thun Group (a self-declared informal group of representatives from the seven leading European banks),[11] for example, issued two Discussion Papers (in 2013 and 2017) on the implications for banks of the 2011 *UN Guiding Principles on Business and Human Rights* (the GPs).[12] In fact the Discussion Papers were restricted to those GPs (Nos. 16–21) that urge all corporations, including banks, to exercise "due diligence" in assessing potential adverse human rights impacts of their business in order to prevent and mitigate such impacts and to address effectively any resultant human rights damage. Though it is commendable to see banks wrestling with what it means to do "the right thing" by "respecting human rights," including in the financial supply chain,[13] the Thun Group is nevertheless especially keen to stress the entirely voluntary nature of its venture into new territory. Both Discussion Papers omit to refer to other apposite GPs, such as GP 11, which underscores the need for corporations to abide by their existing human rights obligations under relevant national laws—obligations that certainly encompass banks.[14] Furthermore, while the Thun Group declares that one of the central aims of the discussion papers is to prompt proactive engagement between banks and human rights issues instead of "waiting for legal requirements,"[15] it presents a decidedly cautious, even cynical, approach to doing so by appending extensive legal disclaimers to both documents. For example, 2013 Discussion Paper proclaims:

> [i]n assessing compliance with any of the policies and guidelines, the standards applied are subjective and any decision in relation thereto remains within the banks' discretion. The banks do not accept liability for whatever consequences may result from their not adhering to these policies, procedures, criteria, instructions, statements and guidelines.[16]

It is, in fact, now common for major financial institutions to adopt statements or policies that refer expressly to a commitment to protecting human rights, including, for example, ABN AMRO, Credit Suisse, Deutsche Bank, Goldman Sachs, ING, JP Morgan, and Royal Bank of Scotland.[17] That said, these declarations (and there are many other global banks who have made no such commitments),[18] should not be mistaken for deep understanding either of human rights or how they relate to the core business of finance. Banks' corporate social responsibility (CSR) programs, within which such human rights commitments are likely to be found, are typically peripheral concerns, "rarely linked to the defining purpose and core strategy of the company or the expected values, conduct and behaviors of employees," as a Group of Thirty report on the need to reform banking culture observes.[19] The elite membership of the Group of Thirty includes many former central bankers, financial power-players, and leading financial thinkers. That its report, being trenchantly critical of prevailing banking culture and stressing that "[b]anks have a broader responsibility to society," fails even to mention human rights in its eighty-four pages further underlines how little human rights concerns register on the finance sector's radar.[20]

It seems, therefore, that the breadth and depth of the relationship between the management of private sector wealth and human rights remains poorly understood by those within finance, just as it is by those outside it. This is a serious and somewhat surprising situation, as it reflects something of a missed opportunity.

Alongside a record of human rights abuse caused by the pursuit of private wealth (which is certainly one of the reasons that makes finance wary of engagement), there is also ample evidence of widespread human rights benefits brought about by private wealth (which should encourage such engagement). Both sides of the rights protections ledger must be recognized in order to understand the complicated relationship, especially as presently, these effects—whether good or bad—seem to be inadvertent rather than intended.

It is by way of explanation and illustration of these circumstances that we turn now to a consideration of, first, the relevant components of the generation and investment of private wealth, and second, the implications of its distribution.

The Generation and Investment of Wealth

There is a symbiotic relationship between the generation of wealth and its investment. One often begets the other, such that the two become, effectively, the same thing. Take, for example, the fact that the principal aim of capital investment in shares, bonds, other financial instruments, or any of their synthetic derivatives, is to see their value increase. And any income derived from these investments may itself be reinvested in the same assets, thereby perpetuating the intermingling of wealth generation and investment. As individuals and societies become more affluent, a larger share of their wealth is derived from capital, including capital transfers through inheritance, as well as from savings such as pension funds and the like.[21] But for the vast majority of people on Earth, their capital assests are few or non-existent, in which case income comprises their main or, more likely, only source of financial wealth.

Income

One's ability to generate an income is, typically, directly related to one's capacity to work—often referred to as "human capital," as distinct from "financial capital." Such capacity is dependent on a host of factors, including one's skills, education, aptitude, stamina and strength, and, of course, opportunity. Being employed in an income-paying job, or otherwise deploying one's skills in ways that attract an income, is one of the most direct and effective ways to procure basic human rights protections for individuals, families, and whole communities. "Jobs," according to the World Bank, "are the most important determinant of living standards around the world."[22] Employment income is evidently an important utility. The very fact of employment, however, is also an essential feature of rights protection. Work constitutes so much of so many people's lives that it often defines them to a significant degree. It "forms an inseparable and inherent part of human dignity," as the UN Committee on Economic, Social and Cultural Rights puts it,[23] and directly contributes to workers' "feeling[s] of self-esteem," as the International Labour Organization adds.[24]

It comes as no surprise, therefore, that the right to work is itself a free-standing human right recognized across many international human rights instruments, most especially in Article 6 of the ICESCR.[25] It is not in fact a right *to* work, in the sense that the states (still less private employers) are required to provide work for everyone, but rather, as Article 6(1) declares, "the right of everyone to the *opportunity* to gain his living by work which he freely chooses or accepts" (my emphasis). To that end, states are obliged to facilitate conditions that optimize the availability of such opportunities, including through the encouragement of private-sector enterprise that develops and expands employment options.[26]

The importance of jobs and the essential role of the private sector in generating them are well recognized by the World Bank. Introducing the Bank's World Development Report 2013, which focused on the role of jobs in promoting prosperity and fighting poverty, Bank president Jim Yong Kim declared: "It's critical that governments work well with the private sector, which accounts for 90 per cent of all jobs. Therefore, we need to find the best ways to help small firms and farms grow."[27] One might be forgiven for thinking President Kim grandiloquently indulgent when he then adds that "jobs equal hope. Jobs equal peace. Jobs can make fragile countries become stable." Yet, these are the very outcomes that the data collected for the report point to.[28] They also reflect the conclusion that economist Paul Collier's reaches based on his work on the impact of income on development—namely, that there exists a "trigger point" for many states when average income per head reaches approximately $2,700 per annum, after which evidence indicates that countries are likely to break the cycles of internecine conflict and dysfunctional government.[29]

While private sector investment and job creation occur in agrarian, industrial, and postindustrial economies alike, the twin phenomena of industrialization and urbanization in the last two centuries (but especially globally, in the last eighty years or so) have shifted the workplace out of the fields and villages and into the factories and offices of towns and cities. The result is that working for others and being paid a wage or salary, rather than subsistence labor (working for oneself or family), is now by far the most common income-generating vehicle. Therefore, private sector investment has become the single most important aspect of job creation and maintenance. This is true both nationally and internationally. The third great economic and social phenomenon that has changed the face of income, development, and human rights, has been globalization.

Remittances and Credit

With respect to income, globalization has created one of the most dramatic of all changes in the generation and transferral of wealth, through the enormous and still-growing global flows of remittances. The idea of leaving home to make your fortune (or just to find a better job) and then to send some of one's newfound wealth back home is hardly new. In pre- and early Bronze Age Mesopotamia, notes anthropologist Justin Jennings,[30] large numbers of stone masons, artisanal miners, and farmers migrated south to exploit the mineral- and soil-rich alluvial plains of the Tigris and the Euphrates, remitting a portion of this wealth either directly (via the physical carriage of their spoils), or indirectly, through inter-mediaries in physical form or via early versions of money. The opportunity for abuse of such methods, alongside the difficulties of travelling long distances and remaining in contact, ensured that for a long time, remittances were rare and insignificant. But with the onset of greater opportunities for economic migra-tion, alongside more secure means of financial communication, remittances gained greater significance in the latter half of the nineteenth century and into the twentieth century.[31] But it is in its modern phase, over the past twenty-five years or so, that we have witnessed their exponential growth.

World Bank data shows that total global remittances in 2015 amounted to $581 billion, of which $431 billion flowed into developing countries—nearly three times the official development assistance (ODA) received by those same countries.[32] These are substantial increases since 1995, especially for developing countries whose total remittances inflows were then only $55 billion.[33] For some countries, the quantities of personal remittances are nothing short of financial lifelines, constituting sizeable income streams as compared to states' GDP. In Haiti, Honduras, Moldova, and Samoa, for instance, remittances inflows fluctu-ate around the equivalent of 20% of GDP, and in Liberia, the Kyrgyz Republic, and Nepal the figure is around 30%.[34] There have been figures in recent times that are even more impressive, such as for Tajikistan in 2013, when remittances equalled 49.6% of GDP. But without doubt it is the historic data for Lesotho that is truly staggering; at 106% in 1983, remittances exceeded the country's total GDP, and were still enormous at 62% in 2000. Today the figure is more sedate at 17%.[35] Such levels represent both a blessing and a curse. For while it is a long-term problem for all of these countries that their primary export is the country's labor force, there is no denying the short-term benefits to families, communities, and the states themselves of the remitted income.

The marginal utility of cash transfers sent directly to individuals and families can be very significant—helping to reduce poverty and better protect human rights. In their study of the microeconomic impact of remittances in Africa, finance specialists Cerstin Sander and Samuel Munzele Maimbo note that they are "primarily used for consumption and investment in human capital" such as education, health and better nutrition, as well as for investments in "land, livestock and housing." Group- or community-based remittances also tend to be used for welfare purposes such as to upgrade schools or health facilities, or to contribute to church activities.[36] In addition, there is also evidence of remittance income being used for debt repayments and (increasingly) investment in business opportunities and even savings.[37]

Clearly, these income streams promote the financial literacy of recipients and provide them with access to financial services, which goes some way toward explaining the marked rise in levels of private credit in low- and middle-income countries in recent years.[38] Remittance receipts can be used to establish one's creditworthiness when seeking microcredit or microinsurance,[39] facilities that in turn promote both the earnings potential and financial security of the poor.

Heiko Fritz and Günter Lang, two economists from the German University in Cairo, found this to be the case in their analysis of data collected from a survey of 670 low-income households from different areas in Cairo on the impact of microloans on poverty and income distribution.[40] Their survey sample included veteran and neophyte, male and female, and borrowers spread across three broad income bands: those living on less than $1.25 per day; those living on income between $1.25 and $2 per day; and those living on more than $2 per day. The researchers concluded that there was indeed a clear positive correlation between the presence of microloans and earning potential. But there were also a number of interesting contributory and qualifying factors. First, they noted that some 5% of households revealed that they had a simultaneous loan from a source other than the microfinance institution focused on in the survey, but there were likely "many more [that] probably concealed this information strategically." They observed that the marginal impact of a loan or loans was greatest for those who were relatively richer—that is, especially, among the more than $2 per day group. Furthermore, and unrelated to the preceding point, the earning potential of individual borrowers was consistently greater for men than for women. This last issue is of some importance to understanding the relationship between respective levels of income and human rights.

Fritz and Lang point out that if you want to foster economic growth, then the evidence from their study indicates that allocating more loans to men is desirable. They leave aside the question of whether economic growth will necessarily lead to enhanced human rights protections, which, as the discussion in the following section on capital demonstrates, is a moot point. More importantly, however, are the reasons they offer for why male borrowers produce higher returns, at least presently. "Males," they note "have a higher capital stock" (as in years of schooling and business connections), "allowing them to better exploit the opportunities from loans." They add that men also benefit from the fact that endemic discrimination in Egyptian society both provides men with the opportunity to increase their capital stock and prevents women from making the most of the loans. Their concluding suggestions, therefore, are that if you want to empower women and obtain the same level of marginal impact as men (both desirable human rights outcomes), then loan providers should be encouraged to continue targeting women, but to do so in schemes that offer "*microfinance plus education* [their emphasis]," which would help offset women's inherent disadvantage vis-à-vis men, and improve overall economic benefits of such financial services.

State intervention and regulation are necessary if the benefits of financial inclusion are going to assist income generation among the poor who currently have access to formal financial services, and if they are to be extended to the estimated 40% (or approximately 2 billion adults) of the world's poor who do not.[41] While supporting lenders and intermediaries in the services they provide, governments must also encourage or oblige them to act in ways that yield wide social benefits. Market tendencies are unlikely to guarantee such benefits on their own. For all the vaunted praise for, and the enormous growth of, both remittances and microfinance over the past fifteen years or so, these two financial pathways are far from perfect.

Rent-seeking

Rent-seeking, it is clear, is an opportunity too tempting for many of these financiers to resist. A serious and persistent problem for the poor who use these services are the costs they incur, especially interest rates and loan fees, as compared to those incurred by rich clients. A 2013 report compiled by a group of analysts from three specialist microfinance research agencies charting global movements in microcredit between 2004 and 2011 found that in 2011, the worldwide average microcredit loan fees and interest rate was 27%, with the highest rate recorded in Latin America (30%), and the lowest in South Asia (21%).[42] And while these were lower rates than those recorded in 2004, when the global average was 30% (with the highest rates in Africa [39%] and the lowest in South Asia [28%], they are evidently still far higher than the interest rates typically charged in Western economies. The authors of the report accepted that interest rates on microcredit loans are always higher "because it inevitably costs more to lend and collect a given amount through thousands of tiny loans than to lend and collect the same amount in a few large loans." "But," they wanted to know, "how much higher?" Were the current (and past) interest rates unconscionable profit-making, or the unavoidable price of access to finance? Their overall conclusion was that if previously the profits made by microlenders had been on the generous side (in 2004 the average percentage of borrowers' interest payments that went to microfinanciers' profits was around 20%), that was no longer the case (the same figure in 2011 had dropped to less than 10%).[43]

Still, the fact remains that the cost of microfinance borrowing remains very high relative to the commercial rates charged by banks in the West. Just as we saw with subprime mortgages, and as we shall see later in this chapter in the context of capital, and further regarding taxation in the next chapter, financial systems are cheapest and most effective for the rich and relatively rich. For the poor, access to financial services is nearly always much more expensive, even if it does offer the possibility of leverage up to a level where advantages accrue.

The cost of sending money is also high, though here the rent-seeking by the relevant bankers and brokers is more evenly spread across the rich and the (relatively) poor, as everyone suffers from slow and expensive money transfer services. As economist Jeffrey Tucker laments, our transmission technologies for moving money between countries are stuck in the 1950s.[44] The global average cost of remitting money has stubbornly persisted above 8%, largely due to the generally higher costs throughout Africa (around 12%)—in some cases, outrageously so (such as nearly 20% when sending money from South Africa to Zambia)[45]—as well as high-cost remittance corridors in the Pacific (as with a cost of 20.6% to transfer money from Vanuatu to Australia).[46] These costs have remained high despite the increased volume of transactions (as a consequence of which one would normally expect economies of scale to bring costs down), and despite a G8 pledge in 2009 (and reiterated by the G20 in 2014) to reduce that figure "in five years" to 5%.[47]

Even the onset of mobile money (or e-money)—using Internet and mobile telephone services to execute financial transfers—has hardly dented this figure. Growth in the numbers of mobile money accounts is accelerating, especially in developing countries, as competition between service providers lowers transaction costs for consumers.[48] It is true, as the World Bank points out, that some of the high costs for remittances transfers by whatever means are due to the regulatory requirements designed to counter money laundering and terrorist financing,[49] but in light of the fact that it is transfers into, rather than out of, rich-state banking systems that are the preferred route for illicit funds (precisely because of the whitest-of-whitewash they provide for dirty money),[50] it is perverse to maintain that poor, small-scale users of international financial transfers into poor states should bear disproportionately higher costs.

Nonetheless, income, and the various means by which it is generated, leveraged, and transferred, is only part of the story of how private wealth impacts on human rights. An even bigger tale to tell in this regard is how private capital is raised and deployed.

Capital

Globalization has also wrought incredible changes in cross-border capital investment. Investments overseas have existed for as long as there have been borders.
But the breadth and depth of FDI[51] have expanded enormously over the past
few decades, especially in developing nations.[52] Total world inflows of FDI have
grown from $200 billion in 1990, to just under $1.75 trillion in 2016, though
the latter figure is still short of the peak of $1.9 trillion in 2007, immediately
before the GFC. In fact, for developed economies, both the 2007/08 crisis and
the Asian financial crisis in the late 1990s were watershed events. FDI inflows
and outflows rose sharply for developed states leading up to both events, and
then fell precipitously during and after them, and remained low for many years.
Thus, for example, in 2014, total FDI inflows for developed states stood at $563
billion (compared to $1.28 trillion in 2007), and total FDI outflows at $707 billion (compared to $1.84 trillion in 2007).

These rollercoaster movements are perhaps to be expected. The real story
in FDI, however, has been in developing countries. Here, trends in both FDI
inflows and outflows have been steadily upward,[53] starting from negligible
total inflows into developing states in 1990 of $34 billion, to as much as $752
billion in 2015. Evidently, many developing economies, especially those graduat-
ing into middle- income or emerging-economy status (such as Brazil, China, and
India), have become attractive destinations for foreign investment. The changes
in FDI outflows from developing countries are even more dramatic. From a total
of $13 billion in 1990 (and still only $48 billion in 2003), they rose to $472 bil-
lion in 2014 (though dropping to $383 billion in 2016). Developing economies,
in other words, have become major contributors to cross-border capital investment, and while some of that has certainly been directed toward rich nations, the
bulk has been invested in other developing economies. These include, notably,
investments in countries otherwise effectively locked out of the (Western) international financial system, as, for example, was the case with Chinese investments
in Argentina, Ecuador, and Venezuela in the early 2000s.[54] This so-called "South-
South" investment is the reason why the above total FDI inflows into developing
countries have remained on an upward trajectory despite the severe and lasting
reductions to investments coming from developed economies.[55]

So, on the face of it, developing states should be benefiting from growing foreign investment in their domestic economies by way of more jobs, greater skills
transfers, higher incomes, and increased tax revenues. Such hopes and expectations, however, are seldom borne out in practice; or at least, not as fully as
they could be. For the people of developing countries, especially the poorest
and marginalized, many obstacles stand between them and the economic, social,
and human rights advantages that might flow from heightened levels of financial

investment in their economies. For instance, some are simply consequential, as noted by the UN Special Rapporteur on the right to housing: "Even where developing countries have successfully attracted a large increase in private capital flows, the rapid growth of cities typically outpaces the provision of adequate housing, resulting in an increased number of the poor living in squatter settlements with no security or civic services."[56]

Other obstacles are regulatory, such as the form and substance of investment laws often adopted by developing economies that stress the attractiveness of their economies to foreign investment unencumbered by nonfinancial demands and conditions. After some fifty years as an international Pariah state, one of the first and most controversial subjects that the Myanmar legislature turned its mind to as the country opened up was a new foreign investment law regime, which was eventually enacted in 2012.[57] Typical of many laws of this kind in newly emerging economies, the Myanmar law has been criticized for not garnering sufficient tax revenues from foreign investors; not providing adequate protection of land rights against expropriation; and for permitting too much opportunity for corruption and cronyism among the political elite.[58]

The protection of human rights is seldom a priority concern when developing state governments are considering their own investment laws, and this is reflected in the nature of the international investments agreements (IIAs) that they sign with their trading partners in ever-increasing numbers. Of the estimated 3,400 IIAs now in existence worldwide (most of which are bilateral investment treaties [BITs]), few make any reference to human rights.[59] Some labor rights, for example, are protected under Article 13 of the United States 2012 Model BIT, which requires both state parties to "reaffirm" their existing commitments under International Labor Organization Conventions, and, exceptionally, Norway's Model BIT refers not only to labor rights, but also sustainable development, democracy, the rule of law and international human rights standards.[60] But by and large, BITs are concerned exclusively with the commercial conditions under which investments are made and protected (or "stabilized"),[61] as well as the process by which investment disputes are to be resolved. They empower transnational corporations in ways that are typically indifferent—and sometimes in opposition—to states' obligations to protect human rights under international law.[62] While it is true that this conflict has occasionally been recognized in investment dispute settlement fora,[63] the peculiarity of such occasions underlines how exceptional the matter is still considered to be within international investment circles.[64]

The scant regard for the bigger picture of states' responsibilities in the enforcement of investment treaty obligations can result in such perversities as the notorious case of *CME v. Czech Republic* (2003) in which a BIT arbitral tribunal ordered the Czech government to pay compensation of $355 million to a jilted foreign investor, a sum equivalent to the entire annual budget of the Czech Ministry of Health.[65] Based on the facts of the case, there is little doubt that the government was complicit in the blatant expropriation of CME's investment by its local corporate partner, but for the tribunal to take no heed whatsoever of the wider public welfare consequences of its award (estimated to cost $40 per person in a country where the average monthly wage was then $600) is blinkered to a point near absurdity.[66] The fact that these arbitration tribunals are private, closed affairs designed with only the settlement of investment disputes in mind neither excuses nor exempts them from being held to greater account for decisions that have such wide-ranging public effects. That, further, there are questions raised over the independence and neutrality of the "small clique of arbitrators and lawyers" that effectively control the whole process, adds to the reasons why it cries out for greater scrutiny.[67] The commercial convenience and prevalence of the system, however, mitigates against this happening willingly or quickly. In the meantime, there will remain the pressing need to reconcile the legitimate objects of BITs with the no-less-legitimate concerns to protect the human rights of people who are, after all, innocent bystanders to any dispute.[68]

Capital and Tyranny

There are further obstacles, however, that are less defensible. Financial investments in repressive regimes, whether by way of public sector aid or private sector capital, can perpetuate human rights abuses.[69] The complicity of the investor in these situations may be inadvertent—the result of indifference rather than malevolence—but it is assistance nonetheless, and the cause of it does not matter to the victims of oppression. Careful due diligence on the part of investors is necessary if they are to minimize the chances of such connivance. "Money is not neutral," notes Juan Pablo Bohoslavsky in his study of the impact of financial investment in dictatorships. "Whether . . . given to directly finance the crimes (for example, financing death squadrons or transactions to buy weapons to repress the population) or to add financial resources generally available to the government (contributing to make the regime politically stronger or its life longer) is a question to which a combined micro and macro analysis of the situation could help to answer."[70]

Such introspection likewise applies to the international oil trade, given how Western governments help sustain a string of malicious autocracies, stretching from Russia in the north through the Gulf States to Angola in the south, by buying their oil.[71] The reconciliation of procuring profits and aiding oppression that this implies is also something very familiar to the many foreign corporations who invest in China. Google, Yahoo, and Microsoft have all faced this challenge regarding censorship and disclosure of users' details, and have suffered or prospered accordingly: Google, for example, (alongside other major Western social media platforms such as Facebook, Twitter, Instagram, Tumblr, and YouTube) is blocked inside China after it refused to continue self-censorship in 2010.[72]

There are, however, situations in which no amount of due diligence would help. History is littered with examples of the pillage and squander of a country's resources and assets by way of the malice, avarice, and incompetence of foreign investors and host state governments alike. From the British East India Company's monopolistic and harsh militaristic control of commerce and much of government from Bengal to Beijing in the eighteenth century, and King Leopold II's barbaric trade in ivory and rubber in the "Belgian" Congo in the nineteenth century,[73] to the carelessness and intimidatory tactics of today's corporate behemoths like Shell (oil exploration in Nigeria), Trafigura (dumping toxic waste in Côte d'Ivoire), and Nestlé (marketing of breast milk substitutes in Asia, Africa, and Latin America),[74] foreign investors have shown little hesitation in exploiting their hosts, immiserizing local communities, and repatriating profits. Host state governments-cum-autocracies have also demonstrated their kleptocratic relish, often conniving with foreign corporations in the process. From Suharto's Indonesia, Mobuto's Democratic Republic of Congo (DRC) and Baby Doc Duvalier's Haiti of yesteryears, to Dos Santos's Angola, Obiang's Equatorial Guinea, and Hun Sen's Cambodia of today, they have ravaged their nation's resources for their own and their families and friends' gargantuan gain.

All of these nations have exploitable physical assets and have hosted decades of substantial foreign investment, yet their people remain poor while their leaders possess (literally) untold wealth.[75] It is no accident that the DRC has languished for more than twenty-five years at the very bottom of the UNDP's *Human Development Index* given that the country was so systematically looted first by Leopold and then Mobutu, as well as by a host of extractive resources corporations in between.[76] For more than a century, there has seldom been a shortage of foreign investment flowing into the country and yet today its 70 million people suffer the lowest annual per capita GNI in the world (at $444, compared to the global average of $13,723); can expect a life expectancy of fifty years, which is also the world's lowest (the global average is 70.8 years); and average only 3.1 years of schooling for its children (the global average is 7.7).[77]

FDI, therefore, can be associated with, or directly cause, systemic abuses of rights to education, health, labor conditions, and an adequate standard of living (including rights to adequate food, water, and housing). It can also support or promote violations of civil and political rights by corrupt and/or dysfunctional host state governments such as the rights to physical safety, nondiscrimination, self-determination, freedom of expression, association, and movement, as well as privacy, fair trial, and representative government.

Capital Gains

Examples of benign and even highly effective FDI in developing states do exist. "Sustainable development depends as much on the quality of investment as on the quantity,"[78] as the Organisation for Economic Co-operation and Development (OECD) puts it, and quality, in turn, depends on the aims and competencies of both investors and host states. What one hopes for in terms of human rights are, at the very least, beneficial spill-over effects from foreign investment. That is where, for the local population, FDI yields more jobs, better skills, higher tax receipts, improved infrastructure, and responsible and effective government, all of which promote, directly or indirectly, human rights standards. Certainly, there are countries whose socioeconomic and human rights fortunes have risen in line with increasing inflows of FDI across their borders. Some of these states were poor and small—such as Cape Verde, Costa Rica, Mauritius, and Singapore—while others were poor and large—such as Brazil, China, India, and South Korea. There have also been variations on these themes, with, for example, relatively richer countries (both small and large) such as Chile, Estonia, Ireland, Malaysia, Mexico, and Poland, as well as present-day emerging economies such as Indonesia, South Africa, and Vietnam all reflecting the same correlation between improving living and human rights standards, and pronounced increases in FDI inflows. Yet, crucially, evidence of direct causal linkages between the indicia is more circumstantial than solidly definitive.

Scholars in human rights,[79] economics,[80] and political science[81] have all pointed this out and warned against too-hasty conclusions about correlations—whether positive or negative—between increasing FDI and levels of human rights protection. The challenge here lies in the fact that human rights-impacting outcomes (currently a live issue in intellectual and human rights policy circles)[82] can be difficult to measure, but it also arises from the sheer complexity of charting clear lines of cause and effect between such large and amorphous phenomena as a country's aggregate FDI inflows and the levels of human rights protection enjoyed by its people.[83]

One researcher who has nonetheless tried to bridge the gap in development finance and human rights has been economist and former director of global programs at the World Bank Institute (the Bank's in-house think-tank) Daniel Kaufmann. Drawing on the mass of data that he and his colleagues Aart Kraay and Massimo Mastruzzi collected from the application of their innovative "worldwide governance indicators" to more than two hundred countries and territories,[84] Kaufmann argues that "success in socio-economic development . . . requires particular focus on governance and integrity issues. These issues, in turn, are dependent in part on voice and civil liberties, as well as on domestic politics."[85] Development projects have greater prospects of success, he

concludes, in countries where "participatory citizen voice" is protected and promoted and governments are more accountable and effective. The result can be a
virtuous circle whereby better-governed states attract more foreign investment,
and more investment leads to higher incomes, which, in turn, improve human
rights standards. Kaufmann summarizes such beneficial impacts as a "300 per
cent development dividend: a country that improves governance by one standard deviation—which is a realistic improvement where political will exists—can
expect to more or less triple its annual per capita income in the long run."[86]

Kaufmann's focus was on publicly funded international development projects
(in particular, those sponsored by the World Bank), but his conclusions resonate
with those of Robert and Shannon Blanton, who have been studying the social,
political, and economic impacts of FDI for more than a decade. Thus, for example,
in their review of empirical surveys of what U.S. investors are looking for in potential destination countries, they find that "a 'build up' approach, in which a country that protects the rights of its citizens and makes long-term investments in the
quality of its human capital,"[87] is the most effective in attracting (financial) capital.

Responsible Capital

Questions about the nature and effects of the relationship between FDI and
human rights have increasingly drawn the attention of scholars, policy-makers,
legislators, and activists alike over recent years, which, if nothing else, has meant
that the overseas activities of corporate investors and the banks behind them
have been scrutinized like never before. Much of the global business and human
rights debate has focused on transnational commerce, and especially that of
multinational corporations (including banks), as reflected in the UN *Guiding
Principles on Business and Human Rights* (2011) discussed above.

"Transparency"—especially of financial dealings between investing corporations and host states—has become a catchphrase in the field. Aided by
the expanding power of information technology and by the desire to expose
that which should be known but had previously been successfully hidden,
Transparency International (TI) has grown into the world's leading nongov-
ernmental organization combatting global corruption. Established in Berlin in
1993 by lawyer and retired World Bank official Peter Eigen, TI is perhaps best
known for its annual publication of the "Corruption Perceptions Index." The
Index ranks 176 countries according to the levels of public sector corruption as
perceived by a set of independent international organizations that specialize in
governance and business climate analysis, including the Economist Intelligence
Unit, Freedom House, the World Economic Forum, and specialist programs in
the African Development Bank and the World Bank.[88]

TI's modus operandi of naming and shaming has strongly influenced subsequent, more targeted disclosure initiatives, such as the *Extractive Industries
Transparency Initiative* (EITI)—a coalition of governments, resources corporations, and civil society that has set a global standard for disclosure that seeks to
"promote open and accountable management of natural resources" both by governments and corporations working in the sector.[89] The civil society–inspired
global coalition Publish What You Pay is another enterprise dedicated to greater
transparency. Working under the rubric "resource-rich but poor" it, too, aims to
unlock states' development potential by exposing what revenues, incomes, royalties, and taxes are paid by resource corporations and to host state governments
and thereby "influence key stakeholders and drive policy and practice change."[90]

The degree to which these schemes directly achieve their objectives is hard
to gauge. In respect of the EITI, for example, Andrés Mejía Acosta, a specialist
in the management of natural resources revenues, observes that "[i]t remains
an empirical challenge to demonstrate that more revenue transparency and
improved budgeting standards could lead to improved fiscal performance or better income redistribution."[91] In other words, even if states and corporations are
today less willing or able to conceal what they can, and instead feel more pressure to publish, the challenge remains to convert less opacity into more money
for developing states, and more money into better human rights protections.
The promise of change is certainly there; it is just not clear (at least not yet) if
and when changes in practice will follow.

The same sense of hope above expectation stands behind those voluntary human rights compliance schemes specifically aimed at the international
finance and investment sectors. The UN's *Principles of Responsible Investment*
(PRI) have attracted some 1,600 signatory financial institutions. While broad
in membership,[92] the initiative's six principles are exhortatory rather than exculpatory (which is one reason why the signup numbers are so healthy), and their
incorporation of human rights concerns implicit rather than explicit. In a section
entitled "What is responsible investment," for example, the PRI proclaims that
"the whole investment chain" should focus more "on long-term value creation . . .
[to] help ensure that investors preferentially invest in companies that have better
ESG [economic, social and governance] performance and thereby make a real
contribution to addressing the sustainability challenges that we face."[93] The con-
verse is true for the coverage of the *Equator Principles* (EPs). Here, the breadth of
coverage is relatively narrow (that is medium- to large-scale project financing)[94]
and membership is relatively small (eighty-five financial institutions),[95] but the
EPs do focus on member financial institutions conducting human rights due diligence when assessing applications for finance.[96]

Neither initiative possesses any enforcement teeth, nor are their member
financial institutions obliged to provide remedies for breaches of their respective

principles. The two schemes are intended instead to promote responsible deci-sion-making and management of risk. That may not be enough for some, but it is certainly an advance. Many large financial institutions today possess complex compliance processes covering social and environmental risk, as well as com-mercial risk,[97] and the fact that these have been designed more in response to the risk of sanction through anti-money-laundering regulation rather than actively to promote environmental or human rights goals should not detract from the result that these latter goals may nonetheless be served.[98]

The Business of Impact

In a similar vein, in recent years there has emerged a distinct "business case" for better human rights awareness and protection in the private sector regarding capital investments. If, in other words, responsible investment can lead to prof-itable investment, then mutual benefits might be assured. Indeed, the socially responsible investment sector (alongside its environmentally sustainable sib-ling) has grown enormously in recent years. In 2014, more than 30% of all finan-cial assets under management worldwide were classified as socially responsible (for Europe alone, the figure was an astounding 58.8%). The global percentage represents an enormous leap in just two years, from 21.5% in 2012.[99]

Large institutional investors such as pension funds are key drivers behind this continuing push as they respond to demands of their members and clients, even if at times what is and what is not "social responsible" is not always clear.[100] Yet, as veteran responsible investment advocate Rory Sullivan argues, much remains to be done if such matters as human rights impacts are to become mainstream concerns for investors. Sullivan—who has experience as an advisor both to non-governmental organizations (NGOs) and to investors—argues passionately that civil society must show a greater commitment to understanding the finance sector if it is to be taken seriously and thereby possibly persuade finance to heed its arguments.[101] As is so often the case with the divide between human rights and finance, hands and minds from both sides must be extended across the gap, if mutual benefits are to be truly attained.

The rise of social impact investing (or "innovative financing," as it is usually referred to in the context of private sector investment in development projects in developing countries) is another example of financial investment inspired by "business case" reasoning that can directly benefit human rights. The nature and forms of such finance are incredibly varied—from issuing bonds for reducing recidivism rates among juvenile offenders in London and New York, through expanding mobile money services in Kenya and the delivery of water and elec-tricity via renewable energy sources in rural communities in India, to funding

the manufacture of generic (and therefore affordable) medicines in Brazil and
South Africa and using air ticket levies to fund the treatment and diagnosis of
HIV/AIDS, tuberculosis, and malaria across the developing world.[102] But what
they all have in common is their concern to achieve certain defined social or
environmental outcomes, not just to return a profit. The balance between profit
and nonprofit goals also varies from scheme to scheme. The OECD calls this
"a spectrum of capital," with "financial only" concerns at one end and "impact
only" concerns (which is, in fact, philanthropy) at the other, and gradations in
between of greater or lesser financial returns versus ESG (environmental, social,
and governance) returns.[103]

The pitch that is often used by advocates of social impact investing is that
it seeks to ensure that private investment contributes to public benefit.[104]
Certainly, this is evident when applied in the context of development, where
the concern is to hitch the capital and skills of the private sector onto the public
sector wagon of overseas aid. Three UN conferences on innovative financing for
development—the first in Monterrey in 2002, a follow-up in Doha in 2008, and
the third in Addis Ababa in 2015—have sought to collate existing and encourage
new ways by which this integration can be achieved to the satisfaction of both
sectors.[105] And if there was any doubt of the importance of the private sector
to achieving development's goals, even in the minds of those dedicated to pub-
lic-sector-funded development assistance, the unambiguous declaration that
"only private-sector investment can end extreme poverty" made by Raj Shah in
February 2015, as he finished his tenure as the head of one of the world's largest
state aid agencies, USAID, surely puts them to rest.[106]

What is perhaps more surprising about how impact investing is presented
today is the trumpeted proclamation that the private sector may be willing or
keen (or even feel compelled) to contribute to the public good, *at the expense
of profit* (here recalling the OECD spectrum of capital discussed above). The
idea is presented as both novel and noble on the part of private sector investors.
Many, both inside and outside the world of impact investing, believe this to be
so.[107] Yet, profit alone is the reward system in what might be called a pure market economy—that is, one completely free of interference from forces outside
the market itself. As no such hermetically sealed economic system has ever (or
could ever) exist within societies governed as we know them—as Karl Polanyi
and his many followers have forensically demonstrated[108]—capitalist investors
have always had other goals or conditions thrust upon them. The methods and
means of production sustained by capital investment have long been regulated,
including by labor laws, environmental standards, taxes, and criminal sanctions.
Industries and services have also been variously encouraged, discouraged, or
even prohibited (by way of revenue or fiscal incentives, and licensing laws).
And the standards as well as prices of products themselves have been prescribed

through compliance and inspection processes, consumer protection laws, and competition policies.

No matter that all of these techniques have been and still are unevenly applied, they are nonetheless profit-impacting conditions, borne of expectations that commerce, and investment in it, contributes to public good and is not simply an exercise in private gratification. Rather than "novel and noble," for which praise or gratitude is apparently sought, the more accurate, if mundane, description of impact investing should be "desirable and necessary." The phenomenon of social impact investing is not to be criticized per se—undoubtedly it can produce great benefits of the kind I advocate in this book—but it should not be presented as a luxury benefit of capitalism. On the contrary, it is precisely the sort of core beneficial outcome that Joseph Schumpeter's "creative destruction" definition of capitalism anticipates, and what Adam Smith intended the market's "invisible hand" to deliver.[109]

Equity and Inequality

George Bernard Shaw is credited with the quip that England and America are two nations separated by a common language.[110] So it is in the worlds of finance and human rights. The term "equity," for example, in finance and commerce refers to a share or ownership interest in a company or asset (including real estate). In human rights parlance, the idea of equity connotes a fair share of, or access to, the basic necessities and amenities of social existence.[111] And yet the two need not, indeed must not, be incompatible.

Further on the matter of terminology, it must be made clear that the notion of "equality" in international human rights law is in fact much closer (but not identical) to the above description of human rights "equity." As drafted, understood, and applied in all the main international instruments of the modern, postwar human rights era, references to equality are made in the context of access to rights in ways that do not discriminate against individuals and groups on such designated illegitimate grounds as gender, race, religion, political belief, or economic status. The 1948 *Universal Declaration of Human Rights* and its progeny are products of their particular histories, and given that nearly all of these conventions and covenants were conceived during the decades when Cold War politics dictated so much of international relations, including the philosophy behind human rights treaty-making, it is unsurprising that the term "equality" did not carry collectivist connotations of absolute equality. Rather than equality of outcomes (substantive, or absolute equality), the preference has been for equality of opportunity (formal equality), though in both legal and policy practice, elements of the former have been promoted within or alongside the latter.

With specific reference to economic (or wealth) equality, the picture has been especially opaque. For in addition to equality/equity, the second great pillar upon which the modern edifice of human rights has been built is that of freedom. From the Western perspective this entails both economic freedom of market-based capitalism, as much as political freedom of democratic government. The tensions that exist between these two freedoms, as well as between the notions of freedom and equality, are unavoidable and interminable. Importantly, in the present context, this circumstance amounts to the fact that wealth *in*equality is not itself considered to be a human rights violation. So fundamental is the feature of the necessity of wealth differentials to the idea of freedom within its economic (and social) contexts that, as human rights scholar Martha Davis argues, it is inconceivable that the United States or any other Western nation would have acceded to any of the international human rights agreements formulated during the past seventy years if they had "jeopardize[d] the ascendancy of a market-based economy."[112] Financial gain is capitalism's reward system. But what, precisely, does it reward? That is the question at the heart of the burgeoning debate about wealth inequality and the seismic effects it has on relative standards of living and levels of rights protection.

Rewarding Capital

Proliferating wealth gaps are evident between individuals on a global scale, between individuals within states, and between rich and poor nations or regions. Drawing on data collected by *Forbes* magazine, French economist Thomas Piketty shows how the wealth of the world's billionaires has accelerated over the past twenty-five years, not just in absolute terms, but, crucially, in relative terms. Where in 1987, this group commanded 0.4% of private global wealth, by 2013 that proportion had risen to 1.5%.[113] Further, he calculates that the average annual real growth rate of wealth between 1987 and 2013 for the planet's richest (that is, the top one in twenty-millionth percentile)[114] was 6.4%, as compared to 1.9% for the world's adult population as a whole,[115] a difference that, through the power of compound interest, is very significant. The resulting disparity is stark. Data compiled by Credit Suisse in its Global Wealth Report 2015 suggest "that the lower half of the global population collectively own less than 1% of global wealth, while the richest 10% of adults own 88% of all wealth, and the top 1% account for half of all assets in the world."[116]

Obviously, some of this extreme wealth is to be found outside the West, especially in Brazil, China, India, Russia, and oil-rich states in the Middle East, as well as in the hands of potentates dotted all over the world, but the fact remains that it is highly concentrated in the developed economies. Analyzing the distribution of world GDP in 2012, for example, Piketty finds that the EU, with 8% of the world's population, possesses 21% of its GDP; Japan, with 2% of the population, holds 5% of GDP; and the USA and Canada together command a whopping 20% of the world's GDP with only 5% of its population. Contrast this with the world's poorest states or regions: sub-Saharan Africa has 13% of the globe's population, but only 3% of its GDP; India has 18% of the world's population with only 6% of GDP; and even China, with 19% of the population and 15% GDP. Latin America breaks even (just), with 9% of global population and 9% of its GDP.[117]

Beyond measuring the wealth of rich individuals and of states, a third metric of widening wealth inequality is comparing wealth between individuals in particular states. Here again, the exemplars are rich Western countries. According to OECD data, the gap between the wealthy and the rest has widened in all rich states in the last two decades, though in terms of both the magnitude and rate of change, the differential has been greatest in the United States.[118] The most recent annually published Global Wealth Reports show that the wealth inequality in the United States is now reaching levels that have not been recorded since the early part of the last century, when, for example, in 1910, the top decile's share of the country's total wealth was just over 80%. This share dropped after both the First and Second World Wars to hover around 65%, until the late 1990s, when it began to rise sharply. It has been rising ever since.[119] OECD data indicate that the richest 10% of Americans now account for 76.4% of their country's wealth.[120]

Some of this personal wealth can be attributed to generous incomes, which for the highest earners have been increasing rapidly in recent years while the income levels of the middle and lowest paid have actually decreased. Using U.S. Census Bureau statistics for the period 1979–2009, the Institute of Policy Studies Inequality Project shows that the top quintile of income earners in the United States enjoyed an aggregate rise in real terms of 48.8% (for the top 5% it was a rise of 74.9%). The corresponding figure for the lowest quintile of income earners was minus 12.1%, and for the second quintile, minus 0.1%. The figures for the third and fourth quintiles were 8.4% and 20.3%, respectively.[121] For those at the very top of the income tree, the gains have been truly astonishing. The average remuneration package of CEOs of the largest 350 corporations in the United States in 2014 was $16.3 million, representing 303 times the average pay of American workers in that same year (the ratio had previously peaked at 376:1 in 2000). Over the period 1978–2014, top executives' compensation packages grew by 997.2%, as compared to 10.9% growth in a "typical worker's pay" over the same period.[122]

Yet, despite all that, income wealth tells only part of the story, and not even the main part. Piketty argues that the principal source of accelerating wealth disparity lies in the ownership of capital (which of course may be fueled by high incomes) and the exponential returns it delivers over time. By extrapolating current trends, he estimates that by 2030, capital wealth held by the top decile in the United States will reach the stratospheric levels that the wealthiest 10% in Europe enjoyed around 1910, which at 90%, exceeded even the wealth of top decile in the United States at that time.[123] What is being rewarded, therefore, to return to the questioned posed earlier, is capital; or more specifically, the *possession* of capital, whatever uses the holder may, or may not, be putting it to.

Consequences of Unequal Wealth

The significance of such wealth inequality is not confined merely to economic considerations. Its implications are keenly felt across social and political spheres as well. This much is already apparent from popular reactions to outrageously conspicuous wealth—from "Occupy" movements (most notably in Wall Street and the City of London in 2011),[124] to moral outrage over the extent of tax avoidance opportunities made legally available to rich individuals and corporations in nearly all developed economies.[125]

For Piketty, too, it is where this might be leading that is of particular concern—to the accumulated sense of injustice felt by individuals and the social instability that both reflects and propagates what in 2014 Piketty called a "potentially explosive process" of excessive wealth accumulation.[126] Barely two years later, the potential was emphatically translated into practice by the waves of electoral anger and despair that swept Donald Trump into the White House and pushed the UK onto a path out of the EU. It was and is not so much the disparities in income that concerns Piketty, but rather the consequences of "excessive and long-lasting concentration of capital."

Exaggerated and unmerited income levels may pique senses of fairness and foment discontent, but it is the systemic bias in favor of capital that most seriously distorts the economy[127] and undermines social cohesion. "No one denies that it is important for society to have entrepreneurs, inventions, and innovations," he protests, nor that their success be financially rewarded. The problem is that the "entrepreneurial argument" can justify neither the scale nor the scope of resulting wealth inequalities, most especially when fortunes initially gained from innovation then self-perpetually expand, with little or no added social utility, to levels of personal wealth that are both unconscionable and indefensible.[128] It is the systemic predisposition toward capital accumulation that inclines "entrepreneurs . . . to turn into rentiers,"[129] and that strips the currently prevailing version of financial capitalism of its economic rationalization.

Such wealth differentials are not just economically inefficient. They also seriously retard progress toward development goals in all countries, but especially in low- and middle-income states, where data collected by the UNDP show a "highly statistically significant negative correlation" between levels of economic inequality and levels of health, education, and life expectancy.[130] In its most extreme forms of capital concentration (which, as noted above, we are again approaching), the fallout for rich states also stretches far beyond the economy to jeopardize social and political order.

The wealthiest 1% fundamentally rely on the stoicism and stability of the 99%, argues economist Joseph Stiglitz—"the rich do not exist in a vacuum."[131] It is on the shoulders of the masses that the few stand. The assumption is that the majority will continue to believe in established social norms, to support the institutions of government, and to adhere to the rule of law. "It is amazing to me the degree of inequality that exists without people really getting upset," commented Warren Buffett on the fragility of such an assumption.[132] Indeed, evidence points to the fact that such forbearance is not unending. Where, relative to the rich, the wealth of the rest falters or falls, incomes stagnate, education and health services degrade, and standards of living decline, a society's givens are shaken by increasing civil conflict and criminality.[133] In other words, the stability of the social contract is threatened when people's commitment to community is replaced by the disposition to grab all you can.

Economists, as well as political and social scientists, will all point to the same basic response to this problem, namely, that some level of wealth redistribution must occur in order to promote both economic efficiency and social harmony. Transfers through a myriad of taxation and benefit schemes administered by public bodies is the most obvious way this can be achieved. And it is to that matter that the next chapter is dedicated in part. However, there is also a time-honored private means by which some redistribution occurs, namely, philanthropy.

Wealth and Giving

Philanthropy is now big business. So much so that the term "philanthrocapitalism" has been coined to try to capture the growing propensity for applying private sector corporate methods to achieving public interest and welfare goals.[134] The total value of global philanthropy is very difficult to estimate given its many and various forms (from numerous small, individual donations, to large grants from behemoth foundations) and the wide range of destinations and ends to which it is put. But it is certainly large. *Giving USA: The Annual Report on Philanthropy*, for example, estimates that in 2014 Americans donated a total of $358 billion[135]—which is both the largest sum (by far) of any country, and the largest per capita.[136] Most of that went to charitable causes inside the United States, including religious programs (easily the largest recipient

category), education, health and human services, and philanthropic foundations themselves.[137] Using separate and earlier data, it is estimated that approximately $39 billion of that total was spent on development projects overseas.[138]
This amount was higher than the total overseas development assistance from
the U.S. government (approximately $33 billion in 2014), and also constitutes
by far the largest contribution of international private philanthropy from any
country worldwide.[139] The Washington DC–based Hudson Institute's Center
for Global Prosperity estimates that around $60 billion in private donations
flows annually into developing countries—a figure that, in addition to the U.S.
contributions and those from other Western nations, also includes the still
small but growing totals for private giving in emerging economies.[140]

The Givers

Of course, not all of this private giving comes from the very wealthy, nor does
all of it go to the most needy, whether they live in the same country or overseas. In 2015 in the United States, for example, it was reported that the wealthy
were giving less and the middle class more. Analyzing data held by the United
States Internal Revenue Service on claims made for tax deductions for charitable donations, the *Chronicle of Philanthropy*, an independent news organization that charts giving in the United States, calculated that between 2006 and
2012 wealthy Americans (those earning $200,000 per annum or more) reduced
the share of income they gave to charity, while the share contributed by those
who earned $100,000 per annum or less rose by 4.5%. On average, American
households give about 3% of their disposable income to charity, a figure that *The
Chronicle* notes "has not budged significantly for decades."[141]

That said, in terms of raw dollars, some of the very rich appear to be the biggest donors, and some actually are. Wealth-X and Arton Capital—two research
and advisory services specializing in financial services for the very rich—have
estimated that the typical ultrahigh net worth (UHNW) philanthropist donates
approximately $28.7 million over the course of his or her lifetime.[142] Individuals
are classified UNHW if their investable assets exceed $30 million, in which cat-
egory the two consultancies' most recent annual "Philanthropy Reports" calculate there are some 200,000 such individuals worldwide.[143] On the face of it,
their donating capacity is vast. However, on closer examination, the figures are,
in relative terms, anything but impressive.

For a start, not all of these 200,000 UHNW individuals give back, even minimally. While Wealth-X estimates that some 65% of this cohort donates "at least
$1 million throughout their lifetimes," that still leaves more than one-third of the
world's richest who give nothing or only a tiny fraction of their wealth.[144] I was

unable to find any published data on what this translates into in terms of annual giving, and giving as a percentage of wealth, for this ungenerous cohort of some 35%. But if we assume that the "*less* than $1 million" is spread over twenty years, this equates—at its most generous—to an annual donation of $50,000 (that is, $1 million divided by 20). Taking the 2015 Philanthropy Report's estimate that the global average net worth of UHNW individuals is $141 million (and this figure remains fairly stable year on year), then their annual giving as a proportion of their wealth is less than one-tenth of 1%, at just 0.0354%. This percentage compares miserably with the charity of an average American household noted earlier, at 3% of disposable income.[145]

Of the 130,000 or so UHNW individuals who give more than $1 million in their lifetime—dubbed as "philanthropic" in the Report—the picture is a little clearer. As noted above, it is estimated that the average member of this group gives away $28.7 million of his or her fortune during their lifetime. It also appears that the individuals in this group are richer than UHNWs as a whole, with an average net worth of $236 million (as opposed to $141 million for the whole).[146] If, once again, we assume that the amount each of them gives away is spread over a twenty-year period (that is, at $1.18 million per annum), then annual giving as a proportion of wealth for the typical UHNW philanthropist is still less than 1%, at just 0.5%. So while, in raw dollar terms, UNHW philanthropists may be more than ten times more generous than average UHNW individuals, they are still a long way short of the average American.[147]

As one might expect, when you expand the calculus to cover the estimated levels of giving for the whole of the UHNW cohort as against their collective net worth, the results are even more alarming. Wealth-X and Arton Capital note that the while the 200,000 UHNW individuals constitute just 0.003% of the world's population, they command 13% of the world's total wealth—that is, approximately $27.7 trillion.[148] If we combine the annual levels of charity assumed above for the 65% of the world's UHNW philanthropists and the 35% marginally (or not at all) philanthropic UHNW individuals, the total is $156.9 billion per annum (that is, $1.18 million x 130,000 + $50,000 x 70,000). This is a substantial sum (and though calculated crudely, does not appear inconsistent with the figures of global giving discussed earlier in this section). As a proportion of the cumulative net worth of these individuals, however, it equates to a mere 0.5664%.[149]

Given the stark reality of what these figures represent, it is perhaps not surprising that the annual Philanthropy Reports do not spell them out. Indeed, there is a somewhat exculpatory note struck by the authors throughout the reports and elsewhere when they suggest that UHNW individuals in fact give back in all sorts of other ways, "such as impact investing, micro-financing, or simply job creation."[150] This is presented as going "beyond 'traditional' philanthropy,"[151] but is in truth not philanthropy at all. Profit-yielding "entrepreneurialism" that is also socially beneficial may well be a most desirable and laudable form of business, but it is business nonetheless. To seek to classify it as philanthropy, or even new philanthropy, is grasping at straws, or worse, calumny.[152]

The Receivers

As to the causes to which these charitable monies from all sources are put, it is not always easy to be certain how much reaches those most in need, let alone whether the donations serve human rights ends. It is perhaps easiest to calculate with respect to the global annual total of $60 billion (including $39 billion from the United States)[153] of private giving dedicated to overseas development projects, the central aims of which are to help the poor in poor countries by establishing better health care and education services, providing access to water or power, ensuring better sanitation or housing, or providing humanitarian or disaster relief.[154] The task, however, is more difficult with respect to charity spent at home.

For example, of the categories of recipient causes to which Giving USA's estimate of $358 billion in private donations in the United States were allocated in 2014,[155] only one—so-called human services—is unambiguously targeted at the poor, being wholly concerned with providing essential services to low-income families.[156] This amounted to 11% of the total. Other classifications, such as health and education (a combined total of 23% of the $358 billion)[157] are less obviously dedicated to alleviating poverty. For while building better hospitals, school rooms, and university libraries may indeed benefit the poor, the not so poor and indeed the wealthy may also gain from them.[158] Much the same can be said of the single biggest recipient category of all: religious organizations and projects, which garnered 32% ($117 billion) of all private giving in the United States in 2014.[159] Thus, while the considerable investments made by the Catholic Church—the largest religious organization in the United States—in health care services and education facilities clearly provide for the poor and disadvantaged, they serve richer and privileged individuals as well.[160] Whether the redistribution of wealth, let alone promotion of human rights goals, is effectively achieved through an institution whose finances are so opaque and thoroughly mismanaged and that continues to weather storms of protest over its handling of widespread sexual abuse of minors by its priests, is a moot point.[161]

There are, in fact, few large philanthropic enterprises that do not court some degree of controversy about the effectiveness, methods, or objectives of the projects they sponsor. The Gates Foundation, for instance, has been criticized for marginalizing concern for certain health issues by the simple fact of deciding to invest its very considerable resources into combatting one or other disease or medical problem. That is despite the fact that by so doing much has been achieved. Access to and the provision of vaccines and other treatments specifically for tuberculosis, measles, hepatitis B, rotavirus, and AIDS have been revolutionized through the investment of some $6 billion into such health-related projects by the Gates Foundation and others.[162]

Criticism has also been leveled at the current vogue of so-called venture philanthropy for behaving too much like venture capitalism, albeit at the same time bringing life-saving drugs to markets quicker than would otherwise be the case. The case of the Cystic Fibrosis Foundation's speculative investment in a small biotech start-up in 2000 that yielded enormous dividends when, fourteen years later, it sold the royalty rights to groundbreaking drugs developed by the firm for $3.3 billion is the exception that proves the rule. More often—given the nature of these speculative investments—such ventures yield little or no profit for the charity, or a complete or partial loss of its original investment. Even if impressive financial returns do eventuate, they are often perceived to be tainted, especially, for example, if they are a result of consumers paying high prices for the resultant product. [163]

Mixed Motivations

The complexities and problems of philanthropy as a means of effective redistribution of wealth and benefits, as well as the relative paucity of its contributions, are existential questions for philanthropic foundations. For instance, the world's three largest such entities—the Gates, Stichting INGKA, and Wellcome Foundations (in that order)—each variously talk of their goals being to combat poverty, understand inequities, create lasting and substantial beneficial change, and improve health and education levels. And with combined assets of nearly $90 billion and annual divestments of around $9 billion, they clearly have the financial capacity to pursue them.[164] But how effectively are these funds put to use? How do we measure that? And is it enough? Seeking ways to answer these questions was a key motivation behind the formation of the *Giving Pledge* in 2010.

The objectives of the *Giving Pledge* are somewhat similar to, if more open-ended than, those of the three funds mentioned above. Launched by Warren Buffett and Bill and Melinda Gates, the Pledge is presented as a vehicle by which to "address society's most pressing problems," and as a forum to "inspire conversations, discussions and action" about how much to give and for what purposes.[165] While the "what for?" question is, naturally, critical, as it is for all philanthropic enterprises, it is the "how much?" question that makes the *Giving*

Pledge so distinctive. Aimed exclusively at fellow billionaires and inspired by their own public commitments to give the vast majority of their fortunes away, the Pledge's single condition for others to join the founders is that they too commit to donating more than half of their wealth "to philanthropic causes or charitable organizations either during their lifetime or in their will."[166] Of the world's some 2,043 billionaires, 168 from twenty-one countries have now signed the Pledge. Their cumulative wealth is estimated to be more than $800 billion, so the potential is clearly enormous.[167]

Seeing that potential flowing through to practice is another matter. For while Warren Buffett and Bill and Melinda Gates may have already given away close to their 50% threshold (and made clear their intentions to give away much more),[168] other pledgers have not. The Giving Pledge is a moral obligation only and not legally enforceable, on top of which there are also significant questions about how wealth is calculated and therefore how much constitutes 50%.[169] But at least the intention has been publicly declared, which is more than can be said for the other 90% or so of the world's billionaires, including Donald Trump (dubbed, pre-presidency, as America's least charitable billionaire);[170] Liliane Bettencourt, who pointedly refused to join the Pledge; and China's cohort of some 600 billionaires (now, since 2016, ahead of the United States in number), only one of whom has made the pledge.[171]

Givers' motivations vary. If there is one abiding impulse behind the charity of all philanthropists, whatever their level of wealth or giving, it is that they want to do good. How precisely they express this desire in words and deeds, however, differs significantly across wealth categories. Thus, a survey of a number of studies and reports[172] that chart the motivations of donors makes clear that for those on relatively modest incomes (roughly $50,000 to $100,000 per annum), their primary concerns are to help meet the basic needs of those less fortunate and to help the poor help themselves. For the more wealthy (incomes of between $100,000 and $200,000 per annum) and/or with higher educational qualifications, the greatest concerns are to make their immediate communities and the world better places to live in.

There is some evidence from this latter group that the promotion of equity is another motivating factor. The very rich and the ultrarich (HNW and UHNW individuals, respectively) also express their altruistic desire to make the world better for all, but most commonly they declare themselves to feel a sense of obligation to share their wealth, and to "give back"; capitalism's noblesse oblige, as it were. One report suggests further that concern over community reaction to growing inequalities of wealth also plays some part in motivating the richest among us.[173] What is especially striking from reading the testimonies of the wealthiest— as found in the veritable treasure trove of personality traits and worldviews that is the collection of letters nearly all of the Giving Pledge billionaires have made public—[174]is that for them there is also a profound sense of personal fulfilment ("pleasure," "joy," and "satisfaction" are the words used most frequently) they experience when engaging in their philanthropic activities.

Human rights protections are seldom specified as motivating factors or even necessarily as goals for donors. It was clear to me from my interviews with senior policy directors in two large foundations—Atlantic Philanthropies and the Gates Foundation—[175] that the former's use of human rights as a framework for analyzing both the objectives and impacts of its projects was an exception to the norm. Typically, philanthropic organizations adopt the Gates Foundation's perspective, whereby outcomes are analyzed without express reference to human rights, even if human rights benefits are otherwise apparent. This accords with the results obtained by a joint study conducted by Bank of America, US Trust, and Indiana University's Lilly School of Philanthropy of issues driving charitable giving by the wealthy. Asked to nominate "the three issues that currently matter the most to you, whether you fund them or not," education, poverty, and health care were preferred by HNW donors far ahead of all others.[176] "Human rights" issues were identified as one of the top three by 13% of participants, behind disaster relief and the environment, but also behind arts and culture and the economy. That said, there were a number of categories surveyed by the study that were clearly rights-oriented, including women's rights, race relations, and LGBT rights (all lower down the list). Further, and consistent with the theme of this chapter, many of the issues, including the top three nominated, can and often do impact positively on human rights protections, no matter their specific labels.

A final point to make on the matter of the motivations behind giving is to look at the motivations behind *not* giving. If one accepts that a central objective and effect of philanthropy is to provide relief from poverty and disadvantage, then the implications of not giving when one has sufficient disposable wealth to satisfy one's own basic needs and comforts, might be considered very grave. Philosophers such as Peter Singer and Thomas Pogge have argued that in such circumstances there exists a moral and possibly even legal obligation to give and/ or to act. Singer holds that we have a personal moral obligation to give where we can,[177] and Pogge maintains that we have a duty to seek to change the global economic system, stemming from a human rights obligation not to perpetuate poverty by contributing to system that is inherently biased toward the interests of the wealthy and powerful.[178] In constructing his argument, Singer rebuts common objections to giving, such as "poverty cannot be solved" (poverty levels have already been substantially reduced); "poverty is a government's responsibility" (poor states' inability to fund welfare programs and rich states' shortfalls in aid provision are chronic problems); "I cannot afford it" (globally, we spend $59 billion on ice cream each year, nearly twice the estimated cost to provide basic sanitation and health care for all); and finally, "charity creates dependency" (not if you are starving or sick or unable to break the poverty cycle).[179]

How Much is Enough?

The question of how much is enough is both a moral and practical matter. Ruminating on the different levels of giving, Peter Singer wonders whether there is "a line of moral adequacy" that would assist us in answering the question. He concedes that the question is a difficult one to answer precisely and comprehensively, but that said, he argues that "it should be seen as a serious moral failure when those with ample income do not do their fair share toward relieving global poverty."[180] At a minimum, Singer believes that a fair share for most of us would be to commit 1% of our income to charity (which he has since promoted as an opportunity to pledge as much).[181]

The redistribution of private wealth by massively increased philanthropy may well be desirable, and certainly there are no shortages of calls for such, whether by philosophers, Oxfam or Irish rock stars.[182] But the harvesting of the financial wherewithal is only half of the story. The recipients of charity—big or small, local or global, newly created or longstanding—all face the same broad problems of capacity, efficiency, and efficacy. These are issues that must also concern us, at least as earnestly as how much, why, and where the money is coming from. Lawyer and philosopher Leif Wenar encapsulates this problem on the international plane in what he calls "the donor's question," namely, "how will each dollar I can give to aid [public or private] . . . affect the long-term well-being of people in other countries?" [183] The paths and processes by which each dollar must travel from your pocket to reach those in need are often uncertain and seldom direct, and when they do reach the recipient, it is difficult to gauge whether and how they help. The financing of development is dependent on the plumbing system of development, to borrow economist Jeffrey Sachs's terminology.[184] No matter how much money may be pumped into the system, it won't work well if it has too many twists and turns, blockages, and bottlenecks.

The Private/Public Connection

Who or what we should entrust with the task of managing and maintaining the system to ensure it does function effectively is a question that brings us to the junction between this chapter and the next. Should it be private actors and a market economy, or public agencies and by way of regulation? Or if, as seems unavoidable, it is to be a combination of the two, how is the balance of responsibilities between them to be determined? It is perhaps no surprise that wealthy philanthropists have remarkably little faith in the organs of government (or even, interestingly, in large corporations) to deliver in this respect, whereas they invest much greater confidence in individuals and nonprofit organizations "to solve domestic or global problems," including poverty. [185]

The accumulation and expenditure of financial assets can be for private or public purposes, and in both respects the outcomes can promote, as well as harm, human rights guarantees. Any single individual's standard of human rights enjoyment is typically dependent on a combination of their level of personal wealth acquired by personal means and their access to essential social commons financed by way of public funds. He or she looks to secure minimum levels of individual safety, security and liberty, education, shelter, and health care, as well as the freedom to express opinions, protect privacy, move and associate freely with others, be subject to a fair legal system, and practice one's religion. All of these desirable attributes require not only effective public institutional protection, but also minimum private individual facilities to be able to claim them, or otherwise benefit from them. All, to greater or lesser extents, require financial accommodation.

So, while this chapter has focused on the private means and methods of finance that aid human rights—by way of investment, access, transference, and charity—the next chapter concentrates on the how the public structures of finance advance or retard the goals of human rights.

|| 5 ||

Public Affairs

"The fancies and intricate contrivances of men, following contrary
and hidden interests put into words; for so truly are a great part of the
municipal laws of countries."
—John Locke, *Second Treatise on Civil Government* (1689)

Duty

Somewhat unusually for his profession, the American jurist Oliver Wendell
Holmes, Jr., fashioned an articulate argument for a much wider notion of justice
than that dispensed by the courts. He saw the need for "Big Government," and
the wide and deep laws that come with it, as essential to securing not only equality, but also freedom for the people of the United States and beyond. Holmes
was a forerunner in the art of extracurial pronouncements and public speaking
by judges, while in his judgments maintaining a strong line of judicial restraint
and deference to the elected arms of government.

As an old-style liberal, Holmes advocated passionately for respect for what
governments can achieve while being ever-vigilant of what they actually do. But
at its root, this balancing exercise is only possible if one concedes the salient
financial (and sociological) fact that that we, the people, have to pay for it. "Taxes
are what we pay for civilization," was how he neatly put it.[1] Holmes lived just
long enough to witness the first years of Franklin D. Roosevelt's New Deal. He
thus learned to appreciate the fundamental importance of the financial under-
writing of government programs to support and provide for those not otherwise
able to afford basic services. Access to minimal levels of education, health care,
social welfare, and housing are not only desirable, they are essential elements
of today's international human rights regimes (being expressly protected by the
ICESCR),and increasingly also featured in states' laws and constitutions. The
funding of these social expectations and rights standards is therefore a quintes-
sentially public affair. It is a relationship that must be played out in the open if its
integrity is to be respected and its outcomes are to be effective.

Important though it is, the link between finance in the public sphere and human rights is not all about taxation. This is partly due to the fact that in many developing countries formal taxation regimes are absent or wholly inadequate. It is also because there exists a range of other public financial streams that impact upon human rights standards, or that have the capacity to do so. In this chapter, therefore, in addition to taxation, I also consider the role played by international aid and development of the traditional kind (that is raised and expended by and through purely public authorities), as well as means of so-called alternative financing, which increasingly and significantly join private sector financial resources with public processes. As such, I examine the role of public institutions (using public funds) in co-opting private finance to achieve social ends, and thereby complement the discussion in the previous chapter of privately sourced funding that seeks social impacts independent of any public sector engagement.

Before moving on to discuss these issues, however, let us first consider what international human rights law has to say on the question of a state's financial resources. Unusually, this is a matter upon which it speaks directly.

The Voice of Human Rights

Article 2(1) of the UN's *International Covenant on Economic, Social and Cultural Rights* (ICESCR) states the following:

> Each State Party to the present Covenant undertakes to take steps, individually and through international assistance and co-operation, especially economic and technical, to the maximum of its available resources, with a view to achieving progressively the full realization of the rights recognized in the present Covenant by all appropriate means, including particularly the adoption of legislative measures.

In legal, political, and economic terms, this provides much to chew on, but for our present purposes I want to focus on two important elements. First, the instruction that states must employ "the maximum" of their "available resources" in their efforts to realize the rights to food, health, housing, education, and working conditions such as are protected by the Covenant. By "resources," it has been made clear that the intention is much broader than merely finance—though, in the context of this book, I shall be confining the discussion in this chapter largely to financial matters. Even then, which financial resources are "available," and what is their "maximum" use in pursuing human rights goals, are difficult to questions to answer—not least because who or what has the competence and authority to answer them, as well as how they do so, are matters of contention. The second element concerns the role of states in helping each other, as reflected in the direction to operate "through international assistance and cooperation." This, too, is a phrase open to a breadth of interpretation.

The UN Committee on Economic, Social and Cultural Rights (ESCR Committee), which oversees the Covenant, has offered some guidance, but no definitions, as to what these terms mean in practice.[2] "Available resources," it maintains, comprise both those existing within a state and those potentially available from international sources, and they also encompass private sector resources when directed toward rights protections. The Committee further notes that maximizing the use of resources is not predicated on the need for any particular sort of political economy, whether "socialist or capitalist system, or mixed, centrally planned, or *laissez-faire*."[3] As regards the exhortation that states must help each other, the Committee has matter-of-factly noted that the full realization of economic, social and cultural rights will remain "an unfulfilled aspiration" in many countries, in the absence of substantial international assistance and cooperation.[4]

The rules of the relationship are somewhat open-ended. What precisely is expected of governments as regards their funding of economic, social, and cultural rights (as well as civil and political rights) is not made clear. Nor can it ever be. In the manner of all important and complex international legal affairs, what is necessary or desirable in any one state, let alone in all, comes down to context and the specific circumstances prevailing at a given time. Over the years, the ESCR Committee has suggested how the determination and division of funding levels might be better managed by states to achieve better human rights outcomes.[5] Various other UN human rights bodies, including Special Rapporteurs on the issues of extreme poverty, debt forgiveness, and the rights to food, water, housing, and health, have also commented on the dimensions of states' financial commitments to rights protection.[6] We encounter specific examples of all of these throughout this chapter.

Public Funding of Human Rights

What is important for our purposes at present is to emphasize just how challenging it is to sustain, let alone increase, the levels and effectiveness of public funding for human rights. Principles are important, but sometimes they clash and often they must yield to practical demands. Pragmatism is a valuable and necessary strategy, and compromise is often helpful in moving toward goals rather than a sign of failure. The sheer size and intricacy of a state's financial relationship with the promotion and protection of human rights mean that the manner of their intersection is nothing less than a state of perpetual contestation. If there is one certainty in national politics it is that we will argue for what we think are good uses to which public funds are put and against those we believe are bad. Human rights concerns are part of that mix, yet while the commands of Article 2(1) of the ICESCR may be open-textured, they are not so rubbery as to be meaningless. Let me illustrate this point by reference first to the extent of a modern state's financial capacity to address human rights matters, and then with a discussion of two recent examples of how the relationship has been interpreted by two adjudicatory bodies whose purposes and expertise are very different.

The financial resources available to many states today are enormous, and their potential (will and competency permitting) to fund the many social services that promote human rights enjoyment is therefore substantial. The size of the modern state in purely monetary terms is impressive compared to one hundred years ago. One indication of how much larger monetary resources are today harks back to our discussion of philanthropists' largesse at the end of the last chapter. Consider, for example, the fact that Andrew Carnegie's endowment to establish his foundation (the Carnegie Corporation) in 1911 was equivalent to one-third of the entire budget of the U.S. federal government at that time. Generous and unprecedented though that figure then was (worth just over $3 billion in today's dollars), it is dwarfed by the Gates Foundation endowment, which today stands at more than $40 billion. Meanwhile, the U.S. federal budget has grown much faster, being now equivalent to nearly one hundred times the value of the Gates Foundation. In public budgetary terms alone, government today really is big. Furthermore, when one considers in addition the private sector financial resources that governments are able to employ or direct or guide in ways that can promote human rights protections (as was the subject of chapter 4), the pot grows even larger.

Whether or not financial capacity is directed toward human rights goals and, when it is, whether in sufficient (or "maximum") quantities, fairly, and effectively, are ultimately questions of judgment. That judgment, what is more, may differ according to the perspective of the multitude of actors interested in or affected by the process of financial allocation. One category of such actors whose very purpose is to adjudicate on these matters is that of dispute-settlement institutions and mechanisms—courts, committees, tribunals, and others. At the level of international adjudication, both the International Centre for the Settlement of Investment Disputes (ICSID) and the UN's ESCR Committee perform functions that require interpretation of competing legal claims as to the proper allocation of public finances and impacts on private interests, including the protection of both financial investments and human rights.

As noted in the previous chapter, international investment disputes are increasingly sites of human rights concerns, no matter that the legal texts involved (namely, commercial contracts between parties and relevant international investment treaties) seldom make any reference to human rights at all. A prolonged series of investments disputes involving Argentina offers a telling example of what French private international lawyer Horatia Muir-Watt calls this "human rights ordeal" now facing investment arbitration.[7] The cases were initiated by a coalition of water and sanitation corporations disputing the Argentinian government's decision in 2006 to foreclose on agreements it had made with the companies to supply water and sewerage treatment facilities to the city of Buenos Aires.[8] The relevant contracts were among a long list of commercial casualties (many of which are still before ICSID)[9] that followed Argentina's sovereign default in 2001 and ensuing economic crisis.[10] The necessity to cut public spending, the government argued, forced it to freeze the tariff levels at which the corporations were to be paid for the provision of their services. This, claimed the complainant corporations, contravened the government's contractual obligations and violated terms of the applicable bilateral investment treaties (BITs) guaranteeing fair and equitable treatment of investors and guarding against expropriation by the state.[11]

Among the arguments advanced by Argentina in defense of its actions was the specific claim that it had taken the measures "in order to safeguard the human right to water of the inhabitants of the country."[12] Argentina promoted this argument by way of the international legal principle of a "defense of necessity," rather than under the more specific obligations of the ICESCR to uphold people's right to an adequate standard of living, including access to water and sanitation.[13] While the relevant BITs referred to neither the necessity defense nor to international human rights obligations, the latter nonetheless could have been argued as comprising part of the former, in that it is a necessity for the state to ensure people's adequate access to water.[14] In any event, the complainant corporations were dismissive of any human rights–based arguments, going so far as to assert that human rights law is "irrelevant" to the determination of whether Argentina breached its legal commitments under the BITs.[15] The ICSID Tribunal did not agree on that point, but it did rule that "[u]nder the circumstances of this case, Argentina's human rights obligations and its investment treaty obligations are not inconsistent, contradictory, or mutually exclusive. Thus . . . Argentina could have respected both types of obligations."[16]

This conclusion is, in the end, a matter of judgment, and one that clearly differs from that held by the government of Argentina, and others.[17] What is "necessary" in order for a state to fulfill its human rights obligations, including how and on what it deploys its financial resources, *and* whether such actions are pursued alongside or instead of a state's other international obligations (including under investment treaties), cannot be determined in isolation. This is very significant for developing and middle-income countries, not only because nowadays the majority of investment disputes are brought against them,[18] but also because the dilemma for these nations of trying to attract foreign investment at the same time as preserving and hopefully promoting the human rights standards of their citizens, is especially acute.[19] When all of these questions are considered within the full context of their circumstances, it is clear how difficult they are to answer.[20]

The challenge is no less difficult when approached from the other side of the legal spectrum. Under the ICESCR, the obligations regarding rights to adequate water, food, health, housing, and education (among others) do not require the state to provide these goods and services to everyone—which would neither be realistically possible (in terms of finance or political philosophy), nor desirable. Rather, they require such direct provision by the state only at the most basic level, or to those otherwise unable to provide for themselves. Instead of acting as *the* direct provider, the expectation in international human rights law is that in the main, states facilitate, oversee, or regulate the effective fulfilment of these rights by nonstate actors—that is, by the private sector. The obligations on states are thus not any less onerous in financial or any other terms, it is just that they are differently focused. Once again, questions of perspective and competing interests similar to those facing the ICSID tribunal are at issue.

In 2014, a woman with the anonymized initials "IDG" became the very first individual to have a complaint determined under the Optional Protocol (the complaint procedure) to the ICESCR. The ESCR Committee that oversees the Covenant was asked to consider whether Spain had complied with its Covenant obligations regarding the right to adequate housing in the particular circumstances of Ms. IDG.[21] The case concerned the adequacy of legislation and the role of courts in the process by which a bank can, when a mortgagee is in default, repossess a property over which it holds a mortgage, evict the mortgagee, and sell the property. Ms. IDG had failed to make a number of mortgage payments, and the bank had initiated legal proceedings that eventually led to a court order authorizing the bank to take possession of the mortgaged property and evict the complainant. However, the court had failed, despite several attempts, to take all reasonable steps to notify the complainant of the proceedings and orders against her, with the result that she was unable adequately to construct her defense to the actions. The Committee thereby found that the state had failed in its obligation to take all appropriate measures (as per Article 2(1)) to protect the complainant's right to housing under Article 11 of the Covenant.[22]

The wider context in which this action was brought is important. At the time of its commencement (in May 2013) the Spanish economy was in dire straits, with an estimated 400,000 mortgage foreclosures occurring between 2008 and 2012, a national housing budget that had shrunk by nearly 50%, and the number of unemployed approaching 6 million (or 26% of the working population).[23] The issues raised by the case reflect well the complex nature of the juncture between public and private responsibilities for human rights protection referred to above. For while it is clear that under international law the right to housing does not prohibit eviction from one's home (even forced evictions are permissible under certain conditions),[24] nor does it require the state to provide substitute housing (unless one's circumstances are such that no alternative is available),[25] the state is obliged to ensure that the legal procedure by which eviction is effected meets certain standards of fairness and due process.

Here again, one might ask whether this is the best (or "maximum") use of the state's financial resources in protecting the right to housing. Or, are there other ends to which they might be put that are equally, or more, important than ensuring due process, such as investing more in public housing, for example, or in assisting the homeless?[26]

The point is that, as illustrated by both of these cases, questions about the allocation of a state's financial resources to achieving human rights goals— among many others—are not, nor ever will be, easy to answer. Yet, even before one reaches this stage, states must first have acquired the financial resources to allocate. It is to this prerequisite that we now turn.

Taxation, Representation, and Rights

Traditionally, tax gets a lot of bad press. This is not just because it is a state-sanctioned impost on the activities of private entities and persons—though that, for many people, is sufficient reason to resent and resist it. It is also because of the many and various ways in which the tax is imposed. As Charles Adams notes at the beginning of his splendid work on the subject, *For Good and Evil*, the analog of tax and robbery was as popular and pervasive in ancient times as it is today. The meaning of the word "taxation" itself—that is, "forced exaction"—hammers home the connection between tax collectors and robbers, if for no other reason than, as Adams points out, "a tax is owed because a government orders it to be paid. Nothing else is required."[27]

Certainly, those on the Right have always rebelled and railed against it. Isabel Paterson—who together with Ayn Rand is credited with establishing the philosophical foundations of modern American Libertarianism—considered "a tax-supported, compulsory educational system" to be no less than "the complete model of the totalitarian state."[28] Her modern-day political successors, Tea Party supporters across the United States, would agree. One prominent offshoot, the so-called Tea Party Express, includes "stop raising our taxes" and "reduce the size and intrusiveness of government" as two of the "six simple principles" in its mission statement.[29]

Just about any exercise of public power that raises revenue may be seen as a tax, no matter how agencies choose to label it (whether as fees, charges, duties, or even fines).[30] While the filling and replenishment of states' coffers may be the outcome, the purpose of the exercise may be for any number of other reasons. Tax is used to control or curb social behavior (tobacco and alcohol consumption); to license, permit, or pay for certain activities or services (registering births, deaths, marriages, and property sales); executing health care levies and social insurance charges; and licensing (casinos, clubs and taxi cabs), or to fund the provision or facilitation of basic public utilities (water, power, sanitation, communications, public transport, security, courts, and law and order).

The Consequences of Levying Tax—A Brief History

It is the perceived incursion on an individual's liberty to be as free as possible from interference by others, especially the state, that so disturbs many who oppose systems of taxation. Plainly, taxes can be used in ways that oppress, both in the manner and form in which they are levied, and in how the resultant revenue is spent. Taxes are raised to wage war (from Medieval Europe back to the Romans, that was their raison d'être); they can be used to persecute (Nazi Germany used the 1931 *Reich Flight Tax* to strip Jews emigrating prewar Germany of nearly all their wealth); to punish (in King Leopold II's Congo, the "with-holding tax" on local communities meeting rubber-collection quotas comprised the abduction of women and children, and the severing of hands was the result of failure to meet the quotas); to subjugate (British taxes on Indian salt production were so heavy during the nineteenth century that they enabled salt imported into India from Britain to be sold locally at a lower price than the cost of the Indian product); and to suppress freedoms (both Russia and China use tax laws to strangle civil society organizations' finances and quell dissent). They can also discriminate, whether by intent or not (regressive taxes are a classic example of disproportionately taking from the less well-off). With tax, as Adams reminds us, "we are dealing with fire, and without proper controls and care, we can easily burn down everything we have built."[31]

In fact, throughout history, tax injustices have fueled fires that have destroyed empires and launched revolutions. Of these injustices, perhaps the most keenly felt and the most inflammatory has been when taxes are levied without sufficient or any input from those who have to pay them. There is, then, a strong democratic rights dimension to the legitimization and efficacy of any tax regime. The slogan "no taxation without representation" was coined by Jonathan Mayhew, a firebrand Bostonian preacher instrumental in the fomenting of discontent that led to the American Revolution. However, the resentment reflected in Mayhew's words had burned just as fiercely in the breasts of many of those unilaterally compelled to pay taxes under Egyptian, Roman, and Aztec Empires, and was a contributory factor in each of these empires' respective downfalls.[32]

The forces that led to King John of England turning up for a meeting with some rebellious barons at Runnymede on June 15, 1215, included widespread (at least among the tax-paying nobility) antipathy to John's arbitrary and extortionate tax-raising. The *Magna Carta* that he duly consented to and sealed that day contained a prohibition against the imposition of taxes (or "scutage") "unless by common counsel," which though admittedly imprecise, nonetheless represented an important step toward accountable government based on rights and not just duties. The English *Bill of Rights* (1689) cemented and extended this limitation on royal power by specifying that only Parliament had the authority to levy taxes. The French and American revolutions underlined the necessity of popular (and, in America's case, local) consent in even more dramatic fashion. As discussed earlier in Chapter 2,[33] the perceived injustices of tax burdens—shouldered, in France, by the peasantry and bourgeois, to the benefit of the aristocracy and clergy; and in America, by local traders, to the benefit of their British colonial masters—precipitated revolution.[34]

The crude or unwarranted imposition of taxes continued to elicit mutinous responses wherever it was pursued, with the ensuing upheavals yielding some impressive human rights results. In Australia, for example, the "Eureka Stockade" in 1854 involved a rebellion by thousands of prospectors ("diggers") working in the gold fields of central Victoria against having to pay 30 shillings each month for a miner's license. It was a simple means by which the Victorian government taxed the miners; however, not only was it extortionate (average weekly wages at that time were around 10 shillings), it was also seen as inherently unfair as it had to be paid regardless of whether one found any gold or not. Less successful prospectors, therefore, found it especially hard, if not impossible, to pay the fee.

When, among other draconian actions, the government instituted twice-weekly license checks, the miners rebelled, publicly burning their licenses and erecting a stockade around the Eureka diggings. Their defiance and demands—that the licensing system be dispensed with and that miners (most of whom were foreign immigrants from Europe, North America, China, and the Pacific Islands) be given voting rights—were initially met with a swift and brutal response. The stockade was stormed by government troops and police, twenty-two diggers were killed, as well as five policemen, and most of the ringleaders were arrested. It was all over in twenty minutes. However in the aftermath, a Government Commission of Inquiry was appointed that eventually led to the diggers' demands being largely met. The license system was replaced by the combination of the requirement to possess a miner's right (one-off cost and much cheaper) and payment of tax on gold found, and the franchise was extended to all those who held a valid miner's rights. For many Australians, this iconic event and its consequences are considered to be the birth of democracy in the then-still-British colonies.[35]

The key demand today—as we see it has been throughout history—is that if you are compelled by a government to pay tax, then it has to be seen as fair. The best way that can be ensured is for you to have some say in who comprises the government. In short, the democratic, or representational, insistence that people have the authority to choose their leaders must lie behind any legitimate governmental authority to levy taxes. Still, even when such legitimacy is established and widely respected, a more serious problem lies in making sure that taxes levied are duly paid.

Of Ghosts and Icebergs—The Consequences of Lost Tax

The loss of tax revenue is a serious issue. Worldwide, the cost of tax evasion per year is estimated to be more than $3 trillion (or about 5.1% of global GDP).[36] The total stockpile (built up over decades) of wealth held offshore coming from developing and emerging economies alone is now estimated to be worth more than $12 trillion (out of the $24 trillion–$36 trillion approximate for all countries), and while there may be legitimate and legal reasons why the money may be parked there, it is believed that much of it comes from tax evasion and criminal activities.[37] Using World Bank data, the Tax Justice Network provides an insight into the sheer size and significance of private pilfering of public dues. Tax evasion in Europe accounts for half of the lost $3 trillion, with Asia, North America, and South America making up the bulk of the remaining half.[38] These raw dollar figures are certainly impressive, but it is when they are presented in terms relative both to annual GDP totals and annual health care budgets that one truly begins to understand their gravity. Thus, for example, while estimates of tax evasion losses in Africa and Oceania are small in dollar terms, they nonetheless represent 5.7% of Africa's yearly GDP and 97.7% of health spending, and for Oceania, 4.4% of GDP and 50.9% of health care expenditure. For Asia the losses equate to 3.4% of total GDP and 61.8% of total health care expenditure. The most shocking figures of all are those for South America, where tax evasion is equivalent to 10.3% of GDP and a monumental 138.5% of health care costs.[39]

Nor are the rich countries immune in these respects. Europe loses tax revenue equivalent to 7.9% of its total GDP, and 86.6% of its health care budgets, and North America the figures are 2.6% of GDP and 18.5% of health budgets. The regional disparities can be explained in part by the fact that, for example, the tax base in Europe is much higher than elsewhere (an average of 38.9%, as compared to South America's average of 28.2%, North America's average of 24.1%, and Asia's and Africa's averages of below 20%), which tends to increase the extent of losses by stretching the gap between how much is owed and how much is paid. The total spending on health care in North America (that is, especially the United States) is also much higher than elsewhere. When, in the case of the United States, this is combined with its relatively small average base tax rate, it results in comparatively less impressive tax loss percentages,[40] no matter that in terms of raw dollars, the losses from tax evasion in the United States are shocking—running at some $450 billion per annum, according to the Internal Revenue Service.[41]

The perpetrators of this vast larceny of the public purse have been dubbed by IMF economist Michael Keen "ghosts" and "icebergs." [42] The former are either unregistered for tax or are unknown to the authorities, while the latter are registered but do not pay what they should. Together, the impact of their illegal actions on the financial capacity of states to do their job, including the protection and promotion of human rights, is profound. "Simply put," declares the International Bar Association in a 2013 report on tax, poverty, and human rights, "tax abuses deprive governments of the resources required to provide the programs that give effect to economic, social and cultural rights, and to create and strengthen the institutions that uphold civil and political rights."[43] How and why this craven circumstance has come about are matters that I investigate at length in the next chapter. In this chapter we now turn our attention to another dimension of the problem of lost tax revenue that is at least as troubling as the out-and-out criminality of tax evasion, namely, the legalized facilitation of its avoidance.

The fair and full apportionment of tax liability was a key concern for Adam Smith. In *The Wealth of Nations*, Smith espouses four maxims on taxation, the first of which begins:

> The subjects of every state ought to contribute towards the support of government, as nearly as possible, in proportion to their respective abilities, that is, in proportion to the revenue which they respectively enjoy under the protection of the state.[44]

His concern was not just that the liability ought to be proportionate, but that it should result in sufficient financial support for the government to work effectively. Therefore, where tax systems are distorted in ways that greatly and disproportionately favor certain classes of taxpayers over others, not only are they unjust, they are also ineffective. When—as is so often the case—the favored are the richer and more powerful, the impact is exacerbated. For some economists, such systemic bias is essentially antidemocratic, amounting to "a form of civil disobedience."[45] For John Maynard Keynes it squanders what he considered to be one of the key utilities of direct taxation—that it can be used to combat the "arbitrary and inequitable distribution of wealth" that otherwise constitutes, in his view, one of the "outstanding faults of the economic society."[46]

No nation can easily afford the consequences of gross and systematic abuse of its tax base, but the poorer the state, the greater the cost. Such is the case with Guatemala. Though classified as a middle-income country, the country suffers from "astonishingly high rates of maternal death, child stunting . . . and primary school incompletion"[47] as compared to other middle-income economies worldwide, as well as to its neighboring Central American states, all of which have smaller economies.[48] Asking the question whether Guatemala was maximizing all its available resources in its efforts to protect fundamental economic and social rights, a European-based human rights organization in collaboration with a Central American–based fiscal studies institute mounted a two-year study of the state of the nation's tax system.

What they found was that the state budget was indeed relatively impoverished—dubbed a "bonsai state" by the researchers, because its budget equates to a mere 15% of GDP, as compared to the regional average of just under 27% of GDP. The stunted budget led directly to the state's meager spending on health, education, and welfare services.[49] The principal cause of the state's threadbare coffers, the study found, was a very low tax base (equivalent to 12%–13% of GDP, when the regional average is just over 28%), which had changed little since the country had emerged from a long and devastating civil war in 1996. Not only was the tax system riven with tax privileges for the country's most profitable business sectors, it was also highly regressive, based largely on indirect taxes on consumption, rather than direct taxes on income and capital. What is more, the report concluded, "[f]or decades, attempts at fiscal reform have been systematically thwarted by the politically powerful business sector," such as to cause former President Alvaro Colom to lament that his country had become a "fiscal paradise that benefits a select few."[50]

Entrenched elite capture of the organs or processes of government is not the only difficulty facing developing states trying to raise revenue through taxation. Data collected by economists Timothy Besley and Torsten Persson suggest that a combination of weak institutions of governance, lack of transparency (often accompanied by an enfeebled media), and the lack of a strong culture of norm compliance are among the chief reasons why developing countries tax so little compared to rich ones.[51] The fact that the state is thereby deprived of the financial capacity that might help mitigate some of these drawbacks makes clear how vicious this circle can be.

A further paradox that developing states often struggle with is their need to strike a balance between constructing a tax regime that will, on the one hand, encourage local investment and attract foreign investment, while, on the other, still raise sufficient tax revenue for the state to function effectively and efficiently—which includes upholding human rights standards. The OECD has calculated that certain tax incentives hamper economic efficiency and can reduce government revenues by 1%–2% of GDP.[52] Another difficulty developing states face is the establishment and subsequent maintenance of a regulatory system that is sophisticated and robust enough to reach all designated taxpayers, treat them equitably, and make sure that they pay what they owe. Given that even developed economies encounter significant problems in these respects, it is little wonder that developing states do too.

The array of preferences and privileges that are built into the tax regimes of Western states is a constant source of contestation and debate. While the resultant regulatory tinkering can reach almost farcical proportions (the U.S. federal tax code, for example, is nearly 4 million words long—double what it was in 2000)[53] there are certain staple concessions extended to the rich (in particular, the capital rich), corporations (especially multinationals able to exploit the extraordinary benefits of transfer pricing that can turn a company's tax department into a profit center),[54] and property holders. There also exist vast armies of accountants and tax lawyers (the "new masters of the universe," as accountancy scholar Prem Sikka puts it)[55] who are very willing and able to assist such privileged categories of taxpayers to take advantage of these legalized loopholes.

The impact of such tax edifices is not confined to Western economies, but is also felt in developing countries, especially by way of their embrace of multinational corporations in their economies. The UN Conference on Trade and Development (UNCTAD) estimates that while foreign corporations contribute annually some $730 billion in tax and royalties revenues to developing countries, at least a further $100 billion is forgone through corporate profit-shifting offshore.[56] Additionally, this lost tax revenue translates into an annual total "development finance loss" of $250–$300 billion when one factors in the added losses flowing from those profits not being reinvested for productive purposes in the host developing countries.[57]

There is no doubt that developing economies appreciate the importance of taxation as the "new frontier," not only in state building,[58] but also in providing the capacity to raise standards of human rights protection, even if, at the same time, they are acutely aware of the many difficulties surrounding the raising and spending of tax revenue. How developing countries manage the delicate balance between the possibilities and the problems of tax policy was a question Ahmed Shahid, a brilliant young economist from the Maldives, set out to answer when he embarked on a PhD with me in 2012. What he found after scouring states' reports to the UN Committee on Economic, Social and Cultural Rights for references to tax matters was widespread and increasing evidence of developing countries' awareness of the links between tax and their capacity to meet their international human rights obligations.[59] Some states have raised minimum income tax thresholds to increase the disposable income of the lower paid (and thereby reduce welfare costs), or they have provided tax breaks for business enterprises to encourage job creation and training, including greater participation of disabled people in the workforce. There was, however, less evidence of developing states actively tackling the endemic problems of compliance and enforcement that surround tax revenue collection. While Shahid noted that there was, at least, some sign of greater frankness about these problems,[60] it was evident that developing states still struggle, often desperately, to design tax regimes that are comprehensive, fair, and effective.

It is clear then, that adequate representation of the taxed in government and also their compliance in paying taxes in the first place are both important aspects of the relationship between tax and human rights. But they are not the whole story. For a no less significant consideration is the matter of the ends to which the tax receipts should be put. And if to human rights goals, which ones, with what effect, and to what extent?

Tax as a Force for Good

Taxation is the lifeblood of a state, and as such it is essential for all that a state can and should do for the benefit of its people, including the standards of human rights they enjoy. Despite all its undoubted wrongs, indiscretions, and facility for abuse, tax is nonetheless also a force for good. It is no accident that the states with the highest percentage of tax revenues are also freer, more democratic and governed more fairly, and have better human rights records. They also tend to be wealthier. Counting only taxes (and excluding "compulsory transfers such as fines, penalties, and most social security contributions") World Bank calculations show that the majority of Western economies command tax revenues equivalent to between 20% and 27% of GDP.[61] The main exceptions are Germany (11%), the United States and Japan (both around 10%—the same level as China), and, at the other extreme, Denmark (around 33%).[62] Most emerging economies command tax income between 10% and 20% of GDP, and the majority of poorer states beneath 10%, or do not possess sufficient data for the calculation to be made.

Better governance and a deeper public purse tend to correlate, and both together yield higher standards of human rights protections. In the end, the task of turning public funds into support for human rights depends on the choices made by governments. These do not reduce simply to choosing between weapons or welfare, though, certainly, such first-tier decisions are important.[63] But

just as important are the questions that follow. What is the balance of allocation between them (and all the other demands on public funds)? How and by
whom (or what) will the money be spent? And, what are the processes for holding them to account and for evaluating the expenditure? More profoundly, still,
these choices—regarding outcomes, as well as manner and form—will substantially legitimize the exercise of the power to tax. "It is through respecting, protecting and fulfilling civil, political, economic, social, cultural and environmental
rights that the state earns its legitimacy to tax," as *The Lima Declaration on Tax
Justice and Human Rights* (a 2015 civil society initiative) puts it.[64]

It is, therefore, by analyzing what governments actually do—that is, what
they fund—more than what they say they will do or how much they promise
to spend, that one begins to comprehend the true nature and extent of a state's
commitment to human rights.[65] In this, the situation of tax echoes that of finance
generally: the relationship with human rights outcomes is both unavoidable and
intimate. It also echoes the inherent complexity of really making the relationship
work. In many ways examining financial intent, while vital, is the easy part. The
allocation of funds to where they are most needed and where they will have the
greatest beneficial human rights impact, while remaining mindful of alternative
or competing interests and striving to make decisions as fairly and as openly as
possible, is more challenging. However we might wish it otherwise, the fulfillment of human rights is more an art than a science, driven by considerations of
fairness and equity no less than by economic concerns of efficiency.

There is no final solution to this monumental problem. It is, in fact, the very
stuff of politics and principle, as much as law and economics, so it is unsurprising
that even the most impressive and influential allocative theories tend to bend or
break in the inevitable mess of practice. This, of course, does not mean that they
are wrong or useless; merely that they are incomplete. John Rawls's first principle of social justice, for example, is implementable at the tier-one level of decision making. All basic freedoms ought to be distributed equally, as indeed is the
express proclamation of human rights law. Rawls's second principle, however,
adds important qualifications. It permits differential allocation of freedoms on
grounds that benefit the poorest and most marginalized.[66] And here, of course,
is the difficulty. How are the poorest and most marginalized to be defined and
identified? The continual parsing of apparently equally valid competing interests in circumstances that are seldom static is never easy and is, therefore, more
prone to pragmatism than principle in its execution.[67] This is the fate of affirm-
ative action.

Much the same fate befalls putting into practice the "minimum core obligations" of states that the UN Committee on Economic, Social and Cultural Rights
has sought to establish as a floor beneath which no state should sink. Thus, for
example, state parties are expected, at the very least, to ensure people's access

to adequate food and water, to primary health care, to basic housing, and to primary education.[68] Yet, in the very same document in which the committee makes this stipulation, it acknowledges the inevitable, if undesirable, reality that the economic and political circumstances of many states are such that this floor will be breached.

When this happens, the committee insists that offending states demonstrate that they have in fact made every effort to use all available resources, no matter how scarce, to fulfill their responsibilities.[69] Here again we see an international human rights body take the only viable road open to it when its noble aspirations are rudely interrupted by realpolitik.[70] In fact, the committee has demonstrated increasing levels of "principled pragmatism" in its communications with states' parties on their funding and implementation of social security measures. It now regularly engages with states on the directions and the details of their welfare policies in areas such as housing, health, education, and unemployment support.[71]

All states struggle with establishing, sustaining, and making effective their social welfare programs. World Bank data show that across all low- and middle-income economies, the average safety net transfers to the extreme poor amount to 30% of their consumption or income, while the average consumption or income of the same extreme poor in those states is approximately two-thirds (65.2%) of the (former) World Bank international poverty line of $1.25 per day.[72] Behind these averages there are some very significant differences between countries. "There is a negative relationship with the size of needs," noted the same World Bank study one year earlier,[73] with the bigger and better welfare schemes being found in the relatively richer states where poverty is shallow. It is, however, the poorest in the poorest states who need it most, and yet often it is those states that have the least success in providing welfare. Some states suffer from chronically low levels of spending on social security (Papua New Guinea commits only 0.01% of GDP to social safety net programs and Sudan only 0.08%),[74] while for others the problem is delivery.

The collection of data on the efficacy or impact of welfare programs is somewhat sketchy (as acknowledged in the cited World Bank report), so definitive conclusions are hard to obtain. But it is clear that even when comparing markedly different state approaches to the funding and delivery of welfare, the human rights implications of poverty alleviation are not always obvious or benign. As one World Bank economist has remarked, compared to India, welfare programs in China are much more effective in reaching their target communities (the Indian government's own Planning Commission admitted that less than 20% of its welfare subsidies reach the intended recipients),[75] but at the expense of individual privacy and democratic accountability. The difference, as he put it to me, is that in determining eligibility, Chinese authorities "will know the contents of your sock drawer."[76]

The continuous need to refine even relatively successful programs also poses practical problems. Consider, for example, the generally good-news story we encountered in Chapter 1 of Brazil's *Bolsa Família*—a scheme for direct cash payments to poor families. It works especially well in rural communities, where evidence shows it contributing directly to better nutrition, health, and education among recipients. But in urban communities the problems facing the poor are often different—more drugs, violence, family breakdowns, and child labor, on top of higher living expenses. In the *favelas* of Rio de Janeiro and São Paulo, for example, not only does this calamitous cocktail apparently dull the impact of the scheme, the percentage of families actually receiving *Bolsa Família* payments is substantially lower (less than 10%) than in rural areas (41%), despite the need being at least as great.[77] Once again, the fact of this entrenched problem is not necessarily a criticism of the scheme, or of the Brazilian government (though some consider it to be both); rather, it illustrates another level of complexity to the task of spending public funds effectively, efficiently, and fairly.

There is one public financing choice that is especially peculiar on account of its focus beyond, rather than within, a state's territorial boundaries. That is whether—and if so, where, on what basis, and how—to fund overseas aid, or "Official Development Assistance" (ODA).

Aid and Debt

We will not enjoy development without security, we will not enjoy security without development, and we will not enjoy either without respect for human rights.[78]

This was how Kofi Annan, the then United Nations Secretary-General, captured the essence of an important report he submitted to the UN General Assembly in March 2005. Entitled *In Larger Freedom: Towards Development, Security and Human Rights for All*, the report sought to recapture some of the aspirant aims of the UN Charter (in the Preamble of which the words "in larger freedom" appear), while reflecting upon more recent lessons of what happens when one or more of the three nominated ingredients is missing. The events of September 11, 2001, and the threat of global terrorism had cast a shadow over all manner of international relations; the HIV-AIDs epidemic still raged worldwide; the 1997 Asian financial crisis that had plunged millions into poverty remained fresh in the memory; and progress toward the *Millennium Development Goals* (MDGs), then one-third of the way through their tenure, was in many countries woefully inadequate.

In terms of the human rights responsibilities of the global community, the point Annan was making resonates with the chorus from both development and human rights communities that greater international assistance and cooperation between states is needed if development and human rights goals are to be advanced. The 2005 report amplified the point by noting:

> Even if he can vote to choose his rulers, a young man with AIDS who cannot read or write and lives on the brink of starvation is not truly free. Equally, even if she earns enough to live, a woman who lives in the shadow of daily violence and has no say in how her country is run is not truly free.[79]

But in fact, intent of Annan's words was broader than that. Namely, that international assistance by way of committing public funds to ODA is not to be seen merely as an act of altruism, or just an exercise in helping other countries realize their human rights obligations. Rather, in its potential to dilute the economic causes of alienation and revolt, it also contributes, in a very self-interested way for the donor state, to global security.[80]

Development and Human Rights: More Awkward than Intimate

Yet, despite this reasoning, there has long been tension, and sometimes conflict, between the development and human rights camps. This is especially apparent when looking at institutional competences and behavior. In characteristic fashion, Philip Alston, the UN Special Rapporteur on Extreme Poverty and Human Rights, pulls no punches when, referring to the World Bank, he declaims: "The existing approach taken by the Bank to human rights is incoherent, counterproductive and unsustainable. For most purposes, the World Bank is a human rights-free zone. In its operational policies, in particular, it treats human rights more like an infectious disease than universal values and obligations."[81] Though more colorful than most, this is merely the latest in a long line of criticisms of the ephemeral manner in which human rights are treated not only by the World Bank (especially pertinent as it is the standard setter in international development), but also by other multilateral and bilateral aid and development agencies.[82]

The problem is often one of political sensitivities (within the Bank, and throughout development circles generally, there are those who view human rights with suspicion as a Trojan Horse for Western interests), or legal demarcation (as is the case with the so-called political prohibition clause within the World Bank's Articles of Agreement, which instructs the Bank and its officials not to "interfere in the political affairs of any member" and that "only economic considerations shall be relevant to their decisions").[83] While these last-mentioned provisions have been long and roundly criticized as being anachronistic and unworkable, they nonetheless continue to hold sway inside the Bank, as the Alston report makes clear. A similar political prohibition has also been incorporated into the legal documents establishing the two new development institutions on the global scene—the New Development Bank (operated by the BRICS countries, based in Shanghai) and the Asian Infrastructure Investment Bank (with global membership—except, notably, the United States—based in Beijing).[84]

But the mutual dissatisfaction between the two specialisms also runs deeper, reflecting what are often fundamentally different approaches to the same problems. Both are broadly aligned in their concerns to address poverty and support the powerless, but they go about doing so by different means. Development specialists tend to be more interested in economic outcomes, are goal-oriented and pragmatic in their approach, and are much more amenable to molding programs to fit political circumstances and cultural sensitivities. Human rights activists, on the other hand, tend to be more legally minded, are process-oriented and principled in their approach, and are more inclined to insist that political particularities give way to the universal application of human rights.[85] Such variances in perspective and practice matter in terms of public finances because they establish the grounds upon which funding options are chosen and against which projects are monitored and evaluated.

Political scientist and development practitioner Peter Uvin explores these differences in his refreshingly frank and thoughtful book *Human Rights and Development*. He recounts a story of a phone call with a colleague who had recently returned from a mission to assess the rates of vaccinations and access to basic health care in Zairean refugee camps following the genocide in neighboring Rwanda in 1994. His colleague had proudly reported that the rates in the camps were in fact better than they had been before the refugees had fled their homes. Uvin continues:

> As I put the phone down, I realized that my colleague had just described the basic needs and even "human development" approach as implemented by the main development actors: great attention had been paid to healthcare, nutrition, vaccinations, and other so-called basic, human dimensions of development. If that is true then, according to the progressive vision of development then in vogue, people in these camps were 'more developed' than before. We intuitively feel that this is nonsense, of course. When people are deprived of their freedom, live in constant fear, cannot move or work as they wish, and are cut off from the communities and lands that they care about, development has emphatically *not* taken place."[86]

Echoing Amartya Sen, among others, Uvin concludes that the story shows how "there is no way to separate human rights and human economic and social improvement; the terms mean nothing without each other and can only become meaningful if they are redefined in an integrated manner."[87]

In fact, it is precisely this philosophy that lies behind many of the policies and practices advocated and pursued in the development field over the last twenty years or so, including the ill-conceived idea that the human rights family should include a "right to development." There exists, in fact, a UN *Declaration on the Right to Development* endorsed by the UN General Assembly in 1986, but it is so riven with textual incoherencies as to be unworkable.[88] Even the very idea of development as a human right is fundamentally problematic. It is, as human rights scholar Jack Donnelly argued at the time the Declaration was being negotiated, an unattainable myth, the propagation of which endangers human rights precisely because such an empty promise devalues their currency.[89] Alas, however, none of this has deterred ongoing attempts to flog this particular dead horse (including via a longstanding UN intergovernmental working group on the matter established in 1998), and the textual and political problems facing the idea remain as insurmountable today as they were thirty years ago.

Another policy movement that tries to bridge the gap between human rights and development has evolved out of so-called Human Rights–Based Approaches to Development (HRBAD). The essence of the idea behind these is to use human rights standards as the frame of reference in the design and implementation of development programs, and thereby to empower the individuals and communities targeted. The UN implemented a "Common Understanding" on such a human rights approach in 2003 that embraces all relevant UN agencies working in the fields of development,[90] and several bilateral aid agencies have also expressly adopted the approach.[91] The OECD and the World Bank have put their shoulders to the HRBAD wheel in a jointly authored report surveying the experiences of bilateral and multilateral agencies that try to integrate human rights into development programming, concluding that "all development actors should leverage their expertise and comparative advantage to better understand the synergies between human rights and development."[92]

While it remains the case that there are difficulties in translating human rights norms into concrete guidance for development policymaking,[93] this has not stopped the continued pressure for greater convergence. Following the long and sustained criticism of the absence of any explicit recognition of human rights standards in the UN's 2000 MDGs,[94] concerted pressure was exerted throughout the drafting process of their successor template—the 2015 Sustainable Development Goals (SDGs)—to adopt a more human rights perspective. Several of the SDGs' seventeen enumerated goals focus on human rights concerns, namely equality, labor rights, and, broadly, rule of law rights.[95] It remains to be seen, however, whether the "catch-all" format of the SDGs (its seventeen goals are amplified by 169 targets that cover just about every significant aspect of human endeavor) manages to excite anything more than peripheral interest in an HRBAD.[96] That does not look likely if one considers the way in which the SDGs approach the macroeconomic dimensions of development. SDG 17, which aims to foster strong global partnerships, for example, has nineteen associated targets that range across a broad spectrum of international cooperation matters, including tax reform, debt management and relief, innovative financing and public/private partnerships, and increases in aid, trade, and FDI for developing nations. Yet in none of these are human rights concerns raised or even alluded to.[97]

It comes as no surprise, therefore, that where public funding of international development impacts on human rights, it tends to be directed toward initiatives that play an auxiliary, or supporting, role in their protection. Perhaps the most obvious example of this has been expanding focus in development thinking on promoting good governance and law and justice reform programs, including, for instance, providing technical assistance and training for judges, police, Treasury officials, parliamentarians, accountants, tax officers, human rights commissioners, anticorruption administrators, and other government officers. The remits of these programs encompass such issues as the rights to fair trial, participation in government, and nondiscrimination, as well as social and economic rights to education, food, health, housing, and adequate labor conditions. The proportion of ODA directed toward these programs has risen correspondingly. Today, around 35% of all ODA from OECD countries is bracketed as "social and administrative infrastructure," by far the largest category (the next largest is "economic infrastructure" at 19%), comprising support for government and civil society, health, education, water supply, and sanitation services.[98] Indeed, the size of these two infrastructure categories reflects the fundamentally changing role of development finance in today's global economy. In its movement away from directly funding service provision by government agencies, and toward the funding of institutions, procedures, and processes by which governments are made more stable, effective, and accountable, development finance is looking toward a future in which developing states are better able to procure the services themselves.

This desired outcome is dependent on a symbiosis between good governance and good economic growth, as a historical comparison between the respective fortunes of neighbors Zimbabwe and Zambia graphically illustrates. In 1990 Zimbabwe's per capita GDP was $677, just above Zambia's, which stood at $642, though below that for the sub-Saharan region as a whole (at approximately $800).[99] Zimbabwe's worsening levels of respect for civil and political rights (its Freedom House classification moved from "partly free" to "not free" in 2001, where it has remained)[100] accompanied an economy that went in the opposite direction to its neighbors, plummeting to a per capita GDP of $326 in 2008, before rising to $455 in 2014. Meanwhile Zambia, accompanied by improving Freedom House ratings (moving from a low-end to a high-end "partly free" classification), has seen its economy thrive in comparison—sitting on a per capita GDP of $1,032 in 2014, and almost equal to that of the sub-Saharan region as a whole, at $1,045.[101]

Partnering with the Private Sector

The facilitative role now played by development agencies has necessarily involved the co-option of the private sector in the pursuit of development goals. I say "necessarily" because the size of private sector financing has grown exponentially in recent decades as compared to ODA. As recently as 1998, commentators were still talking of the "sheer size of aid compared to foreign investment," with ODA accounting for the bulk of international financial flows into developing countries.[102] Today, the annual totals of net ODA from OECD countries have climbed to around $140 billion.[103] They are dwarfed by total FDI inflows into developing economies, which at more than $700 billion per annum, are now on par with (or exceeding) FDI inflows into developed states.[104] The private sector today is actively courted by aid agencies, not just as an essential partner in promoting development goals, but as a substitute for publicly funded initiatives. The privatization of public services, for instance, reached near cult status among international financial institutions (led, in particular, by the IMF) in the late 1980s and 1990s.[105] A derivation of the privatisation campaign has been the growth in "public-private partnerships" (PPPs). These are designed to utilize public funds in ways that attract greater private sector investment, typically by promising generous, long-term returns (as in the Buenos Aires water contract discussed earlier in this chapter), or by issuing government-backed "vaccine bonds" on the capital markets, as does the aid organization Global Alliance for Vaccines and Immunization (GAVI).[106] PPPs aim to make business work for the poor by "unleashing entrepreneurship," as the UNDP optimistically puts it.[107]

Leveraging the relatively small public sector financial inputs (in the form of ODA) by drawing on the much larger private sector investment pool is obviously financially and developmentally attractive, and provides the main impetus behind the enthusiastic emergence in recent years of innovative financing for the development movement. The spectacular growth of the International Finance Corporation (IFC)—the so-called private sector arm of the World Bank Group—reflects the same trend. Empowered to provide investment and advice services so as to encourage private sector ventures and projects in developing countries, the IFC "work[s] with governments, corporations, foundations, and other multilateral organizations and development institutions to foster innovative partnerships that create prosperity and eradicate poverty."[108] From its relatively modest beginnings in 1956, with just twelve full-time staff, a capital base of $100 million, and authority only to provide loans and not make equity investments, the organization has expanded enormously. It now employs more than four thousand, has the power to invest as well as write loans, and commands total assets worth $87.5 billion. In the fiscal year 2016 alone, the IFC's long-term disbursements in developing countries of loans, equity investments, and guarantees spread across a wide range of sectors totaled $18.8 billion, of which nearly $8bn was provided (or "mobilized") by its private partner investors.[109]

The watershed Monterrey Consensus on Financing for Development in 2002 set out a broad aspirational agenda to eradicate poverty and promote economic growth and development by mobilizing the effective use of financial resources.[110] Removing any doubt as to the democratic and, above all, free market foundations of the enterprise, the heads of state, finance ministers, and representatives from all major economic and financial institutions who signed the consensus underscored the importance of good governance to their enterprise by stipulating that it necessitated respect for human rights and the rule of law as well as the promotion of democratic institutions and "market-oriented policies."[111]

Two subsequent meetings of relevant state and nonstate parties—one in Doha in 2008 and the other in Addis Ababa in 2015—have sought to advance the initiative by focusing on specific macro- and microeconomic goals. Notably, these include international cooperation in tax matters and combating both corruption and illicit financial flows. But they also comprise increasing public and private investment in the keys areas of agriculture, infrastructure, job creation (especially for women), and access to basic financial services, as well as boosting the capacity of developing states to establish and maintain adequate social protection programs.[112]

The 2015 Addis Ababa Action Agenda in particular stresses the importance of states taking primary responsibility for the mobilization and effective use of their own domestic resources, as generated by economic growth and private sector investment. First and foremost, the agenda notes, these resources are generated by economic growth, as supported by private sector investment, both local and overseas. But it also underlines the importance of "an enabling *international* economic environment," that is, one that includes coherent and mutually supporting global trade, aid, and financial systems.[113] The WTO-led "aid for trade" initiative exemplifies this approach. "Aid 4 Trade" (as aficionados are wont to label it) aims at redressing the trade-related constraints suffered by many poor countries, such as poor infrastructure and weak or inappropriate government support. Thereby, the argument goes, these countries will be better able to enjoy the fruits of increased international trade.[114]

Getting the Mix Right

It is clear that the game plan here is oriented toward the long-term. Public finances play a critical facilitating role in all this, and for developing states, their own public finances are importantly supplemented by ODA from wealthier states. An abiding theme throughout the UN's financing for development agenda has been the exhortation of rich states to increase their levels of ODA, at least to meet the long-established target contribution of 0.7% of gross national income (GNI)—currently achieved by only seven states (Denmark, Luxembourg, Netherlands, Norway, Sweden, the UK, and the United Arab Emirates).[115] Certainly, there remains skepticism surrounding the motives behind developed countries' aid-giving. Critics allege that too much "boomerang aid" is doled out to home-state consultants and businesses, and that donors are more concerned with securing self-interested geopolitical security and stability than with addressing the fundamentals of poverty.[116] The manner and efficacy of the delivery of aid are also much maligned, with too much aid being lost through "leaky bucket" intermediation, and accusations of "phantom aid," when donor-states inflate their aid budgets by including their costs of hosting refugees, their relief or forgiveness of previous debts, and their own aid administration costs.[117]

Even accepting these manifest problems, the need for aid is indisputable, both for purposes of immediate humanitarian and disaster relief, and also for longer-term structural and institutional strengthening in developing countries. Arguments like those of former World Bank consultant and former Goldman Sachs employee Dambisa Moyo to do away with aid altogether are more melodramatic than prescient.[118] Moyo's proposed cure for what she sees as the destructive dependency of much of Africa (her home continent) on aid is that by turning off the aid tap, corrupt and inept African leaders would be forced to raise the funds they need on the international capital markets. This, Moyo argues, would allow market forces to punish or reward states accordingly. The fact that she delivered this broadside in early 2009, when the international financial markets had just demonstrated so graphically their incompetence at assessing and controlling risk and were, in any case, at that time squeezing, not expanding, credit, was a sensational misjudgment. Moreover, Moyo ignores the inconvenient truth that under such a scheme the heaviest burdens will inevitably be shouldered by the poorest and the most powerless—especially in the most dysfunctional states—as the coffers of market-punished states are emptied and the poorest are left with no backup, however compromised, from international aid.[119] In any case, aid's increasing push, then and now, into partnering with or promoting private sector investment renders such a critique of aid (or "caricature," as the *Economist*, of all reviewers, caustically put it)[120] somewhat otiose.

Does "New" Aid Work?

The important question is whether or not new aid's combination of using public monies to court the private sector while at the same time addressing systemic problems of governance and economic management, works. Does it, or will it, strengthen both the capacity and willingness of states to achieve development goals and improve human rights outcomes? Answering such questions has been a perennial problem for the monitoring and evaluation of aid programs, spawning what has become a growing industry of measuring aid effectiveness.

Articulating clear lines of cause and effect in aid and development has never been easy, so answering these questions is bound to be partial at best. There are, however, certain features of the new aid landscape that provide some indication of whether progress is being made or not.

Poorly

Some indicators show poor or even retrograde results. The perception that incorporating private sector investment and enterprise into development programs by way of the privatization of public utilities, for example, has had an especially checkered history. "Does privatization make the world a better place or not?" was a question that the World Bank posed itself in a study it undertook some thirty years ago. In the report that followed, published in 1992, the bank declared: "[O]ur case studies answer this question with a resounding 'Yes.'"[121] But that was in 1992. Evidence to the contrary has since not been hard to find.

The extensive pursuit of multilateral and bilateral aid–supported water and sanitation privatization programs has been notably problematic, not least because of the fundamental importance of water as a resource and its adequate access as a human right.[122] The ongoing impasse over the nature and extent of the proposed privatization of water supply to the 21 million inhabitants of Lagos in Nigeria, for example, is just the latest in a long list of controversial mega water privatization projects.[123] There can be no doubt that the state of water supply to the metropolis is unsustainable. Up to 80% of Lagos's water supply is wasted or stolen; only a tiny fraction of it is piped into people's houses; and its sanitation is seriously defective or nonexistent. The ineffable difficulty in Lagos, as with all major plans to privatize water supply in poor countries across the globe over the past thirty years, lies in striking a balance that will, as John Vidal puts it, "satisfy corporate demands, raise the billions of pounds inevitably needed, and convince the . . . public that international companies would fulfill their contracts and not make unreasonable profits from the sale of what was widely seen as a public resource."[124]

Concocting a recipe for fair, safe, affordable, and economically viable systems of water management has proven to be a major challenge for the World
Bank, and especially the IFC, which has been at the forefront of the privatization
push. They have long been aware of the associated human rights problems.[125]
According to the Bank's own data, the economic performance of water privatization projects in particular has been very disappointing, with 26% of the Bank's
total investment in water and sewerage privatization projects between 1990 and
2014 being distressed or cancelled.[126] Privatization remains in the economic
toolbox of the Bank, but its use is now very much on the wane. What is more,
there is compelling evidence of widespread deprivatization (or "remunicipalization") of water supplies in many conurbations all over the world.[127] Neither the
World Bank nor the IMF laud the virtues of privatization in anything like the
assured terms they did fifteen years ago,[128] and, in the case of the Bank's IFC,
new performance standards require it to pay more heed to the environmental
and social implications of its operations.[129] Indeed, while the IFC is still at the
forefront of the negotiating process over how to engage the private sector in fixing Lagos's water supply problems, the fact that it has repeatedly redrafted the
proposal is itself a reflection of sensibilities that were thoroughly absent in the
earlier, more fevered days of privatization propaganda.

Promising

Other funding features of new aid have been more positive. While there is still
a long way to go before the unconscionable burdens of sovereign debt and their
legacies are removed from least developed states, there is cause for some optimism over what has been achieved thus far. That progress has been made is
due to some significant degree to the depths we have come from. It is truly a
matter of financial disgrace and moral failure that in the 1970s through to the
early 1990s, the levels of sovereign debt borne by some of the world's poorest
and most dysfunctional states were allowed to become so onerous that these
countries were spending far more on servicing the loans from rich states and
their banks than they were on health, education, and social welfare. Zambia, for
example, spent nearly 20% of its GDP servicing external debt between 1990 and
2000, while allocating only 2% for health and 3% for education during the same
period.[130] In 2006 the Philippines government spent 1.3% of its annual budget
on health services and 14% on education, while in the same year spending 32%
just on servicing interest payments; and when repayments on the principal debts
themselves are added in, the total for debt repayments amounted to a staggering 68.5%.[131] Overall, the total annual debt repayments made today by low- and
middle-income countries to creditors in rich states are still equivalent to nearly
six times what they receive annually in ODA from those same states.[132] For many

indebted states it is added salt to the wound that the debt they are paying off was illegimately incurred by a previous crooked or "odious" regime (hence the term "odious debt").[133]

However, by the early 1990s moral outrage finally began to challenge the enforcement of contractual obligations as the primary motivator behind the international community's approach to the poorest states' external debt, and a series of debt relief and cancellation schemes were put into motion.[134] Foremost among these was the IMF- and World Bank–backed Highly Indebted Poor Countries (HIPC) initiative established in 1996, subsequently supplemented by the Multilateral Debt Relief Initiative (MDRI) in 2005. Together, these programs first identify countries whose external debt obligations are unsustainable under their present terms, and then restructure those terms, including cancelling some or all of the debt. Certain standards of proven and planned good economic governance are also required of eligible states, including "develop[ment] of a 'Poverty Reduction Strategy Program' through a broad-based participatory process in the country," for the debt relief to be fully implemented.[135] As of September 2015, the IMF reported that thirty-six countries (including Zambia, but not the Philippines) have been approved for HIPC debt relief amounting to $75 billion in total, which has resulted in a decline of about 1.8% of debt service paid by those countries between 2001 and 2014.[136]

There is no doubt that relief for these states has helped their balance sheets, increased their governments' autonomy and financial competence, and provided the policy space and funds for improved social conditions of their peoples. The IMF, for instance, estimates that on average, expenditure on health, education, and social services in HIPC-initiative states has increased to "about five times the amount of debt-service payments."[137] But in the eyes of many experts it is too little too late and still leaves many low- and middle-income states that are seriously debt distressed outside the initiative and exposed to the financial incompetence or corruption of their governments, as well as the venality of some creditors who are less forgiving. UNCTAD has highlighted these problems, stressing, in particular, the destructive consequences of the lack of international coordination between major sovereign creditors.[138] For while the IMF, the World Bank and regional development banks, and the twenty largest bilateral lenders (under the so-called Paris Club)[139] have been prepared to cancel or significantly restructure debts (for those states deemed eligible), this is not the case with other bilateral lenders and many private sector creditors,[140] which together account for around one quarter of poor countries' sovereign debt holdings.

A further complicating factor is that some of these creditors have sold their debts, at discount prices, to so-called vulture funds, whose explicit mandate is to recover from the debtor state as much of the outstanding debt as they possibly can, often by way of relentless litigation, and regardless of any human rights consequences for the citizens of the indebted state.[141] Recognizing the dislocating impact such mala fides can have on the whole process of international debt management, the UN General Assembly has formulated a set of *Basic Principles on Sovereign Debt Restructuring Processes* that underline "the obligation of sovereign debtors and their creditors to act in good faith and with a cooperative spirit to reach a consensual rearrangement of the debt of sovereign States."[142] Some states, such as Belgium and the UK, now have legislation that effectively prohibits vulture funds from litigating within their respective jurisdictions,[143] though the practice is still alive and well in U.S. courts.[144]

Whatever progress has been made in addressing some of the worst cases of unconscionable or odious debt, the need to insist on good faith dealing, alongside the legal obligations under the ICESCR that debtor and possibly also creditor states bear, remains pressing.[145] The combined debt burdens of all 134 low- and middle-income countries have been rising, seemingly inexorably, both before and after the onset of international debt relief arrangements—from $500 billion in 1980, to $1 trillion in 1985, to more than $2 trillion in 2003.[146] The latest available World Bank data show that the total rose to $6.7 trillion in 2015.[147] It is the principal reason why human rights bodies, including the UN, continue to be so concerned with how the sovereign debt of developing countries is handled. For, as international lawyer and financial specialist Danny Bradlow points out, despite the various sovereign debt-restructuring initiatives now in existence, none of them "provide detailed guidance to the parties on how they should deal with the social and political impacts in negotiating and agreeing on a sustainable SODR [sovereign debt restructure]."[148]

It is also the reason why the UN Independent Expert on the Effects of Foreign Debt and Human Rights, Juan Pablo Bohoslavsky, has opted for a more legalistic tack. He has argued for the reconciliation of a state's sovereign debt obligations with its human rights obligations through the foundational international law principle of *pacta sunt servanda* (literally, "agreements must be kept").[149] Debt and human rights obligations are, on their face, equally imposing on states. However, there are crucial differences. A state's debt will, typically, be established by way of a contract between the state and the creditor, whether a private bank or another state. Human rights obligations under international law, on the other hand, are established through international agreements entered into directly with other states, and indirectly with the state's own people. Though debt obligations are normally binding, they are not absolute, he argues. They can, and must, be subject to limitations where such grave concerns as the state's capacity to protect basic human rights would otherwise be seriously threatened. This situation may be exceptional, but it is nonetheless important and necessary. Sovereign debt obligations under the notion of *pacta sunt servanda* are "thus limited by the sovereignty of human rights," Bohoslavsky concludes.[150]

Possibly

New aid's potential to stimulate development by combating corruption and enhancing taxation regimes is presently more latent that imminent. As we shall see in the next chapter, what international efforts have achieved thus far is to identify the size and complexity of the problems, rather than to make any significant headway in addressing them.

Another new aid phenomenon that holds great promise and that possesses the distinct advantage of already having the money in hand, is the activities of Sovereign Wealth Funds (SWFs). SWFs are state-owned financial entities that are usually established using fiscal or balance-of-payments surpluses, or the proceeds of sales of public utilities or resources.[151] Though, strictly speaking, state pension funds, foreign currency reserves, and other state-controlled assets are not included in the definition of SWFs, the same principles of ethical investment as discussed in this section also apply to them. In any event, these funds are big and getting bigger. There are currently six SWFs with assets in excess of $500 billion—two located in China, and one each in Kuwait, Saudi Arabia, UAE, and the largest (at $873 billion in 2015) in Norway. Two national pension funds—one in the United States and the other in Japan—are even larger, at $2.79 trillion and $1.15 trillion, respectively.[152] The top fourteen pension and sovereign wealth funds alone have assets of more $10 trillion,[153] and SWFs as a whole have grown rapidly, nearly doubling in size in the five years between 2009 and 2014.[154]

On the face of it SWFs function in ways that are indistinguishable from any other large global investor, investing "in real and financial assets or in alternative investments such as private equity or hedge funds."[155] They are, however, as law scholar Larry Catá Backer puts it, "projections of public economic power in private form."[156] From a human rights and development point of view, it is their institutional status that is significant. As emanations of the state, SWFs are subject to the obligations borne by states under international human rights law, no matter the largely private sector forums in which they operate.[157]

Each fund has its own mandate and operating principles, though generally it can be said that all are concerned to provide financial resources for the national benefit by appropriate investments and sustainable growth. The Santiago Principles for SWFs provide some measure of common (though voluntary) standards that relate, almost entirely, to matters of management practice and financial probity.[158] That is, their governance structures are established by law, operate transparently and independently, manage risk and measure performance in appropriate ways, and are audited according to internationally accepted standards. The Santiago Principles do refer to ethics but only regarding professional and accounting standards. The extent to which SWFs are committed to broader standards of ethical investment in terms of international development goals or the protection and promotion of human rights is a matter determined by the mandates of each fund.

In this respect, according to Edwin Truman, an economist and leading commentator on SWFs, "only a few . . . (30 percent overall) make a public statement adhering to guidelines for corporate social responsibility."[159] By far the most prominent and active (if still imperfect)[160] of these is the largest, Norway's Government Pension Fund Global (GPFG).[161] The fund has an Ethics Council that oversees the implementation of a set of guidelines regarding the GPFG's investments. Specifically, the guidelines exclude investment in companies engaged in the production or sale of weapons or tobacco, as well as those whose operations cause severe environmental damage, are involved in gross corruption, or participate in humanitarian abuses during times of conflict. They also preclude investing in any company that "contributes to or is responsible for . . . serious or systematic human rights violations, such as murder, torture, deprivation of liberty, forced labour and the worst forms of child labour."[162] The GPFG publishes a list of excluded companies, which presently includes Wal-mart (for human rights abuses), and Barrick Gold, Daewoo, Freeport-McMoRan, and Rio Tinto (all for severe environmental damage).[163] As the fund holds about 1% of all company stocks worldwide, these prescriptions have the capacity not only to affect companies directly, but also more broadly, to benchmark what can be done by SWFs to promote both good corporate governance *and* environmental and human rights goals, where the political will exists.

In terms of the promotion of economic development and the protection of human rights in developing countries,[164] the role of SWFs can be significant, no matter the ever-present dilemma of choosing between saving for future generations and helping the present one.[165] For the time being, however, that role remains largely potential than evidential.[166] The twin facts, as mentioned earlier, that (1) SWFs are state entities (which status carries obligations under international human rights law) and (2) that they are investing public money (which provides the basis for arguing that they are under a fiduciary duty to act in the best interests of the public, including realizing human rights goals),[167] underlines that their rights-respecting role is not simply desirable, but also necessary.

Scourges

The human rights impacts of public funds substantially depend on both the quantity of the funds raised and the uses to which they are put, whether at home or overseas. As this chapter has made clear, the key to states' raising and spending public monies lies very much in how well they are able to leverage and regulate the private sector. The link, therefore, between the focus of this chapter on public finance and the one preceding it on private finance, is now clearer. We move on in the following chapter to consider the enormity of the obstacles that exist for public and private actors alike in their efforts to exploit finance for better human rights results, obstacles borne of the scourges of cheating and dishonesty.

‖ 6 ‖

Cheating

"The greater the wealth, the thicker will be the dirt."
—J. K. Galbraith, *The Affluent Society* (1958)

"The truth is ugly."
—Friedrich Nietzsche, *The Will to Power* (1901)

Consequences

Their faces are gaunt and drawn, their bodies hollowed out. They clutch sad little bundles of all they possess, or, in one case, the body of a child draped across their shoulders. Their eyes are fixed on the ships ahead as they stagger along the quay toward them. They have not eaten for days, and the only creature seemingly half-well-fed is the dog that crouches behind them, watching and waiting for his next meal to fall.

This is how Dublin's Famine Memorial emerges out of the Liffey mist, after you realize that the oddly elongated figures on the path ahead are not merely other folk out for an evening stroll by the river. Ireland had known many famines before it, but the "Great Famine" of 1845–49 was especially devastating. The population was decimated. Of the 8.17 million inhabitants counted in the 1841 census, starvation and disease claimed more than 1 million lives, and at least another million emigrated during the famine years.[1] By 1851 the population had dropped to 6.55 million (growth trends before the famine indicated that the population would otherwise have reached just over 9 million by this time), and continuing hunger and abject poverty stripped another 4.5 million emigrants from the island over the subsequent seventy years.[2] Even today, the combined total population of Northern Ireland (UK) and Southern Ireland (Éire) is still only 6.3 million.[3]

The relationship between finance and the appalling human rights violations these levels of loss of life and livelihood represent lies embedded in the politics and policies of United Kingdom governments at that time. As an integral part of the Kingdom, Ireland was subject to the Corn Laws,[4] which, by imposing high tariffs on imported cereals (mainly wheat), propped up the high prices charged by grain growers in Britain and Ireland. In Ireland this policy mostly benefited absentee (both British and Irish) landlords, while at the same time putting the cost of these alternative staple commodities beyond the reach of the Irish peasantry. The attractive prices had also pushed more and more land into the production of cereal crops for export, leaving subsistence farmers to rely on one crop—potatoes—as their principal food source. The potato provided the best yield for the small plots typically farmed by the poor in Ireland at the time, but equally it exposed them to dire consequences if crops failed, as they did successively from blight during the famine's five years.

While the state's willingness to pursue protectionist policies that favored landholders may have been a significant factor in the creation of the calamity, it was the state's reluctance to interfere in the market to protect the starving that perpetuated the famine even after its scale had become apparent.[5] For the most reprehensible aspect of this dreadful episode was the fact that in the years immediately before and after the onset of the famine, Ireland continued to export huge quantities of wheat to mainland Britain (enough, by one estimation, to feed 2 million people annually).[6] Throughout the famine years, Ireland was also exporting substantial quantities of other foodstuffs, including livestock, meat, poultry and dairy products, vegetables, seafood, beer and spirits, as well as barley, oats, and even potatoes, all raised or cultivated on Irish soil or in Irish waters. Exports of some products even increased during the period—notably, oats, butter, eggs, bacon, and ham—and in many cases food was shipped out under military guard, especially in the west of Ireland where the famine hit hardest.[7] Why was this happening? For the simple reason that there were markets for these goods on the mainland that commanded returns far greater than the Irish could afford. The catastrophe, therefore, was not technically a "famine" at all, as there was no lack of food. It was starvation. What was lacking were, first, the financial means of the poor to purchase the food and, second, the will of the government to step in to provide either the means or the food.[8]

The terrible consequences of such indifference and incompetence represented a gross deception by the state of a section of its population. To cheat, as it were, some of its people out of the right to guardianship that they were entitled to expect, precisely at the time when they most needed it, was a dereliction of duty that the UK government itself acknowledged some 150 years later.[9] An oft-repeated observation of the economist and philosopher Amartya Sen is that no democracy has ever presided over a famine,[10] yet here was the world's wealthiest nation and burgeoning democracy, permitting, through its institutions of government, one of the worst famines in European history to unfold within its borders. If nothing else it taught us, in the words of historian Christine Kinealy, "that money alone cannot solve the problems of starvation and financial inequality . . . famine is a political rather than [only] an economic problem which needs to be addressed within the context of social justice and human rights."[11]

This shameful saga represents a monumental failure of governance: people denied their most basic rights by the lure of lucre. It illustrates the vital importance of the relationship between political authority and economic or financial power, whereby the former is always susceptible to being hijacked by the latter, no matter how dire the consequences. To be sure, governments are and ought to be open to the demands of finance, but such concerns must always be weighed against governments' primary responsibility of protecting the welfare of its citizens. How well governments undertake this balancing task—specifically, the extent to which they permit or encourage financial behavior that compromises human rights standards—is one concern of this chapter. The other concern is with the rights-jeopardizing actions of the financiers and financial institutions themselves.

As this book's journey thus far has shown us, fair, effective, and responsible government is vital if finance is to operate in ways that benefit society as a whole. In the book's final chapter I will suggest how best we might leverage finance in ways to help achieve those ends, now and in the future. In this chapter, however, I examine what happens when these governance features are absent, ineffective, or flouted in ways that negatively impact human rights standards. I do so in two stages. In the first, I look at the *subversion of governance*—that is, how finance subverts governance by flouting, ignoring, or evading regulation. In the second, I look at the *appropriation of governance*—that is, how finance has hijacked the powers of governance and regulation, skewing them in ways that benefit certain private interests at the expense of broader public needs. In the chapter's final section I consider the related and endemic problem of denial and delusion within and between finance and human rights, where hubris in both camps makes dealing with the consequences of cheating all the more difficult.

Deceit and Subversion

All human relationships harbor elements of deceit, both of oneself as well as of others. Indeed, to some degree they sustain relationships, as we may suspend beliefs or supress emotions for the greater good of the union. But there are also forms of cheating that are intolerably destructive, and all the more so when the relationship is interdependent and the consequences profound, as between the human actors that constitute the worlds of finance and human rights. When, in addition, there is a significant imbalance of power between the two, then the consequences are accentuated and the problem even more difficult to resolve. In the politics of the relationship between finance and human rights, there can be no doubting which partner is the more powerful.

Given finance's "bear pit" culture, which encourages behavior that has banks cheating on each other, it comes as no surprise that bankers do not hesitate to cheat on those of us outside the sector whose levels of financial literacy are almost certainly much lower. Finance's internecine savagery was certainly on display in a case before a New York State court in October 2011. An Australian hedge fund (Basis Capital) had sued Goldman Sachs for $1.067 billion, claiming that in 2007 it had been knowingly duped by the Wall Street bank into investing in "Timberwolf," a collateralized debt obligation (CDO).[12] At the time of the transaction a Goldman Sachs executive had frankly, but rather imprudently, described Timberwolf as "one shitty deal" in an email to a colleague, while simultaneously the firm's sales force was being told that selling Timberwolf "is our priority."[13] The Sydney-based fund had duly lost $56.3 million on its $80.8 million investment in the CDO in less than six weeks, though in the lawsuit it claimed a further $1 billion in punitive damages. In a statement responding to the lawsuit, Goldman Sachs flatly denied fraud, pointing rather to the fact that as Basis Capital "advertised itself as one of the world's most experienced hedge funds," it ought to have known better.[14] A more eloquent disclosure of finance's bestial ethics might be hard to find.

Understandably then, when finance's jungle law is let loose in unsuspecting suburbia you can be sure that there will be carnage. The explosion of subprime mortgage loans in poorer neighborhoods across the United States in the 1990s and 2000s was grounded in the simple fact that lenders knew what they were doing and many borrowers did not.[15] Relatively poor, gullible, and financially unsophisticated borrowers were easy prey for mortgage brokers and banks who were interested in how many loans they could write rather than whether their clients could service them. Predatory and discriminatory lending targeted and aggressively solicited borrowers in predominantly low-income, minimally educated communities whose understanding of even basic financial terms such as "interest rate" and the "principal of a loan" was negligible or nonexistent. [16] The practice grew so large as to become a key contributory factor to the pileup on "a highway where there were neither speed limits nor neatly painted lines" that was the 2007/08 financial crisis, as the U.S. Financial Crisis Inquiry Commission chose to frame it.[17]

While the impact of such unscrupulous behavior may have been especially serious and far-reaching for subprime housing loans in the United States, the practice was in fact widespread. In his tragic essay "Who Killed Richard Cullen?" author and documentarian Jon Ronson shows how banks and other lenders in the United Kingdom systematically target the most gullible. Prompted by the suicide of a middle-aged, averagely wealthy, husband and father (Richard Cullen), whose life collapsed under the weight of indebtedness (including twenty-two credit cards and outstanding debts of more than £130,000 at the time of his death), Ronson set out to discover how and why Cullen was deluged with unsolicited credit offers even as his creditworthiness plummeted.[18] Adopting multiple personas (ranging from rich to poor, ethical to venal, gambler to conservative, and debt-free to heavily indebted) he filled out lifestyle surveys, entered magazine competitions, and made purchases online. The personal information he divulged in these ways was picked up by banks and credit card companies (among others), and soon his various personas began to receive unsolicited offers for all manner of products and services. Loan or credit offers were received in the greatest quantities by the persona who had the highest level of relative indebtedness, who showed the greatest willingness to take risks, and who had the lowest credit rating.

When Wall Street cheats Main Street the consequences are always gravest for those who can least handle them. For the stark reality is that no matter the strength of moral and philosophical argument that may be called in aid of human rights, it is money that makes the world go around. Or, more to the point, the world revolves around money. Public power is nearly always and everywhere held in the thrall of the demands made by the private pursuit of financial wealth. It has been so for as long as sophisticated trade and commerce have been with us. In *Wolf Hall*, Hilary Mantel has Thomas Cromwell—early international lawyer, financier, Lord Chancellor of England, and courtier of Henry VIII—say of this circumstance in the Middle Ages:

> The world is run from Antwerp, from Florence, from places . . . never imagined; from Lisbon, from where ships with sails of silk drift west and are burned up in the sun. Not from the castle walls, but from the counting houses, not by the call of the bugle, but the click of the abacus, not by the grate and click of the mechanism of the gun but by the scrape of the pen on the page of the promissory note that pays for the gun and the gunsmith and the powder and the shot.[19]

The exchanges may now be in London, New York, and Shanghai, and the abacus replaced by computer-driven algorithms, but the global power of finance remains. And its track record of creating public as well as private goods is more than matched by its record of damaging or destroying them.

Illicit Finance

Perhaps the greatest capacity of finance to endanger public interests, including human rights standards, comes not from its overweening presence but from its conspicuous absence. The financial black hole represented by the annual totals

of global illicit financial flows to and from developing countries has been growing steadily over the past two decades or so and today stands at an estimated
annual value of between $2 trillion and $3.5 trillion.[20] The detrimental implications for developing states are significant in respect of illicit financial flows
in *both* directions, because in both, illegitimate private interests are benefiting
at the expense of legitimate public interests. The nonprofit research agency
Global Financial Integrity (GFI), which compiles the data, reckons that these
estimates are "conservative" (being illicit, the amounts are nearly always hidden and so are hard to calculate), and that the actual losses are much higher.[21]
Even the figures at the lower end of the range are shocking enough, representing more than sixteen times the global aid provided to developing countries
and more than triple the total inflows of foreign direct investment into their
economies.[22] Levels of illicit financial flows over the past decade have risen,
on average, somewhere between 8.5% and 10.4% per year (far exceeding average annual GDP growth), and in 2014 were equivalent to between 13.8%
and 24% of all trade flowing in and out of developing states that same year.[23]
Neither developing states nor their people can afford to haemorrhage financial
resources on such a colossal scale.

These rivers of illicit finance are fed by corruption, fraud, trafficking, extortion, embezzlement, tax evasion, and terrorism. All are directly or indirectly a
form of theft from the public purse, and as crimes against the state they constitute a subversion of it. For developing countries, the impact can be profound.
Inequality is exacerbated and poverty entrenched, the rule of law is frustrated
(if not crushed entirely), and the opportunity and capacity for people to enjoy
human rights protections severely undermined.[24] A sobering example of the
sort of on-the-ground human rights impact such larceny can have is provided
by a study undertaken by a team of British and Malawian medical researchers,
together with a development specialist, of rates of infant (under five years old)
mortality in thirty-four sub-Saharan African countries, all of which suffer, to
varying extents, illicit financial flows (IFFs).[25]

The team endeavored to calculate how many additional infant lives would be
saved if IFFs no longer existed in each of the subject states. By assuming "that the
relationship between the percentages of GDP lost through IFF, and therefore
gained if IFF [was] completely curtailed, would have had the same impact on
child mortality as the remainder of the GDP," they were able to extrapolate estimates of reductions in mortality rates. Using already-available data for the period
2000–11, they first compared the rates of infant mortality across the thirty-four
chosen states in 2000 with those in 2011. Reductions had been recorded in all
states during that time, with the average annual mortality rate in 2011 (141
deaths per 1,000) being 3.3% lower than that in 2000 (146 deaths per 1,000),

though both figures far exceed the rates typically found in Western states.[26] The research team then "added in" the GDP funds lost through IFF, which averaged 7.41% of GDP for 2011 across all thirty-four countries. These extra funds, they calculated, would have led to an additional reduction in average annual infant mortality rates of 3.31% (or 4.6 per 1,000 fewer deaths).[27] Applied to the sub-Saharan region as a whole, that represents an annual saving each year of approximately 4.5 million additional lives of children under the age of five in the poorest region in the world.[28]

Though the leaching of public monies in developing countries can rightly be blamed on the unscrupulous actions of persons outside governments, it would be a mistake to believe that governments are always merely innocent victims. Typically, government insiders—officials, ministers, politicians, and presidents—are assisting in, or instigating, the fraud. This is, in fact, what makes the many problems of illicit finance so serious and so intractable for developing states. Crimes against the state are being perpetrated from within the apparatus of the state itself, not just from without. As author and former World Bank Executive Director Moisés Naím warned in his pathbreaking 2005 book on the topic, "[i]llicit trade is deeply embedded in the private sector, in politics and in governments."[29]

Even if we look only at the estimates of sums pilfered by the more infamous of the world's kleptomaniac leaders the figures are shocking, especially in the context of the poverty endured by so many of their people. The top five, according to Transparency International, are all believed to have embezzled billions:

1. Mohamed Suharto (President of Indonesia, 1967–98), $15–35 billion;
2. Ferdinand Marcos (President of Philippines, 1972–86), $5–10 billion;
3. Mobuto Sese Seko (President of Zaire, 1965–97), $5 billion;
4. Sani Abacha (President of Nigeria, 1993–98), $2–5 billion; and
5. Slobodan Milosevic (President of Yugoslavia/Serbia, 1989–2000), $1 billion.[30]

The per capita GDP in 2001 in each of these countries ranged between a high of $1,634 (Serbia) and a low of $150 (Democratic Republic of Congo—as Zaire had by then become). The per capita GDP in the United States in that same year was $37,273.[31]

Contemptible though such larcenous leaders are, their raids on the public purse are only one part of a much bigger problem. Widespread and systematic attacks are perpetrated on the world's public revenues every day by much larger and collectively wealthier strata of society. The strata comprise taxpayers and the problem is endemic tax evasion.

Tax Evasion

As a matter of fact, the single biggest component of the illicit funds washing through the global financial system comprises wealth illegally hidden from tax authorities. Here again it is difficult to be precise about the sums involved, not only because of their clandestine nature (like "an exercise in night vision"),[32] but also because the lines between what constitutes illegal tax evasion and legal tax avoidance are so often blurred. I will return to this last point later in the chapter when considering the financial and human rights implications of the state being hijacked by private interests. For now it simply needs to be borne in mind as we contemplate the watchdog group Tax Justice Network's estimate that the global total of wealth accumulated in offshore secrecy jurisdictions stands somewhere between $21 trillion and $32 trillion.[33] These enormous sums represent untaxed funds that might potentially be taxable in the states in which they were generated, or in the home state of their beneficial owners, or both.

The problem is a significant one for developed economies, especially those whose relatively high levels of taxation provide an incentive for taxpayers to shift otherwise taxable income offshore into lower (or no) tax jurisdictions. The issue has attracted much debate and, more recently, widespread community attention and some outrage, but it is at least something that richer states are able to tackle, political will permitting. Certainly, it could be made clearer what constitutes the illegal movement of assets offshore legally—as the OECD's Base Erosion and Profit Shifting (BEPS) program is presently seeking to do[34]—and where illegality is suspected or detected, enforcement measurements should be pursued with greater zeal and efficiency.[35]

Tax Free

The problem for developing economies, however, is in a different league altogether. Their tax systems are already struggling to raise revenue from domestic economies that are informal and unfamiliar with (or resistant to) taxation, on top of the fact that the tax authorities themselves often lack the requisite skills and resources to establish and administer viable tax regimes.[36] Globalization pressures have made this situation even worse. The principal source of tax revenue for most developing states comes from duties on imports and exports because they are easiest to administer and control. Maligned as trade-restricting tariffs, these duties are often among the first casualties when states join multilateral trade regimes such as the World Trade Organization. The proffered hope and expectation is that the economic gains from increased trade will more than make up for the loss of this tax revenue stream. It seems, however, that for many states this simply does not happen. IMF economists have calculated that even after twenty-five years of trade liberalization developing states typically recover only 30% of the revenue, mainly because it takes a long time and significant economic growth to establish and reap the benefits of a sophisticated and comprehensive tax system that covers income, capital gains, sales, and payroll taxes, among others.[37]

In these circumstances any substantial capital flight overseas beyond the reach of domestic taxation of any kind can seriously retard a country's development prospects. Just how serious a problem that might be is graphically illustrated in the Tax Justice Network study mentioned above. The report's author, former McKinsey chief economist James Henry, and his team chose to focus on a group of 139 "mainly low to middle income" countries (that is, excluding the [roughly] 25 richest and 25 poorest states). These 139 they characterized as "capital source countries"—that is, "countries that have seen net unrecorded private capital outflows over time."[38] By the authors' estimations the economic impact of wealth being shipped offshore is truly breathtaking, for it sideswipes not just the developing states themselves, but the entire global financial system. Their calculations are so striking they are worth considering step by step.

First, they estimate the total of accumulated *unrecorded* offshore wealth emanating from these 139 countries for the period from the 1970s to 2010. It amounts to somewhere between $7.3 and $9.3 trillion. Being unrecorded, this figure is necessarily an estimate, albeit, as noted in the report, almost certainly on the conservative side of the true total. But in any case, the furtive manner in which this wealth has been shipped overseas by the private elites in these countries points strongly toward their illicit intent.

Next, the report calculates the *recorded* offshore wealth held by those same developing countries (that is, by their governments, private institutions, and individuals), most of which is held in stocks and bonds in developed economies. In 2010, this figure was $6.88 trillion. So, as of 2010, the developing world had a combined total of at least $14.18 trillion ($6.88 + $7.3 trillion) of wealth held offshore. Even after subtracting the aggregate gross external debt of $4.08 trillion owed by the 139 source states, the offshore treasure chest still amounted to more than $10 trillion.

On the basis of these figures, therefore, the world's poorest states are not debtors to the world's richest states, they are their creditors. The critical point is, however, that "the assets of these countries are held by a small number of wealthy individuals while the debts are shouldered by the ordinary people of these countries through their governments."[39]

The debts in question comprise losses incurred through the blatant theft of public funds as well as forgone tax revenue. There are no precise figures as to the size of the loss,[40] but as noted earlier, the tax revenue lost by developing countries from multinational corporations' profit-shifting activities alone is estimated by UNCTAD to be at least $100 billion annually.[41] While national and international initiatives established to try to locate and recover these stolen assets, such as the joint UN/World Bank–backed Stolen Assets Recovery Initiative (StAR), are to be welcomed, their success has thus far been extremely modest in the face of the size of the problem.[42]

Whatever the overall tax losses, they are certainly significant and the implications profound. But what is of even greater concern is the extent and sophistication of the system that permits, indeed expedites, such gargantuan sums to flow offshore. Here again Henry's report is revealing. He talks of these offshore destinations as together constituting "a brave new 'virtual country,'" which, though lacking physical boundaries, "offers escape routes from many of the taxes, financial regulations, human rights standards and moral restraints that the rest of us take for granted." The "virtual country," what is more, is the creation of a "pirate banking" system that "launders, shelters, manages and if necessary re-domiciles the riches of many of the world's worst villains, as well as the tangible and intangible assets and liabilities of many of our wealthiest individuals, alongside our most successful mainstream banks, corporations, shipping companies, insurance companies, accounting firms and law firms."[43]

The tax havens at the center of this other world are sometimes small economies (but with big reputations), like Andorra, the British Virgin Islands, Cayman Islands, and the Seychelles, as well as mid-sized economies like Singapore, Hong Kong, Luxembourg, and Switzerland. Others, however, are bigger (including the biggest), but their role as tax havens is less well known. These include all major European states, North America, and Australia. Indeed, the permissive regulatory environments of just about every OECD state make it easy for those with something to hide to deposit their wealth in banks within their jurisdiction.[44]

Tax Sport

Political scientist and corruption expert Jason Sharman's illuminating study of the behavior of many offshore banking institutions shows just how casually extensive this phenomenon is in Western states. Posing as a wealthy investor seeking anonymity, tax "minimization," and asset protection, Sharman approached more than 200 offshore providers from both renowned, small state, tax haven jurisdictions, as well as from OECD countries. Of the latter, forty-seven providers gave valid responses (that is, were prepared to discuss options), and of those, no fewer than thirty-five "agreed to form shell companies without requiring any identification documents." Twenty-four of those were from the United States and eight from the UK.[45] All were acting in direct contravention of a requirement mandated by the intergovernmental Financial Action Task Force (of which thirty-four countries are members, including all in the OECD), that states establish and enforce rules to identify "beneficial ownership" in company structures, as well as similar provisions under in domestic laws such as in the UK and the United States.[46]

The audacity of it all is astounding,[47] even if the community-wide reaction to the scale of these illicit activities, if understood at all, approaches something akin to resigned acceptance. In the matter of egregious tax evasion (or avoidance), we tend toward satire rather than revolution. As we laugh wryly at the inimitable Jon Stewart when he quips, ". . . there is one thing that corporations do have in common with the rest of us, they don't like paying taxes . . . fortunately, they rarely have to,"[48] we betray a collective and deeply held attitude toward tax.

Psychologists Erich Kirchler and Valerie Braithwaite have identified and analyzed a range of "motivational postures" that people hold in respect of their obligations to pay tax—from commitment (it's the right thing to do), through capitulation (on balance, best to pay up), to resistance, disengagement, and game-playing. While noting that competing feelings can co-exist in many tax-payers, it is apparent that in states in which, generally speaking, the tax authorities are respected if not exactly loved, the most frequently held perspectives are commitment and capitulation.[49] However, the more complex and ambiguous the tax rules, or seemingly skewed toward or against certain interests (for example, favoring capital wealth over income, or having impacts that are more regressive than progressive, or providing fewer tax breaks to salary-earners than other wealth vehicles), the lower their perceived legitimacy. The lower the regard in which a tax regime is held, Kirchler and Braithwaite found, the lower are the levels of taxpayer commitment to it. In such circumstances, the willingness to pursue strategies of what their colleague John Braithwaite labels the "legal entrepreneurship to manipulate the rules" increases.[50]

Expectations that others will do the same will also, apparently, increase, if governments lose our respect for how they spend the tax revenue they collect. That is, at least, if you heed the late Kerry Packer (formally Australia's richest individual), who with characteristic fortitude once advised his fellow citizens that if they didn't "minimize their tax, they want their heads read," adding, for the benefit of the politicians before whom he was appearing, "because as a government I can tell you you're not spending it that well that we should be donating extra."[51]

It is here that we find ourselves, once again, traversing the gray area between what is legal and what is fair, and from there, constructing explanations and rationales for peoples' attitudes toward their governments. In this we might reflect upon the views of another archetype of the world's wealthiest human beings, Warren Buffett, who has also raised questions about tax minimization, albeit for different reasons and in a different register than Packer. During a television interview some years ago, Buffett told a story of a small but revealing survey he conducted in which he asked the people working in his Berkshire Hathaway office (including management, analysts, administrative assistants, and receptionists) to declare their effective income tax rates. It turned out that he had the lowest (17.7%), with the average being 32.9%. How can this be so? Because, as Buffett explained, such tax leniency for the rich is a cardinal feature of the horrifyingly complex U.S. federal tax code.[52] "I have no tax planning," he points out, "I just follow what the U.S. Congress tells me to do."[53] The bottom line for Buffett is that the current U.S. tax system may be legal, but it is not fair. In his view the wealthy should be paying more tax as a percentage of their wealth than they do presently.[54]

The fact that tax regimes in rich countries, as well as poor, tend (to varying degrees) to treat the wealthy favorably points to a deeper, more insidious challenge to governance. This challenge comes not from countermanding the state, but from commandeering it. This happens when the power and authority of the state are used to legitimize what is prejudicial and demonstrably unfair, clothing it in respectability and protecting it from censure. In short, it aims to recast that which ordinarily would be considered illegal, as legal.

Misappropriation

It was the illegitimate appropriation of public power that so concerned Baron de Montesquieu as he sought to construct and justify a theory of governance that transcended the extreme concentrations of power that accompany the happenstance of monarchies and the domination of despotism. In De l'Esprit des Lois (1748) he advanced arguments for government by institutions that were more representative, empowered and limited by law, and (above all) separate in authority and function.[55] By way of these democratic features, he argued, the powers of government are checked or balanced, rather than dangerously concentrated. Thereby, he believed, they were better able to deliver governance that is free, fair, respected, and legitimate.

For these arguments alone, Montesquieu is lauded as one of the greatest and most influential of Enlightenment thinkers, but it is his prescience as to what can go wrong in democracies that deserves our attention here. In a section of De l'Esprit des Lois entitled "The Corruption of the Principles of Democracy," he warns of the despotic dangers of private interests appropriating the instruments of public power in order to advance their own goals, including and especially, their financial enrichment at the expense of the community at large.[56] Here, Montesquieu is echoing a line of reasoning he had pursued in another treatise written fourteen years earlier and encapsulated in his famous aphorism that "[t]here is no crueller tyranny than that which is perpetuated under the colour of the laws and in the name of justice."[57]

Have the instruments of governmental power today fallen prey to the sectional interests of the rich generally, and finance in particular? Well, "yes," according to Simon Johnson, former chief economist of the IMF; that is, at least in the relationship between finance and successive U.S. governments. In a remarkable piece published shortly after the GFC, Johnson likens the hold that the financial sector has over the political organs of government to a coup d' état, but a "quiet" one, as he puts it, not borne of violence or overt bribery and corruption, but "by amassing a kind of cultural capital—a belief system."[58] The significance of this point can hardly be overstated. At its peak, in the decade leading up to the GFC it amounted to the belief among "Washington insiders" that "what was good for Wall Street was good for the country."[59]

Johnson identifies one obvious channel for this exceptional influence as the sharing of personnel and positions between major private financial institutions and the government agencies charged with the responsibilities for their oversight and regulation. It is what Charles Ferguson refers to as a "revolving door" in his fantastically unforgiving documentary *Inside Job* on the causes of the financial crisis.[60] The list of individuals who have shuffled between jobs in Washington and Wall Street is long and studded with key operators (including Alan Greenspan, Robert Rubin, Hank Paulson, Tim Geithner, and most recently, Steve Mnuchin, Wilbur Ross and Gary Cohn), and it leaves no doubt as to how and why laws and regulatory behavior have so favored financial interests. Johnson relates a story from his time working at the IMF that illustrates the depth of shared beliefs: "I vividly remember a meeting in early 2008—attended by top policy makers from a handful of rich countries—at which the chair casually proclaimed, to the room's general approval, that the best preparation for becoming a central-bank governor was to work first as an investment banker."[61]

Even immediately following the GFC, Johnson, writing in May 2009, could not see significant changes in attitude and behavior on the part either of the financial sector or of the government. The latter's "velvet-glove approach" to banks persisted, and the former continued to exercise what was, in effect, a "veto over public policy, even as that sector loses popular support." In fact, the very scale of the crisis had so spooked governments worldwide, that the political clout of the financial sector had, if anything, increased, as authorities frantically sought counsel to help them understand what had and was going wrong in the financial markets, and what they could do about it.

Despite the collapse or merger of some global banks, a worldwide, but still modest, increase in capital adequacy levels (under Basel III), new disclosure requirements, and new regulatory agencies in the UK and the United States to administer them,[62] and enduring public cynicism as to the sector's ethical standards, the symbiosis between politics and finance remains intact. The same beliefs and attitudes that have sustained the relationship over the past three decades remain prevalent today, even if held a little less ardently.

Consider the fact that a key plank in the global regulatory reaction to the 2007/08 financial crisis was an initiative aimed at addressing a problem believed to be at the core of the crisis. Called the "Systemically Important Financial Institutions (SIFI) Framework," the initiative was intended by its creator (the intergovernmental Financial Stability Board [FSB]) to devise ways to defuse the "too big to fail" (TBTF) problem. This is the invidious circumstance where "the threatened failure of a SIFI leaves public authorities with no option but to bail it out using public funds to avoid financial instability and economic damage."[63] Not only do such rescue packages make egregious demands on the public purse, the very existence of an implied, publicly funded, guarantee against institutional failure instils a sense of recklessness in private financiers— that is the "moral hazard" problem we encountered in chapter 3.[64] There can be no doubting the size and complexity of the task facing the FSB (together with national financial regulatory bodies) in tackling the problem. And yet, it is the very enormity of the task that explains why so many inside and outside the sector still believe in the dispositive power that finance has over governments. The FSB maintains lists of SIFIs of global significance (currently comprising thirty banks and nine insurance companies),[65] and has promoted in these institutions increased levels of supervision, disclosure, and risk management planning, but it also acknowledges its limitations. With few exceptions, the FSB notes, "markets have not yet changed their assumptions of [financial firms'] reliance on extraordinary public support." The reality is, as the board concludes a report on its own progress, that "[i]t will understandably take time to fully establish the credibility of the new framework in addressing TBTF."[66]

Questions of Impunity

Another important reason why finance's torch continues to burn brightly is that while a number of leading banks have been prosecuted and fined for their role in the crisis, the senior management of the same banks have nearly all been able to escape legal sanction.[67] This is a significant distinction, for while prosecution may be embarrassing for a bank, and the fines substantial, both consequences are quickly absorbed and business continues much as usual.[68] Unlike banking corporations, individual bankers do have "bodies to be kicked and souls to be damned."[69] Whatever the legal arguments over the precise legal boundaries of criminal liability—and they have raged hard and long[70]—the fact is that total levels of prosecutions for financial fraud offences as well as other white-collar crimes showed only a small increase following the 2007/08 financial crisis.[71] This was in stark contrast to the marked spike in fraud prosecutions during and following the U.S. "Savings and Loan" crisis in 1983–92, which, by 1995, amounted to an almost twenty-fold increase on prosecutions levels before that crisis.[72]

The impression of impunity is even starker when one looks at the trending figures for referrals by banking regulators to the U.S. Department of Justice (DOJ), upon which the Department principally relies in order to initiate criminal proceedings. According to data collected by Syracuse University's Transactional Records Access Clearinghouse (TRAC) and reported in the *New York Times*, bank regulators referred 1,837 cases to the DOJ in 1995. By 2006, that figure had dropped to 75, and in "the four subsequent years, a period encompassing the worst of the crisis, an average of only 72 a year were referred for criminal prosecution."[73] This decline can be explained largely in terms of the institution of light-touch regulation of the finance sector in the intervening years.[74] The sector had successfully lobbied for less intrusive, more lenient, and flexibly permissive laws, and also, by way of flattery and infiltration, had managed to instill an attitude of submissive somnolence in the sector's supervisory agencies.

On the face of it and some years after the crisis, the DOJ appears to have recovered a semblance of spine by way of a string of high-profile bank prosecutions and some eye-watering fines and settlements. These include the single largest ever criminal penalty of all time ($8.97 billion against BNP Paribas in 2015 for "years-long and wide-ranging criminal conduct," in violating trade sanctions against Sudan, Iran, and Cuba.).[75] The willfulness and flagrancy of the bank's behavior in this case was astounding, continuing even in the face of internal emails from its own compliance and legal officers "expressing concern about the bank's assisting the Sudanese government in light of its role in supporting international terrorism and committing human rights abuses during the [relevant] time period."[76] That said, the huge cumulative settlements recorded by other banks—notably, $77.1 billion for Bank of America in thirty-four total cases, and $40.1 billion by JP Morgan Chase in twenty-six total cases—represent recidivist behavior that is no less shocking in its brazenness.[77]

However, even these results "are not all that they appear," according to criminal law specialist Brandon Garrett. Garrett has spent years sifting through these banking cases, before and especially after the financial crisis,[78] and while he notes the impressive spike in both the number of criminal cases and the size of fines and settlements (in 2015 in particular),[79] he unearths disturbing trends that point more to window dressing than to real reform. His research identifies (i) a marked mismatch between the seriousness of offences and quantities of ill-gotten profits, vis-à-vis the relative leniency of the financial penalties (staggering though they are); (ii) a lack of deterrence as evidenced by serial recidivism of many of the biggest banks over many years; and (iii) the continuing hypersensitivity and reluctance of regulators to press for prosecutions of senior management of banks in their individual capacities.[80]

Stung by a long line of criticism such as this, the DOJ issued a new set of prosecutorial principles in November 2015 that stressed the premise that "[o]ne of the most effective ways to combat corporate misconduct is by holding accountable all individuals who engage in wrongdoing."[81] A cloud of suspicion nonetheless hovers over the DOJ that it still retains a belief that some banks are just too big to jail. Former U.S. Attorney-General Eric Holder once stunned members of the Senate Judiciary Committee in 2013 when he admitted to being concerned about the potential negative economic consequences of pursuing prosecutions of global banks. Such concern "has an inhibiting influence . . . on our ability to bring resolutions that I think would be more appropriate," he declared.[82] Following Mr. Holder's departure, statements by senior DOJ officials, including the then Deputy Attorney-General Sally Yates, stressed that in business cases there existed neither leniency for corporations, nor clemency for individuals, and that criminal activity would not go unpunished.[83]

The walk, however, has yet to follow the talk. Deferred prosecution agreements and nonprosecution agreements are still being negotiated with banks under investigation for egregious and longstanding criminal behavior. Citibank, for example, secured a $97 million "no sanctions" settlement with the DOJ in May 2017, thereby ending a lengthy inquiry into the flagrant money-laundering activities of one of its subsidiaries.[84] And, more generally, the Trump administration has shown little appetite for reigning in errant behavior in the sector; indeed quite the opposite. In moves designed to roll back consumer protections against financial fraud and deceit, President Trump has not only backed legislation to weaken the powers of the Consumer Financial Protection Bureau and to shield financial institutions from publication of data on complaints made about them.[85] He has also signaled his intent to remove protections for consumers against unscrupulous financial advisors who place their own interests above those of their clients.[86] What is more, and in keeping with the Trump administration's fondness for doublespeak, both of these initiatives have been presented as vehicles to improve peoples' opportunities and freedoms of choice.[87]

So, as it presently stands, the record of imposing criminal sanctions on financiers and financial institutions is far from impressive. As compared to the scale of proven individual criminal liability following earlier financial scandals and crises, there has been a marked reduction in the level of chastening experienced personally by those who were at the forefront of the 2007/08 crisis. The prospect of prosecution, let alone conviction and serving a custodial sentence, was so remote as to be effectively disregarded.[88] Certainly, a number of the Titans of

Wall Street spent an uncomfortable day or two before congressional committees in the face of some withering lines of questioning.[89] Yet, even when on such public display, the audacity of some bankers was truly breathtaking. John Stumpf, the then CEO of Wells Fargo Bank, batted not an eyelid when proclaiming "we are frugal," in response to questions concerning his bank's use of publicly funded bailout money, though such parsimony, apparently, did not extend to Stumpf's own pay. His total remuneration package for that year (2009) was valued at $21.3 million, the highest of any banking executive.[90]

As a method of sanction, evidently, the experience cannot be considered especially burdensome. Its deterrent effect is even less so. It simply pales in comparison to the circumstance where one's wrongdoing brings the very real prospect of jail time. As Matt Taibbi reported in one of his characteristically forthright exposés of the finance sector's chicanery: " 'You put Lloyd Blankfein [CEO of Goldman Sachs] in pound-me-in-the-ass prison for one six-month term, and all this bullshit would stop, all over Wall Street,' says a former congressional aide. 'That's all it would take. Just once.' "[91]

Regulatory Capture

All governments, everywhere, are subject to regulatory capture. This occurs when the regulatory organs of government are appropriated by private interests they are supposed to be regulating and are bent to their (the private interests') demands, rather than to the demands of the community at large.[92] It is, to some degree, an unavoidable consequence of the exercise of public power. Ideologies, as much as the exigencies of circumstance, can be powerful determinants of what and who holds sway over what governments think and do. The propagation of "financial exceptionalism" has been especially persuasive in this regard over the past twenty years or so. But has it gone too far? Has it reached the level of psychosis, whereby in policy circles, the financial argument sweeps all before it? Rather than governments using finance as a tool to achieve broad social and economic goals, such as the promotion and protection of human rights standards for all, are governments now bent to the will of finance?

One of the important objects of this book has been to construct a response to the argument that doing whatever it takes to encourage financial innovation and growth is justified by the simple fact that doing so helps the financial pie grow bigger and that therefore, there will be more for everyone. For such a line of reasoning to deliver on its promise, governments responsible for carving up and distributing the pie must be competent, representative, and fair in the way they undertake the task. Moreover, they must also have an eye on the manner and means by which the pie is enlarged—including the allocation of risk, especially

between financial players themselves and the rest of society—and to ensure that
the pie is shared fairly, according to both one's need and the level of one's investment. Here, of course, is the rub.

In the context of my argument, bigger financial pies—nationally and
globally—are desirable insofar as they provide a potential resource for funding
better human rights standards, and as long as in the process of their expansion
they do not pose risks so great as to substantially endanger wider community
interests. In this we must concede that the motivations that drive growth in
national or global wealth are rooted in the prospect of personal financial enrichment. Greed in finance, as discussed in chapter 3, may not be good, but it is to
some extent necessary in this enterprise. Disparities in wealth will, necessarily,
occur. It is, however, the conditions that governments attach to such disparities
that are crucial. Foremost here are the questions of how, and how much, wealth
is taxed. What proportion of the pie, in other words, is made available to the
state for redistribution through the funding of public-interest activities, including human rights fulfillment?

Tax regimes that substantially favor the wealthy are unfair, as Warren Buffett
says, not least because they permit the rich to make a proportionately lower contribution to a state's tax revenue base than the less well-off and yet share many
of the same public benefits. Fundamentally, such regimes contradict the claim
that the larger the pool of wealth, the more everyone will benefit, not just the
few. For in circumstances where the broader public gains are so small relative to
the private gains made by a few, then the system fails to deliver on its promise
and instead reveals the extent to which the state is captured or bought by private, elite interests.[93] "Legal corruption" is how a former director of the World
Bank Institute, Daniel Kaufmann, labels situations where systemic injustice is
instituted by law.[94]

Legal Smoke Screens

I accept that there is a clear difference between using the law in ways it was
intended or at least supports (even if unfair and morally repugnant), and abusing it. The elaborate and highly effective tax-avoidance schemes employed by
Starbucks and Google are an example of the former, while corrupt politicians
or businesses hiding stolen assets in run-of-the-mill corporate structures that
conceal the identities of the 'beneficial owners' reflect the latter.[95] The intentions
may be different (to follow the letter of the law in one, and to hide from it in the
other), but the end results are much the same. In both, the law provides a vehicle by which private or corporate wealth escapes public accountability or even
awareness.

In economic terms, Starbucks and Google are acting perfectly rationally by exploiting the legal options available to them to ship offshore the substantial profits each makes from operations in the UK to jurisdictions with much lower corporate tax rates. A study conducted by Reuters concluded that in the fourteen years between 1998 and 2012, Starbucks paid a total of £8.5 million of UK corporation tax against a cumulative total of UK sales for that period of more than £3 billion (that is, an effective average annual tax rate of 0.283%). It had been able drastically to reduce its notional taxable income in the UK by having the bulk of its UK profits booked as royalty payments to Starbucks entities established in the Netherlands and Switzerland that held the intellectual property rights to the brand name.[96] Google has employed a similar strategy with regard to its UK business, except that the destination jurisdictions were Ireland and Bermuda.[97] There are, it is true, signs of pushback coming from some quarters, but even the most spectacular of these redemptive efforts do more to illustrate how entrenched are the tax privileges of corporate giants, than to bring them to heel.

In August 2016 the EU Commission issued a ruling that Ireland's sweetheart deal with Apple Inc., permitting the company to channel the profits from all of its European sales through two Irish-registered corporations at an effective tax rate (in 2014) of 0.005%, contravened EU competition laws and that Ireland was obliged to recover some €13 billion (plus interest) in lost tax revenue over the previous ten years.[98] The ruling elicited a pantomime of reactions. Some were predictable, such as those from Apple itself, which proclaimed that it was simply following some very accommodating regulations to the letter; others were disingenuous. The U.S. government, erstwhile avid tax hawk, weighed in behind Apple's warning that the ruling jeopardized "the important economic partnership between the U.S. and the EU," despite the fact that it was a U.S. Senate committee's criticisms of Apple's opaque tax affairs that had prompted the EU to pursue its own investigations.[99] Most extraordinary of all was the reaction of the Irish government, which vowed to appeal the ruling, no matter that the forgone taxes amounted to 5% of country's GDP and more than its total annual health care budget.[100] Aside from representing the truly astounding financial reality of modern Ireland as compared to the utter degradation described at the outset of this chapter, the response of the Irish government reflects its long-term perspective. Apple brings jobs to Ireland, (some) tax receipts, and, above all, helps bolster the country's reputation as a desirable corporate tax haven[101] (corporate tax stands at 12.5% in Ireland, compared to 35% in the United States, and between 20% and 30% in many European states).[102] Despite their differences, what all three of these cases share is evidence of the manipulative influence of corporate power.

The symptoms of regulatory capture are, therefore, evident everywhere. Some are serious systemic artifacts, like the above-mentioned legalized business structures used not only by the world's "grand corrupters," but also by rich, savvy, tax-averse individuals and companies. It was all very well for Barack Obama in 2008 to point an accusing finger at the Cayman Islands as home to tens of thousands of shell companies, yet that pales in comparison to the more than one million companies registered in Delaware, "many of which," notes *The Economist*, "are dodgy shells."[103] In the UK, an investigation by *Private Eye* has shown how limited liability partnerships (LLPs) have been used to enable partnerships between anonymous, offshore shell companies to obtain a legalized business presence in the UK and thereby facilitate the undetected shipment of funds out of the jurisdiction.[104]

Other symptoms are brassily opportunistic. Robert Jenkins, when serving as a member of the Financial Policy Committee at the Bank of England, remarked on what he called the "intellectually dishonest" claims and tactics of finance sector lobbyists (an occupation he once held himself) when, following the financial crisis, they sought "to convince pundits, public and politicians that encouraging prudence [in the sector] too soon will hit the economy too hard."[105]Finally, some symptoms are frankly ridiculous, and would be laughable were they not taken so seriously by those in government. The tragicomedy of the 2015 changes to tax transparency laws for corporations in Australia illustrates this point well. The reforms contain an extraordinary exception for large *private* companies (with annual turnovers of more than AUD$100 million), which are exempted from the requirement to publicize their tax records made of all other corporations, both public and private. The initial reason given by the then assistant treasurer Josh Frydenberg, when introducing the change, was that requiring these companies to make public their financial statements would jeopardize the safety of private business people and their families as it may increase the chances of their kidnap.[106] No matter what the reason (and Mr. Frydenberg produced not a shred of evidence to support his), such a blanket exemption, covering some 800 of the total of 2,400 affected companies, is difficult to reconcile with the Australian Tax Office's (ATO's) explanation of tax transparency laws as intended "to discourage large corporate tax entities from engaging in aggressive tax avoidance practices," especially as the ATO disclosed that one in five of these companies paid no tax at all in 2014.[107]

The essential point in all these examples is that "fraud" on this scale and perpetrated in this way is not victimless. Its "legalization" does not change that fact. If anything, laundering the process and its consequences makes the situation even more reprehensible. There may appear to be some distance between, on the one hand, egregious risk taking by banks, or the systematic manipulation of political power by the finance sector, or the tax-dodging antics of individuals and corporations, and, on the other, the impoverishment of people's human rights standards, but that connection is there. It is a connection, what is more, that rests on questions of fairness and equity. When an economic and political system enables individuals or corporate entities to accrue substantial financial wealth, it is incumbent on the state to ensure that they give back to the society that sustains them. Everyone is "a part of the main," as poet John Donne put it in his cautionary "No Man is an Island," so that by contributing your share all stand to prosper, and when you decline to do so, all are diminished.[108]

Denial in Finance

Throughout this chapter (and the book) there has been plenty of evidence of the hubris of financiers and their attendant belief in the exceptional status the financial sector occupies in national and international polities. The result is endemic denial throughout finance that there is anything fundamentally wrong with the system as it is. There is always a need for peripheral tinkering now and again (if only to satisfy popular political demands), as most in the sector would readily concede, but there is certainly no need to raise questions of an existential nature. Liberalized financial markets have created enormous private wealth in which an ever-widening spread of people are directly participating, and from which the public is indirectly benefiting, so leave them be, the argument continues.

Even if it is accepted that such "trickle-down" benefits do accrue, to presuppose that they constitute sufficient justification for maintaining the financial system as it currently operates is to ignore the very substantial costs of retaining the status quo. These include costs associated with gross and growing inequalities of wealth that not only reflect widely differing standards of individual human rights enjoyment, but also represent lost social and economic opportunities that fairer distributions of wealth bring to societies as a whole.

I have spent some time explaining the problematic consequences of such tunnel vision, including the role it plays in inciting financial crises. The persistence of high levels of financiers' conceit even after the experience of the most recent crisis in 2007/08 demonstrates just how embedded the problem is. Where one might have expected to see some sectorwide chastening, the fact of the matter is that evidence of such has been the exception rather than the rule.

This helps explain why financial advisers in the United States[109] and fund managers in the UK[110] today remain so shamelessly and stridently resistant to even the most basic of regulatory reforms, such as the suggestion that they should always put clients' interests first and ahead of their own, including being more transparent about the commissions they receive and the fees they charge. It helps explain how the bankers directly involved in the fixing of the London Interbank Offered Rate (LIBOR) had become so comfortable with this long-standing, systematic rort that they simply couldn't be bothered to try to cover their tracks.[111]

And it helps us understand why even Credit Suisse's apparently well-intentioned annual Philanthropists Forum, representing the bank's "commitment to provide its clients with integrated solutions to meet their philanthropic needs,"[112] must be placed in the context of its equal commitment to facilitating rich Americans to evade taxes on such a massive scale that it was compelled to plead guilty to charges led by the DOJ and fined $2.6 billion.[113]

One would be hard pressed to disagree with Bank of England Governor Mark Carney's rueful reflection on the succession of scandals following the credit crisis: "It is simply untenable now to argue that the problem is one of a few bad apples. The issue is with the barrels in which they are stored."[114] Such frankness is one of the above-mentioned exceptions to the prevalence of denial, but welcome though it is, translating the sentiment into viable options for changes in policy and practice is proving very difficult.

In the final chapter I will be looking at what the options are, or might be, to make finance work better for broader societal goals, including human rights, and thereby help sustain its own future. For the moment, however, my concern is to stress the importance of first winning hearts and minds. Carney's heart may indeed be in a reformatory space, but even he struggles to engage minds with the goal of effecting real change. Despite the fact that he oversees the FSB's reform agenda in his capacity as its chair, the FSB's progress has been, as noted earlier, frustratingly slow.[115] Similarly, the Bank of England's Open Forum, launched in 2015 with the intention to "map a positive future for financial markets" by bringing together "policymakers, financial market participants and users, academics, media representatives and wider society,"[116] has also underwhelmed. While the Background Papers prepared for the event repeatedly stressed the need for markets to operate with a "social license," based on "fairness and accountability" and promoting "the values of society," they were extremely sparing in providing practical guidance as to what these terms mean for the financial system.[117] Proclaiming further that "markets work best when they work in the interests of society, not just market participants," the papers nevertheless seem to relegate "the interests of society" to a matter of merely coincidental concern of what works best for finance.[118] If there is a core message that this book has sought to convey, it is that the conditionality should operate in precisely the opposite direction—what works best for the promotion of people's human rights, operates in the best interests of finance.

Denial in Human Rights

Problems of perspective, however, are not restricted to the world of finance. The relationship between finance and human rights also suffers from the latter's hubris and denial. To some extent this is a product of a broader problem within human rights advocacy and scholarship as the discipline struggles to contend with its own rhetorical success. Long and deep though its roots are, the political popularity of human rights has reached new heights in the post–World War II period, when, through a combination of philosophical argument, global institution building (notably the UN and regional human rights regimes), and domestic and international law-making, human rights have today become common parlance in just about any serious political discussion, at any level of social organization. Their proclaimed universality and perceived preeminence have lent them a "trump" status in many of these discussions.[119] While this status may be warranted in many or even most such cases, its very existence can lead to the presumption that it is always warranted.

It is insufficient merely to invoke the human rights trump without both understanding and explaining how and why it is justified. Indeed, it is intellectually lazy (even dishonest) and ultimately counterproductive not to make the attempt. "To secure acceptance of the primacy of human rights," as one rights-based think tank frankly admits, "human rights advocates . . . have to show that human rights principles are relevant to the solution of economic and social problems." [120] The argument for human rights can or could be decisive in many contexts, but only if the argument is actually made, and made well.

In the context of human rights' intersections with finance this has proven to be a particular problem. My erstwhile colleague and finance expert Mary Dowell-Jones (whom I introduced in chapter 2) and I wrote about the dimensions of this problem in a paper published in 2011 in which we referred to the body of work analyzing the intersections between human rights and finance as occupying "a blank space." Neither side is making any particularly sophisticated and robust attempt to reach across the gap by seeking to understand the demands and complexities of the other. Nor are they helping the cause by explaining frankly what those demands and complexities mean in their estimation of their own field. So, for example, even when presented with the opportunity to influence financial reform following the GFC, the necessary technical understanding of key features of the financial system had not been built within the human rights sphere for principles of human rights law to have much, if any, relevance on the financial reform agenda.[121]

Further, as we argued in another paper published a year later, despite the many codes of conduct and other voluntary initiatives developed in recent years covering corporate social and human rights responsibilities, the integration of such standards into the financial sector has been shallow.[122] This includes the due diligence standards established by the 2011 UN *Guiding Principles on Business and Human Rights*,[123] which regardless of the guidance they provide for nonfinancial corporations, are less relevant to business entities working in finance. The

Guiding Principles' assumption of a relatively straightforward cause-and-effect assignment of responsibility (think of environmental damage caused by mining companies, or the sweatshop conditions of suppliers to major clothing and footwear retailors), ill-fits the convoluted process of how human rights help or harm is generated by the finance sector. Bespoke attempts by banking bodies—such as those of the Thun Group discussed earlier[124]—to retrofit the Guiding Principles to the circumstances banks face every day show how difficult it is to insert a square peg in a round hole. Quite simply, such is the complexity of today's financial system, there exists no "accepted understanding of how to measure and control either the financial or human rights risks it generates."[125]

Just how little understanding is illustrated by the civil society organization BankTrack's survey of the responses of fifteen major banks to the widely publicized human rights breaches by a corporation with which all fifteen had financial dealings—the Malaysian palm oil conglomerate IOI. Driven by large corporations like IOI (as well the likes of Singapore's GAR and Wilmar), the tsunami of palm oil cultivation that has swept across Malaysia and Indonesia over the past ten to fifteen years has devastated local populations. Rich tropical rainforests and vast carbon dioxide–absorbing peatlands have been razed and replaced with palm plantations; farmers have been forced from their lands with inadequate or no compensation; plantation workers must endure atrocious conditions; and communities have been scattered and basic health and education systems have been destroyed or degraded.[126]

Yet, despite—or perhaps because of—the substantial evidence of widespread involvement of many corporations, including IOI, in these human rights abuses the responses from the fifteen banks were pitiful. Of the fourteen banks that did respond, seven did not acknowledge any financial relations with IOI; four refused on grounds of client confidentiality to disclose what, if any, actions they had taken; just three banks were willing to declare that they had taken some remedial action in line with the UN Guiding Principles (engaging with the company, or simply removing it from the bank's "socially responsible" investment products).[127]

Even sector-specific derivations of the Guiding Principles, such as the UN Environment Program Financial Initiative's (UNEPFI) Human Rights Guidance Tool for the Financial Sector, fail in this regard by assuming that finance and the finance sector can be regulated in much the same way as other businesses.[128] The Guidance Tool's description of "human rights and finance" speaks only of the sector's direct impact on human rights "when providing funding or financial advice to a business client," and nothing at all about the indirect impacts of macrofinancial policymaking and practice, or of the principles upon which the financial system is based. The UNEPFI's 2015 collaborative report with U.S. law firm Foley Hoag on banks and human rights is similarly restrained, aiming merely to help readers "better understand the content and implications" of the UN Guiding Principles. The report adds that it provides no analysis of banks' "investment activities" except where incidentally related to "other banking products and services," by which it means, essentially, retail banking. The whole world of shadow banking is therefore beyond its remit.[129] Another attempt to frame the issue in practical terms—this one from the OECD—does hint at the need to extend the scope of human rights due diligence responsibility to encompass fund managers and other financial intermediaries, but beyond "recognis[ing] the complexities around this topic," it adds little by way of detail of what this would look like.[130]

Dealing with this "monster under the bed," at least in terms of setting applicable standards, requires a much deeper and more sophisticated analysis of how the financial system operates as a whole, what human rights impacts it has, and, above all, what role human rights can play in financial policymaking and practice. What can be said with some certainty, therefore, is that it will take some time before workable and effective standards of human rights responsibility will become an established feature in the financial sector.

The online networking initiative Righting Finance, born of the 2007/08 financial crisis, captures the essence of the problem neatly when it says: "The debate on financial regulation, on account of its technical and complex nature, has typically been out of reach for human rights networks, organizations, communities and grassroots groups," and that as a consequence "access and capacity of those organizations to influence such debate has been limited."[131] Despite the best endeavors of Righting Finance (and others) to promote interest in financial matters in human rights thinking, there is today "still a long way to go" in terms of understanding finance in terms beyond high-street banking.[132] Interactions between human rights scholarship or commentary and private sector finance tend to be superficial. With few exceptions (which I cite throughout this book), they take the form of proclamations rather than explanations, designed more to achieve rhetorical impact than to invite and engage in serious dialogue. Not even running into the brick wall of the GFC changed this state of affairs, with human rights "barely figur[ing] in the diagnoses and prescriptions of the international community" that followed the event.[133]

Taking the form of a warning shot across the bows of human rights scholarship and activism, Aoife Nolan, a professor in the discipline, puts this missed opportunity down to a design fault in the prevailing human rights frameworks of laws and institutions. Their state-centric focus, she argues, are ill-suited for application to key nonstate financial actors such as the global financial institutions (the World Bank, the IMF, or the European Central Bank), private banks, and other financial intermediaries. Moreover, a heavy reliance on legal reasoning and a myopic obsession with court-based remedies have made it difficult for human rights actors to engage in wider economic and social policy discussions in any-thing beyond "a very limited degree."[134]

Wishful Thinking

Albeit well-intentioned, talk of international human rights law "provid[ing] a clear and universally recognized framework" that can guide "the design and implementation of economic policies and programs to address this unprece-dented economic crisis"[135] is simply wishful thinking. Such talk invests in human rights, and especially in international human rights *laws*, capacities they do not have, nor could they be expected to possess. It is all very well to lament the det-rimental social impacts of the latest financial crisis, as was the context in which this statement was delivered, but doing so, no matter how sincerely, does not transform human rights laws into a cure for the problem.

For the most part, international human rights laws articulate desirable social, economic, and political outcomes (nondiscrimination, free speech, personal security, and access to adequate health care, education, and housing, among them); they say very little about how these goals are to be achieved beyond mak-ing general references to states using legislative and other means and employing all available resources.[136] They say next to nothing about economic policy, and nothing at all about financial policy. To maintain, nevertheless, that they pro-vide a "framework" for the design and implementation of such policies places the burden of demonstrating how they do so squarely on the shoulders of those making the claim. To put it bluntly—it can hardly be expected that economic or financial policymakers will be able to interpret the framework properly and fully if human rights advocates are themselves are unable to do so convincingly, if at all. As a consequence, financial institutions and relevant policymakers either ignore such human rights proclamations, pay lip-service to heeding them (as in the human rights statements of the Thun Group or Goldman Sachs discussed in previous chapters),[137] or make vacuous promises to reform, as discussed earlier in this chapter. Either way, such insincerity borne of a widening gulf of miscom-munication ill-serves both human rights and finance.[138]

Part of the problem here, as I've argued elsewhere, is the inherent ambiguity, or "bendability," of human rights as expressed in the major international instru-ments.[139] The provisions of international human rights law are products of the necessity of compromise; they attempt, all at once, to enunciate principles of human social conduct that are to apply universally and transcendentally, regard-less of denominators such as race, gender, age, disability, culture, religious or philosophical beliefs, and economic circumstance. Such legal proclamations and "attendant legal obligations, imperatives, instructions and institutionalized dispute settlement regimes, give the impression of rigidity and immediacy."[140] But it is just that, an "impression."

The language used in these instruments is open-ended, comprising bare statements of the rights of individuals and groups, and of the means to be employed by states to meet their obligations to ensure their fulfillment. Many of the rights are qualified by permissible limitations—such as, for reasons of national security, public order and health; "where necessary in a democratic society"; or where they conflict with the rights of others.[141] And in the case of economic and social rights, implementation and protection are dependent on states' capacities and available resources. The flexibility in these provisions is duly reflected in the reality of both human rights policy and practice, as well as in human rights jurisprudence, with such well-established notions as a "margin of appreciation," which tolerates some limited differences between states in their interpretation and implementation of rights protections.

Another part of the problem lies in what legal scholar Mary Ann Glendon maintains is one of the most common and unfortunate misunderstandings of the purpose of the *Universal Declaration of Human Rights* (and by implication all the human rights treaties that have followed it): namely, that the Declaration was meant to impose a single model of right conduct for all mankind. Not so, she argues. Rather, it was intended to "provide a common standard that can be brought to life in different cultures in a legitimate variety of ways".[142] Here, Glendon points to a problem that lies within the human rights community itself. For it is incumbent upon human rights scholars and advocates alike to acknowledge the unavoidable flexibility of what human rights promise and can be expected to deliver. Not to do so hampers both the feasibility and credibility of the already-daunting task of relating human rights to the particular complexities of private finance, including any suggestions for its reform.

The problem of hubris within the field of human rights is not restricted to its engagement with private finance. It exists also in relation to certain aspects of public sector finance as well, despite the fact that in the public sphere one might expect the connections to be better understood and the lines of responsibility more clearly defined. Some of the interactions between human rights and the financing of overseas aid illustrate the point. Indeed, one of the most egregious examples of human rights faith adrift on the seas of political reality is the notion that there exists a legally enforceable "right to development."

To declare "that every human person and all peoples are entitled to a development process in which all human rights can be realized fully" is not the issue.[143] Few would disagree with such a proposition, not least because if human rights values really are universal then "we should be astonished to discover that good development practice did not fairly accurately reflect them."[144] Where the problem lies is in how the right *to* development is expressed. That is, specifically, who or what are the rights holders, and who or what the duty bearers? The 1986 *Declaration on the Right to Development*, mentioned earlier, expressly or by implication nominates individuals, peoples, and states as the entities both holding the rights *and* bearing the duties.[145] Not only is this legal nonsense, it forfeits any hope of securing political consensus by committing to the transformation of "international assistance and co-operation" (as a number of existing human rights treaties exhort) into a full-blown, legally enforceable right to development. Even leaving aside the obvious difficulties of defining "development," and even if it is agreed that something approaching an equal distribution of the world's resources among its people is highly desirable, the entire history of international relations suggests that winning universal agreement for such a proposal is well-nigh impossible .

There should be and there are arguments for why and how development can be more evenly distributed, but the promulgation of a right to development is not one of them. To believe that the push for an instrument of international human rights law would bring about any change in this respect is fanciful (like chasing a unicorn, as Jack Donnelly puts it), or worse counterproductive, because it promises what it cannot deliver and so weakens the rhetorical authority of human rights as a whole.[146]

Measuring Progress

As discussed in the previous chapter, considerable energy and effort are also expended by some in the human rights community who support the so-called human rights–based approach (HRBA) to development.[147] Such an approach, it is argued, would increase the human rights benefits flowing from development's primary objective to alleviate poverty, at the same time as reducing the detrimental human rights impacts of development. Some bilateral aid agencies have explicitly adopted HRBAs to development and others have not,[148] and pressure continues on the World Bank to recognize its human rights impacts, including more recently from certain state representative executive directors within the Bank itself.[149]

Yet, it remains unclear whether the results on the ground can be said to be markedly better in human rights terms when development is approached through an HRBA lens. This begs the question whether the whole HRBA enterprise is worth the effort. Some studies, for example, have even suggested that by signing up to human rights treaties, states might actually see a decline in human rights standards.[150] However, it must be said that the methodologies employed in these studies are plagued by exactly the same problems of indeterminacy as those studies that suggest the very opposite (namely, that states experience increased human rights standards when they sign up to relevant international treaties).[151] There are so many factors at play when contemplating human rights progress within real-world situations that in the end "observers are left with a confusing muddle in which everything matters, at least a little bit."[152] So it is with development projects. The measurement of their success or failure has also provided no clear indication of the impacts of an HRBA to development, let alone any definitive indication that the effects are beneficial. The multidimensional nature of human rights is such that it may simply be impossible "to devise a 'human rights index' of the kind often demanded in the international donor community," as political scientists Todd Landman and Edzia Carvalho conclude in their study of the challenges faced by anyone trying to measure human rights impacts.[153]

Once again, the source of the difficulty here is the extent of legitimate differences in interpretation and application that human rights standards themselves permit. Pinning down what is a good or better human rights outcome is inherently very difficult.[154] Behind the heat and light generated by many who are disturbed about the human rights impact of China's overseas development program, for example, there ought to be a more serious debate as to what precisely China is and is not doing in this regard, and how that compares with the Western aid orthodoxy. As development specialist Deborah Brautigam argues, China's "no-strings attached" approach to providing funding for economic industrialization has allowed recipient "countries to improve poor infrastructure, inadequate services, and weak institutions by focusing efforts on a limited geographical area."[155] Such objectives and outcomes would not sit uncomfortably with any OECD donor trying to achieve development with human rights and governance strings attached.[156]

In the end, a more productive perspective on the problem of integrating development and human rights is to recognize their inexorable convergence. Speaking of a "human rights approach" to development is misleading, argues former UN High Commissioner for Human Rights Mary Robinson. To do so conveys a sense of something wholly new or revolutionary, when as a matter of fact human rights have always been a part of development even if this fact has not always been recognized.[157]

The common feature in all of these critiques of human rights perspectives is the problem of overreach—either in terms of subject matter (a human rights approach to everything?), or in terms of what human rights laws are capable of achieving (they are not unambiguous blueprints for the management of all human affairs), or both. But to understand and accept that human rights have limits is not an admission of weakness or a compromise of the human rights project.[158] Quite the opposite. It represents one of their great strengths, as well as an opportunity to engage with and influence other important aspects of society and the human condition, including economic and financial circumstances. It is a grave mistake to treat human rights as one would a frail child, bubble-wrapping the idea against all possible intrusions.[159] Accommodating difference and debate is not only unavoidable in human rights, it is essential for maintaining their relevance and credibility in all conditions, including financial.

Repair

Denial, then, is as much an obstacle to better understanding and changing the ways human rights and finance relate to each other as are the problems of cheating and deceit encountered earlier in this chapter. Together they present a formidable challenge. Yet it is a challenge we cannot shirk. The interactions between human rights and finance have yielded beneficial outcomes and they can yield more if encouraged to do so. The relationship can be counseled in ways that focus on mutual interests, pay attention to political and legal imperatives, and, above all, draw on lessons learned from past and present mistakes. It is to these matters that we now turn in the concluding chapter.

Counseling and Reconciliation

"The mind will ever be unstable that has only prejudices to rest on, and the current will run with destructive fury when there are no barriers to break its force."
— Mary Wollstonecraft, *A Vindication of the Rights of Women* (1792)

"Because you believed I was capable of behaving decently, I did."
— Paulo Coelho, *The Devil and Miss Prym* (2000)

What Sort of Counsel?

A few years ago, on a live television program aired in the People's Republic of China, a six-year-old girl was asked what she wanted to be when she grew up. "An official," she replied. What kind of official, the interviewer pressed. "A corrupt official. Because corrupt officials have lots of things," she proudly responded.[1]

The type of relationship we maintain or create—or, through our governments, allow to be maintained, or created—between finance and human rights will be inherited by our children and likely copied and propagated by them. It is of the utmost importance, therefore, that we get it right, or at least try to get it right, sooner rather than later. By this stage in the book, we now better understand the nature of the relationship and its importance to many aspects of social and economic prosperity. We are, like well-intentioned friends or concerned stakeholders, in a position to offer counsel regarding those parts of the relationship we believe are not working well, or not working at all. So it is, in this final chapter that I take on this mantle and reflect upon what sorts of reforms are needed to rescue the relationship, ever mindful of the fact that one or the other or both of the parties may not welcome the interference, but they need to hear it nonetheless.

There are a number of approaches I might adopt in performing this role. I could for example, choose not to intrude at all; to smile nervously, shrug my shoulders, and mutter, que sera, sera. But having come this far, and armed with the knowledge gained along the way, that is simply not an option. Alternatively, I might begin the enterprise with earnest and ambitious intentions, only to let them wane when faced with the inevitable political resistance, swallowing my valor and settling for discrete tinkering on the edges. I might reach the same result if, on the other hand, I accepted from the outset that all we can realistically achieve is to paper over the cracks in the relationship. Or perhaps I could jump into the deep end by insisting that the two parties take a good long hard look at themselves and remember why it is that they are together in the first place, and what it takes to make the relationship a happier and more productive one. Corruption, whether "legal" or not, should not be allowed to occupy the mind of a six-year-old as emblematic of how to secure the "lots of things," both financial and nonfinancial, that constitute the good life. It is this path that I will take.

A helpful place to start down this road is with Gordon Brown. On October 14, 2008, one month after Lehman Brothers had filed for bankruptcy in the United States, and one week after the UK government had announced its intention to acquire a controlling interest in three major ailing banks, the then UK Prime Minister and former Treasurer delivered a speech in the Reuters Building in London.[2] The audience was packed with bankers and business leaders anxious to hear what more the government was going to do about the credit crunch and looming economic crisis. What he said may not have been music to their ears, but such were the circumstances that few openly demurred.

As both Brown and the bankers were by then feeling the blowtorch of political pressure to protect society's many small and powerless, as well as its few large and powerful, the Prime Minister did not mince words. He talked of the banking system's fall from grace—built on trust and confidence, both were now in short supply; of the ills of short-termism and the sins of financiers' "unfair incentives for irresponsibility or excessive risk-taking for which the rest of us have to pay"; and of a global financial system "too clouded with opacity [and] conflicts of interest." He underlined the government's responsibility to continue to protect the most vulnerable in these "tough times," and his commitment to addressing the problems of finance, not with bandaids, but with a surgical approach that gets to the root of the problem. His grand plan, he revealed, as supported by other European leaders, was to "build a new Bretton Woods, a new financial architecture."

At that time and later, other world leaders made similar high-minded and thoroughly principled arguments, including, some months later, the then newly elected U.S. President Barack Obama, who remarked: "We're called upon to recognize that the free market is the most powerful generative force for our prosperity; but it is not a free license to ignore the consequences of our actions."[3] There was, nevertheless, a sense that rhetoric was running ahead of reality. A catastrophic collapse of the global financial system was averted only by way of huge injections of public capital. And in the years that followed, regulations have required increases in financial firms' transparency and in their minimum capital holdings; overall levels of bank borrowing and leverage have been cur-tailed; and an international Financial Stability Board (FSB) has been created to coordinate and oversee the broad policies and actions of national financial authorities.[4] However, banking behemoths still thrive and continue to pose sys-temic risk;[5] bankers' pay and proclivity for skullduggery have remained high (or even increased); taxpayers have borne the risk and footed the bill of the financial sector bailouts;[6] and, as detailed in chapter 3,[7] the most vulnerable in society have been hit hardest by reduced social welfare spending at the same time as unemployment rates are rising.

This "reality," however, does not mean that the rhetoric was wrong. It was undoubtedly and evidently hard to translate into practice, but the diagnosis of the problems and recommended remedies were basically sound and still relevant today.

The Long Shadow of Financial Exceptionalism

Of these ailments and their causes, one stands out above all others: the capacity of finance's prevailing culture of self-assured exceptionalism (and the political clout it buys) to resist fundamental change. The world of finance has become so confident of its role as the *élan vital* of the economy that it seldom need con-cern itself with the exogenous consequences of its actions, up to and including the possibility of its own collapse.[8] In large part, it is either indifferent to mat-ters beyond its borders, or dismissive of them with vague references to trickle-down benefits from the expanding wealth it creates. Most of all, this level of self-possession has enabled bankers blithely to neither accept responsibility for the financial market chaos of 2007/08, nor feel the need to "give . . . any indica-tion that they are prepared to alter their business practices sufficiently radically to avoid a repetition."[9]

Even when banks are repeatedly prosecuted and fined for criminal behav-ior and questions are raised about the evidently poor state of financial corpo-rate culture that permits or even encourages such behavior, bankers are prone to react with petulance, sometimes bordering on the absurd. "Adolf Hitler comes to mind,"[10] is how David Murray, one of the Australia's leading bankers,[11] responded to the suggestion made by country's chief financial services regulator (the Australian Securities and Investments Commission [ASIC]) that the bank executives could be held criminally liable if bank culture tolerates or encour-ages breaches of corporate or criminal law.[12] Despite the fact that a string of legal scandals dogged Australian banks at the time—including allegations of rigging of benchmark interest rates, systemic failures to ensure the probity of finan-cial advisory services, and endemic life insurance malpractice[13]—Mr. Murray apparently considered such a response appropriate. Perhaps his indignation stemmed from the fact that he had recently chaired a year-long Financial System Inquiry that, while conceding that "a persistent theme of international political and regulatory discourse has been the breakdown in financial firms' behaviour," had summarily dismissed any notion that bank culture should be regulated by parliamentary legislation or government policy.[14] Or, maybe he was simply comforted by the likelihood that his audience on that occasion would be sympathetic to his remarks (it was a banking and wealth summit). Whatever the case, the episode graphically illustrates the distance that still exists between finance's view of itself and the expectations made of it by the rest of society.

How have we come to this? Money, after all, is nothing more than "an instrument which men have agreed upon to facilitate the exchange of one commodity for another," as Enlightenment philosopher David Hume put it.[15] His explanation of it as oil for the wheels of trade, and that by way of trade and commerce individuals and societies are best able to secure the basic necessities and conveniences of life, is as accurate today as it was 275 years ago.[16] Finance, or the management of money, is but a means. An important, even essential, means to be sure, but its efficient functioning is not an end itself. It is the ends to which we put the facility of finance that really matter, for while finance may be a mere instrument, it is not a neutral one. In the same way as water can sustain or destroy, and a gun can liberate or kill, so money can create and devastate. It all depends in whose hands it lies and what is done with it. As individuals, and through the organizations we engage with and the governments that represent us, we have the power and responsibility to fashion its use in ways that promote widespread human welfare rather than diminish it.

It is this point that has been lost sight of, both inside and outside finance. And it is to the re-argument of the point, as foreshadowed in chapter 1, that much of this book has been dedicated. Finance's facilitative role has to be explicitly reconnected with the goals we want to achieve through its agency; its role as a servant of economic and political processes, not their master, has to be underlined. Human rights can assist in this regard. Not by setting "standards for growth or economic productivity," but by setting "standards for the quality of living that individuals are able to achieve and the caliber of services that they receive," as Magdalena Sepúlveda argued when she was the UN Special Rapporteur on Extreme Poverty and Human Rights.[17]

It should not surprise us that the human rights expressed in international and domestic laws can be held up as goals toward which a financial system ought to strive to contribute. Strong, sustainable economies and safe, stable societies both depend on and promote the very political, social, and economic goods evoked by human rights—the rule of law to defend basic freedoms to life, individual security, nondiscrimination, speech, thought, religion, privacy, and assembly; to be able to vote and to participate in government; and to be assured of minimal welfare rights to food, health care, education, housing, sanitation, appropriate employment, and adequate conditions of and safety at work. Therefore, by way of its key supporting role in the establishment and maintenance of strong economies and stable societies, finance is inextricably committed to these human rights goals.

Levels of human rights protection act as a barometer of the health and success of a financial system precisely because they "underpin development, growth and stable societies through providing accountable institutions, healthy, educated and skilled workers, security in old age, and a safety net in times of economic disruption or transition."[18] So when a gross distortion in one or more of these human rights features is accompanied by severe failure in the financial markets, it signals the connections between the two worlds, even if they are not always immediate or obvious.

If, then, we are to acculturate finance in ways that reestablish its subordinate role in the pursuit of broader economic and social ends, human rights can and must have a part to play. Determining precisely what part is a responsibility to be shouldered by both financial and the human rights communities. Importantly, the process also presents an opportunity for them to do so in ways that are mutually beneficial.

The remainder of the chapter is dedicated to describing how this might be done. First, I explain what cultural and attitudinal changes are required to reorient the prevailing notion of financial exceptionalism such that the importance of promoting human rights goals (among other public goods) is recognized and accepted as a service finance can and must provide. Second, I explain why regulatory intervention is both desirable and necessary to secure and sustain such changes. And finally, I emphasize the responsibilities of engagement and education that both sides of the relationship must share if finance is to better support human rights, and human rights are to be used to legitimize finance.

Attitudes and Culture

As we have seen time and again throughout this book, the size of finance, its complexity, and its pervasion demand respect, if not always admiration, and the functions it serves in modern societies are essential and often appealing. These factors, however, have also been used as the basis for arguing, or more typically asserting, that finance must be treated exceptionally by those very same societies. What is important to finance, the reasoning goes, will be important for society as a whole. Further, given its complexity—no matter that such complexity was self-created and is self-perpetuated—it is best to ensure that societal interference is kept to a minimum. And where regulation is unavoidable or deemed necessary, it should be designed and administered by financial insiders. The abnegation of responsibility to or for external interests that this line of logic leads to is, I argue, precisely the fault we need to repair.

You may recall that in chapter 1 we encountered Roger Altman's interesting thinking on finance. As a former U.S. Deputy Treasury Secretary in the Clinton administration and now a prominent investment banker, Altman held forth on the immense power of global finance today, which, he argued (and despite comparing such power to "unusable nuclear weapons"), benefits society, at least in the long run.[19] He then added two important riders. First, he noted that "whether this power is healthy or not is beside the point. It is permanent;" and second, that "above all, there is no stopping the new policing role of the financial markets." These additional comments are revealing in light of what I am trying to argue. For while on the one hand, it is relatively easy to accept that the size and significance of global finance will be long-lasting, it is quite a different matter to dismiss so glibly the critical question of whether such power is healthy or not.

The permanence of power does not equate to its exercise in any way the power-holder pleases. Still less can Altman assert that it is financial markets that play the policing role (whether of finance itself, or of the rest of the economy, or of the polity?—Altman is not clear on this point), rather than it being the financial markets that are subject to policing. In any event, no matter the extent that finance has *in practice* come to influence or even control parts of our economic systems and social orders, that does not supplant what the line of authority *ought* to be. Democratic governance, even (indeed especially) in capitalist economies, is government by the people and for the people. Ultimately, it is the representative organs of public administration that must control organs of private power. When, in realpolitik, the reverse begins to ring true, it serves not to justify the circumstance, but merely to highlight the aberration and signal the pressing need for its correction.

Nobel Laureate Robert Shiller is another distinguished and sympathetic voice on the need for systemic financial reform. His exposés of the fallacy of assuming rationality in financial markets and the need to address the detrimental consequences that flow therefrom have been foundational to arguments (including my own) for financial reforms that enhance wider public benefits.[20] Yet human rights, in Shiller's view, add nothing to this enterprise; indeed, if anything, he sees them as a hindrance. This would be a significant concern if it were backed up by a serious and well-constructed argument about the nature of human rights in the context of finance. But, as we saw earlier in chapter 2, it is not.[21] In an economist, even one of the world's most respected, we would not necessarily expect to encounter a deep knowledge of the vast and varied subject of human rights (though certainly that has not stopped Amartya Sen). However, having raised the topic in his work on using finance as a powerful instrument for the greater good, it is fair to expect that Shiller would grasp at least the basics of what human rights—and specifically human rights laws—say and do. Alas, the grounds for his dismissal of human rights as being of no use for his project are both superficial and erroneous. To pronounce that human rights are too "absolute" and lack flexibility and compromise is a profound misrepresentation of how they are in fact stated in law and practiced on the ground.[22] International human rights laws expressly accept the existence of financial (and other resource) limitations, while pushing always that they be employed so far as is possible for human rights ends.[23]

As my discussions in chapter 6 illustrate,[24] such absolutist naiveté can also (sadly and unhelpfully) be found within the human rights community itself, so perhaps we might cut Shiller some slack here. Unfortunately, he compounds the mistake by implying that where human rights conflict with "financial reality," then it is human rights that need to change, not finance. There is much to lament here, for as I say, Robert Shiller is an economist who understands well the socially destructive and constructive powers of finance and has said much of importance about how to limit the former and promote the latter. His foray into human rights, therefore—especially in the context of the objectives of this book—ought to be especially welcomed as an attempt to bridge the gap by a leading figure from the side of finance. As it is, however, it serves more to emphasize the gap, than to close it.

Empathy

Human rights, properly understood, do in fact have much to offer financial thinking, especially in terms of any project seeking (to use Shiller's terms) to reclaim finance for the common good. Central to the entire project of human rights is the notion of individual dignity, the assurance of which stems directly from a universal notion of mutual respect.[25] Such respect—that you grant, and are granted—is itself reliant not just on one's capacity to recognize, but also to empathize, with others. "Compassion," is how some have sought to characterize this sort of "active concern for others."[26] It is, in the words of human rights scholar and lawyer Conor Gearty, "that part of human rights that insists on making things better, as well as on stopping things from getting worse."[27] Building on the separate work of philosophers James Griffin and A. C. Grayling, Gearty is concerned to get to the root of what it is that we mean when we talk of human rights today, and specifically, what role compassion for others plays in that process. "We all want the chance 'to make the good life for ourselves,'" he concludes, which necessarily entails not just that each individual possesses autonomy and certain minimal levels of health and education that enable them to take the chance, but also that individuals not be unfairly prevented by others from pursuing their chosen path.[28]

Helping others as well as yourself is what philosopher Richard Rorty so eloquently describes as the essence of "fraternity" (or "empathy" by another name). Rorty invokes a passage in John Steinbeck's iconic anthem on poverty during the Great Depression, *The Grapes of Wrath*, to illustrate his point. The novel records the travails of one family of Oklahoma farmers, including when, impoverished, destitute, and on the road, they share their food with an even more desperate migrant family. "Steinbeck writes: 'I have little food' plus 'I have none.' If from this problem the sum is 'We have some food,' the movement has direction."[29] For Rorty, that direction is one of social hope, "that the promise of American life could be redeemed only so long as Americans were willing to sacrifice for the sake of fellow Americans—only as long as they could see the government not as stealing their tax money but as needing it to prevent unnecessary suffering."[30]

This visceral, human impulse to consider the plight of others is born of reason. We may not employ it as fully and often as we should, but our capacity to reason allows, or even compels us, to empathize at least some of the time, while always providing us with the opportunity to do more. It is the great civilizing effect that reason can have on our broader social relations with each other that has been one of the greatest legacies of the Enlightenment. Acts of self-sacrifice that benefit others, muses Adam Smith, appear to run contrary to what seems to be the natural, human disposition: indifference toward the tragedy of strangers. Yet he suggests that if we were faced with the choice between losing a little finger and the loss of one hundred million people in an earthquake in some far-off land, the vast majority of us would choose to lose the finger. What compels us to do so? asks Smith. What force is "capable of counteracting the strongest impulses of self-love," as he puts it? His answer is as impassioned as it is forthright:

> It is reason, principle, conscience, the inhabitant of the breast, the man within, the great judge and arbiter of our conduct. It is he who, whenever we are about to act so as to affect the happiness of others, calls to us, with a voice capable of astonishing the most presumptuous of our passions, that we are but one of the multitude, in no respect better than any other in it; and that when we prefer ourselves so shamefully and so blindly to others, we become the proper objects of resentment, abhorrence, and execration. It is from him only that we learn the real littleness of ourselves, and of whatever relates to ourselves, and the natural misrepresentations of self-love can be corrected only by the eye of this impartial spectator. It is he who shows us the propriety of generosity and the deformity of injustice; the propriety of resigning the

greatest interests of our own, for the yet greater interests of others, and the deformity of doing the smallest injury to another, in order to obtain the greatest benefit to ourselves. It is not the love of our neighbour, it is not the love of mankind, which upon many occasions prompts us to the practice of those divine virtues. It is a stronger love, a more powerful affection, which generally takes place upon such occasions; the love of what is honourable and noble, of the grandeur, and dignity, and superiority of our own characters.[31]

Though separated by more than 200 years, the social hope expressed by Rorty and by Smith does not amount to mere wishful thinking. There is considerable evidence to show that over time and with education, our faculties for reason have increased, and with them, argues American psychologist Steven Pinker, so has our facility for compassion.[32] Pinker bases his argument on philosopher Jim Flynn's groundbreaking work in the 1980s that gave birth to the so-called Flynn Effect. Realizing that organizations responsible for administering IQ tests were regularly, and always upwardly, resetting the number of correct answers required to ensure that the average test score remained at 100, Flynn surmised that this must be due to increasing levels of IQ. He then set about proving his hypothesis by analyzing IQ datasets from thirty countries around the world (including both his native United States and his adopted New Zealand).[33] The same bracket creep was observed in them all. The Flynn Effect was especially marked in respect of abstract reasoning (as opposed to factual recall and arithmetic), and it was this feature that attracted Pinker's attention.

As part of his grand theory of humanity's steady movement toward greater peace and civility, Pinker sees the rise of reason as a key causal feature. Reason, he argues, has a direct pacifying impact on individuals and, through them, communities. From his own work and that of others he shows the statistical correlation between levels of reasoning ability and self-control, whereby with higher levels in both, violence tends to be abstracted "as a problem to be solved rather than a contest to be won."[34] This diminution in violence is tied up with more sophisticated considerations of the views and circumstances of others and a widespread tendency to make "better moral commitments"—in a word, empathy. Such a propitious circumstance, he suggests, must owe something to our "enhanced powers of reason—specifically, the ability to set aside immediate experience, detach oneself from a parochial vantage point, and frame one's ideas in abstract, universal terms."[35] Echoing Adam Smith's invocation of notions of honor and dignity, Pinker labels the phenomenon a "*moral* Flynn effect" and credits it with being a deciding factor in the rise in the recognition and respect for human rights throughout the last century and into the present one.[36]

Responsibilities

In actively or passively helping others, we all have responsibilities. International human rights law may impose specific obligations on states, but domestic laws, moral pressures, cultural mores, and social expectations spread the burden to all of us to have due regard for each other. There are no exceptions here; no individuals are exempt, no groups or classes are excepted, and no industry sector is excused. Indeed if, as evidence suggests,[37] wealth and access to good education go hand in hand and better education increases one's capacity to reason, then, following Pinker, privileged communities should be expected to be more compassionate and to show more consideration for others. That is, even when we encounter everyday examples to the contrary. The fact that most of us would consider the following example of behavior to be reprehensible, even if familiar, is surely itself a sign that overall, society today is kinder, gentler, and more empathetic—or is at least capable of being so.

In October 2015 a boy from a private school in Melbourne, Australia, inadvertently created a media storm by taunting students at supposedly inferior public schools on the eve of the statewide, final-year exams.[38] The 18-year-old posted on Facebook that he was "externally grateful" to his parents that they had sent him to a good, private school instead of a "poverty stricken shit-hole in Pakenham [another Melbourne suburb]." "You give me hope," he continued, " because [I] know there are so many more retards like you out there that I will easily beat tomorrow and over the next two weeks. I hope you all fuck-up really bad so [I] can see your posts tomorrow." Contemptible though this exhibition of arrogance and spite was, it was the responses of some parents to the story's publication that was especially deplorable. In one of the many media chat shows and forums that ran with this story, one self-declared mother of private school children named "Zara" rang in to tell the show's presenter, who had been critical of a system that produces such nastiness, that she was surprised how naïve he was. Did he not understand "that that's half the reason we send our children to private schools . . . to realize that they are part of an elite group . . . and to walk around with their nose[s] in the air?" The fact that Zara appeared sincerely to believe in what she said is unpleasant enough; more mind-numbing is the fact that she was so willing to advertise it.

Wherever sentiments like this run openly, empathy will always struggle to be heard above the din. Yet even in this example, Pinker's "moral Flynn effect" may provide the answer. For it turned out that the young man's intellect had badly let him down compared to the standards of the public school students he scorned. One of the latter shot back a corrected version of his Facebook message highlighting his many spelling mistakes and grammatical errors, awarding it a "D+" and signing off with "see me after class."[39] Money, it seems, can buy an education, but not always the wit to use it wisely.

When the privileged community we have in mind comprises the exceptionally financially literate, we would expect its members to appreciate how important wealth is to one's security and comfort, especially to those who have neither. Here, once again, we should expect as much despite abundant examples to the contrary. As a society, we cannot afford to condone, still less to promote, a financial system based on claims of exceptionalism that promote indifference to the exogenous consequences of its actions, while at the same time, demanding freedom from interference by reasoning that what is good for finance will be good for all. Human rights goals—the base ingredients of a good life—not only comprise some of the most important ends to which finance must be set to work. Insofar as they depend on compassion as the key driver in their delivery, they also pinpoint the changes required in finance's corporate culture and the individual responsibilities of those within it.

Skeptics might protest that surely such expectations would throw sand in the gears of finance, maybe even destroy the whole machine. Demanding that bankers and banks shoulder greater responsibilities born of compassionate recognition of the plight of those nonbankers and nonbanks affected by their actions would be to rob finance of its cutting edge, its driving force—in short, its greed. Not so, I must respond. Greed, as I made clear in chapter 3, is an indispensable feature of finance, but it must necessarily be controlled. The selfish pursuit of one's own pleasures is in finance, as throughout capitalism, a powerful driving force. It is at the core of each individual's human rights–based pursuit of a good life, albeit qualified to the extent that it unfairly restricts the rights or goals of others and according to agreed standards imposed by community-wide interests. This is the nature of democratic society. It is also, it seems, the nature of the human condition. As Gearty observes, in his foray into a Darwinian analysis of our human animal instincts, we not only hold contradictory impulses, we are also conscious of doing so. Thus, "on the one hand, there is the capacity for acts of compassion, hospitality and kindliness, on the other for cruelty, humiliation and callousness." So integral is this dichotomy to our being that human evolution can be fairly described as " 'a constant struggle, not for existence itself, but between selfishness and altruism—a struggle that neither can win.' "[40]

Capitalism has long battled with this insoluble dilemma. The limits imposed on capitalist enterprise in democratic societies (by way, for example, of laws on taxation, health and safety, environmental protection, nondiscrimination, and labor rights) are drawn from the very same liberal, rights-based principles as those that encourage the enterprise in the first place (freedom of association, movement, and speech; privacy; fair trial; nondiscrimination; and education). Freedom comes with a price. There is an argument, what is more, that man, as an economic (and financial) being, should not wish it otherwise; that a degree of public sanction of one's activities is not just to be tolerated, but is desirable.

Esteem

This is one way to interpret the ever-present yearning for esteem that exists in all of us, including (indeed especially) in respect of our work. To have ourselves and our work valued as worthy, or virtuous, or honorable, or estimable, is one of desires that rules our hearts, as Geoffrey Brennan and Philip Pettit contend in their work on the subject. Economist and philosopher, respectively, Brennan and Pettit have constructed a compelling argument for the power of esteem as a driving force in human economic endeavor. Drawing on an old, but in recent times neglected, tradition of thought on the issue (from Plato through to the Enlightenment philosophers) they argue for its rediscovery, specifically in the context of what economics today should be concerned about. People's desire for esteem, as well as their desire to avoid "disesteem," they maintain, can induce them individually to adjust their behavior. This in turn can lead to changes in the behavior of entire communities, which in time become embedded in and determinate of social relations.[41] Esteem, in other words, is economically significant, so much so that for Brennan and Pettit, it amounts to a "third hand" that influences or determines economic action—the "intangible hand," as they call it, sitting between Smith's "invisible hand" of the market and the "iron hand" of state management of the economy.

What is of interest to us is this capacity to alter, or to entrench, the behavior of individuals and the communities to which they belong, for it holds out the possibility of shifting attitudes and actions in finance away from being self-centered and introspective, toward being cognizant of relevant outside parties and respectful of their interests and demands. However, in finance, as in all fields, the crucial question one must ask of esteem is: "[e]stimable in the eyes of whom?" It is fair to say that most of us seek most avidly the respect of those in whom we invest respect. This can, of course, yield disagreeable outcomes, as when "those in a particular group [seek] to earn credit with each other by behaving in a manner that is detrimental to the population at large or to other groups."[42]

Certainly, there is no shortage of examples of such behavior in finance. The "dog-eat-dog" ethos of the financial markets, as we saw in chapter 3, spawns a culture that reveres the toughest and the meanest players, who, if need be, will ignore ethics and flout the law. A May 2015 report published jointly by the University of Notre Dame and securities law firm Labaton Sucharow details the results of a survey on financial workplace ethics of more than 1,223 financial services personnel working in the United States and the UK (the largest such survey ever conducted). The results, as the report tersely notes, "are not pretty."[43] The data are indeed compelling: "Nearly half (47%) of all respondents find it likely that their competitors have engaged in illegal or unethical activity in order to gain an edge in the market." And even within their own firms, the percentage of those who suspect illegal or unethical behavior among colleagues is alarming at 23%, with those newest to the industry being the most likely to suspect misbehavior. The survey's "cool $10 million" question (whether you'd engage in insider trading to make $10 million if there was no chance of arrest) also yielded high positive responses—32% for UK respondents and 24% for ones in the United States.[44]

But perhaps the most disturbing conclusions to be drawn from the report are, first, that the situation seems to getting worse. The first two figures cited in the last sentence represented marked spikes from the data collected in a previous Labaton Sucharow survey in 2012, "despite three years of significant reforms and high-profile prosecutions." And second, the prospects that this will turn around quickly do not look strong. "An astonishing 17% of all respondents find it unlikely that company leaders would report misconduct to law enforcement," the report notes. It then adds that one in ten of all respondents had been asked to sign confidentiality agreements by their firms that would prevent them from disclosing illegal or unethical behavior to the authorities (a figure that rises to one in four for all those earning more than $500,000 per annum), despite the fact that such restrictive clauses are themselves illegal. That said, the survey did find that 89% of industry professionals "would report misconduct given the incentives and protections such as those offered by the SEC [U.S. Securities and Exchange Commission] whistle-blower program," but this ray of hope is dulled by the fact that "37% of respondents are still not aware of the SEC's program."[45]

Sleaze

Apparently, the esteem sought in this environment is associated with actions that are detrimental to the public interest. Yet financial players, it seems, are quite aware of that. What the study reveals is a classic example of collective cognitive dissonance—the simultaneous holding of contradictory beliefs—that not only permits or excuses the behavior, but actively perpetuates it. Suspending belief in what you see before your eyes is one part of the explanation for the recurrence of financial crises, which are so predictable (as outcomes, if not their precise timing) that they have been labeled "a hardy perennial."[46] It is also the result of what Robert Shiller calls "the unfortunate incentives to sleaziness inherent in finance."[47] This observation is in fact amply borne out in the Notre Dame/ Labaton Sucharow survey, which notes, with some dismay, "that nearly one-third of those surveyed (32%) believe there are compensation structures/bonus plans at their company that incentivize [*sic*] employees to compromise ethical standards or violate the law."[48] The preeminent economic leaders' Group of Thirty (an association of high-level financial actors) reaches a similar conclusion after analyzing the internal supervisory processes (covering corporate culture and ethics) of forty-six major banks worldwide, declaring that

> persistent supervisory action in cases where there has been demonstrably poor behavior . . . has manifested itself through weak adherence to internal codes of conduct or specific conduct-of-business requirements specified by regulators. These cases have included failures to properly test client suitability for a specific product; poor or opaque product documentation; improper sales tactics; and poor post-sales processes centered on fair customer treatment, and breaches of client asset protection. The high-profile cases and other cultural breakdowns demonstrate a failure by banks to consistently promulgate and reinforce desired values and the desired culture within their organizations and staff."[49]

This disdain extends even to criminal laws, where the consequences of flouting them appear to be ignored, or at least quickly forgotten. As we saw in chapter 6, evidence of substantial and widespread recidivism among big banks is provided by criminal lawyer Brandon Garrett's detailed examination of the recent (post-crisis) history of criminal prosecutions of global financial firms in the United States. Reflecting on his findings about the regularity with which some of the world's largest banks are charged with the same or similar offences (and then negotiate settlements), Garrett "wonders how seriously prosecutors take recidivism among major financial institutions and how effective prosecutions have been in changing any underlying culture of law-breaking."[50]

Albeit tainted, the attraction of finance, it seems, still reaches well beyond its boundaries into the wide world of wannabe financiers. As both movie director Oliver Stone (*Wall Street* [1987]) and author Michael Lewis (with *Liar's Poker* [1989]) found, even when the intention is to chasten by exposing the gruesome details of just how mean and unethical bankers can be, rather than being appalled, plenty found the message appealing. As Lewis ruefully noted when emptying his bulging mail bag following the huge success of *Liar's Poker*, "I was knee-deep in letters from students at Ohio State who wanted to know if I had any other secrets to share. They'd read my book as a how-to manual."[51] Oliver Stone's opinion is, if anything, even more pessimistic. In an interview in June 2015 he remarked: "Gordon Gekko [the central figure in *Wall Street*] was an immoral character that became worshipped for the wrong reasons . . . the banks became a version of him, speculating for themselves. To hell with the investor."[52] Those on the inside of finance have made the same charge no less passionately. In *Alchemists of Loss*, Kevin Dowd and Martin Hutchinson (finance scholar and former investment banker, respectively) hold that finance today "focuses on marketing and sales, form over substance, and never mind the client; an obsession with the short-term and the next bonus; a preference for speculation and trading over long-term investment; stratospheric remuneration levels for practitioners, paid for through exploitation of clients and taxpayers, or 'rent-seeking,' the erosion of the old governance mechanisms and out-of-control conflicts of interests."[53]

Against this manifestly challenging backdrop, however, Brennan and Pettit's thesis does offer some grounds for optimism. For if and when esteem is sought on a wider plane—that is, beyond finance—the opportunity to change attitudes and shift cultures becomes apparent. Brennan and Pettit offer a number of examples of such "norm changes," including the acceptance of rubbish recycling, the decriminalization and mainstream embrace of (or, at least, indifference regarding) homosexuality, and the mounting disapprobation of tax avoidance, each of which snowballed once a critical mass of people joined the movement's pioneers in their "approval of conformity." What may start out as "moralizing talk" may be transformed into new or altered norms of action when expressed and reinforced by laws that "signal the expectations of the citizenry in general" and incriminate offenders both by punishment and exposing them to the forces of shame. This "intangible hand" of regulation, the pair argue, is the result of the "activat[ion] of the powerful forces that drive behavior within the economy of esteem."[54]

Capacity for Change

Finance may not be as impervious as it seems to the same forces of positive esteem within it that can yield beneficial results beyond it. There is little in its current structure and cultural proclivities that cannot be altered, even if powerful interests currently sustain them. As we saw in earlier chapters, banking was once boring—simple and rigid, but effective and prudent. Bankers' incentives reflected these circumstances, and the market had much more to say about success and failure, such that bankers' pay was for nearly half a century following the Wall Street Crash in 1929 and ensuing global depression no more spectacular than that of the corporate captains in other sectors. We also saw how, following previous financial crises, banks failed and bankers were jailed; regulators had teeth and they were not shy to use them. Above all, trust—that most essential of financial ingredients—has certainly previously been much greater and more readily acknowledged, both within the sector and in the broader community. Today, the qualities admired in finance (or at least accepted as necessary for success) are not being boring, or prudent, or even trustworthy, but rather are arrogance, an appetite for risk, and a killer instinct.

A narrow ledge upon which arguments for more empathy and altered perspectives of self-esteem might be built is provided by the results of the coin-tossing psychology study I discussed back in chapter 1, which sought to determine whether finance attracted cheats or made them. The data, you may recall, favored the latter explanation.[55] The slim encouragement this provides is that despite any inclinations to the contrary, we are not battling nature, but rather nurture, of a peculiarly financial kind. So, while still a monumental task, it is surely easier to seek to induce or influence change in financial culture than to try to alter the predispositions of individual financiers, still less their wholesale substitution for a new, cleaner cohort of bankers (wherever they may be found).

To be sure, the ultimate goal is to instill new or altered attitudes in the individual actors that comprise the financial system, but that requires cultural change at the systemic level. It is a classic example of a collective action problem—the perception of an inherent disadvantage in being the first to make the move—so for any attempt at cultural change to stand a chance of success in finance it must involve intervention by the state, whether directive and admonitory, or guiding and exhortatory. But it is far from a hopeless quest. At least some banks, it seems, are genuinely wedded to improving their cultural genetics. In its study of how forty-six major banks across the world manage cultural and ethical values internally, the Group of Thirty spotlighted at least one (unnamed) bank that had entrenched systems aimed at "lasting change in culture and behavior." Their report noted:

> Recognizing the first tier of management as critical in facilitating the inculcation of values into the firm, the bank holds dedicated "cultural off sites" for the senior management teams twice a year to allow time for discussion, with an emphasis on cultural issues.... [T]he bank does not present the organization's work on culture as corporate social responsibility, but rather as a broader program closely aligned with its core strategy. The bank includes concrete targets within its behavioral program, ensuring it is taken seriously by investors and referenced in financial communications (quarterly performance reviews, annual reports, and so forth).[56]

Regulatory Intervention and Risk

Cultural change is seldom quick and never easy, especially if there are entrenched interests opposed to it. In the case of finance, no change, or merely superficial change, is not an option. For if we are to make finance more efficient, effective, and "socially useful,"[57] we must necessarily free it from the ruinous introspection of exceptionalism by reasserting its subaltern role to the real economy. From the perspective of finance therefore, such change is as much about reestablishing the social and economic legitimacy of finance, as it about providing better protection and promotion of human rights standards. That it is the organs of the state that must take the lead in effecting or overseeing such cultural reformation is a reflection of their political legitimacy and democratic accountability.[58] Certainly the answer to the problem cannot be to *de*regulate, or rather, to regulate such as to free finance from as many restraints as possible.[59] Freedom unlimited ultimately defeats itself, as it permits the strong to exploit the weak, whether in finance or physical relations. "The freedom of the movement of your fists," as philosopher Karl Popper reminds us, "is limited by the position of your neighbour's nose."[60] Intervention backed by the power of the state, as Popper goes on to argue at length, not only authorizes freedom, it also establishes its boundaries. In this way the state is able to protect the weak, ensuring their freedom is not denied them, and thereby save the whole enterprise from fatal compromise.[61]

In the context of finance, regulatory intervention is required for one matter that lies at the heart of the system—the management or control of risk.[62] For it is with the detrimental consequences for human rights of financial risk management gone wrong that much of this book is concerned and has sought to explain and illustrate. The controlling hand of state, I suggest, is needed both to superintend (but not to supersede) the invisible hand of the market and to guide the intangible hand of esteem, at three levels of finance. First, in the identification of risk—to do so more effectively. Second, in the allocation of risk—to do so more efficiently. And third, in the relationship between risk management and the rule of law—to concede that mismanagement of risk will be subject to legal sanction. The culture of financial exceptionalism has been and remains the major obstacle to reform in all three respects. That is the nature of the challenge for the state to overcome if it is to make any headway in the quest to restore trust and integrity in the financial system and enhance its social utility. Let me explain by way of examples of the sorts of changes—extant, incipient, or mooted—associated with each of these three levels.

Identification of Risk

The financial system's record of identifying essentially nonfinancial risks is poor, even when the consequences of such risks are grave, socially, politically, and economically. As we encountered in chapter 6, despite the gargantuan proportions of the global illicit economy, far from proving a substantial bulwark against its further encroachment, financial institutions have been complicit in its expansion. Filthy lucre—stolen, extorted, or illegally earned, from developed as well as many developing states—is being laundered all too easily through Western banks. Financiers and associated professional services are aiding tax evasion on a mammoth scale (and eagerly facilitating tax-avoidance schemes that sail close to the wind of illegality). And public as well as private financial institutions are complicit in human rights abuses perpetrated by states, not simply by providing financial support to authoritarian regimes (engagement is in most cases preferable to ostracization),[63] but by failing to take adequate steps to ensure that their "support does not facilitate the commission of further gross human rights violations."[64] The due diligence required in identifying and analyzing risk in these circumstances is undoubtedly of a higher order, but that is no excuse for not doing it, or doing it poorly.

The inherent dangers of failure in this regard are most graphically illustrated in respect of terrorist financing, which today manifests itself in many new and sophisticated forms, in addition to its traditional modes of theft, extortion, racketeering, blackmail, and kidnapping for ransom.[65] The intergovernmental Financial Action Task Force (FATF) documented a raft of emerging terrorist financing risks in a 2015 report that includes the use of foreign fighters, social media, digital currencies, Internet payments systems, mobile money, and whole businesses based on the expropriation and sale of natural resources, such as oil, minerals, and metals.[66] Terrorist organizations even run their own banks—at its height, ISIS had taken over and controlled some eighty bank branches in northern Iraq and eastern Syria.[67] In all this, there can be little doubt that illicit finance is entering the licit financial system. The sheer size of ISIS's wealth, for example, which according to a joint report by King's College London and the accounting firm Ernst & Young was up to $1.9 billion at its peak in 2014, points to that inevitability.[68] While one might safely suppose that Western banks are not willingly providing financial services for terrorist organizations (at least not openly), they are almost certainly doing so unwittingly (or at least by turning a blind eye). Such being the case, the same point applies here about the need for far greater due diligence, including, as the FATF puts it, the use of financial and nonfinancial intelligence to "focus on the ultimate recipients of the funds, rather than just the source of the funds."[69] This is a task that must be undertaken by the banks themselves, but carried out according to the demands made of them by state authorities, and as enforced by those same authorities.[70]

Allocation of Risk

Central to all financial models is the question of how it allocates risk. As a byproduct of economic innovation, financial risk is unavoidable and therefore endured. Even when the risk attracts grossly disproportionate financial losses or gains, it can be tolerated when those gains and losses are borne by the risk-takers themselves. When, however, the risk bearers include those far beyond the category of those taking the risk—that is, in economic terms, the risk poses significant negative externalities—then the financial system cannot be so accommodating. Furthermore, when such risks are so large, they constitute a threat to the whole system. Such systemic risk, as we discussed in the previous chapter in respect of strategically important financial institutions, is a front-and-center concern for global finance following the 2007/08 crisis.

That there is such alarm should not surprise us. For the pure speculation that today constitutes so much of the derivatives markets was not so long ago outlawed under gaming control legislation in many countries, including the UK and the United States.[71] As international finance lawyer Ross Buckley neatly explains the prior position: "A contract by which a farmer locks in a price for their wheat crop when it is harvested, or by which an airline guarantees a future price for jet fuel, were both valid, but a contract by which a speculator places a bet on future wheat or fuel prices was not."[72] The reasoning here was simple enough—control speculation and you limit the misallocation of risk. Those beyond the parties to the financial transaction—namely, the rest of society—are not thereby burdened with the risk of transaction's failure.

So when these controls were removed by way of financial deregulation in the 1980s and 1990s, the "rest of society" was exposed to the risks of large speculative bubbles bursting. When enough creditors lose faith in the capacity of certain debtors to repay, it can precipitate a financial crisis that cascades into bank collapses, government bailouts or sovereign defaults, and community-wide austerity measures. As we saw in the early chapters of this book, such events impact directly on levels of human rights protection by limiting the financial capacity both of individuals to obtain or maintain rights standards by themselves, and of the state to provide welfare for those who cannot do so, or who do so inadequately.

The attempts of states to regain some control over the financial system, even if only to limit the volatility of boom/bust cycles, are frequently rebuffed by the depth and strength of the sector's resistance to changes it sees as compromising its privileged status. While today some restraint may have been imposed by higher capital adequacy requirements, the global FSB is only just beginning to come to terms with the systemic risk posed by the still-rampant hedge fund–driven derivatives speculation.[73] The post–financial crisis implementation of substantial restrictions on the extent to which commercial banks are permitted to trade in securities on their own accounts—under the so-called Volcker Rule enshrined in the *Dodd-Frank Wall Street Reform and Consumer Protection Act* (2010)—was repeatedly delayed (as of late 2017 these restrictions are yet to come fully into force), and the coverage has been qualified.[74] That is despite the well-recognized tendency of such "proprietary trading" to perpetuate conflicts of interest and destabilize capital markets.[75] Reforms to the perverting pay-based incentives in the sector have been superficial and ineffective, as has been graphically illustrated by the "business as usual" attitude toward pay adopted since the 2007/08 financial crisis.[76] And proposals to take the heat out of overactive capital markets by imposing a financial transactions tax (FTT) have been successfully resisted ever since the idea in its modern form was first advanced in 1972 by Nobel Laureate (as he was to become) economist James Tobin. This is despite the fact that the proposed tax is tiny (between 0.01% and 0.1% of the value of any share, stock, commodity, or currency transaction) and is aimed principally at transactions in so-called high-frequency trading. However, the imposition of such a tax promises to yield substantial dividends in terms of market efficiency, risk management, and government revenue.[77]

Certainly, governments' resolve in these matters must be stiffened. This requires not only that governments overcome the torpidity of their regulatory capture, as documented in chapter 6, but also that they institute and enforce appropriate laws and regulations.

Risk and the Rule of Law

As stated earlier, at the base of all financial transactions is the essential requirement of trust between the parties, including, and especially, the disclosure of relevant risks. The fiduciary relationship that exists between financiers and their clients is a legal one that can and should be enforced. The problem is, however, that over the past three decades trust has been so eroded in the finance sector that the value of this legally enforceable obligation has been correspondingly reduced. Not only has the relationship become clouded as the variety and complexity of financial vehicles grew and the capacity of legislators and state regulators to understand, let alone control, them diminished. A more pernicious force has also been in play.

As former New York State Attorney-General Eliot Spitzer tellingly observed when interviewed in Charles Ferguson's *Inside Job* about the legality of what was happening on Wall Street during his eight-year tenure: "What used to be viewed as a conflict of interest is now viewed as a synergy! Those in the industry and even most regulators had defined the problem away; . . . it was all a way to handle denial."[78] The whole industry, in other words, was making concerted efforts to redefine the fundamentals of finance in order to justify the perversity of the direction it was taking. The consequence, as Douglas Hodge, the CEO of a leading investment company, puts it, was that "we forgot the most basic principle of our profession: that finance is a means to an end."[79]

The most extreme forms of this systemic breach of trust contravene criminal laws, but for those laws to be effective there must be both adequate detection and prosecution of offenders. We saw in the last chapter that the pursuit of banks in the criminal courts has had mixed results and has not (yet?) achieved the level of deterrence hoped for. Moves to prosecute, let alone to secure convictions of, individual bankers (especially senior ones) have been pitiful, despite apparently sufficient grounds to support such actions.[80] Whistle-blowing is one important source of information that could help in the substantiation of financial wrong-doing, but it is still heavily underutilized. The lack of awareness of, or confidence in, whistleblower protection laws (or their absence altogether), together with a culture of resistance toward the practice within the sector, strongly mitigates against its wider use. The 2015 Swiss case of HSBC pressing criminal charges for industrial espionage against a whistle-blower who had leaked details of the bank's blind-eye approach to large-scale tax evasion among its clients is a striking example of both the hubris of the bank (to go after the complainant, rather than address the complaint) and the cowed and craven demeanor of a state that provides no legal protections for whistle-blowers (Switzerland has failed to enact such legislation despite a draft having been on the table for more than a decade).[81]

The rule of law can be a leader as well as follower in such circumstances. In both cases, the prevailing culture of acceptable or applauded behavior will have a strong influence. In the years following the GFC we have seen banks pontificating over their human rights responsibilities,[82] central bank governors alluding to the importance of taking into consideration social factors (including, per force, human rights protections) in their operations,[83] and even business school graduates taking pledges to "serve the greater good."[84] Yet, as much of this book has striven to demonstrate, an attitude of financial exceptionalism still prevails, with predictable consequences for the rest of the economy and society.

Alternatives

Dissatisfaction with the levels of economic and social services provided by traditional finance has certainly been a factor behind the rise viable alternatives, ranging from the relatively straightforward so-called fintech financial vehicles, which allow peer-to-peer lending, crowd-funding, and nonbank schemes for international money transfers, to the highly sophisticated digital crypto-currencies like Bitcoin.[85] Though all of these disruptor alternatives are still small in scale compared to regular banking operations, they are growing in exposure and popularity precisely because they remove regular banks (and the need for a central bank) from the transaction process. The essential ingredient of trust is provided by the parties themselves rather than by a separate, independent institution such as a bank. Harking back to this book's opening pages, these new financial modes are in fact far better (though not foolproof)[86] representations of the balancing power of mutual self-interests that drive a financial system than Alan Greenspan's misplaced trust in the self-interest of modern bankers as they presently operate.

Still, no matter how intriguing, such innovations are for the moment not the solution to our problem of how to make finance more ethical, empathetic, and effective in its role as a social utility.

Reaching Across the Divide

The first step toward reconciliation between finance and human rights requires finance taking one step back. Finance's special pleading that, due to its size and self-proclaimed systemic importance, it ought to be treated leniently or more favorably than other industry sectors must be abandoned. It lacks justification, as we have seen, on political, social, or economic grounds and amounts to little more than a tremendously elaborate hoax. Yet it has potency. When finance raged and economies thrived, many of us were ready to believe in the emperor's new clothes. Even when finance dried up and economies stalled, our preparedness to see the emperor's nakedness for what it really is has been deplorably lacking. The challenge, therefore, is essentially an educative one. It needs to be made clear how finance's assertions cannot be sustained, even according to their own premises—most notably, contradictory exceptionalist claims demanding freedom from state interference when business is booming are reversed when serious busts occur and the state is called to the rescue.

The educational offensive has to be mounted within the sector itself (that is, by financiers themselves and their industry representative bodies), as well as by its regulatory overseers and political masters. It must be promoted by industry-insider champions and it has to include such important intellectual nurseries of financiers as business schools. The appointment of a genuine and well-credentialed human rights advocate such as Mike Posner to the Stern School of Business at New York University, for example, is a welcome innovation from within a category of educational establishments typically associated with apologia of finance.[87] The very fact that the Dean of the Stern School, in announcing Posner's appointment, stressed how exceptional it was to have a major business school focus on human rights as well as profit because "citizens and consumers around the globe demand both" illustrates how conservative are current attitudes toward human rights in the discipline.[88] There is also a heavy responsibility to be borne by human rights advocates if changes are to be made. The voice of human rights advocacy must be educated and informed, able to engage with finance on its own terms while at the same time explaining fully and clearly the relevant obligations and expectations of human rights standards (legal and otherwise). It must also be candid in its acknowledgment of the inherent nuances and flexibility of human rights. That, as we saw at the end of the last chapter, is presently easier said than done. The few human rights thinkers who have seriously engaged with the subject (as cited throughout the book), are presently the exceptions that prove this rule. That has to be reversed.

Generalist human rights bodies, such as the UN Human Rights Council and most of the human rights treaty committees, the regional human rights institutions, and the national human rights commissions, as well as the field's major civil society organizations, such as Amnesty International and Human Rights Watch, tend to sidestep or merely flirt with the intersection of finance and human rights. Others focus on specific aspects of the relationship, such as the UN Committee on Economic, Social and Cultural Rights (state budgetary expenditure), the Tax Justice Network (tax evasion and avoidance), the Institute for Human Rights and Business (environmental sustainability),[89] and Oxfam and ActionAid (aid and development finance). A few approach finance with broader remits, such as the UN Independent Expert on Human Rights and Debt Forgiveness, and the civil society repository Righting Finance. But all need to dig deeper into the esoteric world of finance, to engage with such systemic issues as the roles of risk and leverage in finance, its introspection, its exceptionalist pretensions, its incentives regimes, and its political power gained through regulatory capture.

Above all, the human rights community cannot rely on codes of conduct (whether generalist like the UN Guiding Principles on Business and Human Rights, or specific like the financial services adaptation of the Danish Institute for Human Rights Compliance Assessment Tool) to do such heavy lifting. They may be useful first steps, but they are not alone sufficient. Worse, they may even be dangerous if human rights advocates and financiers alike rely on them too heavily, as the veneer of compliance checks could mask the need for more substantial and necessary systemic change.

A more proactive "carrot and stick" methodology that supplements the educative approaches needs to be adopted by the relevant institutions. These include *direct* regulators and enforcers. At the international level, this includes the central bankers' collectives that are the Bank of International Settlements and the FSB, and key multilateral financial institutions like the IMF and, to a lesser extent, the World Bank and regional aid banks. And at the national level, it includes the reserve banks themselves (as organs of state and therefore bound by international human rights laws),[90] securities watchdogs, prosecutorial agencies, and prudential monitors (including quasi-governmental ombudsmen-like offices and the industry's self-regulatory bodies). All of these need to shoulder the responsibility to break through the spoilt-child façade that finance has erected over the past twenty years and reestablish their role as collective parents. They need to "set out standards of behavior and hold the child to those standards, [and] . . . not play the role of a friend in [their] relationship with the child," as veteran financier Henry Kaufman has pointedly argued with respect to the U.S. Federal Reserve System.[91]

Corresponding responsibilities must also be taken on by those higher up the command chain—namely, the *indirect* financial regulators and enforcers. These include the global economic agenda-setters of the G20, the OECD, and, more broadly, the organs of the UN (from the General Assembly, through the cross-over development (UNDP) and environmental (UNEP) programs, to the right-focused Human Rights Council and the human rights treaty bodies), as well as state legislatures, governments, and the political parties that operate within them. Their particular duties derive from their overseer status—to provide leadership and guidance on how and why finance and human rights must work together. This is no optional extra, no luxury to be indulged in when times are good. It is a burning necessity. These are the very institutions that loudly trumpet both the verities of global finance and virtues of universal human rights, yet very rarely in the same sentence. The fact is that little is being pursued, let alone achieved, by these organs in linking the two fields in either policy or practice, to the continuing detriment of those whose human rights are adversely affected by systemic financial inequities or by the calamitous fallouts from financial crises.

As in all troubled relationships, the true path to reconciliation and success lies in their respect for each other—both as to their strengths and their weaknesses. To try to appreciate the other's point of view, even while you promote your own, and to work hard with the ground you share, while gently tending your own plot, is what it means to show true respect. In all this, superintendent institutions and regulation will have important parts to play, but they are essentially supporting roles. They set boundaries of acceptable conduct and endeavor to enforce them, both by sanctioning and encouraging greater engagement and better behavior well within those limits.

Accepting the inevitability of the political dimensions of the relationship is essential to moving forward. This is as true of economics and finance as it is of human rights. Neither is a science based on indisputable precepts. As James Tobin remarked of his own discipline in his acceptance speech for the Nobel Prize in Economics in 1981, "A subject so close to politics and policy inevitably blends ideology and science."[92] There are different ideological drivers within and between both the human rights and financial communities. Sometimes these smooth the relationship; at other times they scupper it. But, to borrow from Tobin again, behind politics and ideology lie the vision and energy of new ideas, and from these "free professional scrutiny selects the ideas deserving of survival." We must believe in that process, even when—especially when—we are pushing one idea or another. It is to the elemental creativity of this process that I commit the ideas advanced in this book.

Till Death Us Do Part

This is a book of cautious hope: a hope that finance and human rights can operate in tandem more effectively and fairly, and better understand their own, as well as each other's, objects and methods, limitations, and possibilities. It is cautious because there remains much that separates them, at distances that are truly daunting. However, we have no choice but to reach out, understand, and find ways to bring the two phenomena closer together. The book is my attempt to show why that matters and what needs to be done to make that happen. Ultimately, finance and human rights cannot survive without each other; the challenge is to focus our energies on dissecting what that means in practice rather than on lamenting how difficult it is for the pair to live together. It may never be a match made in heaven, but it is imperative that finance and human rights fully appreciate each other for what they are separately and collectively able to achieve. Finance must find its voice and vocation in promoting human rights goals not just because it would be useful and desirable for it to do so, or because it would also be noble or charitable. Rather, it must be impelled—or, if necessary, compelled—to do so in order to fulfill the great expectations made of it; to justify the license we (society) provide it; and most of all, to validate its own existence. In the end, the profits of finance doing so will be reaped by us all.

NOTES

Introduction

1. See discussion under "Tax free" in chapter 6, 157–8.
2. China's foreign currency reserves have been in excess of $3 trillion since 2011, by far the largest of any economy, being three times larger than the next biggest (held by Japan). See Trading Economics, *China's Foreign Exchange Reserves*, http://www.tradingeconomics.com/china/foreign-exchange-reserves.
3. A worldwide survey of the general public's trust in eight major industry sectors records financial services as having the lowest level of trust across all sectors at 51% in 2016, though that has risen from a low of 43% in 2012; see the Edelman Trust Barometer 2016, *Sector Trends: Trust in Each Industry Sector 2012–2016*, at https://www.scribd.com/doc/295815519/2016-Edelman-Trust-Barometer-Executive-Summary.
4. For a discussion of which, see chapter 4, 106–7.
5. Whereas, as noted below (at n.12), the World Bank estimates that some 766 million people live in extreme or absolute poverty (on less than $1.90 per day), more detailed analyses of poverty register much higher figures. Thus, the UN Development Programme's "Multidimensional Poverty Index" (MPI) for 2015 reports that "[a]lmost 1.5 billion people in the 101 developing countries covered by the MPI—about 29 percent of their population—live in multidimensional poverty—that is, with at least 33 percent of the [MPI] indicators reflecting acute deprivation in health, education and standard of living. And close to 900 million people are vulnerable to fall into poverty if setbacks occur—financial, natural or otherwise"; see http://hdr.undp.org/en/content/multidimensional-poverty-index-mpi. See, further, chapter 1, text at nn.52–53.
6. For details and discussion, see chapter 1, 18.
7. The (inflation adjusted) median U.S. household income in 2015 was $56,516, having fallen from $59,909 in 1999, according to the U.S. Census Bureau's *Poverty and Income Annual Report 2016*; See Josh Zumbrun, "U.S. Income and Poverty in 9 Charts," *Wall Street Journal*, September 13, 2016. In contrast, the richest 5% of American households saw their average income rise from $202,061 in 1999 to $214,462 in 2015 (ibid.); and over the same period the top 1% saw their average income rise from $990,00 to $1,360,000. See Emmanuel Saez, "US Top One Percent of Income Earners Hit New High in 2015 amid Strong Economic Growth," Washington Centre for Equitable Growth, July 1, 2016, at http://equitablegrowth.org/research-analysis/u-s-top-one-percent-of-income-earners-hit-new-high-in-2015-amid-strong-economic-growth/.
8. Having risen from 11.9% in 1999 to 15.1% in 2010, before falling in 2015 to 13.5%; see Zumbrun, "U.S. Income and Poverty."

9. As Michael Kazin put it in an article published one month before the election: "Trump and American Populism: Old Whine, New Bottles," *Foreign Affairs*, October 6, 2016; Kazin added, understatedly, that Trump "is an unlikely populist."

10. William Dudley, "Opening Remarks at the Workshop on Reforming Culture and Behavior in the Financial Services Industry," Federal Reserve Bank of New York, New York (October 20, 2014), as reported in Group of Thirty, *Banking Culture and Conduct: A Call for Sustained and Comprehensive Reform* (July 2015), at 24.

11. In 1990, 66.5% of China's population (then 1.13 billion) were living in extreme poverty; by 2010 (latest available data), that had dropped to 11.1% of a population then numbering 1.33 billion. The drop in the thirty years since 1981 is even more remarkable, when 88.3% of the total population (of 993 million) lived in extreme poverty. The World Bank defines extreme poverty as those living beneath $1.90 a day (at 2011 "international dollar" rates). For poverty levels, see World Bank, *World Development Indicators Poverty Headcount Ratio at $1.90 a day (2011 PPP) (% population)*, at http://data.worldbank.org/indicator/SI.POV.DDAY; for population numbers, see World Bank, *Population, total (China)*, at http://data.worldbank.org/indicator/SP.POP.TOTL?locations=CN.

12. That is 766 million people, or 10.68% of the world's population in 2013 (latest available data), according to the World Bank, ibid., for both poverty and population levels. Using the latest available World Bank data (which for India is from 2011 and 2009 for Nigeria), it has been calculated that the number of people living in extreme poverty in India is 296 million and in Nigeria is 108 million; see bar chart compiled by Max Roser, "Number of People in Absolute Poverty by Country (Latest Data)," *Our World in Data*, at https://ourworldindata.org/world-poverty/.

13. 1 Timothy 6:10, *The Bible (New International Version)*.

14. By Jean-Jacques Rousseau: "The money which a man possesses is the instrument of freedom; that which we eagerly pursue is the instrument of slavery," in *The Confessions of Jean-Jacques Rousseau* (1782) (CreateSpace Independent Publishing Platform edition, 2014), 37.

15. "Wall Street's Economic Crime Against Humanity," *Bloomberg Business Week*, March 20, 2009.

Chapter 1 – Strange Bedfellows

1. Committee on Oversight and Government Reform, "The Financial Crisis and the Role of Federal Regulators," House of Representatives, 110th Congress, 2nd session, Serial No. 110-209, October 23, 2008, available at https://house.resource.org/110/gov.house.ogr.20081023_hrs15REF2154.pdf. Greenspan underlines his unapologetic stance toward his role in precipitating the global financial crisis in the introduction to his book *The Map and the Territory: Risk, Human Nature and the Future of Forecasting* (New York: Penguin, 2013), 1–11.

2. Adam Smith, *An Inquiry into the Nature and Causes of the Wealth of Nations, Volume 1*, (1776) (Elibron Classics edition, 2000, being a replica of a 1786 edition published in London), at 1.2.2.

3. John Maynard Keynes, "Liberalism and Labour," in *Essays in Persuasion* (London: Macmillan, 1931), at 311. He elaborated on this triumvirate in the last chapter of his *General Theory of Employment, Interest and Money* (London: Macmillan, 1936), entitled "Concluding Notes on the Social Philosophy towards which the General Theory Might Lead" (chapter 24).

4. John Kay, *Other People's Money: Masters of the Universe or Servants of the People?* (London: Profile Books, 2015), 143–44.

5. See Michele Braun, Adam Copeland, Alexa Herlach, and Radhika Mithal, *Intraday Liquidity Flows*, Federal Reserve Bank of New York, August 6, 2012.

6. Christine Lagarde, "Economic Inclusion and Financial Integrity," speech delivered at a conference on Inclusive Capitalism in London on May 27, 2014.

7. That is, "to find the right balance between public interests and private gains in global financial management," as Geoffrey Underhill and Xiaoke Zhang put it in "Norms, Legitimacy, and Global Financial Governance," *World Economy & Finance Research Programme*, Working Paper Series (WEF 0013), September 2006, 32.

8. The significance of Greenspan's admission of a flaw in his thinking is notably downplayed by Sebastian Mallaby in his formidable study of the man and the myth: *The Man Who Knew: The Life and Times of Alan Greenspan* (London: Bloomsbury, 2016). Labeling it a mere ""philosophic quip" (at 670), Mallaby convincingly demonstrates why it is inconceivable that Greenspan was not fully aware of the irrationality of financial markets players (668–71). Instead, he argues, all that Greenspan was trying to convey was the (incontestable) fact that all ideologies and personal worldviews have flaws, including his. However, this, to my mind, does not explain the most important consequence of Greenspan's reasoning. Namely, that he appeared to believe that such irrationality would always, *ultimately*, be held in check by the self-preservational concern of financiers to avoid a catastrophic financial meltdown. That was the essence of his flawed reasoning, and its consequences were momentous.

9. See John C. Bogle, *The Battle for the Soul of Capitalism* (New Haven, CT: Yale University Press, 2005).

10. See Lynn Stout, *The Shareholder Value Myth: How Putting Shareholders First Harms Investors, Corporations, and the Public* (Oakland, CA: Berrett Koehler, 2012); not least, Stout argues, this is due to our university business and law schools inculcating this view in their classrooms.

11. As *The Economist* put it: "Mutiny over the Bounty," November 6, 2010.

12. Ibid.: "Investment banks, it seemed, were not being run in the interests of the economy or even of their owners, but for the staff. It was financial mutiny."

13. Ian Verrender, "One of Life's Few Certainties: The Rise of Executive Pay," *Sydney Morning Herald*, November 20–21, 2010, 7.

14. Bogle, *The Battle for the Soul of Capitalism*, xxii.

15. See Karl Polanyi, *The Great Transformation: The Political and Economic Origins of our Time* (1944) (Boston, MA: Beacon Press, 2001), chapters 14 ("Market and Man") and 15 ("Nature and Man").

16. Ibid., 45.

17. Thus, to the question what it is that bankers actually do, John Kay answers, "[t]o an extent that staggers the imagination, they deal with each other"; Kay, *Other People's Money*, 1.

18. For a history of the phenomenon, see Gerald Epstein (ed.), *Financialization and the World Economy* (Cheltenham, UK: Edward Elgar, 2005).

19. The trend may have insidious and troubling implications. Anthropologists Keith Hart and Horacio Ortiz, for example, maintain that "valuation of persons and things through money is never just technical: it is also moral, religious and political, placing everyone symbolically in society according to various orders of reckoning." "The Anthropology of Money and Finance: Between Ethnography and World History," *Annual Review of Anthropology* 43 (2014): 465–82, at 467.

20. BMI is now a common factor taken into account by health and life insurers. The online *BMI Calculator*, for example, has an FAQ page dedicated to the question: "How does BMI affect insurance rates?"; see http://www.bmicalculator.org/how-does-bmi-affect-insurance-rates/.

21. Berkshire Hathaway Inc., Chairman's Letter to Shareholders, *Annual Report* 2002.

22. As Mary Dowell-Jones observes, the total face value of global derivatives amounts to "a staggering $700 trillion, ten times world GDP"; Dowell-Jones, "Financial Institutions and Human Rights," *Human Rights Law Review* 13, no. 3 (2013): 423, at 430. It should be noted that the Bank of International Settlements data upon which Dowell-Jones draws makes a distinction between the "notional amounts" or face value of outstanding derivatives contracts, and their "gross market values" (that is, what it would cost to replace those contacts at *current* market prices), which is much smaller—see http://www.bis.org/statistics/dt1920a.pdf. See further, below, 18, in which market value data are used. The impact and role of derivatives in the mismanagement of financial risk are further explored in Chapter 3, 62–3.

23. That is the "mass destruction" envisaged by Buffett (see Berkshire Hathaway Inc., Chairman's Letter to Shareholders, *Annual Report* 2002). One of the most significant conclusions reached by the National Commission on the Causes of the Financial and Economic Crisis in the United States was that legislative deregulation of "over-the-counter [that is, not traded through regulated exchanges] derivatives was a key turning point in the march toward financial crisis," because "without any oversight OTC derivatives rapidly spiraled out of control and out of sight"; see the Commission's *Inquiry Report* (January 2011), at xxiv.

24. World Bank, *Food Price Watch* (February 2011), at http://www.worldbank.org/foodcrisis/food_price_watch_report_feb2011.html.

25. In the seven years before that (2000–06), the total price rise had been 38%. The relevant annualized figures were, respectively, 2000: 85.8; 2006: 118.9; 2007: 163.4; and 2008: 232.1; see FAO Food Price Index, at http://www.fao.org/worldfoodsituation/foodpricesindex/en/.

26. *Food Commodities Speculation and Food Price Crises*, Briefing Note No. 2 (September 2010), at 2.

27. For example, the size of the U.S. futures stockpiles in staple grains all increased markedly between 2003 and 2008. For wheat the increase during that period was nearly eightfold, for corn tenfold, and for soybean the increase was more than twelvefold; see Testimony of Michael W. Masters before the Committee on Homeland Security and Governmental Affairs, U.S. Senate, May 20, 2008, at 3.

28. Ibid., at 1 (emphasis in the original).

29. Upon which matter I expand in chapter 3 when discussing leverage, 61–4.

30. See Sanjeev Sanyal, "The Random Walk: Mapping of the World's Financial Markets 2014" (April 1, 2014), which is an annual survey conducted by Deutsche Bank of the size and value of global financial assets. The OECD defines Gross Domestic Product (GDP) as "an aggregate measure of production equal to the sum of the gross values added of all resident, institutional units engaged in production (plus any taxes, and minus any subsidies, on products not included in the value of their outputs)"; see OECD's *Glossary of Statistical Terms*, at https://stats.oecd.org/glossary/detail.asp?ID=1163.

31. As economist L. Randell Wray neatly puts it: "The Financialization of Health and Everything Else in the Universe," http://wallstreetpit.com/11110-the-financialization-of-health-and-everything-else-in-the-universe/.

32. Simon Johnson, "The Quiet Coup," *The Atlantic* (May 2009). The problem of regulatory capture is discussed further in chapter 6 below, 165–6.

33. Kevin Dowd and Martin Hutchinson, *The Alchemists of Loss: How Modern Finance and Government Intervention Crashed the Financial System* (Chichester, UK: John Wiley & Sons, 2010), 278–79.

34. Roger Altman, "We need not fret over omnipotent markets," *Financial Times*, 2 December 2011.

35. Which comprised Title VIII of the *Housing and Community Development Act 1977*.

36. Interview with President Bill Clinton, PBS *News Hour*, January 21, 1998. https://www.youtube.com/watch?v=WTZIB6Sika4.

37. Writing in *Foreign Affairs* in early 2009, Altman was adamant that "the collapse of housing prices and the subprime market in the US" were merely symptoms of what was the real cause of the crisis, namely, "the (invariably lethal) combination of very low interest rates and unprecedented levels of liquidity"; Roger Altman, "The Great Crash, 2008," *Foreign Affairs* 88, no. 1 (Jan./Feb. 2009): 2–14. By that time Altman was CEO of Evercore Partners, an independent investment banking advisory firm that he had co-founded in 1996, shortly after he left his position in the U.S. Treasury.

38. In the years immediately after the crisis, the World Bank, the ILO, and the UN all documented marked deteriorations in the living standards and human rights protections of the extremely poor, in particular; for a summation of these and other reviews, see UN *Report of the Independent Expert on The Question of Human Rights and Extreme Poverty*, A/64/279 (August 11, 2009), especially paras. 22–45.

39. UNESCO and Education for All Global Monitoring Report, *A Growing Number of Children and Adolescents Are Out of School as Aid Fails to Meet the Mark* (Policy Paper 22/Fact Sheet 31; July 2015), at 2.

40. Ibid., at 5.

41. UNGEI, *Girls' Education Plays a Large Part in Global Development*, http://www.ungei.org/news/247_2165.html.

42. See UN, *The Millennium Development Goals Report 2015*, "Gender parity index for gross enrolment ratios in primary, secondary and tertiary education in developing regions, 1990, 2000 and 2015," graph at 28.

43. See UN Millennium Development Goals Indicators, *Gender Parity Index (GPI) in secondary level enrolment – India*, at http://unstats.un.org/unsd/mdg/SeriesDetail.aspx?srid=613. The

GPI for 1993 was 0.63, while in 2013 it was 0.95. There are, nevertheless, still more than 17 million children in India attending neither primary nor secondary school; see UNICEF, *Global Initiative on Out-of-School-Children: South Asia Regional Study, Covering Bangladesh, India and Pakistan* (January 2014), at 4.

44. Plan International, *Paying the Price: The Economic Cost of Failing to Educate Girls* (2008); see http://plan-international.org/files/global/publications/education/girls_education_economics.pdf; the report was compiled using data collected by the World Bank and UNESCO.

45. See World Bank, *World Development Report 2012: Gender Equality and Development*, chapter 3.

46. See Benjamin Davis, Sudhanshu Handa, Nicola Hypher, Natalia Winder Rossi, Paul Winters, and Jennifer Yablonski (eds.), *From Evidence to Action: The Story of Cash Transfers and Impact Evaluation in Sub Saharan Africa* (2016), a UNICEF study of unconditional cash transfers programs in eight countries in the region that evidences their beneficial impact on school enrolment, levels of nutrition and health, as well as, importantly, financial literacy.

47. UNGEI and Global Partnership for Education, *Cash Transfer Programs for Gender Equity in Girls' Secondary Education*, Discussion Paper (April 2014), 5.

48. According to the latest figures (for 2013) available to UNESCO's Institute of Statistics, 57.1% of Brazil's tertiary students are female; see country profiles under "Percentage of students in tertiary education who are female," at http://data.uis.unesco.org/Index.aspx?queryid=139.

49. Andersen Antunes, "The 10 Most Powerful Businesswomen in Brazil," *Forbes*, May 29, 2013, http://www.forbes.com/sites/andersonantunes/2013/05/29/the-10-most-powerful-businesswomen-in-brazil/.

50. See OECD, *Education at a Glance 2016: Country Note, Brazil*. This pay gap is much wider than the average for OECD countries, which stands at women earning approximately 85% as much as men; see OECD, *Gender Wage Gap*, at https://www.oecd.org/gender/data/gender-wagegap.htm.

51. Make Poverty History, "Nelson Mandela's Speech to Trafalgar Square Crowd," February 3, 2005, available at: www.makepovertyhistory.org/docs/mandelaspeech.doc (emphasis added).

52. What Arthur Brooks, the president of the American Enterprise Institute, refers to as a "dignity deficit" in his essay on the individual, social, and political consequences of entrenched poverty in America's underclass: Arthur C. Brooks, "The Dignity Deficit: Reclaiming America's Sense of Purpose," *Foreign Affairs* (March/April 2017): 106–17.

53. World Bank, "Poverty Drops Below One Billion, says World Bank," Press Release, April 15, 2007, available via www.worldbank.org/news.

54. Although in August 2008 the World Bank raised the extreme poverty line to $1.25 a day, this does not fully account for the lower than expected reduction in the number of extreme poor. World Bank estimates for 2008 had 1.29 billion people living below the poverty line: World Bank, "World Bank Sees Progress Against Extreme Poverty but Flags Vulnerabilities," Press Release, February 29, 2012.

55. See World Bank, *World Development Indicators Poverty Headcount Ratio at $1.90 a day (2011 PPP) (% population)*, at http://data.worldbank.org/indicator/SI.POV.DDAY.

56. The UNDP's "Multidimensional Poverty Index" (MPI), for example, is based on a more detailed analysis of poverty (one that yields considerably higher levels of global poverty); see Introduction above, 3, at n.5.

57. Daryl Collins, Jonathan Morduch, Stuart Rutherford, and Orlanda Ruthven (eds.), *Portfolios of the Poor: How the World's Poor Live on $2 a Day* (Princeton, NJ: Princeton University Press, 2009), 184.

58. See Sabina Alkire and Gisela Robles, *Global Multidimensional Poverty Index 2016*, available at http://www.ophi.org.uk/wp-content/uploads/Global-MPI-2016-2-pager.pdf.

59. See World Bank, *PovcalNet: an online analysis tool for global poverty monitoring*; available at http://iresearch.worldbank.org/PovcalNet/home.aspx

60. As calculated by the U.S. Census Bureau using 2015 data, the latest available. These figures are an improvement on the previous year (46.6 million people, or 14.8% of the population, in 2014), but still 1% higher than in 2007, the year before the onset of the most recent recession; see U.S. Census Bureau, *Income and Poverty in the United States: 2015* (September 2016),

http://www.census.gov/content/dam/Census/library/publications/2016/demo/p60-256.pdf,
at 12. The 2015 poverty line for an individual was set at $12,331 per annum.

61. On the extent of these rights and their limitations, see chapter 2, 47.

62. In addition, two nonmember entities (The Holy See and Palestine) have ratified the
    Convention. Since Somalia's ratification in 2015, the only UN member state not to have rati-
    fied the Convention is the United States.

63. Figures as of late 2017; for updates, see the UN's *Status of Ratification Interactive Dashboard* at
    http://indicators.ohchr.org/.

64. "The Lion Kings?," *The Economist*, January 8, 2011, 70.

65. Franklin Delano Roosevelt, *State of the Union Message to Congress*, January 11, 1944, available
    via the American Presidency Project: http://www.presidency.ucsb.edu/ws/?pid=16518.

66. See UNDP, *Human Development Report 2012*, 126, available at http://hdr.undp.org/en/
    reports/global/hdr2011/download/. The HDI is a ranking based on a composite of three
    factors: life expectancy, education, and per capita income. The "PPP" figure is based on an
    annualized GNI per capita estimate of $1,200 (drawn from a raw GDP per capita total of
    $587). See IMF, *World Economic Outlook Database* (April 2012), at http://www.imf.org/
    external/pubs/ft/weo/2012/01/weodata/weorept.aspx?pr.x=48&pr.y=13&sy=2009&ey=2
    012&scsm=1&ssd=1&sort=country&ds=.&br=1&c=518&s=NGDPD%2CNGDPDPC%2
    CPPPGDP%2CPPPPC%2CLP&grp=0&a=.

67. Kyaw Kyaw, "Land Reform Is the Key to Burma's Future," *The Diplomat*, August 22, 2012.

68. BBC News, "Myanmar Swears in First Elected Civilian President in 50 Years, March 30, 2016.

69. For regular updated lists of those still detained, see The Assistance Association for Political
    Prisoners (Burma), at http://aappb.org/2016/04/121-current-political-prisoner-list-in-
    burma-2016/.

70. Before the managed flotation of the currency on April 1, 2012, the official exchange rate was
    6 kyat to the U.S. dollar, while the black-market rate was around 800 kyat to the dollar. This
    distortion had provided ample opportunities for corrupt and rent-seeking behavior by the
    country's elite; see International Crisis Group, "Myanmar: The Politics of Economic Reform,"
    July 27, 2012, 3.

71. Reaching a staggering $9.4 billion of FDI inflows for 2015/16, more than doubling in
    two years (from $4.1 billion in 2013/14), according to data compiled by the Myanmar
    Government's Directorate of Investment and Company Administration; see "Myanmar FDI
    Hits Record High of $9.4bn in 2015/15," *Reuters*, April 11, 2016.

72. Asian Development Bank, "What's the Fastest Growing Country in Asia? Surprise! It's
    Myanmar," April 14, 2016.

73. Data collected by the World Bank Institute, for example, shows that although average per capita
    GDP in developing states in sub-Saharan Africa is $3,324 (equating to just over $9 per day for
    every man, woman, and child), the average level of extreme poverty in these states (measured
    at less than $1.90 per day) is running at nearly 43%. Our World in Data, "The share of people
    living in extreme poverty vs. GDP per capita, 2008 to 2014," at https://ourworldindata.org/
    grapher/the-share-of-people-living-in-extreme-poverty-vs-gdp-per-capita?year=1981.

74. See Trading Economics, India GDP Annual Growth Rate 1951–2016, http://www.trading-
    economics.com/india/gdp-growth-annual.

75. World Bank, *India: GNI per capita, Atlas method (current US$)*, at http://data.worldbank.org/
    country/india.

76. World Bank, *Poverty and Equity Databank – India: Country Inequality Trend (distribution
    of income or consumption by quintile)*, at http://povertydata.worldbank.org/poverty/
    country/IND.

77. Ibid.

78. Ranked according to nominal GDP; see International Monetary Fund, *World Economic
    Outlook* (April 2016)

79. The World Bank's *Global Poverty Indicators* estimate that in 2012 there were 902 million people
    worldwide living beneath $1.90 per day; at http://povertydata.worldbank.org/poverty/
    home/. According to the Bank's *Global Monitoring Report 2015/16*, this figure was projected
    to fall by around 200 million in 2015 (the data for which, at the time of writing, was not yet
    available); see http://www.worldbank.org/en/publication/global-monitoring-report.

80. An ambitious program of affordable basic health care available to all, announced in 2013 and slated to be in place by 2020. For an account of its progress thus far, including the inevitable political machinations that have dogged its implementation, see Elizabeth Pisani, Maarten Kok, and Kharisma Nugroho, "Indonesia's Road to Universal Health Coverage: A Political Journey," *Health Policy and Planning*, September 6, 2016, 1–10, available at https://academic.oup.com/heapol/article/32/2/267/2555434/ Indonesia-s-road-to-universal-health-coverage-a?searchresult=1.

81. See generally, Chris Manning and Sudarno Sumarto (eds.), *Employment, Living Standards and Poverty in Contemporary Indonesia* (Singapore: Institute of Southeast Asian Studies, 2011).

82. On the pathological, even perverted, extremes this can reach in the very rich, see George Monibot, "Enough Already," *The Guardian*, May 6, 2013.

83. European Union rules established via a rolling matrix of directives, regulations, and guidelines since 2010 have sought to impose "sound remuneration policies" across all EU-based banks (see European Banking Authority, *Remuneration*, at https://www.eba.europa.eu/ regulation-and-policy/remuneration), by restricting the size of bonuses in relation to base salaries and implementing more rigorous assessment of performance-based rewards by, for example, deferring remuneration and increasing the proportion of it comprising stock. These rules, however, have been effectively sidestepped by banks simply paying higher base salaries and awarding hefty "allowances" to senior staff; see John Glover and Silla Brush, "European Banks' Millionaire Club Swells as Pay Shifts to Salary," *Bloomberg News*, March 30, 2016. Long-awaited proposals from U.S. regulators tabled in mid-2016 recommended the imposition of similar remuneration restrictions (including "claw back" of bonuses provisions that would extend a minimum of seven years after the bonuses were paid), but these too have been met with the same sort of evasive and circumlocutory behavior by banks as seen in Europe; see Donna Borak, Andrew Ackerman, and Christina Rexrode, "New Rules Curbing Wall Street Pay Proposed," *Wall Street Journal*, April 22, 2016.

84. The *average* total annual pay for Wall Street employees in 2014 was $404,800, according to data compiled by the New York State Comptroller; see Christina Rexrode, Justin Baer, and Louise Ensign, "One Expected Casualty of New Compensation Rules: Banker Bonuses," *Wall Street Journal*, April 21, 2016.

85. John Maynard Keynes, *Indian Currency and Finance* (London: Macmillan, 1913), at 192.

86. See Thomas Philippon and Ariell Reshef, *Wages and Human Capital in the U.S. Financial Industry: 1909-2006* (Working Paper 14644, National Bureau of Economic Research, 2009), at 3.

87. In respect of the former, see U.S. Department of Justice (DOJ), "HSBC Holdings Plc. and HSBC Bank USA N.A. Admit to Anti-Money Laundering and Sanctions Violations, Forfeit $1.256 Billion in Deferred Prosecution Agreement," Press Release, December 11, 2011; HSBC also agreed to pay $665 million in civil penalties, as the DOJ noted. In respect of the latter, see Gerard Ryle, Will Fitzgibbon, Mar Cabra, Rigoberto Carvajal, Marina Walker Guevara, Martha M. Hamilton, and Tom Stites, "Banking Giant HSBC Sheltered Murky Cash Linked to Dictators and Arms Dealers," *The International Consortium of Investigative Journalists*, February 8, 2015.

88. This list comprised the following: "Interest rate derivative selling, Libor manipulation, Eurobor manipulation, mis-selling mortgages to Fannie Mae and Freddie Mac, Forex rigging, weakness in money laundering, credit default swaps . . . rigging precious metals," all the while HSBC is facing "various class action lawsuits over the Bernie Madoff fraud." See UK House of Commons, Treasury Committee, "Oral evidence: HM Revenue and Customs and HSBC," HC 1071 (February 25, 2015), at Q60 and Q61.

89. Ibid., Q13. Gulliver conceded that the bank's human resources department and the board of directors would have to know his salary, but no one else in the bank, or beyond.

90. Notably in this context, the U.S. *Dodd-Frank Wall Street Reform and Consumer Protection Act* (2010) mandated that the Securities and Exchange Commission (SEC) issue a rule that requires public companies to disclose the ratio of the compensation of its CEO to the median compensation of its employees. Such a rule was duly adopted by the SEC and came into force on January 1, 2017. See SEC Press Release, August 5, 2015, at https://www.sec.gov/news/ pressrelease/2015-160.html.

91. Alain Cohn, Ernst Fehr, and Michel André Maréchal, "Business Culture and Dishonesty in The Banking Industry," *Nature* 516 (December 4, 2014), 86–89.
92. Ibid.
93. Karen Ho, *Liquidated: An Ethnography of Wall Street* (Durham, NC: Duke University Press, 2009), 39.
94. Ibid., 85.
95. Ibid., 73–121.
96. On which saga see Roger Lowenstein, *When Genius Failed* (London: Random House, 2001).

Chapter 2 – Living Together

1. Uri Gneezy and Aldo Rustichini, "A Fine Is a Price," *Journal of Legal Studies* 29 (2000): 1–18.
2. "The Unpredictable Consequences of Using Money as an Incentive," available at the creative ideas website *99U*: http://99u.com/articles/26185/how-money-makes-us-lazy.
3. Sanctions for financial wrong-doing and their enforcement (or lack of) are discussed further in chapter 6.
4. David Graeber, *Debt: The First 5,000 Years* (New York: Melville House, 2011), Ch. 2, "The Myth of Barter," 21–41.
5. Walter Bagehot, *Lombard Street: A Description of the Money Market* (New York: John Wiley, 1999), 9
6. As captured in Socrates' question: "As wealth and the like, . . . are sometimes good and sometimes evil, do not they also become profitable or hurtful, accordingly as the soul guides and uses them rightly or wrongly; just as the things of the soul herself are benefited when under the guidance of wisdom and harmed by folly?" See Plato, "Meno," in *Five Great Dialogues of Plato*, trans. Benjamin Jowett (New York: Van Nostrand, 1942), 79.
7. As recounted by Henry Waxman, chair of the Committee on Oversight and Government Reform, during questioning of Mr. Greenspan in the Committee's inquiry: "The Financial Crisis and the Role of Federal Regulators," House of Representatives, 110th Congress, 2nd session, Serial No. 110-209, October 23, 2008, available at https://www.gpo.gov/fdsys/pkg/CHRG-110hhrg55764/html/CHRG-110hhrg55764.htm.
8. Officially referred to as the Federal Funds Rate.
9. For an account of these cuts and their consequences, see William Fleckenstein, *Greenspan's Bubbles: The Age of Ignorance at the Federal Reserve* (New York: McGraw-Hill, 2008), 15–26 and 121–50. Perhaps the only rival to the setting of official interest rates in terms of significance of market manipulation is the capacity of the state to control the money supply itself. Ben Bernanke, an acolyte of and immediate successor to Greenspan as head of the Federal Reserve, proved himself even more adept with this sort of intervention, when he instigated three gargantuan programs of Quantitative Easing (QE) between 2008 and 2012, injecting more than $3 trillion into the U.S. economy; see Board of Governors of the Federal Reserve System, "Credit and Liquidity Programs and the Balance Sheet: Recent Balance Sheet Trends: Total Assets of the Federal Reserve," at http://www.federalreserve.gov/monetary-policy/bst_recenttrends.htm. Manipulation of official interest rates was in fact not an option available to Bernanke because the rates were held at effectively zero (0.25%) from January 2009 until long after he departed the position in February 2014.
10. Changes in the yields earned on bond holdings are linked closely to fluctuations in cash interest rates (generally speaking, they move lockstep in opposite directions). Where interest rates are pegged and steady, so are bond yields; but where they fluctuate, or have the potential to do so, then the opportunity to create a market in bonds is presented. The bonds market grew exponentially in size and influence in the decades leading up to the financial crisis, prompting James Carville, the media commentator cum campaign adviser to Bill Clinton, to quip that if he was ever reincarnated he'd want to come back as the bond market because "you can intimidate everybody"; as quoted in the *Wall Street Journal*, February 25, 1993, A1. But after 2008, with interest rates collapsing and governments preferring other means to raise money, the bonds markets have declined precipitously to less than one-tenth of their size immediately before the crisis, and now possessing all the intimidatory power of a "chihuahua in an handbag," as *The Economist* put it in "Who's Scary Now?," October 22, 2016.

11. Niall Ferguson, *The Ascent of Money: A Financial History of the World* (New York: Penguin, 2008), 2–4.
12. That is, in particular, the period following the establishment of the United Nations in 1945 and the Universal Declaration of Human Rights in 1948, as dubbed by Louis Henkin in his iconic book, *The Age of Rights* (New York: Columbia University Press, 1990).
13. Article 1 reads: "Les hommes naissent et demeurent libres et égaux en droits. Les distinctions sociales ne peuvent être fondées que sur l'utilité commune."
14. Under Article I(ii) of the *Articles of Agreement of the IMF (1944)*, and Article I(iii) of the *Articles of Agreement of the IBRD (1944)*. These provisions however, did not deter the framers from trying to restrict either institution from taking into account noneconomic, and especially political, considerations in their deliberations and operations; see in particular, the express (if impractical) prohibition of bank officials being influenced in their decisions by political concerns in Article IV(10) of the *Articles of Agreement of the IBRD*. The problematic consequences for human rights of this attempted segregation are discussed in chapter 5, 134–5.
15. Most especially in Articles 1(3) and 55(c) of the *Charter of the United Nations (1945)*, which proclaim that one of purposes of the organization is to promote "respect for human rights and for fundamental freedoms for all."
16. As Mary Ann Glendon puts it in *A World Made New: Eleanor Roosevelt and the Universal Declaration of Human Rights* (New York: Random House, 2001), 19.
17. Thus, Article 2(7) of the UN Charter provides that: "[n]othing contained in the present Charter shall authorize the United Nations to intervene in matters which are essentially within the domestic jurisdiction of any state." The ambiguity that lies within the provision (that, arguably, egregious violations of human rights are matters of international and not just domestic concern) has been the subject of much intense debate ever since.
18. Indeed Rand applauded individual rights as "the means of subordinating society to moral law": see *The Virtue of Selfishness* (1963) (New York: Penguin, 2011), Kindle location 1608.
19. Milton Friedman, *Capitalism and Freedom* (Chicago: University of Chicago Press, 1976)
20. As Karl Marx and Friedrich Engels put it in *The Communist Manifesto* (1848), (Peking: Foreign Languages Press 1975): "The selfish misconception that induces you to transform into eternal laws of nature and of reason, the social forms springing from your present mode of production and form of property—historical relations that rise and disappear in the progress of production—this misconception you share with every ruling class that has preceded you," 54. For analysis of this perspective, and in particular how it was directed at the *bourgeois* notion of "rights," rather than "human rights" as Marx and Engels understood them (that is, specifically, in a true socialist society where individuals choose to cooperate rather than compete), see Tom Campbell, *The Left and Rights* (Abingdon: Routledge, 1983), 103–22.
21. It is in the context of this dual role of the state that Friedrich Hayek constructed his classic conception of liberty, whereby free societies are attained by "conferring the monopoly of coercion on the state and by attempting to limit the power of the state to instances where it is required to prevent coercion by private persons," such that "[t]he coercion which a government must still use for this end is reduced to a minimum and made as innocuous as possible . . ."; F.A. Hayek, *The Constitution of Liberty* (1960) (London: Taylor & Francis, 2006), 20.
22. Ayn Rand, *Atlas Shrugged* (1957) (New York: Penguin, 2012), which, in its glorification of self-interest, prompted Gore Vidal to remark that it reflected a philosophy "nearly perfect in its immorality," as quoted in Harriet Rubin, "Ayn Rand's Literature of Capitalism," *New York Times*, September 15, 2007.
23. Samuel Moyn, *The Last Utopia* (Cambridge, MA: Belknap Press, 2010), 5, and in graph form, at 231. This surge in the popular use of the term, however, is not to be mistaken for the birth (or even rebirth) of the modern human rights movement as Moyn is wont to argue. Philip Alston, for example, chides Moyn's analysis of the origins of human rights as simplistic, myopic, and failing to "acknowledge the polycentric nature of the human rights enterprise," the roots of which stretch back centuries, not mere decades, in "Does the Past Matter: On the Origins of Human Rights," *Harvard Law Review* 126 (2013): 2043, at 2045.
24. After the only other hold-out state, Somalia, ratified the CRC in 2015.
25. Both covenants were adopted by the UN General Assembly on December 16, 1966, with the ICESCR coming into force on January 3, 1976, and the ICCPR on March 23, 1976.

26. For a comprehensive list of UN human rights treaties and other instruments, see UN Office of the High Commissioner, *Universal Human Rights Instruments*, at http://www.ohchr.org/EN/ProfessionalInterest/Pages/UniversalHumanRightsInstruments.aspx.

27. The Optional Protocol did not, however, enter into force until May 10, 2013, after receiving its tenth ratification.

28. The literature on these various issues of human rights debate is truly vast, but for those looking to explore the field, the following three works would be excellent places to start: Jack Donnelly, *Universal Human Rights in Theory and Practice*, 3rd ed.(Ithaca, NY: Cornell University Press, 2013)—an enduring and comprehensive classic in the field; Makau Mutua, "The Ideology of Human Rights," *Virginia Journal of International Law* 36 (1996): 589–57—a trenchant critique of the philosophical roots and universal aspirations of human rights; and David Kennedy, "The International Human Rights Movement: Part of the Problem?" *Harvard Human Rights Journal* 15 (2002): 101–25—a ribald journey through some uncomfortable truths and thought-provoking accusations about human rights and their advocates.

29. This is a theme we return to in the book's concluding chapters when considering what human rights advocacy must do if its message is to be relevant and credible in the context of finance.

30. Which, Charles Blattberg, argues, constitutes the "ironic tragedy of human rights"; Charles Blattberg, *Patriotic Elaborations: Essays in Practical Philosophy* (Montreal: McGill-Queen's University Press, 2009), chapter 3.

31. Costas Douzinas, *The End of Human Rights* (Oxford: Hart, 2000).

32. By way, principally, of his pathbreaking *Theory of Justice* (1971) (Cambridge, MA: Belknap Press, 1999).

33. For an insightful overview of the genealogy of how human rights concepts have entered development discourse generally, and specifically in regard to rights-based approaches, see Peter Uvin, "From the Right to Development to the Rights-Based Approach: How 'Human Rights' Entered Development," *Development in Practice* 17 (2007): 597–606.

34. As, for instance, it does through the General Agreement on Trade in Services (GATS), which includes financial services (and expressly so in two annexes to the GATS), alongside all other types of services.

35. See *GAVI Celebrates 15 Years of Saving Lives* (January 22, 2015), http://www.gavi.org/Library/Audio-visual/Videos/Gavi-celebrates-15-years-of-saving-lives/. GAVI's unique funding arrangements are described in chapter 5.

36. On the elastic meaning and application of which see further, Ben Saul, David Kinley, and Jacqueline Mowbray, *The International Covenant on Economic, Social and Cultural Rights: Commentary, Cases and Materials* (Oxford: Oxford University Press, 2014),133–72.

37. It is noteworthy that even when proclaiming the Covenant's core minimum standard of rights protection in General Comment 3 (1990), the Economic, Social and Cultural Rights Committee conceded that retrogressive measures taken by states regarding levels of protection of rights under the ICESCR, even if "deliberately" taken, are permissible (albeit under certain conditions).

38. The continuing question mark over the U.S. attitude toward economic and social rights is conspicuously neglected in American scholarship. An exception that proves this rule is Daniel Whelan, "The United States and Economic and Social Rights: Past, Present . . . and Future?" *Human Rights and Human Welfare Working Paper No. 26* (February 28, 2005), available at http://www.du.edu/korbel/hrhw/workingpapers/2005/26-whelan-2005.pdf.

39. See, for example, Human Rights Council, *Report of the Working Group on the Universal Periodic Review: United States of America*, UN Doc. A/HRC/16/11 (January 4, 2011), para. 87.

40. Aryeh Neier, "Social and Economic Rights: A Critique," *Human Rights Brief* 13, no. 2 (2006): 1–3, at 1.

41. For some of the history and reasons for this attitude toward civil and political rights, and an intriguing account of what role Chinese human rights scholars might play in promoting China's ratification of the Covenant, see Shiyan Sun, "The Understanding and Interpretation of the ICCPR in the Context of China's Possible Ratification," *Chinese Journal of International Law* 6, no. 1 (2007): 17–42, especially 34–42.

42. Thus, in the first white paper in 1991, there was no mistaking the defiant "we'll do it our way" tone evident in the very first paragraph: "In old China, aggression by imperialism and

oppression by feudalism and bureaucrat-capitalism deprived the people of all guarantee for their lives, and an uncountable number of them perished in war and famine. To solve their human rights problems, the first thing for the Chinese people to do is, for historical reasons, to secure the right to subsistence"; see *Human Rights in China* (1991), at http://www.china.org.cn/e-white/7/index.htm. The language and approach in the latest white paper in 2015 are much more subtle, simply placing "citizens' access to fair development" and "better protected . . . economic social and cultural rights" ahead of "democratic rights" in the list of the state's priorities and achievements in the field; see *Progress in China's Human Rights* (June 2015), at http://english.gov.cn/archive/white_paper/2015/06/08/content_281475123202380.htm.

43. See, for example, the section on China in Amnesty International, *Annual Report: 2015/2016*, which notes "a massive nationwide crackdown against human rights lawyers," and the enactment of a "series of new laws with a national security focus . . . that present grave dangers to human rights;" 117. Available at https://www.amnesty.org/en/latest/research/2016/02/annual-report-201516/.

44. As enunciated in the "Fundamental Rights and Duties of Citizens" in Chapter II (Articles 33–56) of the *Constitution*. These include many of the core civil and political rights (equality, the right to vote, fair trial, free speech and religion, privacy, and freedom from arbitrary arrest), as well as economic, social, and cultural rights (to work and rest, education, and state-funded welfare assistance) recognized in international law.

45. Including the limited, but much scrutinized, "general exceptions" under Article XX of the *General Agreement on Tariffs and Trade* (1947), which permit trade-restricting measures "necessary to protect human, animal or plant life or health," or "relating to the conservation of natural resources." On the actual and potential for these exceptions to protect and promote human rights standards, see Rachel Harris and Gillian Moon, "GATT and Human Rights: What Do We Know from the First 20 Years?" *Melbourne Journal of International Law* 16 (2015): 431–82.

46. As related by Nigel Grimwade, "The GATT, The Doha Round and Developing Countries," in Homi Katrak and Roger Strange (eds.), *The WTO and Developing Countries* (New York: Palgrave Macmillan, 2004), 25.

47. For coverage of both sides of this argument, see Sarah Joseph, *Blame It on the WTO: A Human Rights Critique* (Oxford: Oxford University Press, 2011), 130–37.

48. David Hume, "Of Commerce," in *Essays, Moral, Political and Literary* (1742) (Indianapolis, IA: Liberty Fund, 1987), Part II.I.11: "Every thing in the world is purchased by labour; and our passions are the only causes of labour."

49. Financial Crisis Inquiry Commission, *The Financial Crisis Inquiry Report: Final Report of the National Commission on the Causes of the Financial and Economic Crisis in the United States* (Washington, DC: GPO, 2011), 402, https://www.gpo.gov/fdsys/pkg/GPO-FCIC/pdf/GPO-FCIC.pdf.

50. Ibid., xvi.

51. The *Equator Principles* (2013) seek to promote such beneficial outcomes by encouraging financial institutions to adopt more robust assessments of the social and environmental impacts of projects, especially in the mining and utilities sectors, before committing to financing them; see http://www.equator-principles.com/resources/equator_principles_III.pdf, and chapter 4 below, 100–1, for further discussion.

52. For an indication of the complexity of relations between finance and human rights in terms of the practical challenges it raises for their scrutiny and assessment, see Danish Institute for Human Rights, *Values Added: The Challenge of Integrating Human Rights into the Financial Sector* (2010), especially 11–25. Available at https://www.humanrights.dk/files/media/billeder/udgivelser/values_added_report_dihr.pdf.

53. On the *Equator Principles* generally, see note 51, above; and on the number and identity of so-called Equator Principles Financial Institutions, see http://www.equator-principles.com/index.php/members-reporting.

54. See table on Historical Tantalite Ore Price, at InvestmentMine, http://www.infomine.com/investment/metal-prices/tantalite-ore/all/.

55. See Nicolas Cook, *Conflict Minerals in Central Africa: US and International Responses*, Congressional Research Service, July 20, 2012.

56. According to the UN, alongside the government of the DRC, somewhere between twenty-five and forty-nine armed militia in and around the DRC and its three neighboring states of Rwanda, Burundi, and Uganda are all lethally squabbling over proprietorial control of the country's natural resources, including coltan. See UNEP, MONUSC & OSESG, Experts' background report on illegal exploitation and trade in natural resources benefitting organized criminal groups and recommendations on MONUSCO's role in fostering stability and peace in eastern DR Congo, *Final report* (April 15, 2015), paras. 9, 10, 25, and 97.

57. It has been estimated that in the EU alone, there are more than 400 importers of conflict minerals, including coltan; see EU Parliament News, "Conflict Minerals: Preventing Military Groups from Funding Their Activities," May 19, 2015.

58. Though it is accepted here that there is a difference in principle between the legal responsibilities of international development banks and agencies (which are governed by international law) and the private banks (which are only 'guided' by international law). In respect of the former, see, for example, chapter 4, 86–7 (re: the World Bank); and in respect of the latter, see chapter 5, 134–5 (re: the Thun Group).

59. On this point the advocacy group BankTrack is especially strong. For instance, in its report *Close the Gap: Benchmarking Credit Policies of International Banks* (2010), it produced a scorecard for forty-nine international banks as regards their policies toward preventing human rights abuses in mining operations that they fund. At that time, only one bank (Rabobank) had a mining policy that included due diligence in respect of human rights factors; at 43. Available at https://www.banktrack.org/download/close_the_gap/100427_close_the_ gap_pdf_for_download.pdf.

60. The *Dodd-Frank Wall Street Reform and Consumer Protection Act* (2010), section 1502, requires persons and corporations to disclose annually whether any conflict minerals originating in the DRC or an adjoining country, are necessary to the functionality or production of their business. It would appear, however, that few corporations are taking the matter sufficiently seriously. Amnesty International analyzed the conflict minerals reports submitted by 100 U.S. corporations in 2014–15 and found that nearly 80% of them failed to meet the standards of disclosure required under the statute; see its report: *Digging for Transparency: How U.S. Companies are only Scratching the Surface of Conflict Minerals Reporting* (2015).

61. For a preliminary attempt to outline various levels of banks' responsibilities for human rights abuses occurring within their often complex commercial relations, see *OHCHR response to request from BankTrack for advice regarding the application of the UN Guiding Principles on Business and Human Rights in the context of the banking sector* (June 21, 2017), 3-10.

62. Mary Dowell-Jones, "International Finance and Human Rights: Scope for a Mutually Beneficial Relationship," *Global Policy* 3, no. 4 (2012): 467–70, at 467.

63. Manuel Couret Branco, *Economics versus Human Rights* (Abingdon: Routledge, 2009), 5.

64. Arthur Pigou, *The Economics of Welfare* (1929; 3rd edn; Macmillan, London), Preface.

65. Nassim Taleb, *Fooled by Randomness: The Hidden Role of Chance in Life and in the Markets* (New York: Random House, 2005). In this context, schadenfreude may compel us to ask: If financiers really are as smart as they claim to be, how come nearly all of them failed to foresee the 2007 credit crisis?

66. Mary Dowell-Jones and David Kinley, "Minding the Gap: Global Finance and Human Rights" *Ethics and International Affairs* 25, no. 2 (2011): 183–210, at 185.

67. Ibid., 206.

68. Centre for Concern, *A Bottom-up Approach to Righting Financial Regulation: Why Is a Human Rights Approach Needed in Financial Regulation* (2012), available at http://www.cidse.org/ content/publications/finance-and-development/reforming-the-financial-system/financial_ regulation_and_human_rights.html.

69. International Network for Economic, Social and Cultural Rights, *Statement on the Financial Crisis and Global Economic Recession: Towards a Human Rights Response* (June 2009), para.14. The unhelpful repercussions of such stark proclamations are further discussed in chapter 6 below, 170–6.

70. Robert Shiller, *Finance and the Good Society* (Princeton, NJ: Princeton University Press, 2012), 239.

71. Though he is surely on much shakier ground when he further argues that the "humanizing" effect of finance encourages charity (ibid., 235). For Shiller, it seems, human nature's lust for power will be somehow confined to the market arena of finance, and outside it, financial actors will abandon their acquisitive edge and voluntarily distribute their gains to the rest of society. Reality would suggest otherwise. Relatedly, I discuss both the problems and problems of philanthropy in chapter 5 below, 107–14.

72. Ibid., 149.

73. Ibid.

74. Ibid.

75. Shiller's singular focus on the UDHR in this respect is a significant oversight. In particular, his assessment of economic and social rights (ibid., 149–50) fails to make any reference to or consideration of the ICESCR, or to any of the work of the various UN Special Procedures mandates that cover economic, financial, and human rights matters. I return to the problematic consequences of such superficiality in chapter 7, 184–5.

76. So, for example, David Kinley, "Bendable Rules: The Development Implications of Human Rights Pluralism," in Brian Tamanaha, Caroline Sage, and Michael Woolcock (eds.), *Legal Pluralism and Development: Scholars and Practitioners in Dialogue* (New York: Cambridge University Press, 2012), 50–65, in which I argue that the bendability of human rights can be used to break down the resistance to human rights legal texts methodologies endemic in such international financial institutions as the World Bank and the IMF.

77. Immanuel Kant, *Critique of Pure Reason* (1791), trans. and ed. Paul Guyer and Allen Wood (Cambridge: Cambridge University Press, 1997), 5:19–30.

78. Martha C. Nussbaum, *Sex and Social Justice* (New York: Oxford University Press, 1999), 41–42.

79. United Nations, *Vienna Declaration and Programme of Action* (1993), para. 5.

80. Richard Rorty, *Philosophy and Social Hope* (London: Penguin, 1999), xxxi. While later in the same work Rorty expands on his concern with the *utility* of human rights as distinct from Kant's focus on their *source* (at 83–88), he nonetheless stresses their shared conviction that human rights are critical to "moral progress," "cultural evolution," and the pursuit of a "human future richer than the human past" (87).

81. It is, rather, as Rorty goes on to argue, that "history and anthropology are enough to show that there are no unwobbling pivots, and that seeking objectivity is just a matter of getting as much intersubjective agreement as you can manage" (ibid., 14).

82. *Voices of the Poor* consists of three books published by the World Bank: Deepa Narayan with Raj Patel, Kai Schafft, Anne Rademacher, and Sarah Koch-Schulte, *Can Anyone Hear Us?* (2000); Deepa Narayan, Robert Chambers, Meera Kaul Shah, and Patti Petesch, *Crying Out Loud for Change* (2000); and Deepa Narayan and Patti Petesch, *From Many Lands* (2000).

83. As of August 2016; see Department of the Treasury/Federal Reserve Board, "Major Foreign Holders of Treasury Securities," October 18, 2016, available at http://ticdata.treasury.gov/ Publish/mfh.txt.

Chapter 3 – Flirting with Risk

1. The extent to which this represents a true depiction of Cleopatra's life is a matter of some contention, not least because it largely reflects just one side of the story. It was an age, as a leading authority on Cleopatra puts it, "when Rome controlled the narrative": Stacy Schiff, *Cleopatra: A Life* (New York: Little, Brown, 2011), 4.

2. As made abundantly clear in the published dairies of his wife, Sofia, which paint "a picture of a cruel and difficult man, indifferent to his family, endlessly critical, who forced his wife to breastfeed all 13 of their children despite the agony it caused her," as one reviewer put it: Alison Flood, "Sofia Tolstoy's Diaries Paint Bleak Portrait of Marriage to Leo," *The Guardian*, June 2, 2009; a review of Sofia Tolstoy, *The Diaries of Sophia Tolstoy* (trans. Cathy Porter) (New York: HarperCollins, 2010).

3. The give-and-take built into this rough formula reflects the complexity of risk within global financial policies and practices, the long and interconnected arms of which are not amenable to absolute terms of responsibility and risk.

4. See, respectively, Christopher Bellringer and Ranald Michie, "Big Bang in the City of London: An Intentional Revolution or an Accident? *Financial History Review* 21, no. 2 (2014): 111–37; and Matthew Sherman, *A Short History of Financial Deregulation in the United States* (Washington, DC: Center for Economic and Policy Research, 2009), 8–10.

5. As quoted by Anat Admati and Martin Hellwig, T*he Bankers' New Clothes: What's Wrong with Banking and What to Do about It* (Princeton, NJ: Princeton University Press, 2012), at 11.

6. David Miles, Jing Yang, and Gilbreto Marcheggiano, *Optimal Bank Capital*, External Monetary Policy Unit of the Bank of England, Discussion Paper 31 (January 2011), 37.

7. Rather than being a feature of mature financial systems, as economic orthodoxy maintains, that appears only after the emergence of the medium of money, anthropologists like Graeber argue that granting credit and obtaining debt were the very actions that necessitated money (as a quantifier of debt) in the first place. Money, in other words, first emerged when simple bartering no longer satisfied the needs of the parties to it; see David Graeber, *Debt: The First 5,000 Years* (New York: Melville House, 2011), 38–41.

8. The phrase is the title of the first chapter in Adair Turner, *Between Debt and the Devil: Money, Credit and Fixing Global Finance* (Princeton, NJ: Princeton University Press, 2015).

9. Based on data drawn from the Bank of England, as cited by Turner, *Between Debt and the Devil*, 63.

10. See Òscar Jordà, Moritz Schularick, and Alan Taylor, *The Great Mortgaging: Housing Finance, Crises, and Business Cycles* (2014), Federal Reserve Bank of San Francisco, Working Paper Series, in which the authors demonstrate the rapid rise of mortgage versus non-mortgage lending since the mid-1980s in seventeen Western economies, at 10–12.

11. Ibid., 15, "Figure 5: Ratio of household mortgage lending to the value of the housing stock."

12. Michael Lewis, "When Irish Eyes are Crying," *Vanity Fair*, March 2011, in which Lewis delightfully describes one prescient Irish economist he encounters as "puckish, unrehearsed, and apparently—though in Ireland one wants to be careful about using this word—sane."

13. John Kay, *Other People's Money: Masters of the Universe or Servants of the People?* (London: Profile Books, 2015), 191–94.

14. On the appalling performance and behavior of ratings agencies in this regard, see the discussion under "Faith no more" later in this chapter, 73–6.

15. Kay, *Other People's Money*, 193.

16. *Final Report of the National Commission on the Causes of the Financial and Economic Crisis in the United States* (2011), xix.

17. Marc Labonte, *Systemically Important or "Too Big to Fail" Financial Institutions?* Congressional Research Service, June 30, 2015, 6.

18. See "The Great Distortion," *The Economist*, May 16, 2015. In an accompanying chart, which draws on data from the IMF and the consulting firm McKinsey's, the authors demonstrate how in nearly every major economy, total borrowings (of governments, corporations, and individuals) have risen since 2000. "The world," they conclude, "is addicted to debt": see "The Tracks of Arrears," *The Economist*, May 14, 2015.

19. See Luigi Buttiglione, Philip Lane, Lucrezia Reichlin, and Vincent Reinhart, *Deleveraging, What Deleveraging?* The 16th Geneva Report on the World Economy (2014), which concludes, chillingly: "Contrary to widely held beliefs, six years on from the beginning of the financial crisis in the advanced economies, the global economy is not yet on a deleveraging path. Indeed, according to our assessment, the ratio of global total debt . . . has kept increasing at an unabated pace and breaking new highs: up 38 percentage points since 2008 to 212%," 11.

20. World Bank, *Country Overview: China*, available at http://www.worldbank.org/en/country/china/overview.

21. That is for 2013; see World Bank, *Poverty Headcount ratio at $1.90% a day (2011 PPP), (% of population): China*, available at http://data.worldbank.org/indicator/SI.POV.DDAY?locations=CN.

22. No matter that their civil and political rights remain stunted, on which see the discussion of China's constitutional protection of human rights in chapter 2, 46–7.

23. See International Labour Organization (ILO), *World Social Protection Report 2014/15*, at 2. Though the global picture is improving, "many countries," the ILO notes, "have significantly

extended their social security coverage during recent years" (ibid.), although they still fall short of comprehensive coverage. On the economic returns and social benefits of investing in adequate welfare systems, see further Michael Cichon and Krzysztof Hagemejer, *Social Security for All: Investing in Global and Economic Development. A Consultation*, Discussion Paper 16, Issues in Social Protection Series, 2006.

24. See Global Financial Integrity's annual *Illicit Financial Flows*, at http://www.gfintegrity.org/issue/illicit-financial-flows/. The human rights implications of illicit financial flows are discussed in chapter 6, 153–5.

25. UN Special Rapporteur on the Right to Housing, Raquel Rolnik, Annual Report: *Right to Housing and the Financial Crisis*, February 4, 2009, UN Doc. A/HRC/10/7, para. 43.

26. For more on the venal practices of banks and mortgage brokers targeting the poor and gullible see the discussion below in chapter 6, 152–3.

27. Data drawn from Realtytrac, "1.1 Million US Properties with Foreclosure Filings in 2014, Down 18% since 2013 to Lowest Level since 2006," January 15, 2015, available at http://www.realtytrac.com/news/foreclosure-trends/1-1-million-u-s-properties-with-foreclosure-filings-in-2014-down-18-percent-from-2013-to-lowest-level-since-2006/.

28. Thereby, it is claimed, states are neglecting their obligation to protect the right to housing under Article 11 of the ICESCR; see UN Special Rapporteur on the Right to Housing, Raquel Rolnik, Annual Report: *Right to Housing and the Financial Crisis*, paras. 43 and 91. On the decline and changing nature of public housing in the West, see Alan Murie, "Public Housing in Europe and North America," in Jie Che, Mark Stephens and Yanyun Man (eds) *The Future of Public Housing: Ongoing Trends in the East and the West* (Berlin: Springer, 2013), 165–80.

29. Mark Blyth, *Austerity: The History of a Dangerous Idea* (New York: Oxford University Press, 2013), 7.

30. UN OHCHR, *Report on Austerity Measures and Economic and Social Rights* (undated), at 7.

31. ICESCR, Articles 9–12.

32. See the UN Committee on Economic, Social and Cultural Rights, General Comment No. 3, *The Nature of State Parties' Obligations* (Art. 2, Para.1, of the Covenant), UN Doc. E/1991/23 (December 14, 1990), para. 9.

33. Ariranga G. Pillay, Chairperson, Committee on Economic, Social and Cultural Rights, *Letter to States Parties*, May 16, 2012; available at http://www2.ohchr.org/english/bodies/cescr/docs/LetterCESCRtoSP16.05.12.pdf.

34. Ibid.

35. See Jane Lethbridge, *Impact of Global Economic Crisis and Austerity Measures on Women*, A report commissioned by Public Services International (2012).

36. See International Labour Organization (ILO), *World Social Protection Report 2014/15*, 2. The ILO cites evidence and documentation in support of this argument from the OECD, the World Bank, and G20 sources, as well its own.

37. In contrast, other European states managed to substantially preserve their levels of social protection—notably, the Benelux and Nordic states, as well as France and Germany. See Colm O'Cinneide, "Austerity and the Faded Dream of a 'Social Europe,'" in Aoife Nolan (ed.), *Economic and Social Rights after the Global Financial Crisis* (Cambridge: Cambridge University Press, 2014), 167, at 184–88.

38. Martin Wolf, "How Austerity Has Failed," *New York Review of Books*, July 11, 2013. Regarding the impact of austerity measures on economic, social, and cultural rights standards in Spain, see Luke Holland, "How Austerity is Eroding Human Rights," *Al Jazeera*, June 27, 2012.

39. See O'Cinneide, "Austerity and the Faded Dream of a 'Social Europe.'" Contrary to popular belief, welfare spending actually *increased* across rich states in the years following the financial crisis, by an average of some 10% in real terms, according to OECD states; see OECD, *Social Spending During the Crisis: Social Expenditure (SOCX) Update 2012*, at 1–2 (Figure 1). It was, however, the fact that the increase in spending was insufficient to meet the increase in demand that brought pain to many. For EU states, the European Commission calculated that this "spending gap" steadily increased to about minus 6% in the years following the crisis, a significantly larger gap, it noted, than in previous recessions; see "Chart 9 – Deviation from trend of public social expenditures and GDP in current crisis and past periods of

below-par performance in EU27 and EA17," in Olivier Bontout and Terezie Lokajickova, *Social Protection Budgets in the Crisis in the EU*, Working Paper 1/2013 (May 2013), at 22.

40. As at July 2015; see http://www.tradingeconomics.com/greece/unemployment-rate.

41. See OECD, *Annual Average Wages 2014*; http://stats.oecd.org/Index.aspx?DataSetCode=AV_AN_WAGE. In comparison, average wages in the UK across the same period remained stable.

42. See OECD, *Government Final Consumption Expenditure in US Dollars* (2014); http://www.oecd-ilibrary.org/economics/government-final-consumption-expenditure-in-us-dollars-2014-5_govxp-table-2014-5-en;jsessionid=27ju70jva01d6.x-oecd-live-03. The relevant figures were, for Greece, 2006: $48.5 billion and 2013: $51.1 billion; and for the UK, 2006: $456 billion and 2013: $496 billion.

43. Jim Edwards, "Greece Just Taught Capitalists about What Capitalism Really Means," *Business Insider UK*, July 5, 2015.

44. See Neil Irwin, "How Germany Prevailed in the Greek Bailout," *New York Times*, July 29, 2015.

45. See European Committee of Social Rights, Collective Complaint no. 65/2011: *General Federation of Employees of the National Electric Power Corporation (GENOP-DEI) and Confederation of Greek Civil Servants Trade Unions (ADEDY) v. Greece*, Decision on the merits, May 23, 2012 (on labor rights), and a collection of five cases based on essentially the same facts led by Complaint no.76/ 2012: *Federation of Employed Pensioners of Greece (IKA-ETAM) v. Greece*, Decision on the merits, December 7, 2012 (on pension and social security rights). For discussion of the reasoning behind these decisions, see Petros Stangos, "A compilation of reasoning and decisions of the European Committee of Social Rights on the social impact of economic crisis and the EU," January 9, 2014, available at http://www.europarl.europa.eu/meetdocs/2009_2014/documents/empl/dv/presentation_stangos_/presentation_stangos_en.pdf. . Such decisions are nonbinding, which is why I placed the word "ruling" in the text in inverted commas. The Council of Europe (which has forty-seven member states) oversees the European Convention on Human Rights as well as the European Social Charter, and is a separate body to the European Union, though all twenty-eight members of the latter are also member states of the former.

46. World Bank, "G20: Financial Crisis: Responding Today, Securing Tomorrow," November 15, 2008.

47. Ibid. Further on the human rights impacts, see the UN Human Rights Council, *Report of the Office of the United Nations High Commissioner for Human Rights on the impact of the global economic and financial crises on the realization of all human rights and on possible actions to alleviate it*, UN Doc. A/HRC/13/38 (February 18, 2010).

48. See World Bank, "World Development Indicators 2016 Maps: Economy," at http://data.worldbank.org/products/wdi-maps.

49. Douglas Alexander, "The Impact of the Economic Crisis on the World's Poorest Countries," *Global Policy* 1, no. 1 (2010): 118.

50. See World Bank, "Global Development Finance 2011: External Debt of Developing Countries," at 1 (Table 1); available at https://openknowledge.worldbank.org/handle/10986/8132.

51. Ibid.

52. See UNCTAD, "Key Statistics and Trends in International Trade 2014," at 1 (Figure 1), available at http://unctad.org/en/PublicationsLibrary/ditctab2014d2_en.pdf.

53. As reported in "Capital Bonanzas: Does Wall Street's Meltdown Show That Financial Globalisation Itself Is Part of the Problem?, *The Economist*, September 25, 2008.

54. *Report of the Special Rapporteur on the human right to safe drinking water and sanitation*, UN Doc. A/HRC/24/44 (July 11, 2013), para. 50.

55. Ibid., para. 51.

56. Adding further that "the crisis may trap those who are unable to afford basic needs during a prolonged period of unemployment and very scarce income in extreme poverty for the rest of their lives, and their children may also face a lifetime of poverty"; *Report of the Independent Expert on the Question of Human Rights and Extreme Poverty*, UN Doc. A/64/279 (August 11, 2009), para. 8.

57. *Report of the independent expert on the question of human rights and extreme poverty*, A/64/279 (August 11, 2009), para. 8.

58. Committee on Economic, Social and Cultural Rights, General Comment No. 3, *The Nature of State Parties' Obligations (Art. 2, Para.1, of the Covenant)*, UN Doc. E/1991/23 (December 14, 1990), para.10.

59. Ibid.

60. World Bank, "G20: Financial Crisis: Responding Today, Securing Tomorrow," November 15, 2008.

61. Ibid.

62. Roger W. Ferguson, Jr, "The Future of Financial Services—Revisited," October 8, 2003, available at http://www.bis.org/review/r031013h.pdf.

63. This is a statistical technique used to measure and quantify the level of financial risk that a firm or a financial product may be exposed to over a given time period.

64. John Maynard Keynes, *General Theory of Employment, Interest and Money* (London: Macmillan, 1936), 161.

65. Alan Greenspan, "The Challenge of Central Banking in a Democratic Society," Remarks at the Annual Dinner and Francis Boyer Lecture of The American Enterprise Institute for Public Policy Research, Washington, D.C., December 5, 1996.

66. Some continue to believe they understand and can predict the market. Hedge fund supremo Ray Dalio, for example, swears by a set of "timeless and universal" rules of economics and finance. These include, he pronounces, the fact that "while in any market there are lots of buyers and sellers, and these buyers and sellers have different motivations, the motivations of the most important buyers are usually pretty understandable and adding them up to understand the economy isn't all that tough . . ."; see his *How the Economic Machine Works*, at http://www. economicprinciples.org/wp-content/uploads/ray_dalio__how_the_economic_machine_ works__leveragings_and_deleveragings.pdf. The key word here is "usually," which, in fact, so qualifies the rule as to rob it of rule-bound usefulness. No matter that Mr. Dalio runs the world's largest hedge fund, he and it are not immune to being "fooled by randomness." See, for instance, reports of his more recent reversals of fortune: Jen Wieczner, "Ray Dalio's McDonald's-Inspired Fund Is Crushing His Flagship Fund," *Fortune*, July 7, 2016.

67. J. C. Chandler, *Margin Call*, Before the Door Pictures (2011).

68. Kevin Dowd. John Cotter, Chris Humphrey, and Margaret Woods, "How Unlucky Is 25-Sigma?," March 2008, available at http://papers.ssrn.com/sol3/papers.cfm?abstract_ id=1517146.

69. Ibid.

70. For those who must know, the 8-sigma event formula is $6.249e + 0.12$ years; and the estimates of time since the Big Bang range between 12 and 14 billion years; ibid.

71. Bill Bonner, "Goldman Sachs Was Wrong and 2 Million Families May Lose Their Homes," *The Daily Reckoning*, November 17, 2007.

72. See the definition offered by the *Financial Times* Lexicon, at http://lexicon.ft.com. For an analysis of the history of CRAs, see Rawi Abdelal, *Capital Rules* (Cambridge, MA: Harvard University Press, 2009), chapter 7, including how the immense power they now wield "epitomize[s] ad hoc globalization" (194).

73. Standard and Poor's *What Credit Agencies Are and Are Not*, at http://www.standardandpoors. com/aboutcreditratings/RatingsManual_PrintGuide.html.

74. That is despite the fact that, for example, Standard and Poor's declares: "Unlike other types of opinions, such as, for example, those provided by doctors or lawyers, credit rating opinions are not intended to be a prognosis or recommendation. Instead, they are primarily intended to provide investors and market participants with information about the relative credit risk of issuers and individual debt issues that the agency rates" (ibid.). That said, it is not unreasonable that investors should use, as they routinely do, these risk assessments as indicators of likely outcomes of future actions, in much the same way as we all do with opinions furnished by doctors and lawyers.

75. *California Public Employees' Retirement System ("CalPERS") v. Moody's Corp. et al.*, A134912, CGC-09-490241 (Sup. Ct. Cal., SF County) (May 23, 2014).

76. On which difference see Caleb Deats, "Talk That Isn't Cheap: Does the First Amendment Protect Credit Rating Agencies' Faulty Methodologies from Regulation?" *Columbia Law Review* 110 (2010): 1818.

77. That is, both in previous cases involving rating agencies (for example, *Jefferson County School District No. R-1 v. Moody's Investor Services, Inc.*, 175 F.3d 848, 856 (10th Cir. 1999), and *Compuware Corp. v. Moody's Investors Services, Inc.*, 499 F.3d 520, 529 (6th Cir. 2007)), and in other fields, such as retail advertising: see *Kasky v. Nike, Inc.*, 27 Cal.4th 939 (2002).

78. That is, it affirmed a lower court's ruling that CalPERS had presented sufficient evidence to establish a probability of prevailing at trial and that the defendants' First Amendment defense did not at this stage protect them from suit; *California Public Employees' Retirement System ("CalPERS") v. Moody's Corp. et al.*, A134912, CGC-09-490241 (Sup. Ct. Cal., SF County) (May 23, 2014), at 34.

79. See *Case Note: CalPERS v. Moody's*, by CalPERS's lawyers, Berman & DeValerio, for details of both settlements; available at http://www.bermandevalerio.com/cases/featured-cases?pid=47&sid=171:calpers-v-moodys. Fitch had previously settled (on undisclosed terms, but reportedly not involving payment) in 2011; see "Calpers Settles Suit with Fitch, Not with Moody's or S&P's," *Reuters*, August 29, 2011.

80. See Department of Justice, Press Release, February 3, 2015, at http://www.justice.gov/opa/pr/justice-department-and-state-partners-secure-1375-billion-settlement-sp-defrauding-investors.

81. Ibid.

82. Namely, in the United States, the Securities and Exchange Commission, pursuant to the Dodd-Frank Wall Street Reform and Consumer Protection Act (2010), issued new rules in 2014 to strengthen transparency, conflicts of interest, and governance controls for CRAs (in summary, see http://www.sec.gov/News/PressRelease/Detail/PressRelease/1370542776658); and the EU established the European Securities and Markets Authority in 2011, which registers and supervises all CRAs working within the EU (see http://www.esma.europa.eu/page/Credit-Rating-Agencies).

83. "Credit where Credit's Due," *The Economist*, April 19, 2014.

84. "'Tis always self, which is the object of pride and humility; and whenever the passions look beyond, 'tis still with a view to ourselves, nor can any person or object otherwise have any influence upon us"; David Hume, *A Treatise of Human Nature*, (1739) (Dumfries: Anodos Books, replica reprint of original, 2017), Book II: Passions, Section III.

85. John Maynard Keynes, *The General Theory*, 156.

86. George Akerlof and Robert Shiller, *Animal Spirits: How Psychology Drives the Economy and Why It Matters for the Global Economy* (Princeton, NJ: Princeton University Press, 2009), 168.

87. Robert Skidelsky and Edward Skidelsky, *How Much is Enough?: The Love of Money, and the Case for the Good Life* (London: Allen Lane, 2012), 86–87.

88. William Shakespeare, *The Rape of Lucrece* (1594), lines 137–40.

89. Capitalism's "driving spirit," as Friedrich Engels called it, adding, disparagingly, where what is sought and gained is "wealth and again wealth and once more wealth, wealth, not of society, but of the single scurvy individual"; Friedrich Engels, *Origins of the Family, Private Property, and the State* (1884), Introduction by Tristram Hunt (London: Penguin Classics, 2010), chapter ix: "Barbarism and Civilization."

90. Joseph Schumpeter, *Capitalism, Socialism and Democracy*, 4th ed. (London: Allen & Unwin, 1961), 81–86

91. Nicholas Phillipson, *Adam Smith: An Enlightened Life* (London: Penguin, 2010), 61–62.

92. As Daniel Bell famously argued forty years ago in his *The Cultural Contradictions of Capitalism* (New York: Basic Books, 1976).

93. Matt Taibbi, "Will Goldman Sachs Prove That Greed is God?" *The Guardian*, April 24, 2010.

94. In early 2010, the Securities and Exchange Commission (SEC) launched a civil suit alleging fraud against Goldman and one of its employees, Fabrice Tourre, regarding a financial product called Abacus 2007-AC1. It was claimed that Goldman misled investors in 2006 and 2007 by selling them mortgage securities chosen with help from one of its clients, hedge fund financier John Paulson, without disclosing that the firm was itself shorting the securities (that is, speculating that their value would decline) and thus giving its other clients a "shitty deal," as one internal email described it at the time. Stemming from a referral by the SEC, a

criminal investigation was also instigated by the U.S. Justice Department. Finally, on April 27, 2010, the Senate Permanent Subcommittee on Investigations conducted hearings into the role of investment banks in the financial crisis, before which seven present and past Goldman employees testified. Goldman settled the civil case against the firm with the SEC in July 2010 for $550 million (see *Securities and Exchange Commission v. Goldman, Sachs & Co. and Fabrice Tourre*, Civil Action No. 10 Civ. 3229 (S.D.N.Y. filed April 16, 2010)), and the criminal investigation did not yield any charges.

95. In the Senate inquiry, the firm was lambasted for its "unbridled greed," and compared to Las Vegas, but "much more dishonest": Permanent Subcommittee on Investigations, United States Senate, *Wall Street and the Financial Crisis: The Role of Investment Banks*, April 27, 2010, Washington, D.C. (Senator John Ensign, R-Nev), webcast available at: http://www.senate.gov/fplayers/I2009/urlPlayer.cfm?fn=govtaff042710&st=945&dur=39420.

96. In his testimony before the Senate, Goldman Sachs CEO Lloyd Blankfein stated that the clients who bought the tainted subprime mortgage securities came looking for risk "and that's what they got"; Marcy Gordon, "Goldman Shares Plunge as Feds Open Criminal Probe," *Daily Finance* (online), April 30, 2010, available at: http://www.dailyfinance.com/story/investing/goldman-shares-tumble-as-public-image-takes-another-hit/19460940/.

97. Lord Adair Turner, then chair of the UK's Financial Services Authority, "How to Tame Global Finance," *Prospect* (online), August 27, 2009, http://www.prospectmagazine.co.uk/2009/08/how-to-tame-global-finance/ (accessed October 18, 2012).

98. Satyajit Das, *Extreme Money: Masters of the Universe and the Cult of Risk* (London: FT Press, 2011), 28.

99. A fear aired explicitly, for example, by theologian Thomas Aquinas in the late thirteenth century, when voicing his support for the Church's laws against usury; see his *Summa Theologica* (written between 1265 and 1274; first published in 1485), II-II, Q.78, A.1.

100. It may be a sense of entitlement borne of an assumption that is itself based on the social isolation of the rich. Matthew Lynn, for example, argues that "investment bankers and hedge-fund managers who make up most of the new rich elite don't have much contact with ordinary people. They assume their wealth is entirely the result of their own brilliance"; "Ultra-Rich in Finance are Meaner than the Rest of Us," *Bloomberg Opinion*, September 7, 2010.

101. *Theory of Moral Sentiments* (1817) (New York: Dover, 2007), vol. I, 78.

102. As per the quote at the head of this chapter.

103. As *The Economist* put it: "Wheatley, Cropped," July 25, 2015, 24.

104. On the dramatic increases in levels of debt globally, across all sectors (household, corporate, government, and financial), see Richard Dobbs, Susan Lund, Jonathan Woetzel, and Mina Mutafchieva, *Debt and (Not Much) Deleveraging*, McKinsey Global Institute, February 2015, especially section 1, 15–34; see also Buttiglione et al, at note 19 above.

105. The loans were necessary for the Irish government to fund the rising costs of the controversial guarantee it had issued for all bank deposits on September 30, 2008, which at the time had exposed the Irish Treasury to an estimated €440 liabilities held by the banks and other financial institutions. See "30 Days in September: An Oral History of the Bank Guarantee," *The Journal.ie*, September 29, 2013, available at http://www.thejournal.ie/bank-guarantee-oral-history-30-september-2008-1103254-Dec2014/.

106. Henri Maurer and Patrick Grussenmeyer, *Financial Assistance Measures in the Euro Area from 2008 to 2013: Statistical Framework and Fiscal Impact*, The European Central Bank, April 7, 2015, 18–24; see especially, Table 2 at 19.

107. Under an *EU/IMF Programme of Support* (2010), comprising two Memoranda of Understanding between Ireland and the EU and the IMF and various bilateral creditors. For details, see Central Bank of Ireland, *Quarterly Bulletin Q1* (2011), 63–64.

108. See the *Report of the Special Investigation Commission to the Icelandic Parliament*, April 12, 2010, 16, where the commission estimates that at the time of the banks' collapse, their total collective assets were worth approximately 40% of their booked value; available at http://www.rna.is/eldri-nefndir/addragandi-og-orsakir-falls-islensku-bankanna-2008/skyrsla-nefndarinnar/english/.

109. See Martin Hart-Landsberg, "Lessons from Iceland: Capitalism, Crisis and Resistance," *Monthly Review* 65, no. 2 (2013), 26-44. https://monthlyreview.org/2013/10/01/lessons-iceland/#fn2.

110. Interview with *Al Jazeera*, at World Economic Forum, Annual Meeting, January 26, 2013; see https://youtu.be/3sDgkFalIqo?t=37.

111. A state of self-deception that pervades the finance sector worldwide, as argued by Admati and Hellwig, *The Bankers' New Clothes*.

112. "Report on Mission to Iceland (December 8–15, 2014) of the Independent Expert on the effects of foreign debt and other related international financial obligations of states on the full enjoyment of all human rights, particularly economic, social and cultural rights," Juan Pablo Bohoslavsky, UN Doc. A/HRC/28/59/Add.1 (March 20, 2015), para. 74.

113. A so-called Stand-By Arrangement agreed between Iceland and the IMF. The program comprised access by Iceland to an IMF loan worth $2.1 billion; see IMF Press Release, November 19, 2008, available at https://www.imf.org/external/np/sec/pr/2008/pr08296.htm.

114. A guarantee, what is more, that in Australia's case neither the depositors nor banks have to pay for. Despite having initially supported the introduction of a modest bank levy (of 0.05% on deposits up to AUD$250,000—the limit of the government's unconditional guarantee), the Australian government caved in to banking sector lobbying and announced on September 1, 2015, that it would not proceed with the proposal. The banks were delighted; and with good reason. What other sector in a supposedly free market economy can command such comprehensive insurance on such generous terms?

115. See "Report of the independent expert on the question of human rights and extreme poverty," Magdalena Sepúlveda Carmona, Mission to Ireland (January 10–15, 2011), A/HRC/17/34/Add.2 (May 17, 2011); and Committee on Economic, Social and Cultural Rights, *Concluding Observations on the Fourth Report of Iceland*, E/C.12/ISL/CO/4 (December 11, 2012).

116. As reported in Kerry Capell, "The Stunning Collapse of Iceland," *Bloomberg Business*, October 9, 2008; available at http://www.bloomberg.com/bw/stories/2008-10-09/the-stunning-collapse-of-icelandbusinessweek-business-news-stock-market-and-financial-advice.

117. In the words of Iceland's finance minister Steingrímur Sigfússon, as reported in "Iceland's Unorthodox Policies Suggest an Alternative Way out of the Crisis," *IMF Survey Magazine*, November 3, 2011; available at http://www.imf.org/external/pubs/ft/survey/so/2011/CAR110311A.htm.

118. Ibid.

119. Ibid. See also Paul Krugman, "The Path Not Taken," *New York Times*, October 27, 2011.

120. "Iceland's Unorthodox Policies."

121. See *Report of the Special Investigation Commission to the Icelandic Parliament* (April 12, 2010), Appendix 3, "Iceland's Failed Banks: A Post-Mortem," by Mark Flannery, 91; available at http://www.rna.is/eldri-nefndir/addragandi-og-orsakir-falls-islensku-bankanna-2008/skyrsla-nefndarinnar/english/.

122. "Iceland's Unorthodox Policies."

123. As alternatively dubbed by "Schott's Vocab" in the *New York Times* (November 12, 2009), and defined as "a virtueless circle in which banks take ever-greater risks to boost returns (secure in the knowledge the state will underwrite them), and governments are forced to break their promises 'never again' to bankroll losses (further encouraging banks to take dangerous risks)."

124. "Report on Mission to Iceland," para.77.

125. John Quiggin, *Zombie Economics* (Princeton, NJ: Princeton University Press, 2010), 242.

126. Ibid.

127. "The Gods Strike Back," *The Economist*, "A Special Report on Financial Risk," February 13, 2010, 5.

128. The question of regulation generally, and, specifically, what criminal and civil law sanctions are necessary, are matters we return to in chapter 6 (at 162–5) and chapter 7 (at 198–9).

129. John Gray, *False Dawn: The Delusions of Global Capitalism* (London: Granta, 1998), 17.

Chapter 4 – Private Matters

1. See H. W. Brands, *The First American: The Life and Times of Benjamin Franklin* (New York: Doubleday, 2000), especially chapters 1 and 5.
2. Doudney's quote in full reads: "Money never made a man happy yet, nor will it. There is nothing in its nature to produce happiness. The more a man has, the more he wants. Instead of its filling a vacuum, it makes one. If it satisfies one want, it doubles and trebles that want another way"; see David Alfred Doudney, *Old Jonathan's Jottings, Or Light and Lessons* (Bonmahon: 1870), 19.
3. As represented by many of Franklin's aphorisms in his *Poor Richard's Almanack* (published annually between 1732 and 1758), such as "if you know the values of money, go and borrow some" (#272), and "if you know how to spend less than you get, you have the philosopher's stone" (# 99).
4. Michael Sandel, *What Money Can't Buy: The Moral Limits of Markets* (New York: Penguin, 2012), 3.
5. The phrase was apparently used by Émile Zola in his preparatory notes to his novel *L'Argent* (1891), as noted by Valerie Minogue in the introduction to her translation of the work, *Money* (Oxford: Oxford University Press, 2014), at xii.
6. In 1996, a class action suit was filed in the U.S. District Court (EDNY) by victims, their families, and descendants against the two banks for laundering, funding, and profiting from Nazi money. The case was settled in 1999 for $1.25 billion; see *Class Action Settlement Agreement* (January 26, 1999), available at http://www.swissbankclaims.com/Documents/Doc_9_ Settlement.pdf.
7. That is under the U.S. *Alien Torts Claims Act* (1789); *see Khulumani v. Barclay Nat. Bank Ltd PLC*, United States Court of Appeals, Second Circuit (Nos. 05-2141-CV, 05-2326-CV), January 27, 2007. While the plaintiff was unsuccessful in this case and in a subsequent, amended action (*In re South African Apartheid Litigation*, 617 F. Supp. 2d 228 [S.D.N.Y. 2009]), it has since been argued that legal perspectives on the liability of banks for gross human rights abuses have changed in recent years to be less accepting of arguments that financiers cannot be held responsible for the human rights–abusing actions of their clients; see Sabine Michalowski's penetrating analysis of this jurisprudential shift: "No Complicity Liability for Funding Gross Human Rights Violations?" *Berkeley Journal of International Law* 30 (2012): 451.
8. See U.S. Department of Justice, "BNP Paribas Agrees to Plead Guilty and to Pay $8.9 Billion for Illegally Processing Financial Transactions for Countries Subject to US Economic Sanctions," Press Release, June 30, 2014. A civil suit under the *Alien Torts Claims Act* (1789) has also been brought against the Jordanian-based Arab Bank (on the jurisdictional basis that it has a branch in New York) alleging tortious liability for knowingly promoting terrorist activities by providing banking services to Hamas for many years. The case was heard before the U.S. Supreme Court on October 11, 2017 ; see *Jesner v. Arab Bank PLC*, Petition for Writ of Certiorari, filed on October 5, 2016; see http://www.scotusblog.com/case-files/cases/ jesner-v-arab-bank-plc/.
9. See U.S. Department of Justice, "HSBC Holdings PLC and HSBC USA NA Admit to Anti-Money Laundering and Sanctions Violations, Forfeit $1.256 Billion in Deferred Prosecutions Agreement," Press Release, December 11, 2012.
10. On this changing landscape, see David Nersessian, "Business Lawyers as Worldwide Moral Gatekeepers? Legal Ethics and Human Rights in Global Corporate Practice," *Georgetown Journal of Legal Ethics* 28, no. 4 (2015): 1135–87. See also the *IBA Practical Guide on Business and Human Rights for Business Lawyers*, published by the International Bar Association (May 2016).
11. Namely: Barclays, BBVA, Credit Suisse, ING Bank, RBS Group, UBS, and UniCredit.
12. The Thun Group of Banks, *UN Guiding Principles on Business and Human Rights: Discussion Paper for Banks on Implications of Principles 16–21* (October 2013), and *UN Guiding Principles on Business and Human Rights: Discussion Paper for Banks on Implications of Principles 16–21* (February 2017). The *Guiding Principles on Business and Human Rights: Implementing the United Nations "Protect, Respect and Remedy" Framework*, formulated by the UN Secretary-General's

Special Representative on Business and Human Rights, John Ruggie, were adopted by the UN Human Rights Council on July 6, 2011; UN Doc. A/HRC/RES/17/4.

13. Thun Group, *UN Guiding Principles on Business and Human Rights: Discussion Paper for Banks on Implications of Principles 16–21* (October 2013), 3; though, in respect of the supply chain, adding the caveat that "the degree to which it is feasible for banks to exert influence on their clients' behaviour is a matter of complexity," 5.

14. In fact, the commentary to GP 11 declares that corporations' responsibility to respect international human rights standards "exists *over and above* compliance with national laws and regulations protecting human rights" (my emphasis); see *UN Guiding Principles on Business and Human Rights: Implementing the United Nations "Protect, Respect and Remedy" Framework* (2011). For criticism of this and other perceived deficiencies of the first Discussion Paper, see Damiano De Felice, "Banks and Human Rights Due Diligence: A Critical Analysis of the Thun Group's Discussion Paper on the UN Guiding Principles on Business and Human Rights," *International Journal of Human Rights* 19, no. 3 (2015): 319–40.

15. Thun Group, *UN Guiding Principles on Business and Human Rights: Discussion Paper for Banks on Implications of Principles 16-21* (October 2013), 3.

16. Ibid., 24; similar wording is used in the second document; see Thun Group, *UN Guiding Principles on Business and Human Rights: Discussion Paper for Banks on Implications of Principles 16-21* (February 2017), 26. See further, on this point, David Kinley, "Artful Dodgers: Banks and Their Human Rights Responsibilities," March 2017, at https://papers.ssrn.com/sol3/papers.cfm?abstract_id=2926215, and John Ruggie, "Comments on Thun Group of Banks Discussion Paper on the Implications of UN Guiding Principles 13 & 17 in a Corporate and Investment Banking Context," February 2017, at https://business-humanrights.org/sites/default/files/documents/Thun%20Final.pdf.

17. See BankTrack, *Banking with Principles* (December 2014), 15–16. Consider, for example, Goldman Sachs's "Statement on Human Rights," in which it declares that it "takes seriously its responsibility to help protect, preserve and promote human rights around the world" and its desire to "play a role in championing these fundamental rights." More specifically, the firm claims to place a high priority on its human rights due diligence procedures such that its business decisions are informed by analyses of "new and existing clients for a wide array of possible human rights-related issues, including labor practices, impacts on indigenous peoples, and proximity to conflict regions"; see http://www.goldmansachs.com/investor-relations/corporate-governance/corporate-governance-documents/human-rights-statement.pdf.

18. In a 2016 updated edition of the BankTrack report referred to in note 17, BankTrack noted that still only twenty-seven out of forty-five banks surveyed possessed "a clear statement of policy to 'respect' human rights," 7. Across the full set of criteria against which the organization measured banks (policies, due diligence commitments, reporting, and access to remedy), the report concluded that while banks were making some progress, it was slow and that there were "many laggards; no true leaders," 3. BankTrack, *Banking with Principles: Benchmarking Banks against the UN Guiding Principles on Business and Human Rights* (June 2016).

19. Group of Thirty, *Banking Culture and Conduct: A Call for Sustained and Comprehensive Reform* (July 2015), 24.

20. Ibid.; for membership of the Group, see http://group30.org/members.

21. See World Bank, *World Development Report 2013*, 77–78.

22. Ibid., 76.

23. CESCR, *General Comment 18* (2005) on the Right to Work, E/C.12/GC/18 (February 6, 2006), para.1

24. Preamble to *ILO Convention No. 168* (1988), on Employment Promotion and Protection against Unemployment.

25. Though the ILO also recognizes the right to work, the focus of its many work-related instruments is on rights at work—that is, conditions, treatment and pay, among other things; see *ILO Declaration on Fundamental Principles and Rights at Work* (1998).

26. CESCR, *General Comment 18* (2005) on the Right to Work, E/C.12/GC/18 (February 6, 2006), para. 52. On which, see further, Ben Saul, David Kinley, and Jacqueline Mowbray, *The International Covenant on Economic, Social and Cultural Rights: Commentary, Cases and Materials* (Oxford: Oxford University Press, 2014), 361–65.

27. "Jobs are a cornerstone of development, says World Development Report 2013," World Bank Press Release, October 1, 2012.

28. World Bank, *World Development Report 2013*, chapter 4, "Jobs and Social Cohesion."

29. Paul Collier, *Wars, Guns and Votes* (London: HarperCollins, 2009), 20–22.

30. Justin Jennings, *Globalizations in the Ancient World* (Cambridge: Cambridge University Press, 2014), 68–72.

31. Consider, for example, the estimated 9 million Italians who emigrated in the fifty or so years between the unification of Italy in 1861 and the First World War, and whose remittances proved to be vital to their many families at home, and indeed to the state itself; see Mark Choate, *Emigrant Nation: The Making of Italy Abroad* (Cambridge, MA: Harvard University Press, 2008), 76–78.

32. See World Bank, "Remittances to Developing Countries Edge Up Slightly in 2015," Press Release, April 13, 2016.

33. Data from World Bank, *Migration and Remittances Factbook* 2011, at 19. It is estimated that up to a further 50% of these totals flow through informal remittances channels, both to avoid the punishing transaction costs and the transparency of formal routes; see Dilip Ratha, "Remittances: Funds for the Folks Back Home," in the Finance and Development section, IMF, March 28, 2012, available at http://www.imf.org/external/pubs/ft/fandd/basics/remitt.htm.

34. Using 2015 figures; data drawn from World Bank, *Personal Remittances, Received (% GDP)*; available at http://data.worldbank.org/indicator/BX.TRF.PWKR.DT.GD.ZS/countries?display=default.

35. Ibid.; the interactive data sets provide historical as well as current data.

36. Cerstin Sander and Samuel Munzele Maimbo, "Migrant Remittances in Africa: A Regional Perspective" in Samuel Munzele Maimbo and Dilip Ratha (eds.), *Remittances: Development Impact and Future Prospects* (Washington, DC: The World Bank, 2005), 63–64.

37. See Yéro Baldé, "The Impact of Remittances and Foreign Aid on Savings/Investment in Sub-Saharan Africa," *African Development Review* 23, no. 2 (2011): 247–62.

38. Between 2000 and 2013, the ratio of private credit to GDP in low-income countries increased from an average of 19% to 33%, and from 52% to 82% in middle-income countries; see *Report of the UN Secretary-General: Follow-up to and implementation of the Monterrey Consensus and Doha Declaration on Financing for Development*, A/69/358 (August 27, 2014), para.10.

39. World Bank, *Migration and Development: Recent Developments and Outlook. Special Topic: Financing for Development*, Migration and Development Brief 24 (April 13, 2015), 17.

40. Heiko Fritiz, and Günter Lang, *Microcredit, Human Capital, and Personal Income Distribution: Empirical Evidence from Greater Cairo*, Working Paper No. 30 (2012), German University in Cairo, Faculty of Management Technology, available at http://EconPapers.repec.org/RePEc:guc:wpaper:30.

41. That is, some 62% of adults reported having an account with a bank or other financial institution; see Asli Demirguc-Kunt, Leora Klapper, Dorothe Singer, and Peter Van Oudheusden, *The Global Findex Database 2014 Measuring Financial Inclusion around the World*, World Bank Policy Research Working Paper 7255 (April 2015), 4. The report notes that the number of "unbanked" poor had significantly decreased between 2011 and 2014—that is, by about 20%, or some 700 million adults; ibid.

42. Richard Rosenberg, Scott Gaul, William Ford, and Olga Tomilova, *Microcredit Interest Rates and their Determinants 2004–2011* (Washington, DC: Consultative Group to Assist the Poor, 2013), 5–7. The report was based on data drawn from a survey of 866 microfinance institutions (MFIs).

43. Ibid., 29, Figure 26—which shows that the 29.6% interest yield on loans in 2004 was made of 5.8% profit, 2.4% loan losses, 5.2% financial expenses, and 16.8% operating costs, while the corresponding figures for the 26.9% interest yield on loans in 2011 were 2.6% profit, 3.6% loan losses, 7.8% financial expenses, and 14% operating costs.

44. Jeffrey Tucker, "Mission Truly Impossible: Easily Moving Money between Countries," *Newsweek*, August 15, 2015.

45. See World Bank, *Migration and Development: Recent Developments and Outlook. Special Topic: Financing for Development*, Migration and Development Brief 24 (April 13, 2015), 9–14.
46. For an overview of money-moving costs and their reasons in the Pacific (one of the least-banked regions in the world), see Rebecca Stanley and Ross Buckley, "Protecting the West, Excluding the Rest: The Impact of the AML/CTF Regime on Financial Inclusion in the Pacific, and Potential Responses," *Melbourne Journal of International Law* 17, no. 1 (2016): 1–24, at 9–11.
47. See *Responsible Leadership for a Sustainable Future*, Outcome Document, G8 Summit 2009, L'Aquila, Italy; para. 134; and the G20, *2014 Financial Inclusion Action Plan* (September 2, 2014), at 2. Overall costs have costs have dropped since 2009, just not as quickly as was hoped for and the drop has now tailed off—see The World Bank's *Remittances Worldwide Index*, which keeps a running tally of aggregate and disaggregated transaction costs for all the main remittance corridors worldwide: https://remittanceprices.worldbank.org/en.
48. On the exponential growth of mobile money accounts in developing countries, especially in sub-Saharan Africa, see World Bank, *Global Payment Systems Survey 2015* (October 2016 update), 7–8.
49. World Bank, *Migration and Development: Recent Developments and Outlook. Special Topic: Financing for Development*, Migration and Development Brief 24 (April 13, 2015), 11; and on the costs involved, see Stanley and Buckley, "Protecting the West, Excluding the Rest."
50. As discussed further in chapter 6 below, 157–9.
51. Using the UNCTAD definition of the term, FDI comprises three components: equity capital, reinvested earnings, and intracompany loans; see UNCTAD, *FDI Flows*, at http://unctad.org/en/Pages/DIAE/Investment%20and%20Enterprise/FDI_Flows.aspx.
52. The data referred to in the following paragraphs are taken from UNCTAD, *World Investment Report 2017*, Annex Tables 1 and 2 (June 7, 2017), available at http://unctad.org/en/Pages/DIAE/World%20Investment%20Report/Annex-Tables.aspx.
53. Both total FDI inflows and outflows for developing states experienced downward corrections after the Asian and Global financial crises; they were neither severe nor long-lasting; see ibid.
54. See Kevin Gallagher, Amos Irwin, and Katherine Koleski, *The New Banks in Town: Chinese Finance in Latin America*, Inter-American Dialogue (February 2012), available at http://ase.tufts.edu/gdae/Pubs/rp/GallagherChineseFinanceLatinAmericaBrief.pdf.
55. In 2012, for the first time, developing countries' proportion of total FDI inflows into other developing countries exceeded that sourced from developed countries. See Michael Gistrin, "Putting Foreign Direct Investment to Work for Development," chapter 5 in OECD, *Development Co-operation Report 2014*, Figure 5.1, 73.
56. Special Rapporteur on the Right to Adequate Housing, Report to the Commission on Human Rights, E/CN.4/2005/48 (March 3, 2005), para. 25, to which the Special Rapporteur adds, that as "homelessness is often intimately linked to barriers to income generation" (ibid., para. 33), people get trapped in downward spirals of poverty.
57. "The Foreign Investment Law" (The Pyidaungsu Hluuttaw Law No. 21, 2012; November 2, 2012); since amended: Law No. 40, 2016.
58. See Sean Turnell, an economist and veteran commentator on Myanmar, "Legislative Foundations of Myanmar's Economic Reforms" in Melissa Crouch and Tim Lindsay (eds.), *Law, Society and Transition in Myanmar* (Oxford: Hart, 2014), 184–87. The 2012 law has since been amended repeatedly in an effort, partly, to address some of these social concerns, while maintaining a favorable investment climate; see Achara Deboonme and Khine Kyaw, "Myanmar Kicks off Investment Law Modernisation," *The Nation*, March 9, 2015. For commentary on the latest version of the law (enacted in late 2016), see World Bank, *New Investment Law Helps Myanmar Rebuild its Economy and Create New Jobs* (January 25, 2017).
59. See UNCTAD, *IIA Databases*, at http://unctad.org/en/pages/DIAE/International%20Investment%20Agreements%20(IIA)/IIA-Tools.aspx.
60. This is taken from the Preamble in Norway's 2015 Model BIT, which, as of late 2017, is still in draft form—see https://www.regjeringen.no/contentassets/e47326b61f424d4c9c3d470896492623/draft-model-agreement-english.pdf. The *Investment Agreement for the Common Market for Eastern and Southern Africa* (2010) also expressly protects bona fide regulatory measures taken by member states "that are designed and applied to protect or

enhance legitimate public welfare objectives, such as public health, safety and the environ-ment," against claims by investors of expropriation (Article 20 (8)).

61. So-called "stabilization clauses" seek to render more predictable the regulatory landscape in which the investment is made; see Antony Crockett, "Stabilisation Clauses and Sustainable Development: Drafting for the Future," in Chester Brown and Kate Miles (eds.), *Evolution in Investment Treaty Law and Arbitration* (Cambridge: Cambridge University Press, 2011), 516–38.

62. See Megan Wells Sheffer, "Bilateral Investment Treaties: A Friend or Foe to Human Rights?" *Denver Journal of International Law and Policy* 39 (2011): 483.

63. For an overview of this intersection, see Ursula Kriebaum, "Foreign Investments and Human Rights—The Actors and Their Different Roles," *Transnational Dispute Management* 10, no. 1 (2013): 1.

64. Consider, for example, the inherent conflict that exists between different approaches to water. That is, as a commercially exploitable resource on the one hand, versus its access as a funda-mental human right on the other. See Emma Truswell, "Thirst for Profit: Water Privatisation, Investment Law and a Human Right to Water," in Brown and Miles, *Evolution in Investment Treaty Law and Arbitration*, 570–85.

65. *CME Czech Republic B.V. v. The Czech Republic* (2003), available at http://www.italaw.com/cases/281.

66. See Mihir Desai and Alberto Moel, "Czech Mate: Expropriation and Investor Protection in a Converging World," *Review of Finance* 12, no. 1 (2008): 221–51, at 238–39.

67. See *Report prepared by the Special Rapporteur on the right of everyone to the enjoyment of the highest attainable standard of physical and mental health, Anand Grover*, UN Doc. A/69/299 (August 11, 2014), paras. 60–70.

68. An imperative underlined by the UN Committee on Economic, Social and Cultural Rights in its *General Comment 24 on State Obligations under the International Covenant on Economic, Social and Cultural Rights in the Context of Business Activities*, UN. Doc. E/ C.12/GC/24 (June 23, 2017), para. 29. Some scholars like Benedict Kingsbury and Stephan Schill have suggested that there are legal techniques available that could permit such reconciliation to occur; see their "Public Law Concepts to Balance Investors' Rights with State Regulatory Actions in the Public Interest—The Concept of Proportionality," in Stephan W. Schill (ed.), *International Investment Law and Comparative Public Law* (Oxford: Oxford University Press, 2010), 75–104.

69. See David Shea Bettwy, "The Human Rights and Wrongs of Foreign Direct Investment: The Need for an Analytical Framework," *Richmond Journal of Global Law and Business* 11, no. 3 (2012): 239–72; and on the intersection of FDI, democracy, and human rights, see Liesbeth Clen, Miet Maertens, and Johan Swinnen, "Foreign Direct Investment as an Engine for Economic Growth and Human Development," in Olivier De Schutter, Johan Swinnen, and Jan Wouters (eds.), *Foreign Direct Investment and Human Development: The Law and Economics of International Investment Treaties* (New York: Routledge, 2013), 112–15.

70. Juan Pablo Bohoslavsky, "Tracking Down the Missing Financial Link in Transitional Justice," *International Human Rights Law Review* 1 (2012): 54–92, at 70; and see further his "Another Brick in the Uruguayan Transition: Financial Complicity," in Sabine Michalowski (ed.), *Corporate Accountability in the Context of Transitional Justice* (New York: Routledge, 2013), 189–207.

71. As prodigiously argued by Leif Wenar, *Blood Oil: Tyrants, Violence, and the Rules That Run the World* (New York: Oxford University Press, 2016), 123–32, in which he details both the pas-sive and active complicity of Western states in this travesty.

72. For a compilation of all website and service providers blocked in China, see https://zh.greatfire.org/.

73. Remarkably, Leopold possessed the Congo in his personal capacity—that is, neither as the King of Belgium, nor on behalf of the Belgian state—as per the provisions of a treaty known as *The General Act of the Berlin Conference on West Africa* (February 26, 1885), *Annex 1, Protocol 8*. Demonstrating levels of deceit matched only by his capacities for greed and bru-tality, Leopold named the territory *État Indépendant du Congo*, which he controlled through his own private army, *La Force Publique*.

74. For an excellent portal into the details of corporate abuses (and support) of human rights, see the Business and Human Rights Resource Centre, at https://www.business-humanrights.org/.

75. For grim catalogs of these thefts and the enormous difficulties encountered trying to calculate their extents, see Tom Burgis, *The Looting Machine: Warlords, Oligarchs, Corporations, Smugglers, and the Theft of Africa's Wealth* (New York: Public Affairs, 2016). I return to the huge problem of illicit financial flows out of developing countries in chapter 6 below, 153–8.

76. King Leopold's ghost, as Adam Hochschild so eloquently puts it in his book so entitled, haunts the country still. The DRC's vast mineral resources continue to attract multinational corporate exploitation amid violence and corruption; see, for example, Global Witness, *Faced with a Gun, What Can You Do?* (2009), available at https://www.globalwitness.org/en/campaigns/democratic-republic-congo/faced-gun-what-can-you-do/.

77. These figures are drawn from the UNDP, *Human Development Report 2015*, Table 1: Human Development Index (HDI) and its components, available at http://hdr.undp.org/en/content/table-1-human-development-index-and-its-components. For the DRC Country Profile, including data showing the country's unbroken occupation of the lowest rungs on the HDI ladder since 1980, see http://hdr.undp.org/en/countries/profiles/COD.

78. Carole Biau and Mike Pfister, "Creating an Environment for Investment and Sustainable Development," chapter 12 in OECD, *Development Co-operation Report 2014*, 146.

79. For example, Bettwy, "The Human Rights and Wrongs of Foreign Direct Investment: The Need for an Analytical Framework."

80. See Cem Tintin, "Does Foreign Direct Investment Spur Economic Growth and Development? A Comparative Study" (August 2012), available at http://www.etsg.org/ETSG2012/Programme/Papers/73.pdf.

81. See Robert Blanton and Shannon Blanton, "Rights, Institutions, and Foreign Direct Investment: An Empirical Assessment," *Foreign Policy Analysis* 8, no. 4 (2012): 431–51.

82. For an account of this debate in the particular context of human rights–based approaches to development, see discussions in chapter 5 (136–7) and chapter 6 (176–7).

83. See Elisa Giuliani and Chiara Macchi, "Multinational Corporations' Economic and Human Rights Impacts on Developing Countries: A Review and Research Agenda," *Cambridge Journal of Economics* 38 (2014): 479–517.

84. On which project, see Daniel Kaufmann, Aart Kraay, and Massimo Mastruzzi, *The Worldwide Governance Indicators: Methodological and Analytical Issues*, World Bank Policy Research Working Paper No. 5430 (September 2010).

85. Daniel Kaufmann, *Human Rights, Governance and Development: An Empirical Perspective*, World Bank Special Report (October 2009), 19.

86. Ibid., 15.

87. Blanton and Blanton, "Rights, Institutions, and Foreign Direct Investment," 446.

88. For a complete list of the twelve source organizations whose data is used to compile the Corruption Perceptions Index (CPI), see http://www.transparency.org/cpi2014/in_detail#myAnchor4. Access to the annual CPIs is available at http://www.transparency.org/research/cpi/overview.

89. The resources sector being, principally, the commercial extraction of oil, gas, metals, and minerals. For more on the EITI and on the standard it has set, see https://eiti.org/eiti.

90. See http://www.publishwhatyoupay.org/.

91. Andrés Mejía Acosta, *The Extractive Industries Transparency Initiative: Impact, Effectiveness, and Where Next for Expanding Natural Resource Governance?* U4 Brief (May 2014) No. 6, 3. In his conclusions, Acosta reflects a similar finding of indeterminacy by independent analysts "Scanteam" in their 224-page final report: *Achievements and Strategic Options: Evaluation of Extractive Industries Transparency* (May 2011).

92. Coverage is by no means comprehensive, as many retail banks are not signatories. So, for example, despite substantial investment services, neither Citibank in the United States nor Royal Bank of Scotland in the UK, nor any of Australia's oligopolistic "Big Four" banks (ANZ, Commonwealth Bank of Australia, National Australia Bank, and Westpac) have signed up; see http://www.unpri.org/signatories/signatories/.

93. See UN Principles of Responsible Investment: http://2xjmlj8428u1a2k5o34l1m71. wpengine.netdna-cdn.com/wp-content/uploads/1.Whatisresponsibleinvestment.pdf.

94. The EPs define "project finance" as a method of financing whereby the lender looks to the revenues generated by a specific project both as the source for repayment of the loan and as the security against which the loan is written; see *The Equator Principles: Implementation Note* (July 2014), 34.

95. Though the Equator Principles Association claims that these eighty-five members together cover more than 70% of international project financing debt in all emerging economies, there are some noticeable omissions. The Chinese banking sector, for example, which comprises some of the world's largest and fastest-growing financial institutions, has almost completely ignored the EPs: see David Kinley and Fiona Cunningham, "The Trinity and the Dragon: Reconciling Finance, Human Rights and the Environment in China," *Journal of Human Rights and the Environment* 3, no. 1 (2012): 116–40. The solitary Chinese bank signatory is the Industrial Bank.

96. This feature was introduced in a revision of the EPs in 2013 (now *Equator Principles III*), which in effect incorporated the due diligence aspects of the UN's 2011 *Guiding Principles Business and Human Rights*, on which see note 12 above.

97. See Christopher Wright, "Global Banks, the Environment, and Human Rights: The Impact of the Equator Principles on Lending Policies and Practices," *Global Environmental Politics* 12, no. 1 (2012): 55–67.

98. A similar argument is made by the Institute for Human Rights and Business, in its *Human Rights and Sustainable Finance: Exploring the Relationship*, Inquiry Working Paper 16/01 (February 2016), prepared for the UN Environmental Program Inquiry on the Design of a Sustainable Financial System, at 49–51.

99. See Global Sustainable Investment Alliance, *Global Sustainable Investment Review 2014*, 7. The growth in four years was even more impressive: the figure for so-called ESG ("environmental, social, and governance") funds in 2010 was just 7% according to the *Report of the UN Intergovernmental Committee of Experts on Sustainable Development Financing* (2014), 9.

100. For a description of some of the technical difficulties in defining the term and its attendant vocabulary ("exclusionary screening," "ESG integration," and the like), see JP Morgan Chase, *Decoding the Elements of Sustainable Investing* (2016).

101. Rory Sullivan, "Financial Sustainability: Why NGOs are Failing to Engage Investors," *The Guardian*, May 16, 2013.

102. For a general overview of the subject see the I-8/LIFE Group, *Innovative Financing for Development* (2009)

103. OECD, *Social Impact Investing: Building the Evidence Base* (2015), 13, Figure 2.1.

104. See, generally, Emily Gustafsson-Wright, Sophie Gardiner, and Vidya Putcha, *The Potential and Limitations of Impact Bonds: Lessons from the First Five Years of Experience Worldwide* (Washington, DC: Brookings Institution, 2015).

105. See the *Monterrey Consensus on Financing for Development* (2002), the *Doha Declaration on Financing for Development* (2008), and the *Addis Ababa Action Agenda* (2015). Paragraph 9 of the last-mentioned reads: ". . . national development efforts need to be supported by an enabling international economic environment, including coherent and mutually supporting world trade, monetary and financial systems, and strengthened and enhanced global economic governance." Innovative finance, development and human rights are discussed further in chapter 5, below, 138–40.

106. See transcript of interview with Raj Shah by the Centre for Global Development's Rajesh Mirchandani, February 2, 2015, available at http://www.cgdev.org/blog/only-private-sector-investment-can-end-extreme-poverty-raj-shah-tells-cgd-0.

107. See, for example, from the inside, Jeremy Balkin, *The Noble Cause: Positively Influencing the Allocation of Capital*, TEDx Talks, available at https://www.youtube.com/watch?v=rXyRlfI8Tvo, and from the outside, the former UK Prime Minister, David Cameron, "Social Investment Can Be a Great Force for Social Change," speech delivered at the Social Impact Investment Forum, London, June 6, 2013.

108. See Karl Polanyi's seminal text *The Great Transformation: The Political and Economic Origins of our Time* (1944) (Boston, MA: Beacon Press, 2001).

109. Indeed it was, specifically, the promotion of the public interest that Smith considered to be the great value of the invisible hand that guides the economic actions of self-interested individuals. The market in which the hand invisibly worked was for Smith a vehicle by which to obtain the greatest economic wealth (as represented in his *An Inquiry into the Nature and Causes of the Wealth of Nations* [1776]) that could then be used for wider social good (reflecting his concern in his earlier *The Theory of Moral Sentiments* [1759]).

110. The first recorded reference to the epigram was in the *Reader's Digest* in November 1942, attributed (but unsourced) to Shaw. The *Oxford English Dictionary of Quotations* (1999) records the same reference under a section entitled "Misquotations," adding that the phrase is not, however, to be found in any of Shaw's published writings. Something very similar is verifiably attributed to another great Irish wit, Oscar Wilde, in *The Canterville Ghost* (1887), when describing (the American) Mrs. Otis.

111. This, for example, was the connotation intended in the Preamble to the *Convention on the Elimination of Discrimination Against Women* 1979 (CEDAW): "Convinced that the establishment of the new international economic order based on equity and justice will contribute significantly towards the promotion of equality between men and women." Though, thereafter, the CEDAW refers only to "equality" in its text, which distinction has given rise to some confusion and much debate; see Alda Facio and Martha Morgan, "Equity or Equality for Women? Understanding CEDAW's Equality Principles," *Alabama Law Review* 60 (2009): 1133.

112. Martha Davis, "Occupy Wall Street and International Human Rights," *Fordham Urban Law Journal* 39 (2012): 931, at 943.

113. Thomas Piketty, *Capital in the Twenty-First Century*, translated by Arthur Goldhammer (Cambridge, MA: Belknap Press, 2014), 433.

114. Piketty notes that this was approximately 150 adults per 3 billion people in the 1980s, and about 225 adults per 3 billion people in the 2010s; ibid., 435.

115. Ibid.

116. Credit Suisse, *Global Wealth Report 2015*, 13.

117. Piketty, *Capital in the Twenty-First Century*, 62. Figures from the *Global Wealth Report 2014* show that the rate of increase in wealth for rich states (specifically, Europe and the United States/Canada) remains far ahead of that of middle-income and poor states; at Table 1, 5. Though wealth increases continued for the United States/Canada in 2015 (4.4% growth), Europe had a marked reversal in fortune (decreasing by 12.4%), and China surged ahead with an increase of 7% (though its total and per capita wealth figures still languish far behind North America and Europe); see *Global Wealth Report 2015*, 5.

118. See OECD.Stat, *Poverty and Income Distribution: By Country – Inequality: U.S.*, at http://stats.oecd.org/Index.aspx?DataSetCode=IDD#. In terms of *all* states, the greatest rate of expanding inequality in recent years (2000–14) has been recorded in China (an increase across that period of 15% in the proportion of the country's wealth owned by its richest 10% (to 64% in 2014), and the largest proportion of national wealth held by a country's top 10% is an astonishing 84.8%, in Russia; *Global Wealth Report 2014*, 33 (Table 2).

119. See *Global Wealth Report 2014*, 29–30.

120. See OECD.Stat, *Wealth Distribution: Wealth by Measure: U.S.*, at http://stats.oecd.org/Index.aspx?DataSetCode=IDD.

121. See Table entitled "Changes in Real Family Income" at http://inequality.org/income-inequality/.

122. See Lawrence Mishel and Alyssa Davis, *Top CEOs Make 300 Times More Than a Typical Worker*, a report of the Economic Policy Institute (June 2015; Issue Brief 399); the authors define a typical worker as a "private sector production/non-supervisory worker."

123. Piketty, *Capital in the Twenty-First Century*, Table 7.2, 248.

124. It is estimated that at their height, there existed nearly one thousand such "occupations" in commercial and financial centers in more than eighty countries worldwide; see Derek Thompson, "Occupy the World: The '99 Percent' Movement Goes Global," *The Atlantic*, October 15, 2011.

125. As expressed by parties as disparate as Warren Buffett and the Tax Justice Network. See further discussion on tax and human rights in chapter 6 below, 156–60.

126. Piketty, *Capital in the Twenty-First Century*, 444. In the same vein, billionaire and capitalist skeptic, Nick Hanaeur has warned that extreme levels of inequality will inevitably lead to catastrophe: "The Pitchforks are Coming . . . For us Plutocrats," *Politico*
(July/August 2014); available at http://www.politico.com/magazine/story/2014/06/
the-pitchforks-are-coming-for-us-plutocrats-108014.

127. See Era Dabla-Norris, Kalpana Kochhar, Frantisek Ricka, Nujin Suphaphiphat, and Evridiki
Tsounta, *Causes and Consequences of Income Inequality: A Global Perspective* (IMF Report,
June 2015), in which the authors point to the economic detriments of too great a concentration of wealth, including undermining growth, dampening investment, and hampering
poverty reduction; at 6–8.

128. Piketty, *Capital in the Twenty-First Century*, 443.

129. Ibid.

130. UNDP, *The Rise of the South: Human Progress in a Diverse World*, The Human Development
Report 2013, 29–33.

131. Joseph Stiglitz, *The Price of Inequality: How Today's Divided Society Endangers Our Future*
(New York: W. W. Norton, 2013), 105.

132. As reported in *The Economist*, "Spreading the Gospels of Wealth," May 19, 2012.

133. Stiglitz, *The Price of Inequality*, chapter 4, "Why It Matters," 83–117, on the dire threats to
"social cohesion" posed by extreme inequality.

134. See "The Birth of Philanthrocapitalism," *The Economist*, February 23, 2006. Following
which article the chief business writer of the *Economist*, Matthew Bishop, together
with Michael Green, published *Philanthrocapitalism: How the Rich can Save the World*
(New York: Bloomsbury, 2008), in which, among other things, they argue that the vast
array of opportunities for giving that the philanthropy industry offers (including via
online peer-to-peer facilities like *GlobalGiving*) means that "we are all philanthrocapitalists
now" (238).

135. See Giving USA 2015: *The Annual Report on Philanthropy for the Year 2014*, Press Release,
29 June 2015: http://givingusa.org/giving-usa-2015-press-release-giving-usa-americans-
donated-an-estimated-358-38-billion-to-charity-in-2014-highest-total-in-reports-60-year-
history/. Without any hint of irony, Giving USA (which runs the byline: "A public service
initiative of the The Giving Institute"), makes the full version of the report available only by
purchase— for $89.95 (digital version) or $119.95 (paperback and digital package)!

136. See Ted Hart, "Leading the Way to Greater Global Giving," *Stanford Social Innovation
Review*, March 14, 2014.

137. Giving USA 2015, *The Annual Report on Philanthropy for the Year 2014*.

138. Hudson Institute, Center for Global Prosperity, *Index of Global Philanthropy and Remittances
2013*, 9–10.

139. Ibid.

140. Hudson Institute, Center for Global Prosperity, *Index of Global Philanthropy and Remittances
2016*, 11. While acknowledging difficulties in accurately measuring levels in other countries, the report does make clear that the other major philanthropic contributors are Japan,
the UK, and Canada, and of the emerging economies, donations from India are on the rise,
while in China they are, apparently, almost nonexistent.

141. Alex Daniels, "As Wealthy Give Smaller Share of Income to Charity, Middle Class Digs
Deeper," *The Chronicle of Philanthropy*, October 5, 2015.

142. Wealth-X and Arton Capital, *Philanthropy Report 2015*, 5.

143. See Wealth-X, "8 Myths about the Super Rich," *Business Insider*, June 13, 2014, and Wealth-X
and Arton Capital, *Philanthropy Report 2014*, Table at 31.

144. See Wealth-X and Arton Capital, *Philanthropy Report 2015*, 5. The fact that just one year
earlier Wealth-X had noted that "only a third of the world's UHNW individuals are estimated
to have donated at least $1m" (Wealth-X, "8 Myths about the Super Rich,") is, strangely, not
even mentioned in the 2015 report, let alone explained.

145. For even if we were to use disposable/investible income instead of net worth, the giving percentage for the average UHNW individual, is still tiny. With a mean liquidity (that is, disposable income) of $35 million per annum for UHNW individuals as a whole (see *Philanthropy
Report 2015*, 17), their average annualized philanthropy amounts to 0.1428% of disposable

income. The average American household's contribution to charity is 3% of disposable income; see discussion at 108, above.

146. Wealth-X and Arton Capital, *Philanthropy Report 2015*, 17.

147. And here again (as per note 145, above), even when we use disposable income instead of total wealth as the metric, the average American remains ahead in terms of their relative generosity. As the mean liquidity of UHNW philanthropists is $62 million (see *Philanthropy Report 2015*, 17), their average annualized philanthropy equates to 1.90% of their disposable income.

148. Wealth-X and Arton Capital, *Philanthropy Report 2014*, 31. Other interesting findings in the report include: (1) of those who engage in major philanthropy, the most numerous, generous, and most frequent givers are found in the United States (followed by the UK and China); and (2) women UHNW philanthropists are 26% more generous than their male counterparts.

149. Further down the wealth scale, the merely wealthy (HNW) individuals seem to be more generous. Data collected for *The 2014 US Trust Study of High Net Worth Philanthropy* shows (at 28) that for those households with net wealth between $1million and $5 million, the average amount given in 2013 was $24,955, which equates to between 0.5% and 2.5% of their total wealth.

150. See Wealth-X, "8 Myths about the Super Rich."

151. Wealth-X and Arton Capital, *Philanthropy Report 2014*, at 37.

152. That is despite the authors spending some time trying to explain how these activities amount to philanthropy; ibid., 37–51.

153. See discussion at 107–8 above.

154. See Carol Adelman and Yulya Spantchak, "Foundations and Private Actors," in Bruce Currie-Adler, Ravi Kanbur, David Malone, and Rohinton Medhora (eds.), *International Development: Ideas, Experience, and Prospects* (Oxford: Oxford University Press, 2014), 810–11.

155. Above, at note 135, and accompanying text.

156. As defined by Giving USA 2015, *The Annual Report on Philanthropy for the Year 2014*.

157. Ibid.

158. On the unfairness of which when charity favors the already well-off at the expense of the poor, see Robert Reich, "The Failure of Philanthropy," *Stanford Social Innovation Review* (Winter 2005): 25–33.

159. Giving USA 2015, *The Annual Report on Philanthropy for the Year 2014*. It is notable that with wealthy donors (the HNW and UHNW individuals), the proportions differ—much higher levels of funding for education (especially university, but also high school and primary school), and lower levels for religion (and in the case of UHNW individuals, negligible). Funding of health and community and human services are broadly similar. See *The 2014 US Trust Study*, 16, and Wealth-X and Arton Capital, *Philanthropy Report 2014*, 24.

160. See "Earthly Concerns," *The Economist*, August 18, 2012, which estimates that in America alone, the Catholic Church spent nearly $150 billion on health care and all levels of education in 2010, out of a total budget of $171 billion for that year.

161. Ibid. *The Economist* article wryly concludes that while "the sins involved in its book-keeping are not as vivid or grotesque" as those exposed in the various sexual abuse cases it faces, the finances of the Catholic Church in America are, nevertheless, in "an unholy mess."

162. See, on the one hand, Andrew Bowman, "The Flip Side to Bill Gates' Charity Billions," *New Internationalist Magazine*, April 2012, in which leading AIDS activist Gregg Gonsalve is quoted as saying, "Depending on what side of bed Gates gets out of in the morning, it can shift the terrain of global health"; and on the other, Matthew Herper, "With Vaccines, Bill Gates Changes the World Again," *Forbes Business*, November 2, 2011.

163. Jen Wieczner, "Charities Are Making Big Money by Behaving like Venture Capitalists," *Fortune Magazine*, May 27, 2015.

164. See the mission or vision statements and financial accounts readily available on the websites of all three foundations. Regarding the annual divestment of grants, it must be noted that the Stichting INGKA (established by Ingvar Kamprad, who founded IKEA), despite its

enormous assets (only just short of those of the Gates Foundation), contributes very little to this combined figure (just $120 million in 2013).

165. See http://givingpledge.org.

166. Ibid.

167. For the running total of 'pledgers' and their countries of origin, see Glass Pockets, *Eye on the Giving Pledge*, at http://glasspockets.org/philanthropy-in-focus/eye-on-the-giving-pledge. The total number of billionaires worldwide is drawn from *Forbes 2017 Billionaires List*, at https://www.forbes.com/billionaires/#5be4ec1d251c.

168. Mark Zuckerberg has also indicated his intention to give away most of his wealth by pledging to donate 99% of his shareholdings in Facebook (valued, at the time, at $45 billion) during his lifetime through the Chan Zuckerberg Initiative he created with his wife, Priscilla Chan. See the pair's "Letter to our Daughter" posted on Zuckerberg's Facebook page on December 1, 2015.

169. On some of the difficulties in these respects, see Brendan Coffey, "Pledge Aside, Dead Billionaires Do Not Have to Give Away Half Their Fortune," *Bloomberg Business*, June 4, 2015.

170. By the investigative website, *The Smoking Gun* in April 2011, as reported by John *Cassidy*, "Trump and the Truth: His Charitable Giving," *The New Yorker*, September 24, 2016.

171. That is according to the 2016 *Hurun List of the Richest People in China*, see http://www.hurun.net/EN/HuList/Index?num=612C66A2F245. According to the *Forbes Billionaires List Map: 2017*, however, China has only 319 billionaires compared to 565 in the U.S.; see Luisa Kroll and Kerry Dolan, "Forbes 2017 Billionaires List: Meet The Richest People On The Planet," *Forbes*, March 20, 2017. The almost complete absence of Chinese pledgers (see Glass Pockets, *Eye on the Giving Pledge*) is despite a concerted effort to woo them at the outset of the Giving Pledge in 2010 with a highly publicized invitation to fifty Chinese billionaires to attend a dinner in Beijing hosted by Buffett and Gates.

172. In particular, I consulted the following: Center of Philanthropy, Indiana University, *Understanding Donors' Motivations* (October 20, 2009); *The 2014 US Trust Study of High Net Worth Philanthropy*; Wealth-X and Arton Capital, *Philanthropy Report 2014*; and Forbes Insights, *2015 BNP Paribas Individual Philanthropy Index*. My remarks in this section draw largely from the data and commentary contained in these reports.

173. The Wealth X and Arton Capital *Philanthropy Report* 2014 contains a whole section dedicated to this question, including what impact such protests as the Occupy movements have had on the motivations of UHNW philanthropists; at 31–37.

174. All of which are accessible at http://givingpledge.org/.

175. Interviews with Martin O'Brien, Senior Vice-President for Programmes, Atlantic Philanthropies (on November 22, 2012), and Mark Suzman, Head of Development Policy, The Bill and Melinda Gates Foundation (on October 21, 2010).

176. *The 2014 US Trust Study of High Net Worth Philanthropy*, at 17.

177. Peter Singer, *The Life You Can Save: Acting Now to End World Poverty* (New York: Random House, 2009).

178. Thomas Pogge, *World Poverty and Human Rights*, 2nd ed. (Cambridge, UK: Polity, 2008).

179. Singer, *The Life You Can Save*, chapter 3; also see The Life You Can Save organization, at http://www.thelifeyoucansave.org/learn-more/common-objections-to-giving.

180. Peter Singer, "What Should a Billionaire Give—and What Should You?" in Patricia Illingworth, Thomas Pogge, and Leif Wenar (eds.), *Giving Well: The Ethics of Global Philanthropy* (Oxford: Oxford University Press, 2011), 20 and 23.

181. See http://www.thelifeyoucansave.org/Take-the-Pledge.

182. See, respectively, Oxfam, "The Cost of Inequality: How Wealth and Income Extremes Hurt Us All," Media Briefing, January 18, 2013, and, more fully, Oxfam, "An Economy for the 99%," Media Briefing Paper (January 2017); and Bono's entry in *Look to the Stars: The World of Celebrity Giving*, at https://www.looktothestars.org/celebrity/bono.

183. Leif Wenar, "Poverty is No Pond: Challenges for the Affluent," in Illingworth, Pogge, and Wenar, *Giving Well*, 106.

184. Jeffrey Sachs, *The End of Poverty* (New York: Penguin, 2005), 269–70.

185. *The 2014 US Trust Study of High Net Worth Philanthropy*, 84, where it reports that "high net worth households have the most confidence in non-profit organizations (91.6% reporting either 'some' or 'a great deal') and the individuals supporting these groups (90.8% reporting 'some' or 'a great deal'). Individuals attracted the largest proportion of households' 'great deal' of confidence (40.6%). Sizeable proportions of the wealthy households surveyed held 'hardly any' confidence in Congress (74.8%), the Federal Executive branch (46.3%), and large corporations (42.5%)."

Chapter 5 – Public Affairs

1. *Compañia General de Tabacos de Filipinas v. Collector of Internal Revenue*, 275 U.S. 87, 100 (1927).
2. On the reasons for and consequences of which, see Ben Saul, David Kinley, and Jacqueline Mowbray, *The International Covenant on Economic, Social and Cultural Rights: Commentary, Cases and Materials* (Oxford: Oxford University Press, 2014), chapter 3, 133–72.
3. See Committee on ESCR, *General Comment No. 3, The Nature of State Parties' Obligations (Art. 2, Para.1, of the Covenant)* ("General Comment No. 3"), E/1991/23 (December 14, 1990), para. 8 (see also para.13); and Committee on ESCR Statement *An Evaluation of the Obligation to Take Steps to the "Maximum of Available Resources" under the Optional Protocol to the Covenant*, UN. Doc. E/C.12/2007/1 (2007), paras 5 and 7.
4. Committee on ESCR, *General Comment No. 3*, para.14.
5. That is through the Committee's Concluding Observations on individual state reports; for an overview of some of these, see Saul, Kinley, and Mowbray, *The International Covenant on Economic, Social and Cultural Rights*, 141–72. These suggestions include addressing the problems of excessive bank secrecy and permissive corporate tax rules that can directly impact the ability of states "to meet their obligation to mobilize the maximum available resources for the implementation of economic, social and cultural rights"; Committee on ESCR, *General Comment 24 on State Obligations under the International Covenant on Economic, Social and Cultural Rights in the Context of Business Activities*, UN.Doc. E/ C.12/GC/24 (June 23, 2017), para. 37.
6. In respect of some of these, see Dianne Elson, Radhika Balakrishnan, and James Heintz, "Public Finance, Maximum Available Resources and Human Rights," in Aoife Nolan, Rory O'Connell, and Colin Harvey (eds.), *Human Rights and Public Finance: Budgets and the Promotion of Economic, Social and Cultural Rights* (Oxford: Hart, 2013), 13–39.
7. Horatia Muir-Watt, "The Contested Legitimacy of Investment Arbitration and the Human Rights Ordeal: The Missing Link," in Walter Mattli and Thomas Dietz (eds.), *International Arbitration and Global Governance: Contending Theories and Evidence* (Oxford: Oxford University Press, 2014), 214–39.
8. *Suez, Sociedad General de Aguas de Barcelona, SA and Vivendi Universal, SA v. Argentina*, ICSID Case No. ARB/03/19, Decision on Liability, July 30, 2010.
9. See ICSID: Cases: Argentina, at https://icsid.worldbank.org/apps/ICSIDWEB/cases/Pages/AdvancedSearch.aspx?rntly=ST4.
10. On which see, generally, Paul Blustein, *And the Money Kept Rolling In (And Out): The World Bank, Wall Street, the IMF and the Bankrupting of Argentina* (New York: Public Affairs, 2005).
11. Namely, BITs concluded by Argentina separately with France, Spain, and the UK.
12. *Suez*, ICSID Case No. ARB/03/19, para. 252.
13. The right to an adequate standard of living is contained in Article 11 of the Covenant. Argentina has been a state party to the Covenant since 1986.
14. Which was precisely the argument advanced by a number of NGOs in a joint *amicus curiae* brief submitted to the Tribunal; see *Suez*, ICSID Case No. ARB/03/19, para. 256. For a review of whether and how an appeal to international human rights obligations can be used as the basis for the defense of necessity in international law in the related context of non-payment of sovereign debts, see August Reinisch and Christina Binder, "Debts and State of Necessity," in Juan Pablo Bohoslavsky and Jernej Letnar Černič (eds.), *Making Sovereign Financing and Human Rights Work* (Oxford: Hart, 2014), 115–28.

15. *Suez*, ICSID Case No. ARB/03/19, para. 255. Such an assertion seems to stand in contrast to the following statement made by another ICSID tribunal just one year before: "... Nobody would suggest that ICSID protection should be granted to investments made in violation of the most fundamental rules of protection of human rights"; *Phoenix Action, Ltd. v. Czech Republic*, Award, April 15, 2009, para. 78.

16. *Suez*, ICSID Case No. ARB/03/19, para. 262.

17. For discussion, see Emma Truswell, "Thirst for Profit: Water Privatisation, Investment Law and a Human Right to Water," in Chester Brown and Kates Miles (eds.), *Evolution in Investment Treaty Law and Arbitration* (Cambridge: Cambridge University Press, 2011), 570–85.

18. UNCTAD notes that in 2014, developing countries were the respondents in 60% of international investment arbitration cases, which percentage "is on the rise"—from 47% in 2013, 34% in 2012, and a historical average of 28%. See UNCTAD, *IIA Issues Note: Recent Trends in IIAs and ISDs*, No.1, February 2015, at 5.

19. As noted in the *Report prepared by the Special Rapporteur on the right of everyone to the enjoyment of the highest attainable standard of physical and mental health, Anand Grover*, UN Doc. A/69/299 (August 11, 2014), paras. 55–57. This question of balance and the problems associated with it are also discussed in chapter 4, 94–5.

20. For an exploration of this point, see Diane Desierto, "Calibrating Human Rights and Investment in Economic Emergencies: Prospects of Treaty and Valuation Defenses," *Manchester Journal of International Economic Law* 9, no. 2 (2012): 162–83; and for some suggested guidelines to help arbitrators to understand the legal implications of the often complex interrelationship between investment and human rights, see Susan Karamanian, "The Place of Human Rights in Investor-State Arbitration," *Lewis and Clark Law Review* 17 (2013): 423–47.

21. *I.D.G. v. Spain* (Committee on ESCR, Communication 2/2014), September 17, 2015.

22. Ibid., paras. 15.1–2.

23. See third-party intervention made by ESCR-Net to the ESCR Committee in the case: Intervención de Tercero, February 24, 2015, available at https://www.escr-net.org/sites/default/files/intervencion_de_tercero_-_red-desc_comunicacion_2-2014_2.pdf.

24. As expressly noted in *I.D.G. v. Spain*, at paras.11.2–4 and 12.1, when referring to the Committee's *General Comment 7 (1997), The Right to Adequate Housing (art. 11 (1) of the Covenant): Forced Evictions*.

25. See ESCR Committee, *General Comment 7*, para.16.

26. The Madrid-based RAIS Fundación estimates that in 2014, there were 40,000 homeless people in Spain and some 1.5 million living in sheltered accommodation; see *Innocación con las Personsas sin Hogar* (2014), at https://www.raisfundacion.org/es/que_hacemos/personas_sin_hogar.

27. Charles Adams, *For Good and Evil: The Impact of Taxes on the Course of Civilization* (Lanham, MD: Madison Books, 1993), 1.

28. Isabel Paterson, *The God of the Machine* (New Brunswick, NJ: Transaction Publishers, 2009 [1943]), 258.

29. Tea Party Express, *Mission Statement*, at http://www.teapartyexpress.org/mission.

30. The Oxford English Dictionary defines tax as a compulsory contribution, fee, or due levied by government on persons, groups, or businesses.

31. Adams, *For Good and Evil*, 3.

32. Erich Kirchler, *The Economic Psychology of Tax Behaviour* (Cambridge: Cambridge University Press, 2007), 182.

33. At 39–40.

34. For an excellent overview of these antecedent interconnections between paying tax and gaining rights, see Rory O'Connell, "Rediscovering the History of Human Rights: Public Finances and Human Rights," in Nolan, O'Connell, and Harvey, *Human Rights and Public Finance*, 108–15.

35. See Gough Whitlam and Canberra Dept. of Immigration, *Eureka: The Birth of Australian Democracy* (Canberra: Dept. of Immigration, 1974).

36. Tax Justice Network, *The Cost of Tax Abuse: A Briefing Paper on the Cost of Tax Evasion Worldwide* (November 2011). This accords broadly with a later study by Gabriel Zucman of the Paris School of Economics of unrecorded assets held in tax havens; see his article

"The Missing Wealth of Nations: Are Europe and the U.S. Net Debtors or Creditors?" *The Quarterly Journal of Economics* 128, no. 3 (2013): 1321–64; see especially Figure 1 and accompanying note at 1323.

37. See David Cay Johnston, "How the Kleptocrats' $12 Trillion Heist Helps Keeps Most of the World Impoverished," *The Daily Beast*, March 5, 2016, reporting on as-yet unpublished research conducted by economist James Henry. See further James Henry, "Let's Tax Anonymous Wealth! A Modest Proposal to Reduce Inequality, Attack Organized Crime, Aid Developing Countries, and Raise Badly Needed Revenue from the World's Wealthiest Tax Dodgers, Kleptocrats, and Felons," in Thomas Pogge and Krishen Mehta (eds.), *Global Tax Fairness* (Oxford: Oxford University Press, 2016), 32–95, at 88 for the global estimate cited.

38. Tax Justice Network, *The Cost of Tax Abuse*, Table entitled "The Continent-by-Continent View," at 3.

39. Ibid.; these statistics are drawn from the table cited, and also the one following, at 4, entitled: "The Biggest Losers."

40. Ibid.

41. See Inland Revenue Service, *Tax Gap Estimates for Tax Years 2008–2010* (April 2016), 1.

42. Michael Keen, *Taxation and Development— Again*, IMF Working Paper No. WP/12/220 (September 2012), at 16.

43. International Bar Association, *Tax Abuses, Poverty and Human Rights* (London, 2013), 93.

44. Adam Smith, *An Inquiry into the Nature and Causes of the Wealth of Nations* (1776) (Elibron Classics edition, 2000, being a replica of a 1786 edition published in London), Book 5, chapter II, part 2.

45. See Grahame Dowling, "The Curious Case of Corporate Tax Avoidance: Is it Socially Irresponsible?" *Journal of Business Ethics* 124, no. 1 (2014): 173–84, at 183. Here Dowling is referring in particular to the aggressive tax avoidance strategies employed by corporations.

46. John Maynard Keynes, *General Theory of Employment, Interest and Money* (London: Macmillan, 1936), 372.

47. Ignacio Saiz, "Resourcing Rights: Combatting Tax Injustice from a Human Rights Perspective," in Nolan, O'Connell, and Harvey, *Human Rights and Public Finance*, 87. Saiz is the executive director of the Center for Economic and Social Rights.

48. Guatemala was ranked 128 out of 188 countries in the UNDP's *Human Development Index 2015*.

49. Center for Economic and Social Rights and Instituto Centroamericano de Estudios Fiscales, *Right and Privileges: Fiscal Commitment to the Rights to Health, Education and Food in Guatemala* (2009), 16–17.

50. Ibid., 18–19.

51. Timothy Besley and Torsten Persson, "Why Do Developing Countries Tax So Little?" *Journal of Economic Perspectives* 28, no. 4 (2014): 99–120.

52. See OECD, *International Investment Perspectives* (2004), 98–100, based on a survey of a number of ASEAN countries.

53. National taxpayer advocate Nina E. Olson in her 2012 *Annual Report to Congress*, see *Executive Summary*, p. vii. This is "nearly as long as seven versions of *War and Peace* or . . . just under four times the number of words in all of the Harry Potter books put together," as Kelly Phillips Erb helpfully puts it: "Tax Code Hits Nearly 4 Million Words, Taxpayer Advocate Calls It Too Complicated," *Forbes*, January 10, 2013.

54. General Electric (GE) is a global leader in this respect. Consider, for example, that in 2010 the company reported global profits of $14.2 billion, $5.1 billion of which came from its U.S. operations, and yet its U.S. tax bill for that year was zero. "In fact," as was reported in the *New York Times*, "GE claimed a tax benefit of $3.1 billion." GE's giant tax department, the article continues "is often referred to as the world's best tax law firm": David Kocieniewski, "GE's Strategies Let It Avoid Taxes Altogether," *New York Times*, March 24, 2011.

55. Prem Sikka, "Enterprise Culture and Accountancy Firms: New Masters of the Universe," *Accounting, Auditing and Accountability Journal* 21, no. 2 (2008): 268–95.

56. UNCTAD, *World Investment Report 2015*, 185, for the corporate contributions to tax revenues, and at 200, for the tax losses through corporate tax avoidance.

57. This is development economist Alex Cobham's estimate, calculated using UNCTAD's data; Alex Cobham, "UNCTAD Study on Corporate Tax in Developing Countries," March 26,

2015, http://uncounted.org/2015/03/26/unctad-study-on-corporate-tax-in-developing-countries/.

58. See Deborah Bräutigam, "Introduction: Taxation and State-Building in Developing Countries," in Deborah Bräutigam, Odd-Helge Fjeldstad, and Mick Moore (eds.), *Taxation and State-Building: Capacity and Consent* (Cambridge: Cambridge University Press, 2008), at 1.

59. Ahmed Shahid, *For Want of Resources: Reimagining the State's Obligation to Use "Maximum Available Resources" for the Progressive Realisation of Economic, Social and Cultural Rights*, doctoral thesis, University of Sydney (February 2016), chapter 4; available at https://ses.library.usyd.edu.au/handle/2123/14369.

60. In more recent years, some states, such as Angola, Cambodia, Indonesia, and Tanzania, have provided more revenue detail in their reports to the Committee; ibid.

61. World Bank, *Data: Tax Revenue (as % of GDP)*; available at http://data.worldbank.org/indicator/GC.TAX.TOTL.GD.ZS.

62. Though it must be noted that when all other sources of compulsory transfers to governments are added in, OECD data show that the percentages of tax-to-GDP rise significantly more for Germany, Japan, and the United States, bringing them much closer to the tax revenue percentages of other major Western economies; see OECD, *Revenue Statistics tax to GDP ratio changes between 2007 and provisional 2013 data, Table A: Total tax revenue as a percentage of GDP*, available at http://www.oecd.org/ctp/tax-policy/revenue-statistics-ratio-change-latest-years.htm.

63. As political historian and author Don Watson writes about President (and former General) Eisenhower: "Here was an American President who began his first term [in 1953] by reminding Americans that every dollar spent on weapons was 'in the final sense, a theft from those who hunger and are not fed, who are cold and not clothed' "; Don Watson, *American Journeys* (Sydney: Vintage, 2008), 195.

64. Available at http://www.cesr.org/downloads/Lima_Declaration_Tax_Justice_Human_Rights.pdf.

65. Or as Klaus Schilder puts it: "The true priorities of policies are often revealed more clearly by budgets and tax legislation than they are by declarations and action programmes," in "Tax justice: The significance of emerging human rights instruments," posted on www.rightingfinance.org, March 15, 2013.

66. John Rawls, *Theory of Justice* (1971), rev. ed. (Cambridge MA: Belknap Press, 1999), 52–65.

67. For a compelling analysis of how these difficulties play out in the roles governments play in the highly contested fields of race relations, gender equality, euthanasia, and drug control, see Martin Carcieri, *Applying Rawls in the Twenty-First Century: Race, Gender, the Drug War, and the Right to Die* (New York: Palgrave Macmillan, 2015).

68. Committee on ESCR, *General Comment No. 3: The Nature of States Parties' Obligations (Art. 2, Para. 1, of the Covenant)*, E/1991/23 (December 14, 1990), para. 10.

69. Ibid., para.11.

70. See further, Audrey Chapman and Sage Russell (eds.), *Core Obligations: Building a Framework for Economic, Social and Cultural Rights* (Cambridge: Intersentia, 2002), and Saul, Kinley, and Mowbray, *The International Covenant on Economic, Social and Cultural Rights*, 143–51.

71. See Ahmed Shahid's survey of the specifics of such engagement with a wide range of states; Shahid, *For Want of Resources*, chapter 3.

72. World Bank, *The State of Social Safety Nets 2015*, 46–47.

73. World Bank, *The State of Social Safety Nets 2014*, 31.

74. Ibid., Annex D3, at 121–25. The average for all 120 low- and middle-income countries surveyed was 1.6% of GDP (Figure 2.1, at 22), with Georgia and Lesotho committing the highest levels (7% and 6.58%, respectively). The figure for China was 0.7%, and for India, 0.72% (a substantial increase on 0.24% the year before).

75. See "Rajiv Was Right: Montek Says Only 16p of Re Reaches Poor," *Times of India*, October 14, 2009. On the dimensions of the problem, but also signs of improvement, see Nandan Nilekani and Viral Shah, *Rebooting India: Realising a Billion Aspirations* (Gurgaon: Allen Lane, 2016), chapter 4, "Mending our Social Safety Nets."

76. Discussion with Philip O'Keefe, Lead Economist, Social Protection and Labor Global Practice in the World Bank, September 2016. The same uncomfortable truth is apparent in Timothy Garton Ash, "Come On, India! Show Us That Freedom Can Outdo Tyranny," *The Guardian*, January 31, 2013.

77. As reported in "How to Get Children Out of Jobs and Into School: The Limits of Brazil's Much Admired and Emulated Anti-Poverty Programme," *The Economist*, July 29, 2010.

78. *In Larger Freedom: Towards Development, Security and Human Rights for All*, UN Doc. A/59/2005 (March 21, 2005), para.17.

79. Ibid., para.15.

80. Ibid., para.16.

81. *Report of the Special Rapporteur on extreme poverty and human rights* (August 4, 2015), UN Doc A/70/274; Summary, 2.

82. See for example, Mac Darrow, *Between Light and Shadow: The World Bank, the IMF, and International Human Rights Law* (Oxford: Oxford University Press, 2003), 113–23, and Galit Sarfaty, *Values in Transition: Human Rights and the Culture of the World Bank* (Stanford, CA: Stanford University Press, 2012), 51–74. In 2001 a nonstate group of experts also drafted *The Tilburg Principles on the World Bank, the IMF and Human Rights*, which seek to make the Bank and the Fund more transparent and accountable, and thereby more respectful of human rights; see further, Giuseppe Bianco and Filippo Fontanelli, "Enhancing the International Monetary Fund's Compliance with Human Rights— The Issue of Accountability," in Bohoslavsky and Černič, *Making Sovereign Financing and Human Rights Work*, 216–17.

83. *Articles of Agreement of the International Bank of Reconstruction and Development* (1944), Article IV, section 10.

84. As per *Articles of Agreement of the New Development Bank* (2014), Article 13(e), and *Articles of Agreement of the Asian Infrastructure Investment Bank* (2015), Article 31(2). In respect of the latter, as at December 15, 2015, when "permanent founding membership" closed, the Bank had fifty-seven signatory states, comprising all major economies (except the United States) and many smaller ones.

85. It is these opposing perspectives on handling political circumstances that is encapsulated in the above reference to, and criticisms of, the World Bank's "political prohibition" provision in its Articles of Agreement (at 134–5).

86. Peter Uvin, *Human Rights and Development* (Bloomfield, CT: Kumarian Press, 2004), 123.

87. Ibid.

88. As I have argued elsewhere: see David Kinley, *Civilising Globalisation: Human Rights and the Global Economy* (Cambridge: Cambridge University Press, 2009), 34 and 106–107.

89. Jack Donnelly, "In Search of the Unicorn: The Jurisprudence and Politics of the Right to Development," *California Western International Law Journal* 15 (1985): 473–509.

90. *The Human Rights Based Approach to Development Cooperation: Towards a Common Understanding Among UN Agencies*—available at http://hrbaportal.org/the-human-rights-based-approach-to-development-cooperation-towards-a-common-understanding-among-un-agencies#sthash.tsucyaGH.dpuf.

91. Most notably those of Denmark (DANIDA), Germany (BMZ), Sweden (SIDA), and the UK (DFID). See further Siobhán McInerney-Lankford, "International Development Actors and Human Rights," in Malcolm Langford, Andy Sumner, and Alicia Ely Yamin (eds.), *The Millennium Development Goals and Human Rights: Past, Present and Future* (New York: Cambridge University Press, 2013), 160–207.

92. OECD and World Bank, *Integrating Human Rights into Development: Donor Approaches, Experiences, and Challenges*, 2nd ed. (2013), xxxviii.

93. As Louise Arbour, the then UN High Commissioner for Human Rights, puts it in her foreword to Office of the High Commissioner for Human Rights, *Frequently Asked Questions on a Human Rights-Based Approach to Development Co-operation* (2006), iii.

94. For overviews of which see Malcolm Langford, Andy Sumner, and Alicia Ely Yamin, "Introduction: Situating the Debate," and Sakiko Fukuda-Parr and Joshua Greenstein, "Monitoring the MDGs: A Human Rights Critique and Alternative," both in Langford, Sumner, and Yamin, *The Millennium Development Goals and Human Rights*, at 1–36 and 439–60, respectively.

95. That is, SDGs 10 (on reducing inequalities generally) and 5 (on gender equality); 8 (on decent work and economic growth); and 16 (on peace, justice and strong institutions). Additionally, a number of other SDGs encompass human rights concerns, even if not expressly so—namely, SDGs 2 (on zero hunger); 3 (on good health and well-being); 4 (on quality education); and 6 (on clean water and sanitation).

96. See Bertrand Ramcharan, *Human Rights and the SDGs: A Sidelined Priority?* Future UN Development System, Briefing 31 (July 2015).

97. See SDG 17 and targets 17.1–19 at https://sustainabledevelopment.un.org/sdg17; and nor are human rights referred to in any of the 44 specific 'indicators' associated with SDG 17 that have been designed to help measure progress in achieving the goal; see UN, *Report of the Inter-Agency and Expert Group on Sustainable Development Goal Indicators* (E/CN.3/2017/2), Annex III, available at https://unstats.un.org/sdgs/indicators/indicators-list/. At times the language of the SDGs targets is so opaque as to render them near meaningless, or worse. Consider targets 17.13–15, grouped under the heading "Systemic issues," which contain the head-spinning, "enhance policy coherence for sustainable development" (17.14), and the eminently corruptible "respect each country's policy space and leadership to establish and implement policies for poverty eradication and sustainable development" (17.15).

98. These two categories are followed by humanitarian assistance at 10%, and support for production (agricultural, industrial, and tourism) also at 10%. See *OECD Statistics on Resources Flows to Developing Countries* (updated December 2016), Table 19: *Aid by Major Purposes in 2015*, available at http://www.oecd.org/dac/stats/statisticsonresourceflowstodeveloping-countries.htm.

99. These figures and those that follow in the paragraph, are drawn from the World Bank's *World Development Indicators 2015*, available at http://data.worldbank.org/indicator/NY.GDP.PCAP.KD/countries/1W-ZF?page=1&display=default. The figures are expressed in constant 2005 U.S. dollars.

100. Indicators used by Freedom House include the right to vote and to stand for election, freedoms of association and expression, and standards of the rule of law. For more on Freedom House's methodology and historical rankings, see https://freedomhouse.org/report-types/freedom-world.

101. On the importance of governance to rising economic prosperity for all, and the co-dependency of civil and political rights with economic and social rights, see discussion of Daniel Kaufmann's work in chapter 4 above, 98–9.

102. The quote is from William Meyer, *Human Rights and International Political Economy in Third World Nations: Multinational Corporations, Foreign Aid, and Repression* (Westport, CT: Praeger, 1998), 114; see further on this point, David Kinley, *Civilising Globalisation*, 99–100.

103. According to the OECD (using constant 2014 USD prices) total net ODA for 2016 stood at $143 billion; this compares to $121 billion in 2013, $123 billion in 2014, and $131 billion in 2015; see OECD, *Net ODA*, available at https://data.oecd.org/oda/net-oda.htm. These figures exclude aid contributions from non-OECD economies, which, though rising steadily, are still small. Of these aid contributions the only ones of significant size (in 2014 figures) are: China ($3.4 billion), India ($1.4 billion), and Qatar ($1.3 billion (for 2013)); see OECD, *Estimates of concessional finance for development (ODA-like flows) of key providers of development cooperation that do not report to the OECD-DAC: Brazil, Chile, China, Colombia, India, Costa Rica, Indonesia, Mexico, Qatar, South Africa (Table 33a)* (updated December 2016), available at http://www.oecd.org/dac/stats/statisticsonresourceflowstodeveloping-countries.htm.

104. Total FDI inflows into developing states were $703 billion in 2014 and $741 billion in 2015; for developed economies, the corresponding totals were $493 billion and $936 billion; see UNCTAD, *Global Investment Trends Monitor*, No. 22 (January 20, 2016), Table 1.

105. See Thomas Biersteker, "Reducing the Role of the State in the Economy: A Conceptual Exploration of IMF and World Bank Prescriptions," *International Studies Quarterly* 34 (1990): 477–92.

106. GAVI raises more than one-quarter of its total annual budget of around $2 billion in this way. The process is founded on the concerns of donor governments to lift levels of vaccinations

in poor countries by pledging to sell large volumes of vaccine bonds to private investors through major capital markets. The donor governments make the funds raised available immediately to GAVI (through a financial intermediary specifically established for that purpose), and thereafter honor the yield payments due on those bonds. The success of bonds is in effect directly tied to GAVI's performance in meeting its vaccination and immunization targets. See International Finance Facility for Immunization, "Overview," at http://www.iffim.org/about/overview/.

107. UNDP, *Unleashing Entrepreneurship: Making Business Work for the Poor* (2004).

108. See IFC, "Partnerships," at http://www.ifc.org/wps/wcm/connect/CORP_EXT_Content/IFC_External_Corporate_Site/About+IFC_New/Partnerships.

109. See *IFC Annual Report 2016*, at 31, available at http://www.ifc.org/wps/wcm/connect/corp_ext_content/ifc_external_corporate_site/annual+report/2016+online+report/printed+version. While its largest investments by far are in the financial and insurance sectors, it also holds substantial interests in the power, transport, chemical, oil, gas and mining, agriculture and forestry, food and beverage, health services, and education sectors; see *IFC Financials 2016*, 10, available at https://openknowledge.worldbank.org/bitstream/handle/10986/25084/IFC_AR16_Vol_2_Financials.pdf?sequence=2&isAllowed=y.

110. *United Nations, Monterrey Consensus on Financing for Development* (2002), paras.1 & 3, available at http://www.un.org/esa/ffd/monterrey/MonterreyConsensus.pdf.

111. Ibid., para.11.

112. See *Doha Declaration on Financing for Development* (2009), and *Addis Ababa Action Agenda of the Third International Conference on Financing for Development* (adopted by the UN General Assembly on July 27, 2015 [A/RES/69/313]). A New York–based Financing for Development Office was also established by the UN following the Monterrey summit, see http://www.un.org/esa/ffd/overview. The UN's Sustainable Development Goal (SDG) 8 (on decent work and economic growth) also calls on for the expansion of access to banking, insurance and financial services for all, by strengthening "the capacity of domestic financial institutions" to provide such access; see SDG 8 (Target 10) at https://sustainabledevelopment.un.org/sdg8.

113. *Addis Ababa Action Agenda*, paras 9 and 20.

114. See WTO, *Aid for Trade*, https://www.wto.org/english/tratop_e/devel_e/a4t_e/aid4trade_e.htm.

115. The first six states are members of the OECD Development Assistance Committee (DAC), which comprises twenty-eight Western states (plus the EU in its own right); the UAE is not an OECD-DAC state. See OECD, *Net ODA: Total % of GNI 2000-2015* (Table), at https://data.oecd.org/oda/net-oda.htm (using 2015 data). The average ODA commitment by OECD states is just 0.3% of GNI, with the worst performers among the bigger economies, being the United States (at 0.17% in 2015, down from 0.21% in 2009), Spain (0.13% in 2015, collapsing from 0.46% in 2009), Australia (at 0.27% in 2015, down, precipitously, from 0.36% in 2012), and Canada (0.28% in 2015, down from 0.34% in 2010). Italy and Japan have both hovered around 0.2% or below for the past eight years, and South Korea has climbed slowly to 0.14% in 2015. In contrast, the UK has climbed significantly to 0.71% of GNI in 2015, Germany risen from 0.36% in 2009 to 0.52% in 2015, and Norway and Sweden (1.05% and 1.41%, respectively, in 2015) have long been the top donors in proportional terms.

116. For two notably forthright presentations of these and other skeptical arguments, see William Easterly, *The Tyranny of Experts: Economists, Dictators, and the Forgotten Rights of the Poor* (New York: Basic Books, 2014), especially his opening counterfactual story at 3–5; and Graham Hancock, *The Lords of Poverty* (New York: Atlantic Monthly Press, 1989), especially 37–75. In the latter, Hancock coins the phrase "bureaucratic survivalism" to denote the self-perpetuating view of "foreign aid as a vehicle of restitution, of righting wrongs, of buying pardon," 72.

117. Some argue that the process of aid delivery is often so riven with leaden bureaucracy, inefficiency, incompetence, and larceny (the "leaky bucket"), that by the time the aid reaches its intended targets much of it has been lost; see George Ayittey, "Can Foreign Aid Reduce Poverty? 'No'," in Peter Haas and John Hird (eds.), *Controversies in Globalization: Contending*

Approaches to International Relations (Thousand Oaks, CA: CQ Press, 2012), 94–96. Regarding so-called phantom aid, OECD DAC aid figures for 2015 show that of the $94.2 billion total in bilateral aid (a further $37.2 billion contributed by states to aid initiatives in multilateral institutions (such as the UN and the EU) made up the global ODA total of $131.4 billion for that year), $12.1 billion (or 12.8%) was dedicated to hosting refugees in donor countries and $6.3 billion (or 6.7%) to administrative costs; see OECD *Statistics on Resource Flows to Developing Countries* (updated December 2016), *Table 13: Comparison of Flows by Type in 2015*, available at http://www.oecd.org/dac/stats/statisticsonresource-flowstodevelopingcountries.htm.

118. Dambisa Moyo, *Dead Aid: Why Aid Is Not Working and How There Is a Better Way for Africa* (New York: Farrar, Straus and Giroux, 2009).

119. As economist Bruno Gurtner pointed out at the time, the need for international aid was then at its greatest: "Most developing countries had and still have a clearly lower financial-political scope for stimulation programmes and social measures to protect the poorest. Using a special fiscal capacity indicator, a UNESCO team ascertained that 43 of the 48 low-income countries examined have no scope for stimulation packages in favour of the poor. . . . Higher bilateral aid and liquidity aid from the international financing institutions could significantly expand the range of options for such countries." Bruno Gurtner, "The Financial and Economic Crisis and Developing Countries," *International Development Policy | Revue internationale de politique de développement*, 1 (2010), at https://poldev.revues.org/144#tocto3n2.

120. "Voice of Disenchantment," *The Economist*, March 12, 2009.

121. See Ahmed Galal, Leroy Jones, Pankaj Tandon, and Ingo Vogelsang, *Welfare Consequences of Selling Public Enterprises* (Washington, DC: World Bank, 1992).

122. See Sharmila Murthy, "The Human Right(s) to Water and Sanitation: History, Meaning and the Controversy over Privatization" *Berkeley Journal of International Law* 31, no.1 (2013): 89–149.

123. John Vidal, "Water Privatization: A Worldwide Failure," *The Guardian*, January 31, 2015. For a local perspective, see *Lagos Water Summit: "Our Water; Our Right,"* at http://www.ourwaterourright.org/.

124. Vidal, "Water Privatization."

125. For example, my erstwhile colleague Tom Davis and I were commissioned by the World Bank in 2003 to examine the instance and human rights impacts of the bank's private sector and privatization programs; see David Kinley and Tom Davis, *Human Rights Criticism of the World Bank's Private Sector Development and Privatization Projects: A Discussion Paper* (February 2004), available at http://papers.ssrn.com/sol3/papers.cfm?abstract_id=1133179.

126. See World Bank Group, *Private Participation in Infrastructure Database: Sector Snapshots: Water and Sewerage*, available at http://ppi.worldbank.org/snapshots/sector/Water-and-sewerage. This percentage is much higher than is found in other utility privatization projects, such as energy, transportation, and telecommunications.

127. Satoko Kishimoto, Emanuele Lobina, and Olivier Petitjean, *Here to Stay: Water Remunicipalisation as a Global Trend* (2014), a report of the Transnational Institute; available at https://www.tni.org/en/publication/here-to-stay-water-remunicipalisation-as-a-global-trend. The authors estimate that since 2000 there have been some 180 cases in 35 countries of water remunicipalization.

128. Regarding the IMF, for example, compare the positively upbeat account of the impacts of privatization in an IMF paper by Jeffrey Davis, Rolando Ossowski, Thomas Richardson, and Steven Barnett, *Fiscal and Macroeconomic Impact of Privatization* in 2000, with the chastened and guarded tone of privatization consequences in an IMF paper by James Roaf, Ruben Atoyan, Bikas Joshi, Krzysztof Krogulski, and an IMF Staff Team, *25 Years of Transition: Post-Communist Europe and the IMF*, Regional Economic Issues Special Report in 2014, at 22.

129. IFC, *Performance Standards on Environmental and Social Sustainability*, 2012.

130. *If Not Now, When? Urgent Recommendations on Debt Cancellation for a Strong and Prosperous Africa* (2005), A report by the UK All-Party Parliamentary Group on Heavily Indebted Poor Countries for the Commission for Africa, quoting *Jubilee Zambia*, at 38.

131. Cielito Habito and Edsel Beja, *"Beating the Odds?": The Continuing Saga of a Crisis-Prone Economy*, Civil Society Monitoring of the Medium-Term Philippine Development Plan (2006), 11. On the continuing deleterious effects of present-day and historical excessive sovereign debts, see UN Human Rights Council, *Report of the Independent Expert on the effects of foreign debt and other related international financial obligations of States on the full enjoyment of human rights, particularly economic, social and cultural rights*, A/HRC/31/60 (January 12, 2016).

132. Drawing on World Bank data, the combined total of principal and interest payments made by these countries in 2015 was $753.5 billion (see World Bank, *International Debt Statistics 2017*, 27). Total ODA for 2015, as noted earlier in this chapter, was $131 billion. See further, Share the World's Resources, *Financing the Global Sharing Economy, Part 3(9): Cancel Unjust Debt* (October 1, 2012), available at http://www.sharing.org/information-centre/reports/financing-global-sharing-economy-part-three-9-cancel-unjust-debt.

133. On which see, Robert Howse, *The Concept of Odious Debt in Public International Law*, UNCTAD Discussion Paper no. 185 (July 2007).

134. For an account of evolution, see Nancy Birdsall and John Williamson, *Delivering on Debt Relief: From IMF Gold to New Aid Architecture* (Washington, DC: Center for Global Development, 2002), 13–40.

135. See IMF, *Fact Sheet: Debt Relief Under the Heavily Indebted Poor Countries (HIPC) Initiative*, September 20, 2016.

136. Ibid.

137. Ibid.

138. See UNCTAD, *Sovereign Debt Workouts: Going Forward: Roadmap and Guide* (April 2015), 3–4. UNCTAD also formulated (in 2012) a set of draft *Principles on Responsible Sovereign Lending and Borrowing*, which aims "to build consensus around a set of internationally agreed principles to prevent irresponsible sovereign financing"; see http://www.unctad.info/upload/Debt%20Portal/Principles%20drafts/SLB_Principles_English_Doha_22-04-2012.pdf.

139. "An informal group of official creditors whose role is to find coordinated and sustainable solutions to the payment difficulties experienced by debtor countries;" as the Paris Club declares itself to be; see http://www.clubdeparis.org/. Its institutional cousin, the "London Club," is the leading organization for sovereign debt restructuring involving private sector creditors, albeit a much looser, ad hoc, forum than its Gallic relative, having no fixed membership, nor permanent secretariat.

140. "Low-income countries receive little debt relief from private creditors," notes economist Mark Wright; "Restructuring Sovereign Debts with Private Sector Creditors: Theory and Practice," in Carlos Primo Braga and Galli Vincelette (eds.), *Sovereign Debt and the Financial Crisis: Will This Time Be Different?* (Washington, DC: World Bank, 2010), 295–315, at 295. And on the human rights consequences of this parsimony, see Nicola Jägers, "Sovereign Financing and the Human Rights Responsibilities of Private Creditors," in Bohoslavsky and Černič, *Making Sovereign Financing and Human Rights Work*, 179–98.

141. For case studies of the litigious rapacity of vulture funds and examples of their negative impact on human rights, especially as regards the reduced capacity of states to provide basic welfare services in education, health, and housing, see UN *Report of the Human Rights Council Advisory Committee on the activities of vulture funds and the impact on human rights* (A/HRC/33/54; July 20, 2016).

142. See *Resolution adopted by the General Assembly on 10 September 2015*, UN. Doc. A/RES/69/319 (September 29, 2015). Alongside the insistence on the good-faith behavior of both creditors and debtors, the principles also cover respect for the rule of law, and the need to take into account the social, economic, and human rights costs of any restructured agreements entered into.

143. Belgium has two relevant laws—one enacted in 2008, which prohibits litigation involving funds originally disbursed as aid (*Loi visant à empêcher la saisie ou la cession des fonds publics destinés à la coopération internationale, notamment par la technique des fonds vautours*, April 6, 2008), and another, enacted in 2015, which by limiting the amounts recoverable by a litigant to no more than the rate stipulated in any pre-existing debt restructuring agreement,

effectively removes the incentive to sue (*Loi relative à la lutte contre les activités des fonds vautours*, July 12, 2015). This second Belgian law was modelled on the approach taken in UK's *Debt Relief (Developing Countries) Act 2010*.

144. For an example of one notorious and long-running sequence of such litigation, see the U.S. Supreme Court's judgment in *Republic of Argentina v. NML Capital, Ltd.*, 134 S. Ct. 2250 (decided June 16, 2014), which found in favor of the vulture fund.

145. That is, via the "international cooperation and assistance" stipulation in Article 2(1) of the ICESCR; see Sabine Michalowski, "Sovereign Debt and Social Rights—Legal Reflections on a Difficult Relationship," *Human Rights Law Review* 8, no. 1 (2008): 35.

146. See Noel Villaroman, "Debt Servicing and Its Adverse Impact on Economic, Social, and Cultural Rights in Developing Countries," *Journal of Human Rights* 9 (2010): 487, at 488.

147. World Bank, *International Debt Statistics 2017*, 27.

148. Daniel Bradlow, "Can Parallel Lines Ever Meet? The Strange Case of the International Standards on Sovereign Debt and Business and Human Rights," *Yale Journal of International Law Online* 41, no. 2 (2016): 201–39, at 203. In addition to providing details of the above-mentioned existing restructuring initiatives, Bradlow argues for the application of the UN *Guiding Principles on Business and Human Rights* (2011) to sovereign debt restructurings not least because they would "remind the debtor and its creditors that they will need to take all stakeholders who may suffer adverse impacts into account in their transaction" (226).

149. *Report of the UN Independent Expert on the Effects of foreign debt and other related international financial obligations of States on the full enjoyment of all human rights, particularly economic, social and cultural rights* (August 4, 2015), UN Doc. A/70/275, paras. 33–60.

150. Ibid., para. 50.

151. See definition provided by the Sovereign Wealth Fund Institute (SWFI) at http://www.swfinstitute.org/sovereign-wealth-fund/.

152. See the SWFI's "League Table," ibid.

153. Ibid.; data also drawn from OECD, *Annual Survey of Large Pension Funds and Public Pension Reserve Funds: Report on Pension Funds' Long-term Investments* 2014, 9–10.

154. SWFI, *Recent Sovereign Wealth Fund Market Size by Quarter*, ibid: in March 2009, the combined total assets managed by all SWFs was $3.75 trillion; by March 2014 this had expanded to $7.2 trillion.

155. IMF, *Global Financial Stability Report: Moving from Liquidity- to Growth-Driven Markets* (2014), 139.

156. Larry Catá Backer, "Sovereign Investing in Times of Crisis: Global Regulation of Sovereign Wealth Funds, State-Owned Enterprises and the Chinese Experience," *Transnational Law & Contemporary Problems* 19, no. 1 (2009): 101, at 129.

157. For an account of existing and possible legal interpretations of a state's international human rights obligations for the actions of its agents overseas, see Daniel Augenstein and David Kinley, "Beyond the 100 Acre Wood: In Which International Human Rights Law Finds New Ways to Tame Global Corporate Power," *The International Journal of Human Rights* 19, no. 6 (2015): 828, 833–35.

158. The *Sovereign Wealth Funds: General Principles and Practices (2008)*, as the *Santiago Principles* are formally entitled, comprise twenty-four principles covering the above aspects of fund management stipulated above.

159. Edwin Truman, *Sovereign Wealth Funds: Threat or Salvation?* (Washington, DC: Peterson Institute for International Economics, 2010), 83.

160. See, for example, Earth Rights International, *Broken Ethics: The Norwegian Government's Investments in Oil and Gas Companies Operating in Burma (Myanmar)* (2010).

161. Although somewhat confusingly labeled, the fund was established with excess oil revenues (rather than pension contributions), even if it has become pension-focused in its redistributive intentions.

162. See Norwegian Government Pension Fund Global, Ethics Council, *Guidelines*, available at http://etikkradet.no/en/.

163. Ibid.; see *Exclusion of Companies*, available at http://www.nbim.no/en/responsibility/exclusion-of-companies/. In the middle of 2015, the Norwegian parliament also approved the fund's divestment from all companies whose business comprises 30% or more of mining

or burning coal; see John Schwartz, "Norway Will Divest from Coal in Push Against Climate Change," *New York Times*, June 5, 2015.

164. For SWFs' role in economic development, see Eytan Bensoussan, Radha Ruparell, and Lynn Taliento, "Innovative Development Financing," McKinsey's *Insights and Publications* (August 2013).

165. A dilemma facing sub-Saharan states whose nascent and still-small SWFs are under constant pressure to help deal with the undeniably pressing social problems of today; see "Buried Treasure," *The Economist*, March 18, 2017.

166. The Asian Development Bank, for example, has highlighted pension funds and SWFs as potential sources for financing the SDGs, including, in particular, by way of their increased investment in PPPs in developing countries in the Asia-Pacific region; see Asian Development Bank, *Making Money Work: Financing a Sustainable Future in Asia and the Pacific* (April 2015).

167. See Angela Cummine, "Ethical Sovereign Investors: Sovereign Wealth Funds and Human Rights," in Bohoslavsky and Černič, *Making Sovereign Financing and Human Rights Work*, 163–78.

Chapter 6 – Cheating

1. See Cecil Woodham-Smith, *The Great Hunger: Ireland 1845–1849* (London: Penguin Books, 1992), 411–12. However, even these figures are very likely underestimates because of the unreliability of the census data "owing to geographical difficulties and the unwillingness of people to be registered," as Woodham-Smith notes.

2. A marked reduction in birth rates during the famine and in the decades following also further suppressed population growth; see Timothy Guinnane, "The Vanishing Irish: Ireland's Population from the Great Famine to the Great War," *History Ireland* 5, no. 2 (1997): 32–36.

3. The statistics in this paragraph have been drawn from present-day and historical census data for Ireland as a whole and after its partition in 1921, available through the Census page of the Irish Central Statistics Office, at http://www.cso.ie/en/census/index.html, as well as Ministry of Social Welfare (Ireland), *Report of the Commission on Emigration and other Population Problems* (1954), as extracted in Kerby Miller, *Emigrants and Exiles: Ireland and the Irish Exodus to North America* (Oxford: Oxford University Press, 1985), 569. For Northern Ireland census data, see http://www.nisra.gov.uk/census/2011Census.html.

4. The generic name given to regulations imposed under the *Importation Act* 1815. Though the statute was repealed in 1846 (by the *Importation Act* 1846), it come too late to save many Irish as the famine had by then already taken hold, the legacy of high prices and blocked imports was not easily, nor quickly unwound, and, in any case, destitution was so deep and widespread that few could afford to buy grain at any price.

5. The consequence of what historian Jim Donnelly calls "doctrines of inaction"; see *The Irish Famine*, BBC History, available at http://www.bbc.co.uk/history/british/victorians/famine_01.shtml.

6. Christine Kinealy, *The Great Calamity: The Great Irish Famine 1845–52*, 2nd ed. (Dublin: Gill and Macmillan, 2006), Kindle loc. 633. Even in 1847, the worst year of the famine, 145,000 tons of wheat were exported, though this was offset by the then-massive importation of the Indian corn (maize) and wheat (some 836,000 tons) in that year, primarily to supply the soup kitchens that were then feeding an astonishing 3 million people (ibid., Kindle locs. 3718 & 3673).

7. For a review of the variety and extent of exports from Ireland during the famine, see Christine Kinealy, *The Great Irish Famine: Impact, Ideology and Rebellion* (London: Macmillan, 2001), chapter 4, especially 110–16.

8. It is for this reason that some refer to the event as the great "hunger" or "starvation," as does Woodham-Smith, *The Great Hunger*; see also Terry Eagleton, *Heathcliff and the Great Hunger* (London: Verso Books, 1995).

9. The then UK Prime Minister Tony Blair issued a statement commemorating the Great Famine on June 2, 1997, in which he declared that "[t]hose who governed in London at the time failed their people through standing by while crop failure turned into a massive human tragedy."

10. Amartya Sen, *Development as Freedom* (New York: Oxford University Press, 1999), 51.
11. Kinealy, *The Great Irish Famine*, 2.
12. *Basis Yield Alpha Fund (Master) v. Goldman Sachs Group Inc. et al.*, New York State Supreme Court, New York County, No. 652996/2011; 2014 NY Slip Op 31899(U) (July 18, 2014). Reporting on the case (which was one of a number brought by the plaintiff against Goldman Sachs), see Narayanan Somasundaram and Jonathan Stempel, "Goldman Sued for $1.07 Billion over Timberwolf CDO," *Reuters*, May 5, 2011.
13. See *Wall Street and the Financial Crisis: Anatomy of a Financial Collapse* (2011), a Report of the U.S. Senate Permanent Subcommittee on Investigations, at 544 (April 13, 2011).
14. Somasundaram and Stempel, "Goldman Sued for $1.07 Billion."
15. It was, coincidentally, these very subprime mortgages that comprised the bulk of the toxic assets held in the Timberwolf fund.
16. U.S. Department of Treasury and U.S. Department of Housing and Urban Development, *Joint Report on Recommendations to Curb Predatory Home Mortgage Lending* (June 2000), 72, and 58–59, where the report quotes one study in which 12% of subprime borrowers were unfamiliar with these two terms, and one-third were not familiar with the types of mortgage products available. More alarming still is another survey showing that only half of all Americans over fifty correctly answered the following: Assuming you have $100 in a savings account earning 2% per annum, what would be the value of the account after five years? Is it: (i) more than 102; (ii) less than 102; or (iii) exactly 102? See "Teacher, Leave Them Kids Alone," *The Economist*, February 16, 2013. The discriminatory behavior of the banks and brokers was exposed in a lawsuit filed by the City of Miami against the Bank of America in which the U.S. Supreme Court accepted the plaintiff's argument that the bank had engaged in racial discrimination contrary to the *Fair Housing Act* by intentionally targeting African-American and Latino households with mortgage products that were significantly inferior to those offered to other borrowers; see *Bank of America Corp. v City of Miami*, 581 U. S. __ (2017), No. 15-1111, Supreme Court of the United States (May 1, 2017).
17. *The Financial Crisis Inquiry Report*, Final Report of the National Commission on the Causes of the Financial and Economic Crisis in the United States (2011), xvii.
18. Published in Jon Ronson, *Lost at Sea: The Jon Ronson Mysteries* (London: Picador, 2013), 233–64.
19. Hilary Mantel, *Wolf Hall* (London: HarperCollins, 2009), 378.
20. See Joseph Spanjers and Matthew Salomon, *Illicit Financial Flows to and from Developing Countries: 2005–2014* (Washington, DC: Global Financial Integrity, 2017), Table X-1, viii; available at http://www.gfintegrity.org/wp-content/uploads/2017/05/GFI-IFF-Report-2017_final.pdf. The Report breaks down the total illicit financial flows for 2014 as follows: illicit outflows—between $620 billion and $970 billion, and illicit inflows—between $1.39 trillion and $2.54 trillion; ibid.
21. Ibid., at vii.
22. Total global net ODA in 2014 was $123 billion (see OECD, *Net ODA*, available at https://data.oecd.org/oda/net-oda.htm, and total FDI inflows into developing and emerging economies in 2014 was $676 billion (see UNCTAD, *World Investment Report 2015*, at 2).
23. Spanjers and Salomon, *Illicit Financial Flows to and from Developing Countries*, at viii and 3.
24. See Report of the UN Independent Expert on Foreign Debt and Human Rights, Juan Pablo Bohoslavsky, *Illicit financial flows, human rights and the post-2015 development agenda*, A/HRC/28/60 (February 10, 2015), para. 22.
25. Bernadette O'Hare, Innocent Makuta, Naor Bar-Zeev, Levison Chiwaula, and Alex Cobham, "The Effect of Illicit Financial Flows on Time to Reach the Fourth Millennium Development Goal in Sub-Saharan Africa: A Quantitative Analysis," *Journal of the Royal Society of Medicine* 107, no. 4: 148–56.
26. According to OECD data, the infant mortality rates of Western states in 2000 were all well under 10 deaths per 1,000, and by 2011 they were all below 5 deaths per 1,000; see OECD Data, *Health Status: Infant Mortality Rates*, available at https://data.oecd.org/healthstat/infant-mortality-rates.htm.
27. O'Hare et al., "The Effect of Illicit Financial Flows"; the data as presented in the article (principally in Table 2, at 152–53) were not always as clearly explained as they might have been,

so some of these figures are the result of my subsequent calculations using the data that were provided.

28. The World Bank classifies the full complement of developing countries in sub-Saharan Africa as comprising forty-six states with a combined population (in 2014) of 973 million people; see data sets at http://data.worldbank.org/region/SSA. For further details of the economic and social impacts of such levels of financial haemorrhaging, see Christine Clough, Dev Kar, Brian LeBlanc, Raymond Baker, and Joshua Simmons, *Hiding in Plain Sight: Trade Misinvoicing and the Impact of Revenue Loss in Ghana, Kenya, Mozambique, Tanzania, and Uganda: 2002–2011* (Washington, DC: Global Financial Integrity, 2014).

29. Moisés Naím, *Illicit: How Smugglers, Traffickers and Copycats are Hijacking the Global Economy* (New York: Anchor Books, 2005), 217.

30. Transparency International, *Global Corruption Report 2004*, 13, available at https://www.transparency.org/whatwedo/publication/global_corruption_report_2004_political_corruption. To these figures the report adds the rider that they are "extremely approximate," though in compiling them the report's authors note that they drew on "respected and widely available sources," including, in particular, the UN Office of Drugs and Crime and various media outlets such as the BBC, CNN, and the *Financial Times*.

31. These figures are taken from the World Bank, *Data: GDP per capita (current US$)*, at http://data.worldbank.org/indicator/NY.GDP.PCAP.CD?page=2.

32. James Henry, *The Price of Offshore Revisited: New Estimates for "Missing" Global Private Wealth, Income, Inequality and Lost Taxes* (Tax Justice Network, 2012), 3. On the opportunity costs for human rights of tax dodging, see chapter 5 above, 126–7.

33. Ibid., 5. And yet this estimated range, as Henry soberingly adds, is just of financial wealth: "[a] big share of the real estate, yachts, racehorses, gold bricks and many other things that count as non-financial wealth, are also owned via offshore structures where it is impossible to identify the owners;" ibid.

34. This initiative, which comprises some 100 countries and jurisdictions, seeks to clamp down on tax avoidance strategies that exploit gaps and mismatches in tax rules to artificially shift profits to low- or no-tax locations, by systematic information sharing and increasing standardization of tax rules. See "First meeting of the new inclusive framework to tackle Base Erosion and Profit Shifting marks a new era in international tax co-operation," OECD Press Release, June 30, 2016.

35. Such as through the U.S.'s *Foreign Account Tax Compliance Act* 2010, which obliges overseas financial institutions to declare details of their American clients; and the U.K.'s *Criminal Finances Act* 2017, which creates two new corporate offences of failure to prevent facilitation of tax evasion (s.45). See also the OECD-backed *Common Reporting Standard* system of automatic exchange of individual and corporate financial account information between participating countries (one of which, anomalously, is not the United States), and the UNDP/OECD *Tax Inspectors without Borders* initiative, which deploys retired tax officials from Western states to work directly with tax agencies in developing states.

36. See Michael Carnahan, "Taxation Challenges in Developing Countries" *Asia and Pacific Policy Studies* 2, no. 1 (2015): 169–82, highlighting the particular problems of effectiveness of tax collection

37. See Thomas Baunsgaard and Michael Keen, *Tax Revenue and (or?) Trade Liberalization*, IMF Working Paper 05/112 (June 2005).

38. Henry, *The Price of Offshore Revisited*, 5. These figures (and those that follow in the text) are calculated using data available from a number of sources, including the World Bank, the IMF, the Bank of International Settlements, and the UN, as well as from the central banks and national accounts of all the 139 focus group countries; for a full explanation of the methodology employed, see ibid., 27–36.

39. Ibid., 5–6, where it is further noted that all of this is made possible by the "eager (and often aggressive and illegal) assistance from the international private banking industry." For a shocking account of the long and destructive history of such systematic larceny in poor African states, see Léonce Ndikumana and James Boyce, *Africa's Odious Debts: How Foreign Loans and Capital Flight Bled a Continent* (London: Zed, 2011).

40. For a discussion of the problems and different types of modelling and data sets used, see Clemens Fuest and Nadine Riedel, "Tax Evasion and Tax Avoidance: The Role of International

Profit Shifting," in Peter Reuter (ed.), *Draining Development? Controlling Flows of Illicit Funds from Developing Countries* (Washington, DC: World bank, 2012), 109–41.

41. See UNCTAD, *World Investment Report 2015*, 200, and further, in chapter 5 below, 129.

42. For example, in one 2014 OECD review of StAR's operations, the authors acknowledged that "a huge gap remains between the results achieved and the billions of dollars that are estimated stolen from developing countries. Only US$147.2 million was returned by OECD members between 2010 and June 2012, and US$276.3 million between 2006 and 2009, a fraction of the $20–$40 billion estimated to have been stolen each year." See Larissa Gray, Kjetil Hansen, Pranvera Recica-Kirkbride, and Linnea Mills, *Few and Far: The Hard Facts on Stolen Asset Recovery* (Washington, DC: World Bank, 2014), 2.

43. Henry, *The Price of Offshore Revisited*, 10–11.

44. For an exposé of the extent of this willful blindness, see Nicholas Shaxson, *Treasure Islands: Tax Havens and the Men Who Stole the World* (London: Vintage, 2012), chapter 1, "Welcome to Nowhere," 8–32.

45. Jason Sharman, *The Money Laundry: Regulating Criminal Finance in the Global Economy* (Ithaca, NY: Cornell University Press, 2011), chapter 3. Notably, Sharman's experiment revealed only two of thirty-six providers located in tax haven jurisdictions who were prepared to establish companies without proper identification documentation.

46. See The Financial Action Task Force, *International Standards on Combating Money Laundering and the Financing of Terrorism and Proliferation* (2012; as updated October 2015), Recommendation 10.

47. Consider, for example, the brazenness of HSBC's various misdemeanours discussed earlier (in chapter 1, 31 and chapter 4, 86, at note 9). Schadenfreude there may have been in some quarters over HSBC senior management's obvious discomfort, but there is little evidence that it has led to any significant changes in behavior in the company, or indeed in the sector generally.

48. *The Daily Show*, Comedy Central, July 30, 2014.

49. Valerie Braithwaite, "Dancing with Tax Authorities: Motivational Postures and Non-Compliant Actions," in Valerie Braithwaite (ed.), *Taxing Democracy: Understanding Tax Avoidance and Tax Evasion* (London: Routledge, 2003), 18–20, and as further discussed in Erich Kirchler, *The Economic Psychology of Tax Behaviour* (Cambridge: Cambridge University Press, 2007), 96–102.

50. John Braithwaite, *Markets in Vice. Markets in Virtue* (Oxford: Oxford University Press, 2005), 149.

51. Oral evidence given before Australian Parliament, House of Representatives Select Committee on the Print Media, *Inquiry into the Australian Print Media*, March 25, 1992.

52. As discussed earlier in chapter 5, 129, at note 53.

53. Interview with Tom Brokaw, NBC, October 29, 2007, available at http://www.youtube.com/watch?v=Cu5B-2LoC4s.

54. According to Buffett: ". . . I think that people at the high end—people like myself—should be paying a lot more in taxes. We have it better than we've ever had it." Juliann Neher, "Warren Buffett Tells ABC Rich People Should Pay Higher Taxes," *Bloomberg Business*, November 22, 2010.

55. Classically identified as the three separate, but mutually balancing, powers of the executive, legislature, and the judiciary. See Charles Louis de Secondat, Baron de Montesquieu, *The Spirit of the Laws* (1748), translated by Thomas Nugent (New York: Cosimo Classics, 2011), Book XI, chapter 6.

56. Ibid., Book VIII, chapter 2.

57. Baron de Montesquieu, *Considerations on the Causes of the Grandeur and Decadence of the Romans* (1734), translated by Jehu Baker (1882) (Palala Press, 2015), Chapter XIV, 279.

58. Simon Johnson, "The Quiet Coup," *The Atlantic Magazine*, May 2009. All references to Johnson in this section are to this article of his.

59. Ibid.

60. Charles Ferguson (Director), *Inside Job*, Sony, 2010.

61. The belief remains strong. Coincidentally on the very day I write these words, newly elected Nigerian President Muhammadu Buhari swore in first minister of finance—Kemi

Adeosun, a former investment banker with Chapel Hill Denham; see Daniel Magnowski, "Nigeria's Buhari Picks Ex-Banker Adeosun as Finance Minister," *Bloomberg Business*, November 11, 2015. Two years later, she still holds the position.

62. For a review of these reforms (among others), and an assessment of their impact on banks (though only in respect of market perceptions of their profitability and levels of risk exposure), see Alexander Schäfer, Isabel Schnabel, and Beatrice Weder di Mauro, "Financial Sector Reform after the Subprime Crisis: Has Anything Happened?" *Review of Finance* 20, no. 1 (2016): 77–125.

63. Financial Stability Board, *Progress and Next Steps Towards Ending "Too-Big-To-Fail" (TBTF)* (September 2, 2013), Abstract.

64. Chapter 3 above, 82–3.

65. See Financial Stability Board, *2016 List of Global Systemically Important Banks (G-SIBs)*, and *2016 List of Global Systemically Important Insurers (G-SIIs)*, both November 21, 2016. Most of the companies on the list of insurers are either North American or European (one is from China), as are most of the banks (there are three banks each from China and Japan).

66. Financial Stability Board, *Progress and Next Steps Towards Ending "Too-Big-To-Fail" (TBTF)*, 23.

67. For an account of the one senior banker who was successfully prosecuted and convicted, and why others were not, see Jesse Eisinger, "Why Only One Top Banker Went to Jail for the Financial Crisis," *New York Times*, April 30, 2014.

68. It was calculated that between 2007 and early 2014, more than 200 banks were fined for criminal offences or settled civil claims, for a combined total of just under $100 billion, with JP Morgan commanding the single largest restitution of $13 billion (a $2 billion fine and the balance in civil suit settlements with various federal agencies). But even these amounts can simply be absorbed as a "cost of doing business;" see Richard McGregor and Aaron Stanley, "Banks Pay out $100bn in US fines," *The Financial Times*, March 25, 2014. Controversially, the civil settlement amounts may also be tax deductible! See Aruna Viswanatha and David Henry, "JP Morgan Settlement Could Cost Bank Closer to $9 Billion," *Reuters*, October 22, 2015.

69. To paraphrase the oft-quoted quip of the eighteenth-century British Lord Chancellor, Edward Thurlow, regarding a corporation's lack of conscience.

70. For an examination of this debate in the United States, see David Zaring, "Litigating the Financial Crisis," *Virginia Law Review* 100 (2014): 1405–81, in which the Zaring's notably understated conclusion is that "[t]he courts have played an unsubstantial role in the government's response to the financial crisis," 1481. For an analysis of the debate in the UK, see Jonathan Fisher, Marine Blottiaux, Stéphane Daniel, Helena Oliveira, David Green, Ola Osoka, and Agathi Trakkidi, "The Global Financial Crisis: The Case for a Stronger Criminal Response," *Law and Financial Markets Review* 7, no. 3 (2013): 159.

71. That is despite the fact that in its final report in 2011, the U.S. Financial Crisis Inquiry Commission used the word "fraud" (and derivations thereof) 157 times when referring to the causes of the crisis; as noted by Jed Rakoff, "The Financial Crisis: Why Have No High-Level Executives Been Prosecuted?" *New York Review of Books*, January 9, 2014.

72. See "Two Financial Crises Compared: The Savings and Loan Debacle and the Mortgage Mess," data and tables accompanying Gretchen Morgenson and Louise Story, "In Financial Crisis, No Prosecutions of Top Figures," *New York Times*, April 14, 2011.

73. Morgenson and Story, "In Financial Crisis, No Prosecutions of Top Figures." To access TRAC's excellent resources (albeit by subscription or payment only), see http://trac.syr.edu/.

74. Further on which, see discussion in chapter 3, under 'From boring banking to fantasy finance', 60–1.

75. The plea agreement (which also included a "five-year term of probation") was negotiated in June 2014, and then court-sanctioned in May 2015 (*USA v. BNP Paribas S.A.*, Docket No. 1:14-cr-00460 (S.D.N.Y.)). See Department of Justice, "BNP Paribas Sentenced for Conspiring to Violate the International Emergency Economic Powers Act and the Trading with the Enemy Act," Press Release, May 1, 2015. Of the total, some $4 billion was paid to federal prosecuting authorities (including the Department of Justice), and the remainder to other regulators and state prosecutors.

76. Ibid.
77. As reported by Jeff Cox, "Misbehaving Banks Have Now Paid $204B in Fines," CNBC, October 30, 2015, using data compiled by the financial analyst firm Keefe, Bruyette & Woods.
78. Brandon L. Garrett, "The Rise of Bank Prosecutions," *Yale Law Journal Forum* 126 (2016) (posted May 23, 2016), 33, at 39. For a broader treatment of the topic see Brandon L. Garrett, *Too Big to Jail: How Prosecutors Compromise with Corporations* (Cambridge, MA: Belknap Press, 2014).
79. In 2015 no fewer than eighty banks reached prosecution settlements for a grand total of $7 billion, far in excess of any previous year; see Garrett, "The Rise of Bank Prosecutions," 36–37. By mid-2016 the total since 2009 of all bank prosecutorial settlements (in respect of actions brought by all U.S.-based regulators) was 188, at a total value of $219 billion; as reported in "The Final Bill," *The Economist*, August 13, 2016 (based on data from Keefe, Bruyette & Woods). For data on criminal fines and civil settlements combined, see note 68 above.
80. Garrett, "The Rise of Bank Prosecutions," 41–45.
81. U.S Attorneys' Manual, *9-28.000—Principles of Federal Prosecution of Business Organizations* (November 2015), at 9-28.010; available at https://www.justice.gov/usam/usam-9-28000-principles-federal-prosecution-business-organizations.
82. See Danielle Douglas, "Holder Concerned Megabanks are Too Big To Jail," *Washington Post*, March 6, 2013.
83. See Deputy Attorney-General Sally Quillian Yates, *Remarks at New York University School of Law Announcing New Policy on Individual Liability in Matters of Corporate Wrongdoing* (September 10, 2015); available at https://www.justice.gov/opa/speech/deputy-attorney-general-sally-quillian-yates-delivers-remarks-new-york-university-school.
84. This nonprosecution agreement comprised a forfeiture by the bank of $97.44 million. For further details, see Department of Justice, "Banamex USA Agrees to Forfeit $97 Million in Connection with Bank Secrecy Act Violations," Press Release, May 22, 2017.
85. That is, by way of the incongruously named *Financial Creating Hope and Opportunity for Investors, Consumers and Entrepreneurs Act, or Financial CHOICE Act*, H.R.10 – 115th Congress (2017–18); introduced into the House of Representatives on April 27, 2017, and passed by the House on June 8, 2017. For a commentary on those parts of the Act mentioned in the text above, see Aaron Klein, "How the Financial Choice Act Hurts Americans," *Fortune*, June 8, 2017.
86. See The White House, *Presidential Memorandum on Fiduciary Duty Rule*, Press Release, February 3, 2017, and further below, note 109 and accompanying text.
87. For the former initiative, see The White House, *Presidential Memorandum*, which declares that the intent of the review of the protective Fiduciary Rule is to "empower Americans to make their own financial decisions"; and for the latter, the administration obviously considered it worth its while to concoct a title for the statute that would yield the acronym CHOICE (see note 85 above), no matter the invidious nature of the choice it provides people.
88. "[W]ithout holding real people on Wall Street accountable for their wrongdoing in the years leading up to the financial crisis, the message that their behavior is unacceptable goes undelivered," as William Cohan puts it in "How Wall Street's Bankers Stayed Out of Jail," *The Atlantic*, September 2015, available at https://www.theatlantic.com/magazine/archive/2015/09/how-wall-streets-bankers-stayed-out-of-jail/399368/.
89. See "Top Bankers Face Grilling by Dubious Congress," *NBC News*, February 11, 2009.
90. Ibid.; and Marshall Eckblad, "Pay Jumps at Wells Fargo," *Wall Street Journal*, March 4, 2010. Further on the hubris of other bankers, see "Looting Stars," *The Economist*, January 31, 2009.
91. Matt Taibbi, "Why Isn't Wall Street in Jail?" *Rolling Stone*, February 16, 2011.
92. The term is often associated with Nobel Laureate economist and leading light of the Chicago School of Economics George Stigler, who summed up the phenomenon as "the pervasive use of the state's support of special groups"; see George Stigler, "The Theory of Economic Regulation," *The Bell Journal of Economics and Management Science* 2, no. 1 (1971): 18.
93. An extent, that Jane Mayer argues, threatens the very fabric of Western democracies; see her *Dark Money: The Hidden History of the Billionaires Behind the Rise of the Radical Right* (New York: Doubleday, 2016).

94. Daniel Kaufmann, "Daniel Kaufmann on State Capture," *World Policy Journal* 27, no. 1 (2010): 3–4, and for a more mathematically forensic analysis of the issue, see Daniel Kaufmann and Pedro Vicente, "Legal Corruption," *Economics and Politics* 23, no. 3 (2011), 195–219.

95. That is, in particular, limited liability incorporation, limited partnerships, and trusts (a 'beneficial owner' is one who enjoys the benefits of ownership even though the title is in another name); see Emile van der Does de Willebois, Emily Halter, Robert Harrison, Ji Won Park, and Jason Sharman, *The Puppet Masters: How the Corrupt Use Legal Structures to Hide Stolen Assets and What to Do About It* (Washington, DC: Stolen Asset Recovery Initiative, 2010), especially Appendix C for descriptions of these and other corporate vehicles, and Appendix D for ten case studies of notorious "grand corrupters."

96. See BBC News (Business), "Starbucks 'paid just £8.6 million in tax in 14 years,'" October 16, 2012. The fact that by 2015, the company was loudly proclaiming that, henceforth, it will be paying much more UK tax has more to do with the fact that public outrage had severely dented its bottom line than any change in tax laws; see Simon Bowers, "Starbucks Brews Up First UK Profits in 17 Years," *The Guardian*, February 4, 2015.

97. See Lisa O'Carroll, "If Google Is in Ireland for Tax Reasons, Why Are Most of Its Profits in Bermuda? *The Guardian*, March 24, 2011.

98. The Commission concluded "that two tax rulings issued by Ireland to Apple have substantially and artificially lowered the tax paid by Apple in Ireland since 1991 . . . [and that] this selective tax treatment of Apple in Ireland is illegal under EU state aid rules, because it gives Apple a significant advantage over other businesses that are subject to the same national taxation rules"; see European Commission, "State aid: Ireland gave illegal tax benefits to Apple worth up to €13 billion," Press Release, August 20, 2016. Even in 2011, the Commission notes, when the company's effective tax rate was more than ten times higher (at approximately 0.06%), Apple's Irish tax bill was derisorily small—just €10 million, on profits of €16 billion; ibid.

99. James Kanter and Mark Scott, "Apple Owes $14.5 Billion in Back Taxes to Ireland, E.U. Says," *New York Times*, August 30, 2016.

100. Sarantis Michalopoulos, "Apple Ruling Divides Irish Cabinet," *EurActiv.com*, September 2, 2016.

101. Harry McGee, "Apple Ruling Is Aimed at Harming Irish Tax Regime, Claims Noonan," *The Irish Times*, September 2, 2016.

102. See OECD.Stat, "Corporate Income Tax Rate"; at https://stats.oecd.org/Index.aspx?DataSetCode=TABLE_II1.

103. "The Missing $20 Trillion," *The Economist*, February 16, 2013.

104. See Richard Brooks and Andrew Bousfield, "Where There's Muck, There's Brass Plates: How UK Ghost Companies Made Britain the Capital of Global Corporate Crime," Special Report, *Private Eye* (2012).

105. Robert Jenkins, *Remarks on Lessons in Lobbying*, Introduction to the Third Gordon Midgley Memorial Debate, London, November 22, 2011.

106. Lenore Taylor, "Kidnap Fears If Large Private Companies Publish Tax Details, Says Coalition," *The Guardian*, March 17, 2015. The relevant legislation is the *Tax and Superannuation Laws Amendment (Better Targeting the Income Tax Transparency Laws) Act 2015*, which amends, in part, the income tax transparency requirements provided by *Taxation Administration Act 1953*, section 3C.

107. Taylor, "Kidnap Fears If Large Private Companies Publish Tax Details"; and Heath Aston, "Wealthy Business Owners Get Tax Shield as PM Talks Up 'Have a Go' Society," *Sydney Morning Herald*, October 16, 2015.

108. John Donne, "No Man Is an Island" (1624), as it is popularly cited. Official citation: Meditation XXVII, *Devotions upon Emergent Occasions* (1624)

109. The Department of Labor's "Fiduciary Rule" (2016) (which takes the form of an amendment to the *Employee Retirement Income Security Act* 1974) greatly expands the number and categories of financial advisers who are obliged to put their clients' interests ahead of their own. Incredibly, presently many are not required to do so. Opposition from the industry sector to the rule's implementation has been unabashed and fierce (see Insured

Retirement Institute, correspondence to the Department of Labor Review of the Fiduciary Rule, March 10, 2017). It has also been very effective, with President Trump signaling his intention to prevent the rule coming into effect or to eviscerate it if it does; see The White House, *Presidential Memorandum on Fiduciary Duty Rule*, Press Release, February 3, 2017; and Ashlea Ebeling, "The Next DOL Fiduciary Rule Deadline: April 17," *Forbes*, March 23, 2017.

110. The "suggestion" took the form of a provision in a Code of Conduct advanced by the UK's asset management industry body, the Investment Association (IA), which was endorsed by barely more than 10% of the IA's membership, and created so much controversy that the IA's chief executive was forced to resign; see Michael Bow, "Fund Managers: Don't Ask Us to Be Transparent over Fees," *The Independent*, October 8, 2015.

111. Traders at the Royal Bank of Scotland, for example, "left a trail of evidence in a trove of e-mails and audio recordings detailing how they set about trying to manipulate LIBOR, even after they knew investigators were looking into the issue. 'We're just not allowed to have those conversations over Bloomberg anymore;'" as reported in *The Economist*, "The Wrong Stuff," February 9, 2013. Nb. for readers unfamiliar with the antipodean term, a "rort" is a fraudulent or dishonest act or practice.

112. As the firm proclaims in a two-page advertisement it placed in *The Economist*, February 7, 2015.

113. See Robert Wood, "Credit Suisse: Guilty, $2.6 Billion Fine, but Avoids Death in the US— UBS Luckier," *Forbes*, May 14, 2014.

114. Mark Carney, "The Future of Financial Reform," *2014 Monetary Authority of Singapore Lecture*, November 17, 2014, 12, where he credits Bill Dudley and Minouche Shafik for the metaphorical reference.

115. Financial Stability Board, *Progress and Next Steps Towards Ending "Too-Big-To-Fail" (TBTF)*, 23.

116. See http://www.bankofengland.co.uk/markets/Pages/openforum.aspx.

117. Bank of England, *Open Forum: Building Real Markets for the Good of the People*, June 2015, 4. What the bank means by "fairness" is anchored wholly in the notion of maintaining market effectiveness and combating "ethical drift"; ibid., 7–8.

118. See Background, Plenary Session: "The Role of Financial Markets in the Economy," Bank of England *Open Forum*, November 11, 2015, available at http://www.bankofengland.co.uk/markets/Documents/openforumagenda.pdf.

119. Especially in the context of the adjudication of legal disputes, to the extent that human rights have been enshrined in law, as notably advanced by Ronald Dworkin in his landmark *Taking Rights Seriously* (Cambridge, MA: Harvard University Press, 1977).

120. The International Council on Human Rights Policy, *Human Rights in the Global Economy: Report from a Colloquium* (2010), 10.

121. Mary Dowell-Jones and David Kinley, "Minding the Gap: Global Finance and Human Rights," *Ethics and International Affairs* 25, no. 2 (2011), 185. Specifically, we highlighted gaps in the human rights community's understanding of such issues as "capital adequacy, liquidity, risk management, derivatives, financial modeling, ratings, and supervision," despite such issues being "critical to the crisis and [to the] shape [of] the global financial system and its impact on human rights enjoyment in the years to come."

122. Mary Dowell-Jones and David Kinley, "The Monster under the Bed: Financial Services and the Ruggie Framework," in Radu Mares (ed.), *The UN Guiding Principles on Corporations and Human Rights: Foundations and Implementation* (Leiden: Brill, 2012), 193, 195.

123. UN Human Rights Council, *Guiding Principles on Business and Human Rights: Implementing the United Nations "Protect, Respect and Remedy" Framework*, UN Doc. A/HRC/RES/17/4 (July 6, 2011); and on which see chapter 4 above, 86–7.

124. See chapter 4, 86–7.

125. Dowell-Jones and Kinley, "The Monster under the Bed," 207.

126. See, for example, a report produced by the Jakarta-based Institute of Ecosoc Rights, *The Palm Oil Industry and Human Rights: A Case Study of Palm Oil Corporations in Central Kalimantan* (2015); available at http://www.jus.uio.no/smr/english/about/programmes/indonesia/docs/report-english-version-jan-2015.pdf. And for an overview of a number of studies of

the issue, see Benjamin Skinner, "Indonesia's Palm Oil Industry Rife with Human Rights Abuses," *Bloomberg Businessweek*, July 21, 2013.

127. See BankTrack, *Human Rights Impact Briefing No.1: Labour standards violations in IOI Corporation's Malaysian plantations* (February 2016).

128. UNEPFI, *Human Rights Guidance Tool for the Financial Sector* (2014), available at http://unepfi.org/humanrightstoolkit/finance.php).

129. UNEPFI and Foley Hoag, *Banks and Human Rights: A Legal Analysis* (December 2015), at 1 and 2–3, respectively.

130. See OECD Global Forum on Responsible Business Conduct, *Due diligence in the financial sector: adverse impacts directly linked to financial sector operations, products or services by a business relationship* (2014), 10–11.

131. *Righting Finance*, at http://www.rightingfinance.org/.

132. Institute for Human Rights and Business, *Human Rights and Sustainable Finance: Exploring the Relationship*, Inquiry Working Paper 16/01 (February 2016), prepared for the UN Environmental Program Inquiry on the Design of a Sustainable Financial System, at 17.

133. Ignacio Saiz, "Rights in Recession? Challenges for Economic and Social Rights Enforcement in Times of Crisis," *Journal of Human Rights Practice* 1 (2009): 277, 280.

134. Aoife Nolan, "Not Fit for Purpose: Human Rights in Times of Financial and Economic Crisis," *European Rights Law Review* 4 (2015): 360, 365–71. Nolan's further call "to move past our current situation in which human rights actors and economic actors operate in separate, watertight spheres, resulting in human rights being both sidelined and undermined in the implementation of post-crisis measures" (at 371), is one that this book aims to heed.

135. ESCR-Net, *Bringing Human Rights to Bear in Times of Crisis* (March 2010), 18.

136. See under "The voice of human rights," chapter 5, 118–9.

137. See under "What money can buy," chapter 4, 86–7.

138. A caveat human rights scholar Sigrun Skogly has also directed specifically at international human rights lawyers when urging them to "remain realistic and refrain from the temptation to become dogmatic . . . [because] [i]f a gulf develops between the politicians on the one hand and human rights lawyers on the other, the opportunity for much-needed constructive dialogue will be lost"; see Sigrun Skogly, "The Global Financial Crisis: A Human Rights Meltdown?" in *Poverty, Justice and the Rule of Law*, A Report of the International Bar Association's Presidential Taskforce on the Financial Crisis (2013), 78.

139. David Kinley, "Bendable Rules: The Development Implications of Human Rights Pluralism," in Brian Tamanaha, Caroline Sage, and Michael Woolcock (eds.), *Legal Pluralism and Development: Scholars and Practitioners in Dialogue* (New York: Cambridge University Press, 2012), 50–65.

140. Ibid., 50.

141. Such grounds for restricting rights are expressly provided under the *International Covenant on Civil and Political Rights* with respect to: freedom of movement (article 12), the right to a public hearing under the right to a fair trial (article 14), freedom of religious practice (article 18), freedom of expression (article 19), the right to assembly (article 21), and freedom of association (article 22). Article 4 of the *International Covenant on Economic, Social and Cultural Rights* permits limitations on all rights in the Covenant provided that they "are determined by law only in so far as this may be compatible with the nature of these rights and solely for the purpose of promoting the general welfare in a democratic society."

142. Mary Ann Glendon, *A World Made New: Eleanor Roosevelt and the Universal Declaration of Human Rights* (New York: Random House, 2001), xviii. On top of which individual cultures are themselves, inexorably, changing, by possessing, transforming, improving, and forgetting, as Claude Lévi-Strauss puts it in his *Race et Histoire* (Paris: UNESCO, 1961), 66.

143. *Consolidated report of the Secretary-General and the United Nations High Commissioner for Human Rights on the right to development*, UN Doc. A/HRC/27/27 (June 18, 2014), para. 8.

144. Mary Robinson, "What Rights Can Add to Good Development Practice," in Philip Alston and Mary Robinson (eds.), *Human Rights and Development: Towards Mutual Reinforcement* (Oxford: Oxford University Press, 2005), 39–40.

145. See *UN Declaration on the Right to Development* 1986, Articles 1 and 2; and chapter 5, at 136.

146. As argued by Jack Donnelly; see under "Development and human rights: more awkward than intimate," chapter 5, 136 (at note 89).

147. See chapter 5, 136–7.
148. See chapter 5, 136.
149. See, for example, a leaked statement made jointly by the World Bank Executive representing France, Germany, Italy, the Netherlands, Nordic and Baltic States, and the United Kingdom, regarding a 2015 review and update of the bank's safeguard policies, which states: "We believe it is very much the responsibility of the Bank to ensure that its operations do not violate human rights." The statement was dated June 24, 2015, and is available at http://www.bankinformationcenter.org/wp-content/uploads/2015/10/6eds.pdf.
150. For example, Oona Hathaway, "Do Human Rights Treaties Make a Difference?" *Yale Law Journal* 11 (2002): 1935–2042.
151. Thus, Oona Hathaway's postulation that repressive states exploit the "expressive" role of human rights treaty ratification as a cover for continued rights abuses is based on nothing more than superficial coincidences that hide more than they reveal; see especially the contradictory reasoning at ibid., 1989. Coincidences are also evident in the contrary claims made by Christopher Fariss, that there exists a *positive* correlation between human rights treaty ratification and compliance. The difference between Fariss and Hathaway, however, is that Fariss employs a rigorous methodological approach to interpreting the available data and thereby reaches conclusions that are more robust and defensible; see Fariss, "The Changing Standard of Accountability and the Positive Relationship between Human Rights Treaty Ratification and Compliance," *British Journal of Political Science*, 1-33, published online (6 July 2017), available at https://doi.org/10.1017/S000712341500054X.
152. As Jose Alvarez neatly puts it when responding to elegant-looking theories of how states "socialize" (or internalize) human rights standards, in "Do States Socialize?" *Duke Law Journal* 54 (2005): 961–74, at 968.
153. Todd Landman and Edzia Carvalho, *Measuring Human Rights* (Abingdon, UK: Routledge, 2010), at 131.
154. Though that has not, of course, stopped many from trying. In addition to Hathaway, Fariss, Landman and Carvalho mentioned above, see also, notably, the so-called "spiral model" of human rights change as developed in Thomas Risse, Stephen Ropp, and Kathryn Sikkink (eds.), *The Power of Human Rights: International Norms and Domestic Change* (Cambridge: Cambridge University Press, 1999), and the UN Office of the High Commissioner of Human Rights' 170-page, *Human Rights Indicators: A Guide to Measurement and Implementation* (2012).
155. Deborah Brautigam, "Africa's Eastern Promise: What the West Can Learn from China's Investment in Africa," *Foreign Affairs*, January 5, 2010.
156. See Deborah Brautigam, *The Dragon's Gift: The Real Story of China in Africa* (Oxford: Oxford University Press, 2009), where she notes that "like the US, China gives aid for three reasons: strategic diplomacy, commercial benefit and as a reflection of societies' ideologies and values" (15), as filtered through the three layers of state, societal, and international expectations and pressures.
157. Robinson, "What Rights Can Add to Good Development Practice," 40.
158. "A theory of human rights can . . . allow considerable internal variations, without losing the commonality of the agreed principle of attaching substantial importance to human rights . . . and of being committed seriously to considering how that importance should be appropriately reflected," as Amartya Sen argues; see his "Elements of a Theory of Human Rights," *Philosophy and Public Affairs* 32 (2004): 315, 323.
159. See further David Kinley, "Human Rights Fundamentalisms," *Sydney Law Review* 29, no. 4 (2007): 545, 567–68. The "frail child" metaphor is borrowed from David Kennedy, "The International Human Rights Movement: Part of the Problem?" *Harvard Human Rights Journal* 15 (2002): 101.

Chapter 7 – Counseling and Reconciliation

1. As told by Louisa Lim, *The Peoples' Republic of Amnesia* (New York: Oxford University Press, 2014), 103.
2. Gordon Brown, *Speech on the Global Economy*, available at http://www.ukpol.co.uk/2015/10/02/gordon-brown-2008-speech-on-the-global-economy-at-reuters/. The three banks were HBOS, Lloyds TBS, and the Royal Bank of Scotland.

3. The White House, "Transcript of President Obama's Interview with Novaya Gazeta," Press Release, July 6, 2009.

4. For an overview of these regulatory responses, see IMF Working Paper prepared by Stijn Claessens and Laura Kodres, *The Regulatory Responses to the Global Financial Crisis: Some Uncomfortable Questions*, WP/14/46 (March 2014), 8–9.

5. Big banks have struggled to comply with the so-called living wills provisions established under section 165(d) of the *Dodd-Frank Wall Street Reform and Consumer Protection Act*, which require all large banks to submit to the Federal Reserve and the Federal Deposit Insurance Corporation annual reports on their individual strategies for "rapid and orderly resolution" of their assets and activities should they be in danger of failure. When in early 2016 the living wills of five of the largest banks in the United States were rejected as inadequate by the federal regulators, Senator Elizabeth Warren lambasted the banks for continuing to cling to the "revisionist history" that they "weren't really responsible for the financial crisis," adding that "any one of them could crash the economy again if they started to fail and were not bailed out"; see Press Release: *Statement from Senator Warren on Rejection of Banks' "Living Wills" by Fed and FDIC* (April 13, 2016). This view notwithstanding, President Trump has signaled his intention to review and replace the living wills requirements; see Jeff Cox, "Trump Issues Directives That Could Roll Back Post-Crisis Reforms," CNBC, April 21, 2017.

6. Though by 2015, the U.S. bailout balance sheet, at least, was showing a profit return for the government and taxpayer; see Paul Kiel and Dan Nguyen, "Bailout Tracker: Tracking Every Dollar and Every Recipient," *ProPublica*, November 18, 2015, available at https://projects. propublica.org/bailout/.

7. Chapter 3, as discussed under "Rich world austerity" and "Poor world impacts," 66–71.

8. A point made by Martin Wolf in *The Shifts and the Shocks: What We've Learned and Have Still to Learn from the Financial Crisis* (New York: Penguin, 2014), in which he asks, rhetorically, how credible a theory of human biology would be if it did not anticipate heart failure, or a theory of mechanical engineering that did not acknowledge the possibility of collapse, xvii.

9. Sue Konzelmann, Frank Wilkinson, Mar Fovargue-Davies, and Duncan Sankey, "Government Regulation and Financial Market Instability: The Implications for Policy," *Cambridge Journal of Economics* 34 (2010): 929, 952.

10. Karen Maley, James Eyers, and Jemima Whyte, "David Murray Lashes Regulators on Cultural Crackdown," *Sydney Morning Herald*, April 5, 2016.

11. Murray is a former chairman of the Commonwealth Bank of Australia—Australia's biggest, and the world's tenth largest, bank.

12. See James Eyers, "O'Dwyer Backs ASIC Action on Bank Culture," *Sydney Morning Herald*, March 22, 2016. In fact, the Australian *Criminal Code* 1995 already specifies that criminal fault can be attributed to a body corporate where it is shown that "corporate culture existed within the body corporate that directed, encouraged, tolerated or led to non-compliance with the relevant provision," or that "the body corporate failed to create and maintain a corporate culture that required compliance with the relevant provision"; per §12.3(2) (c) and (d).

13. Ibid.

14. *Financial System Inquiry: Final Report* (November 2014), at 7–8. The inquiry had been commissioned by the Australian Government.

15. David Hume, "Of Money," in *Essays, Moral, Political and Literary* (1742) (Indianapolis, IA: Liberty Fund, 1987), II.III.1.

16. Ibid., at II.I.17 on the supply (by the state) of public necessities, and at II.IV.10, on satisfaction of one's wants and needs through trade between individuals.

17. UN Human Rights Council, *Annual Report of the Special Rapporteur on Extreme Poverty and Human Rights*, UN Doc. A/HRC/17/34 (March 17, 2011), para. 56.

18. Institute for Human Rights and Business (IHRB), *Human Rights and Sustainable Finance: Exploring the Relationship*, Inquiry Working Paper 16/01 (February 2016), prepared for the UN Environmental Program Inquiry on the Design of a Sustainable Financial System, 16.

19. Under "Transformative powers," chapter 1, 19–21.

20. See especially Robert Shiller, *Finance and the Good Society* (Princeton, NJ: Princeton University Press, 2012), and George Akerloff and Robert Shiller, *Animal Spirits: How*

Human Psychology Drives the Economy and Why It Matters for Global Capitalism (Princeton, NJ: Princeton University Press, 2009).

21. See under "Missed opportunities," chapter 2, 52–4.
22. See discussion under "Wishful thinking," chapter 6, 174–5.
23. For example, the *International Covenant on Economic, Social and Cultural Rights*, Article 2(1), on which see the discussion under "The voice of human rights," chapter 5, 118–9.
24. Shiller, *Finance and the Good Society*, 149–50. Part of the problem appears to lie in Shiller's singular reliance on the *Universal Declaration on Human Rights*, as that instrument is neither dispositive of what international human rights law entails, nor was it ever meant to be. It is the Covenants that follow it—and which are replete with explicitly flexible and compromising provisions—that are crucial, as a cursory reading of any basic international human rights law text would reveal.
25. "Dignity is what some of our rights are rights *to*; but dignity is also what grounds all of our rights," as Jeremy Waldron puts it in *Dignity, Rank, and Rights* (New York: Oxford University Press, 2012),16.
26. Conor Gearty, *Can Human Rights Survive?* The Hamlyn Lectures 2005 (Cambridge: Cambridge University Press, 2006), 43.
27. Ibid., 48.
28. Ibid., 47; here drawing directly on James Griffin. Griffin has subsequently expanded his thoughts on the foundations of human rights in his *On Human Rights* (Oxford: Oxford University Press, 2009).
29. Richard Rorty, *Philosophy and Social Hope* (London: Penguin, 1999), 248.
30. Ibid., 249.
31. Adam Smith, *The Theory of Moral Sentiments* (1759) (New York: Dover, 2007), Part III, chapter 1, 46.
32. As laid out in Steven Pinker, *The Better Angels of Our Nature* (London: Penguin, 2011), especially chapters 9 and 10.
33. See James Flynn, "Searching for Justice: The Discovery of IQ Gains over Time," *American Psychologist* (January 1999): 5–20.
34. Pinker, *The Better Angels of Our Nature*, 781.
35. Ibid., 793.
36. What he calls the "rights revolution" (ibid., 456–579).
37. UNESCO, *Overcoming inequality: why governance matters* (2009), for example, documents a vast gulf in educational opportunities separating rich and poor countries; see also Johan Norberg, *Progress: Ten Reasons to Look Forward to the Future* (London: Oneworld, 2016), 135.
38. See Henrietta Cook and Marissa Calligeros, "Xavier College Bully Schooled in VCE Facebook Slapdown," *The Age*, October 29, 2015. All quotes and references regarding this story are taken from this source, which includes an audio clip of the radio broadcast.
39. Ibid.
40. Gearty, *Can Human Rights Survive?*, 41, in which he quotes from "The story of man," *The Economist*, December 20, 2005.
41. Geoffrey Brennan and Philip Pettit, *The Economy of Esteem: An Essay on Civil and Political Society* (Oxford: Oxford University Press, 2006), 245.
42. Ibid., 246.
43. University of Notre Dame and Labaton Sucharow LLP, *The Street, the Bull and the Crisis: A Survey of the US and UK Financial Services Industry* (May 2015), 2.
44. Ibid., 3–6.
45. Ibid., 7–8.
46. As Charles Kindleberger and Robert Aliber title their first chapter in *Manias, Panics and Crashes* (Basingstoke: Palgrave Macmillan, 2011). When this classic was first published in 1978, it provided a valuable historical account of the litany of global financial crises from that precipitated by hyper-speculation in Dutch tulip bulbs in 1636, to all major crises since. It has proved its additional worth by effectively predicting the *inevitability* of all financial crisis since then, thereby necessitating its multiple further editions.
47. Shiller, *Finance and the Good Society*, 159.
48. University of Notre Dame and Labaton Sucharow LLP, *The Street, the Bull and the Crisis*, 5.

49. Group of Thirty, *Banking Culture and Conduct: A Call for Sustained and Comprehensive Reform* (July 2015), at 28.

50. Brandon L. Garrett, "The Rise of Bank Prosecutions," *Yale Law Journal Forum* 126 (2016) (posted May 23, 2016): 33, at 42.

51. As he wrote some twenty years later in the prologue to his *The Big Short: Inside the Doomsday Machine* (New York: W. W. Norton, 2010).

52. See Vanessa Desloires, "Oliver Stone Says Wall Street Culture 'Horribly Worse' Than Gordon Gekko's Time," *Sydney Morning Herald*, June 3, 2015.

53. Kevin Dowd and Martin Hutchinson, *Alchemists of Loss* (Chichester: John Wiley & Sons, 2010), 4.

54. Brennan and Pettit, *The Economy of Esteem*, 250, 280, and 284–85. For their discussions on the details of their examples of recycling, see 126–27; homosexuality, 236 and 264; and tax, 313.

55. Under "Incentives and exceptionalism," chapter 1, 30–2.

56. Group of Thirty, *Banking Culture and Conduct*, 32, "Case Study 2."

57. That is to obvert the remark of Adair Turner, the former chair of the UK's Financial Services Authority (since disbanded), that much of finance was in effect "socially useless"; see his speech—"What Do Banks Do, What Should They Do and What Public Policies Are Needed to Ensure Best Results for the Real Economy?" CASS Business School, London (March 17, 2010).

58. On the various dimensions of which in the context of finance, see Sylvia Walby, "Finance versus Democracy: Theorising Finance in Society," *Work, Employment and Society* 27, no. 3 (2013): 489–507; and on the specific concerns of regulating financial markets, see John Quiggin, *Zombie Economics: How Dead Ideas Still Walk Among Us* (Princeton, NJ: Princeton University Press, 2010), 75–76.

59. Thus, the Volcker Alliance (an independent think-tank headed by Paul Volcker, a former head of the Federal Reserve) has made detailed suggestions as to how to reorganize and rationalize, and thereby strengthen, the U.S. federal financial regulatory system to make it a "more adaptive and more resilient" regime, "aimed at achieving sustained financial system stability." See The Volcker Alliance, *Reshaping the Financial Regulatory System* (2015), at 4, and at 4–5 for the "guiding principles" upon which such reform should be based.

60. Karl Popper, *The Open Society and Its Enemies* (Volume 1: The Spell of Plato) (1945) (London: Routledge, 2011), 121.

61. Popper concedes how hard this balancing act is: "[i]t is certainly difficult to determine exactly the degree of freedom that can be left to the citizens without endangering that freedom whose protection is the task of the state" (ibid.).

62. The allocation of risk being that part of the financial system comprising the capital markets, as opposed to the retail banking part, which acts as the mechanism by which the system shifts capital between those who have it and those who need it. Though, of course, in practice, the two often intermingle. The management and mismanagement of risk is the subject of chapter 3 of this book.

63. For a discussion of the pros and cons of engagement with pariah states and the differences between "business as usual" engagement and "principled" engagement, see Morten Pedersen and David Kinley, "Introducing Principled Engagement?" in David Kinley and Morten Pedersen (eds.), *Principled Engagement: Negotiating Human Rights in Repressive States* (London: Routledge, 2013), 1–11.

64. UN Independent Expert on Foreign Debt and Human Rights, Juan Pablo Bohoslavsky, *Report on financial complicity: Lending to States engaged in gross human rights violations*, UN Doc. A/HRC/28/59 (December 22, 2014), para. 2.

65. On the breadth and sophistication of the "business of terrorism," see Louise Shelly, *Dirty Entanglements: Corruption, Crime and Terrorism* (Cambridge: Cambridge University Press, 2014), 173–217.

66. The Financial Action Task Force (FATF), *Emerging Terrorist Financing Risks* (October 2015), available at http://www.fatf-gafi.org/media/fatf/documents/reports/Emerging-Terrorist-Financing-Risks.pdf. On the particular problem of Western money financing terrorism through the purchase of "blood oil," see Leif Wenar, *Blood Oil: Tyrants, Violence, and the Rules That Run the World* (New York: Oxford University Press, 2016), 91–93.

67. See John McLaughlin, "Ending ISIS: An Ex-CAI Chief's Plan," *OZY*, December 28, 2015, which comprises excerpts of his testimony before the U.S. House of Representatives' Armed Services Committee in November 2015; available at http://www.ozy.com/pov/ending-isis-an-ex-cia-chiefs-plan/66504?utm_source=dd&utm_medium=email&utm_campaign=120 72015&variable=c5ddf527f3f6631699ab539270791c50.

68. Stefan Heißner, Peter R. Neumann, John Holland-McCowan and Rajan Basra, *A Caliphate in Decline*: An *Estimate of Islamic State's Financial Fortunes* (2017), 5, available at http://icsr. info/wp-content/uploads/2017/02/ICSR-Report-Caliphate-in-Decline-An-Estimate-of-Islamic-States-Financial-Fortunes.pdf. The report notes that the group's wealth had declined to around $870 million in 2016, ibid.

69. FATF, *Emerging Terrorist Financing Risks*, 44.

70. For an account of the problems and possibilities of "following the money" in the context of terrorist financing, see Marieke de Goede, *Speculative Security: The Politics of Pursuing Terrorist Monies* (Minneapolis: University of Minnesota Press, 2012), 57–93.

71. See Lynn Stout, "Derivatives and the Legal Origin of the 2008 Credit Crisis," *Harvard Business Law Review* 1 (2011): 4.

72. Ross Buckley, "The Changing Nature of Banking and Why It Matters," in Ross Buckley, Emilios Avgouleas, and Douglas Arner (eds.), *Reconceptualising Global Finance and Its Regulation* (Cambridge: Cambridge University Press, 2016), 9–27.

73. The FSB is considering how it might extend its mandate to cover global systemically important financial institutions (currently it encompasses only banks and insurers) to include institutions such as hedge funds (that is, nonbank, noninsurer institutions, or, to use the FSB's inelegant acronym, NBNI G-SIFIs); see FSB, *Next Steps on the NBNI G-SIFI Assessment Methodologies* (July 30, 2015). On the latent and not so latent influence of hedge funds and their role as "the new merchant banks" (privately owned, ferociously focused on risk, and yet lightly regulated) in the financial system, see Sebastian Mallaby, *More Money Than God: Hedge Funds and the Making of a New Elite* (New York: Penguin, 2010), 391.

74. The Volcker Rule is named after Paul Volcker, a former chairman of the U.S. Federal Reserve who proposed it in early 2010. It is embodied in section 619 of the *Dodd-Frank Act* and operationalized through regulations issued by a suite of federal financial supervisory bodies. For an overview and analysis of the rule, the controversy surrounding it, and its impact (both extant and likely), see Kimberly Krawiec and Guangya Liu, "The Volcker Rule: A Brief Political History," *Capital Markets Law Journal* 10, no. 4 (2015): 507–22.

75. See Paul Volcker, "Financial Reform: Unfinished Business," *The New York Review of Books*, November 24, 2011. For an infamous and colorful example of the undesirable consequences of such conflicts of interest in proprietary trading, see discussion of the "Abacus 2007-AC1" case under "Greed in finance," chapters 3, 78.

76. Which incentives, argue Sue Jaffer, Nicholas Morris, and David Vines, have undermined the trustworthiness of the financial services industry; see their chapter "Why Trustworthiness Is Important," in Nicholas Morris and David Vines (eds.), *Capital Failure: Rebuilding Trust in Financial Services* (New York: Oxford University Press, 2014), 3–31.

77. See Ross Buckley, "Introducing a 0.05% Financial Transactions Tax as an Instrument of Global Justice and Market Efficiency," *Asian Journal of International Law* (2014): 153–67. As of late 2017, a proposed FTT involving ten EU countries (including France, Germany, Italy, and Spain, but not the UK) was still under negotiation after repeated delays in its proposed implementation; see Joe Kirwin, "EU Financial Transaction Tax Talks Kicked to End of 2017", *Bloomberg*, July 10, 2017.

78. *Inside Job* (Sony; 2010). Interestingly, these remarks are to be found in the "Special Features/ Deleted Scenes" that accompanied the release of the movie. Some of the most damning things Spitzer has to say about the death of ethics and the loss of perspective in the financial sector are to be found in this somewhat neglected corner of this extraordinary documentary.

79. Douglas Hodge, "Restoring Trust," in John Taft (ed.), *A Force for Good: How Enlightened Finance Can Restore Faith in Capitalism* (Basingstoke: Palgrave Macmillan, 2015), 67.

80. As discussed in chapter 6 (at 162–5), the record of bank prosecutions, settlements, and convictions under U.S. criminal law has risen in recent years, though still overwhelmingly relating to corporate rather than personal wrongdoing, and even when the latter, still not

of the senior-most bankers; see John Wander, "New records in SEC enforcement actions," blog post on *Harvard Law School Forum on Corporate Governance and Financial Regulation* (November 14, 2015).

81. Former HSBC IT employee, Hervé Falciani, was convicted and sentenced, in absentia, to a five-year jail term in 2015; see Juliette Garside, "HSBC Whistle-Blower Given Five Year's Jail over Biggest Leak in Banking History," *The Guardian*, November 27, 2015.

82. See under chapter 4, 86–7.

83. As Bank of England governor Mark Carney has stressed repeatedly as banks' "social license to operate," see, for example, Mark Carney, "The Future of Financial Reform," *2014 Monetary Authority of Singapore Lecture*, November 17, 2014; and for other examples of central banks addressing human rights and social risks, see IHRB, *Human Rights and Sustainable Finance: Exploring the Relationship*, 36–37.

84. "Forswearing Greed," *The Economist*, June 6, 2009.

85. See "The Trust Machine" and the "The Great Chain of Being Sure about Things," *The Economist*, October 31, 2015.

86. Fraud—as in all financial dealings—is unavoidable. In early 2016 a popular online, peer-to-peer service in China called Ezubao collapsed with 900,000 investors losing $7.6 billion, after it turned out that the fund was a Ponzi scheme (the biggest ever, in terms of the number of investors), and the police arrested its senior management; see Neil Gough, "Online Lender Ezubao Took $7.6 Billion in Ponzi Scheme, China Says," *New York Times*, February 1, 2016. Further, the blockchain system at the heart of bitcoin harbors security concerns that threaten the whole enterprise; see Gertrude Chavez-Dreyfuss, "Cyber Threat Grows for Bitcoin Exchanges," *Reuters*, August 29, 2016.

87. Apologist stances that Charles Ferguson so damningly exposed in his interviews with certain business school professors in *Inside Job*.

88. NYU Stern School, "Michael Posner Joins NYU Stern to Establish New Centre for Business and Human Rights," Press Release, February 28, 2013, quoting Dean Peter Henry.

89. Although its *Human Rights and Sustainable Finance* paper, written by Margaret Wachenfeld, Motoko Aizawa, and Mary Dowell-Jones, as the Institute's contribution to the UN Environmental Program's *Inquiry on the Design of a Sustainable Financial System*, is one of the more sophisticated accounts of how finance interacts with human rights.

90. States, in other words, are obliged under international human rights laws to ensure that such state organs as the Reserve Banks do not act in ways that may violate human rights, or do not adequately protect or promote them. What this means in practice is unclear. At a minimum, it would seem to require the development of specific policy guidance from parent governments, as well as a much greater familiarization of central bankers with the relevant demands of both international and domestic human rights laws. See further on this point, IHRB, *Human Rights and Sustainable Finance*, 30–35.

91. Henry Kaufman, *Civility in the Financial Sector*, Carnegie Council's Lecture Series on Civility, June 20, 2011.

92. James Tobin, Speech on the occasion of the award of the Sveriges Riksbank Prize in Economic Sciences in Memory of Alfred Nobel to James Tobin, December 10, 1981.

INDEX